SO CUTE IT HURTS!!
Volume 14

Shojo Beat Edition

STORY AND ART BY
GO IKEYAMADA

English Translation & Adaptation/Tomo Kimura
Touch-Up Art & Lettering/Joanna Estep
Design/Izumi Evers
Editor/Pancha Diaz

KOBAYASHI GA KAWAISUGITE TSURAI!! Vol.14
by Go IKEYAMADA
© 2012 Go IKEYAMADA
All rights reserved.
Original Japanese edition published by SHOGAKUKAN.
English translation rights in the United States of America, Canada,
the United Kingdom and Ireland arranged with SHOGAKUKAN.

The stories, characters and incidents mentioned in
this publication are entirely fictional.

Printed in the U.S.A.

Published by VIZ Media, LLC
P.O. Box 77010
San Francisco, CA 94107

10 9 8 7 6 5 4 3 2 1
First printing, August 2017

www.viz.com   www.shojobeat.com

W9-AOW-244

AUTHOR BIO

Soon it will be five years since the 2011 Tohoku earthquake. I sincerely express my sympathy to everyone living in the disaster area.

I've been donating a portion of the *Suzuki-kun* and *So Cute!* book profits to support reconstruction of the affected areas. I therefore sincerely express my gratitude to everyone who has bought my comics.

I intend to continue to pray for and to support the disaster-stricken areas as long as I keep working as a manga artist.

Go Ikeyamada is a Gemini from Miyagi Prefecture whose hobbies include taking naps and watching movies. Her debut manga *Get Love!!* appeared in *Shojo Comic* in 2002, and her current work *So Cute It Hurts!!* (*Kobayashi ga Kawai Suguite Tsurai!!*) is being published by VIZ Media.

Chapter 67

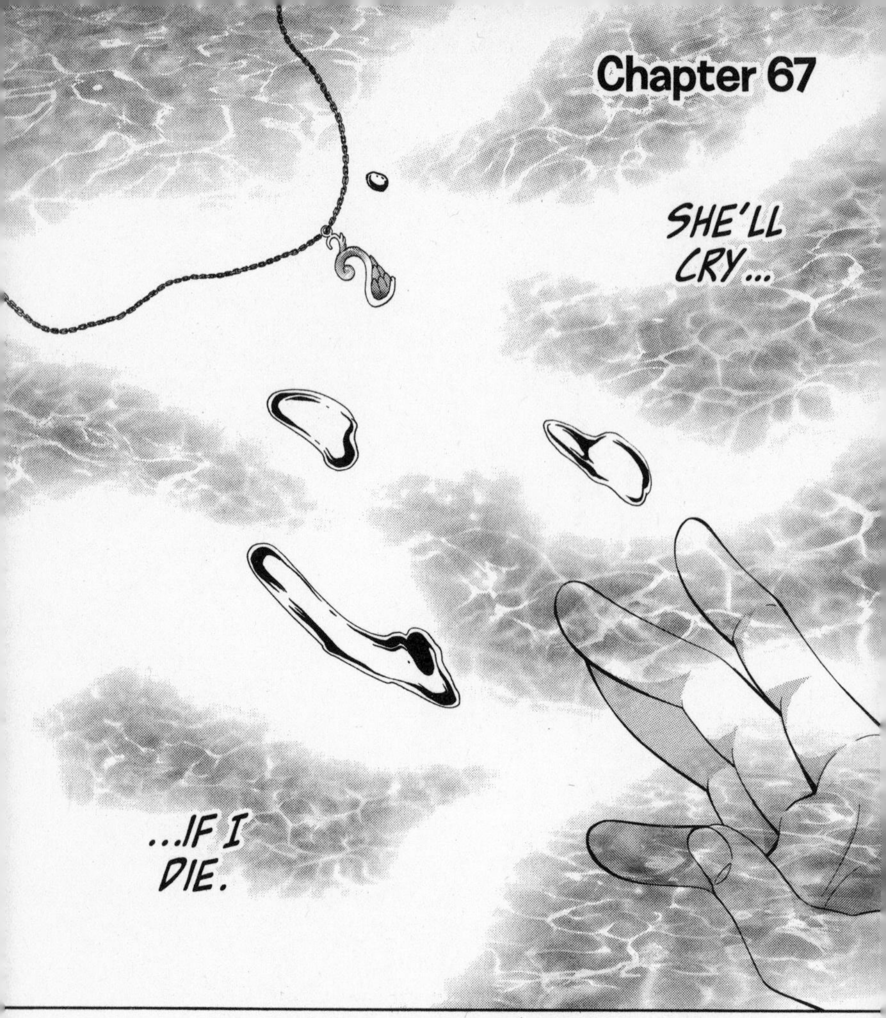
SHE'LL CRY...
...IF I DIE.

NICE TO MEET YOU AND HELLO. I'M GO IKEYAMADA.
THANK YOU FOR PICKING UP MY 57TH BOOK!!
THIS IS VOLUME 14 OF *SO CUTE IT HURTS!!*
THE STORY CONTINUES TO BE VERY SERIOUS, SO I WAS VERY NERVOUS EVERY TIME A MAGAZINE ISSUE WENT ON SALE. HOWEVER, MANY *SHO-COMI* READERS ACCEPTED WHAT I WAS TRYING TO CONVEY WITH THIS WORK AND WARMLY SUPPORTED ME. I WAS THUS FINALLY ABLE TO CONCLUDE THE SERIES. I'M SURE READERS WILL HAVE ALL SORTS OF OPINIONS ABOUT VOLUME 14, BUT I DREW WHAT I COULD WITHIN THE CONSTRAINTS OF SHOJO MANGA. PLEASE KEEP READING UNTIL THE VERY END!

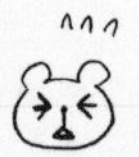

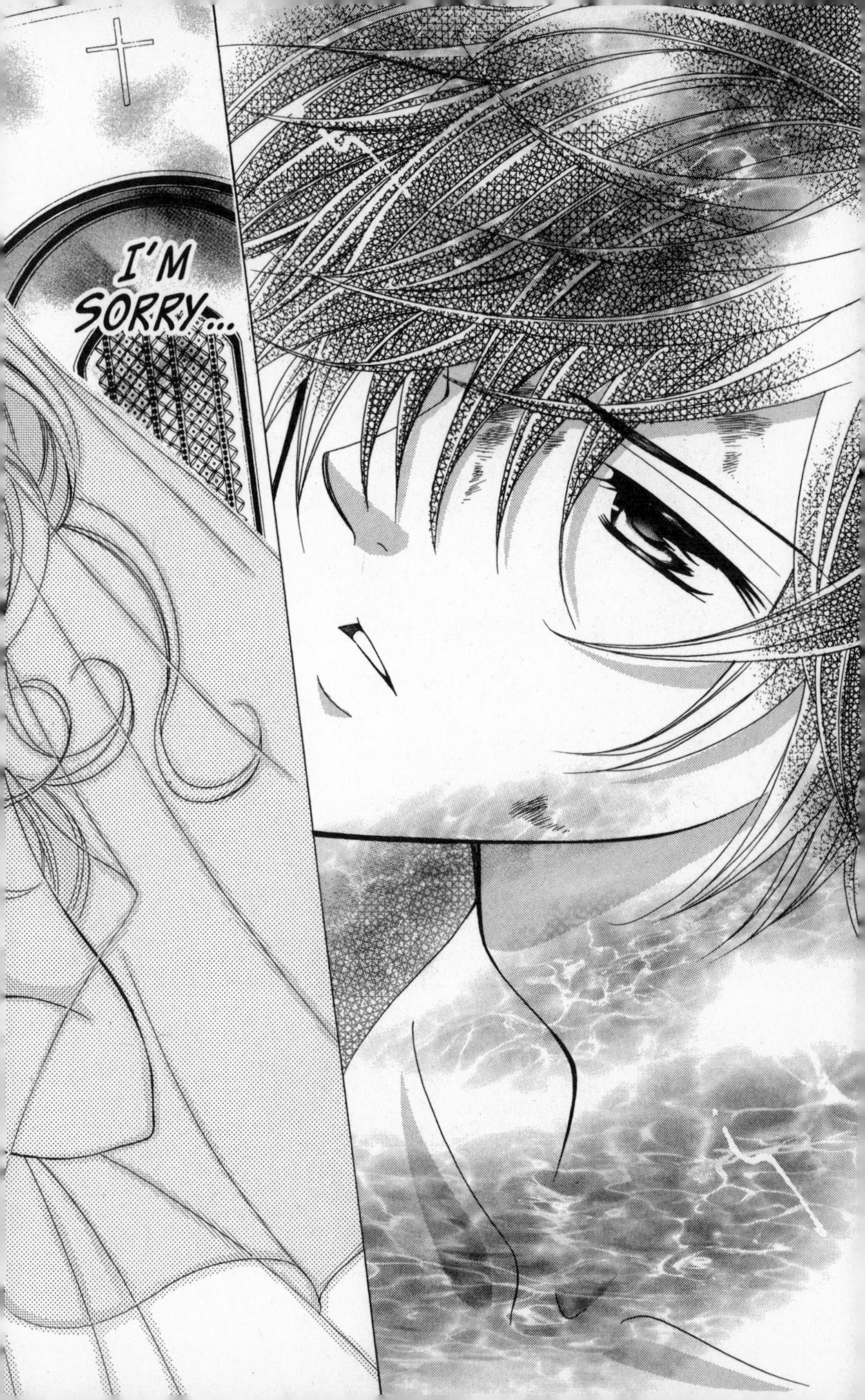
I'M SORRY...

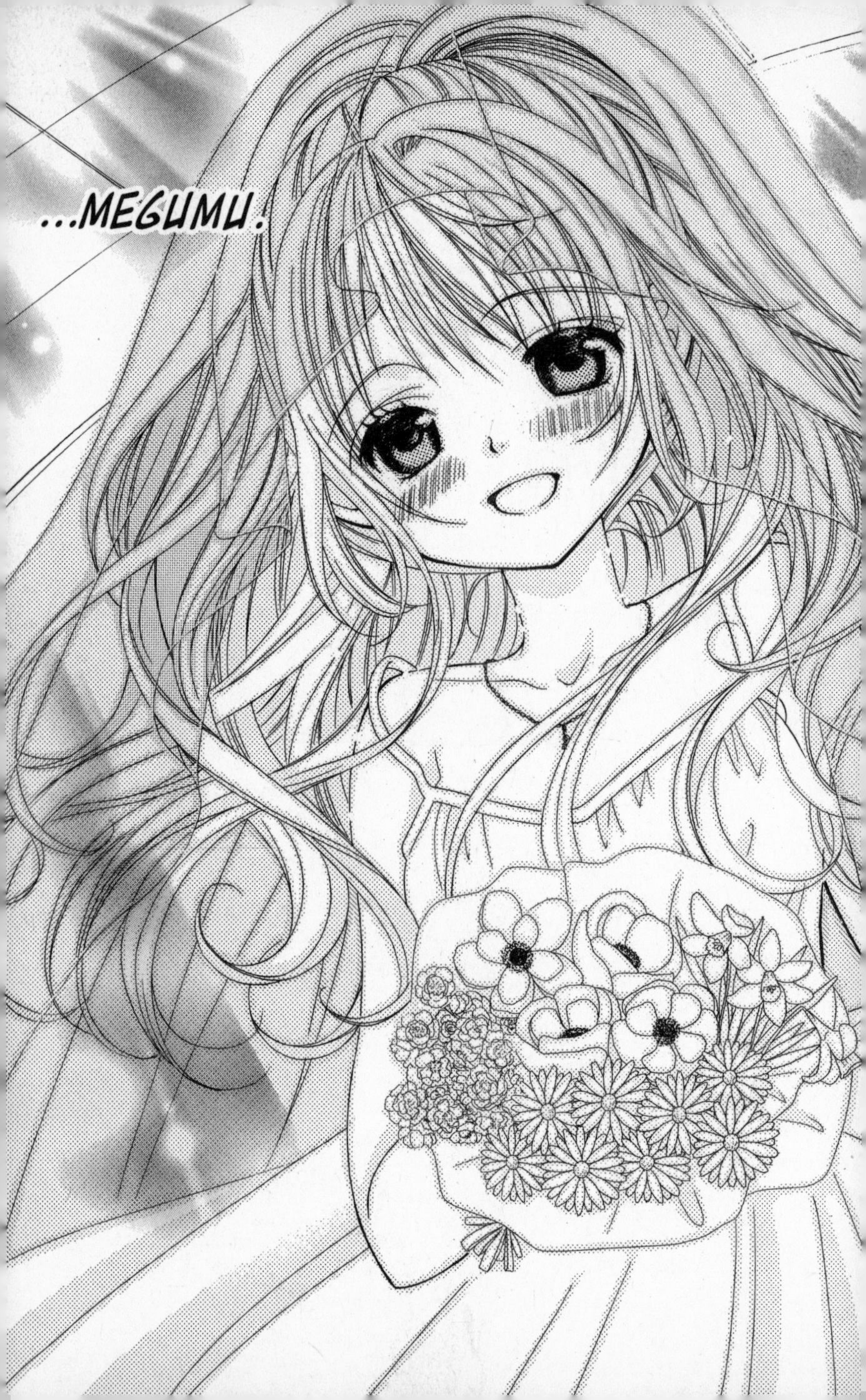
...MEGUMU.

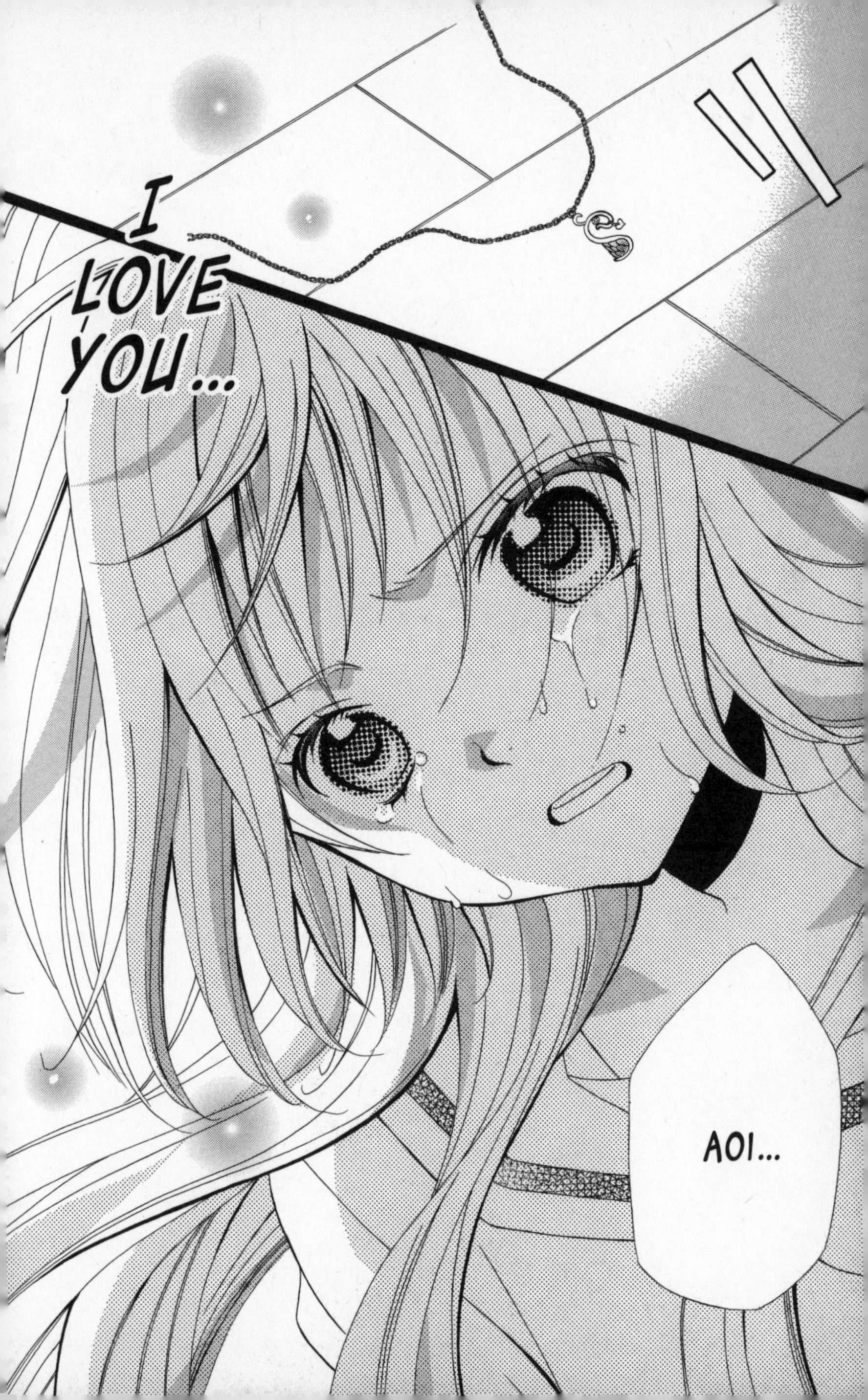
I LOVE YOU...
AOI...

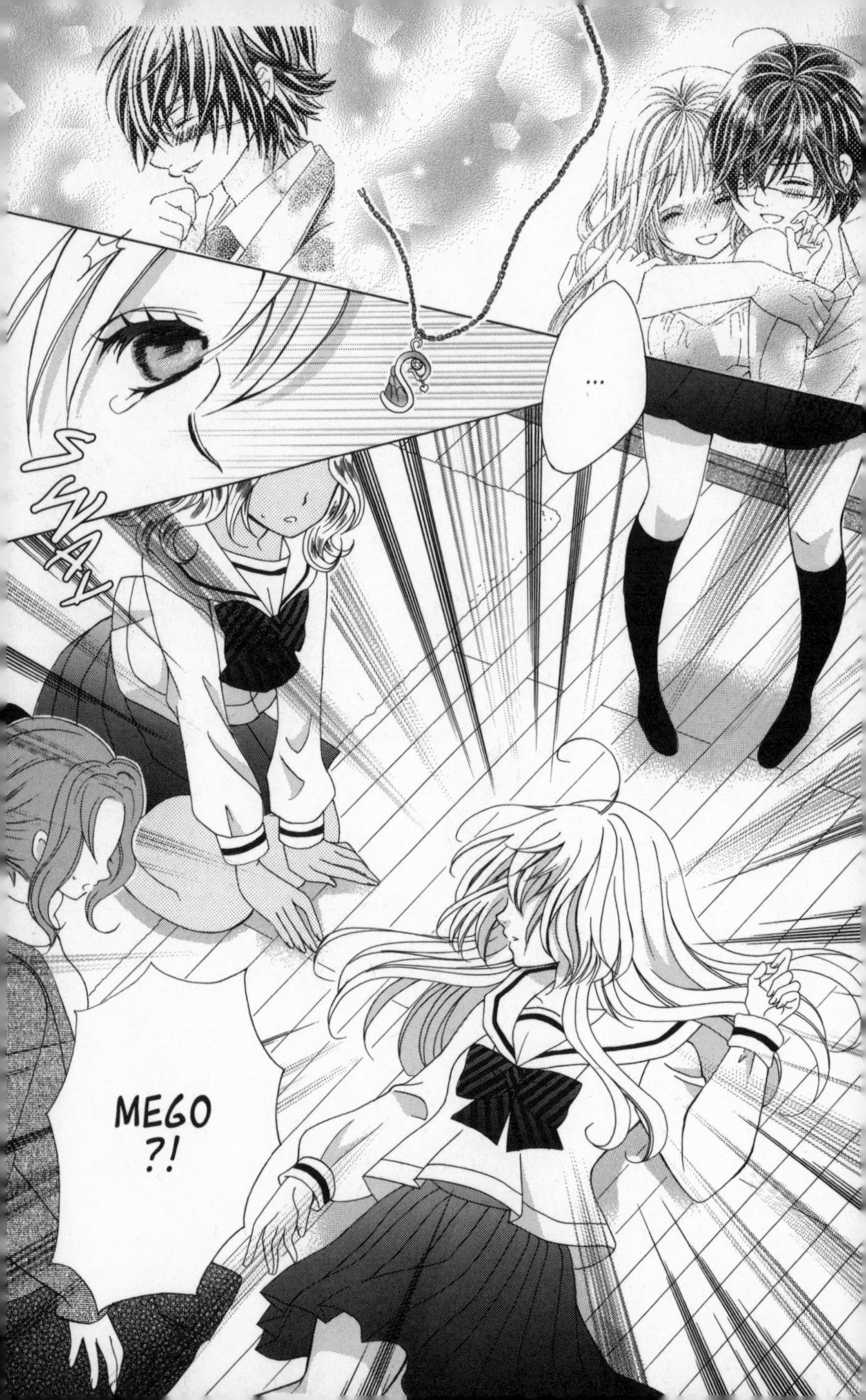
...
SWAY
MEGO ?!

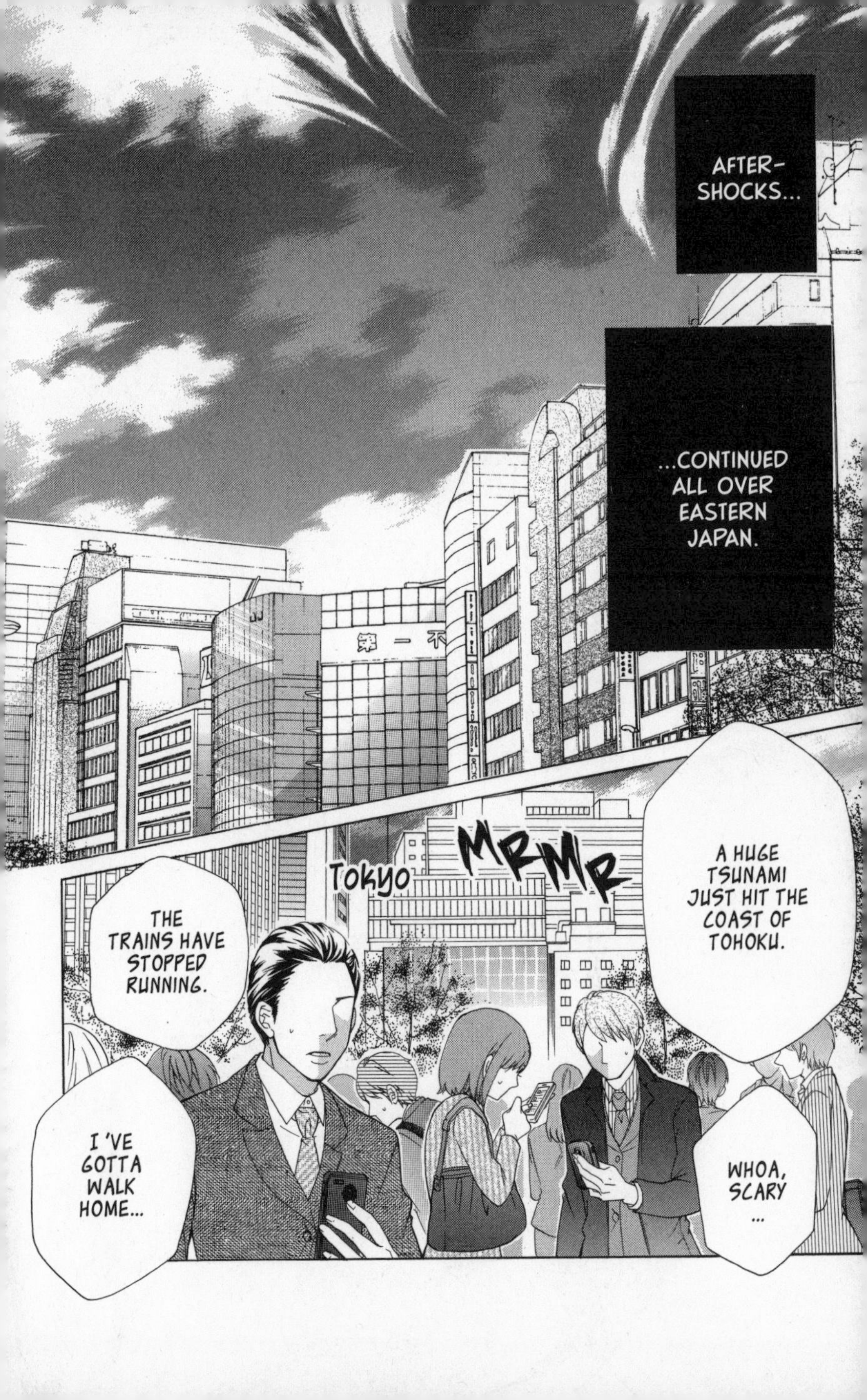
AFTER-SHOCKS...
...CONTINUED ALL OVER EASTERN JAPAN.
A HUGE TSUNAMI JUST HIT THE COAST OF TOHOKU.
MRMR
Tokyo
WHOA, SCARY ...
THE TRAINS HAVE STOPPED RUNNING.
I'VE GOTTA WALK HOME...

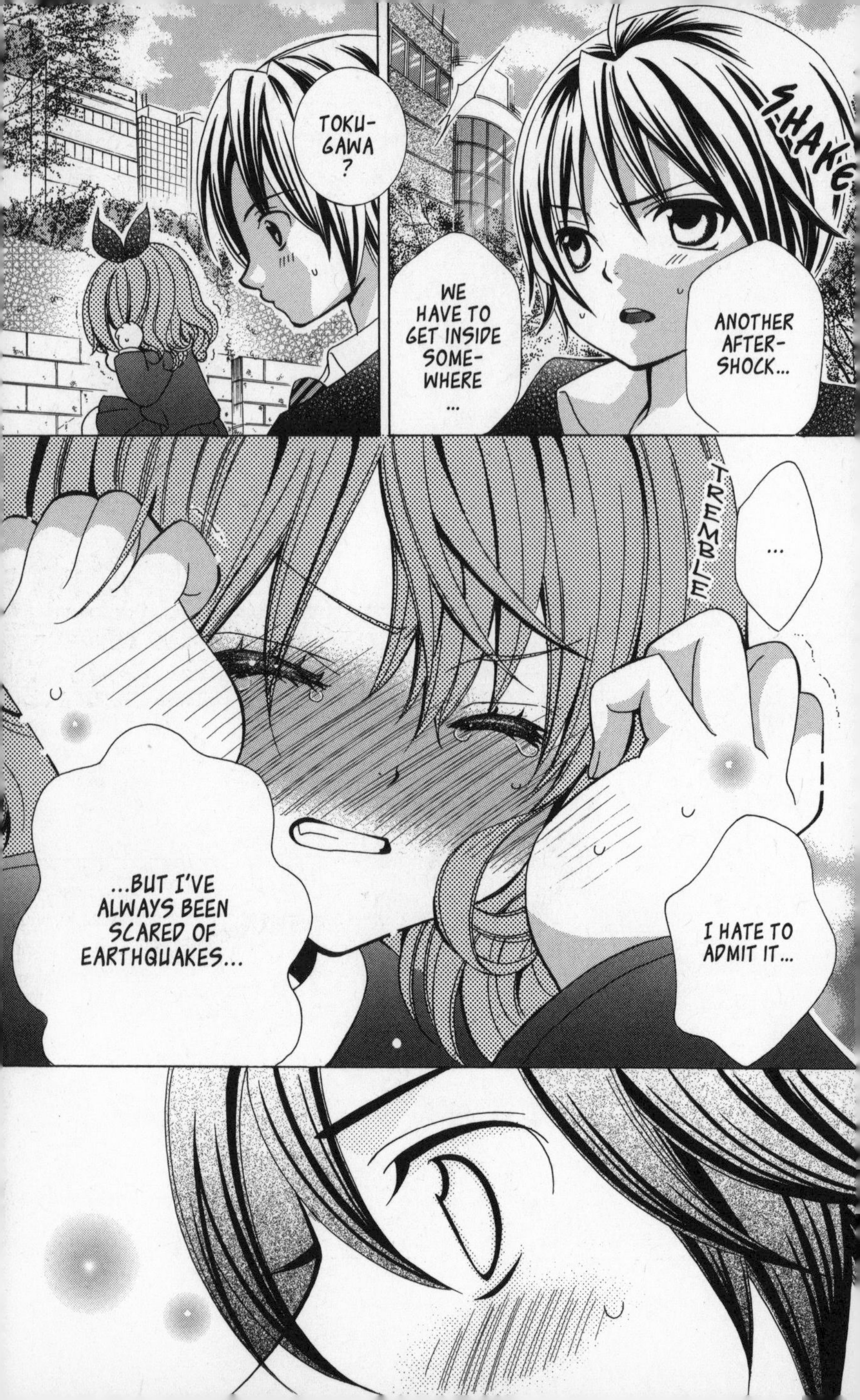
SHAKE
ANOTHER AFTER-SHOCK...
WE HAVE TO GET INSIDE SOME-WHERE...
TOKU-GAWA?
TREMBLE
...
I HATE TO ADMIT IT...
...BUT I'VE ALWAYS BEEN SCARED OF EARTHQUAKES...

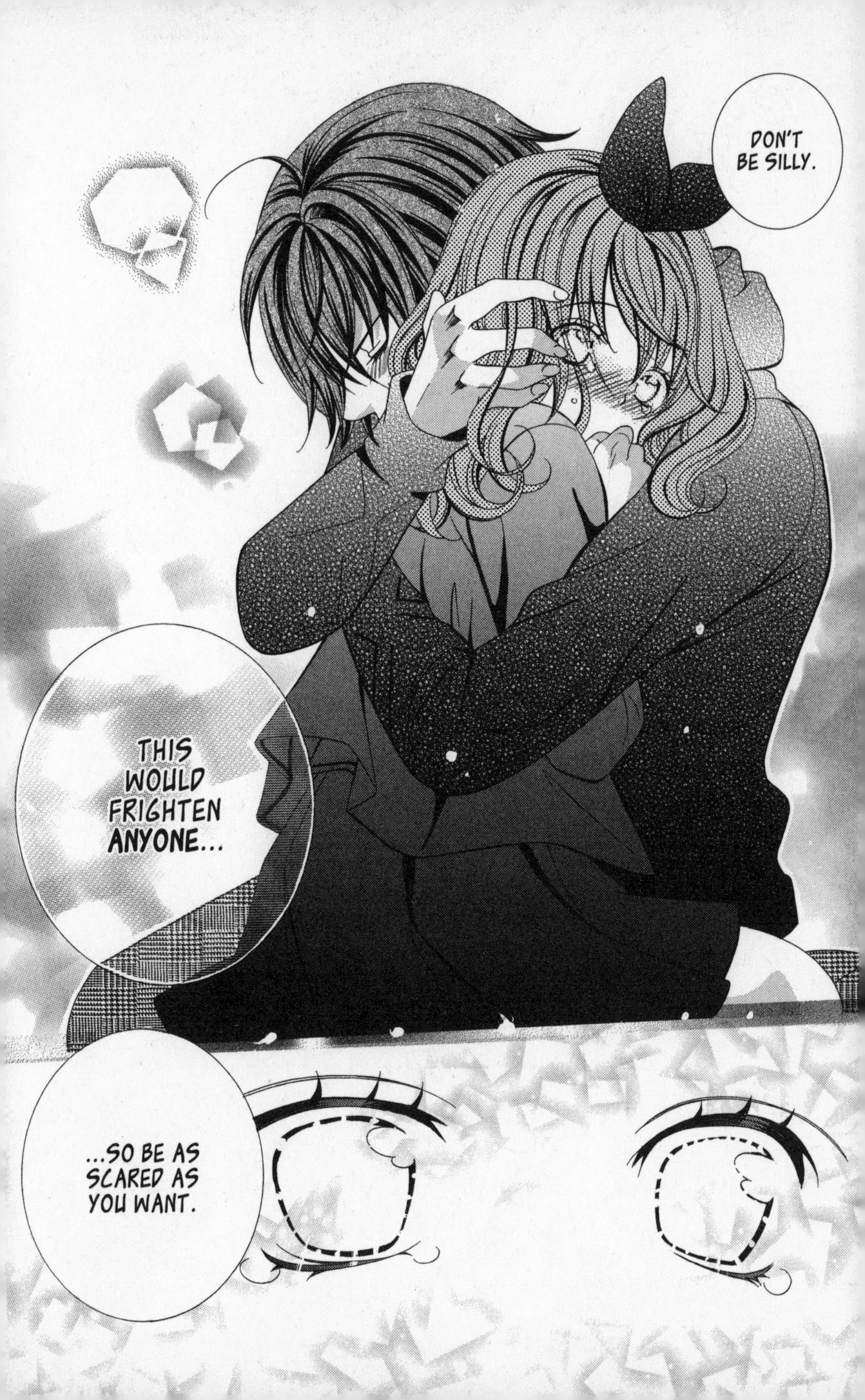
DON'T BE SILLY.
THIS WOULD FRIGHTEN ANYONE...
...SO BE AS SCARED AS YOU WANT.

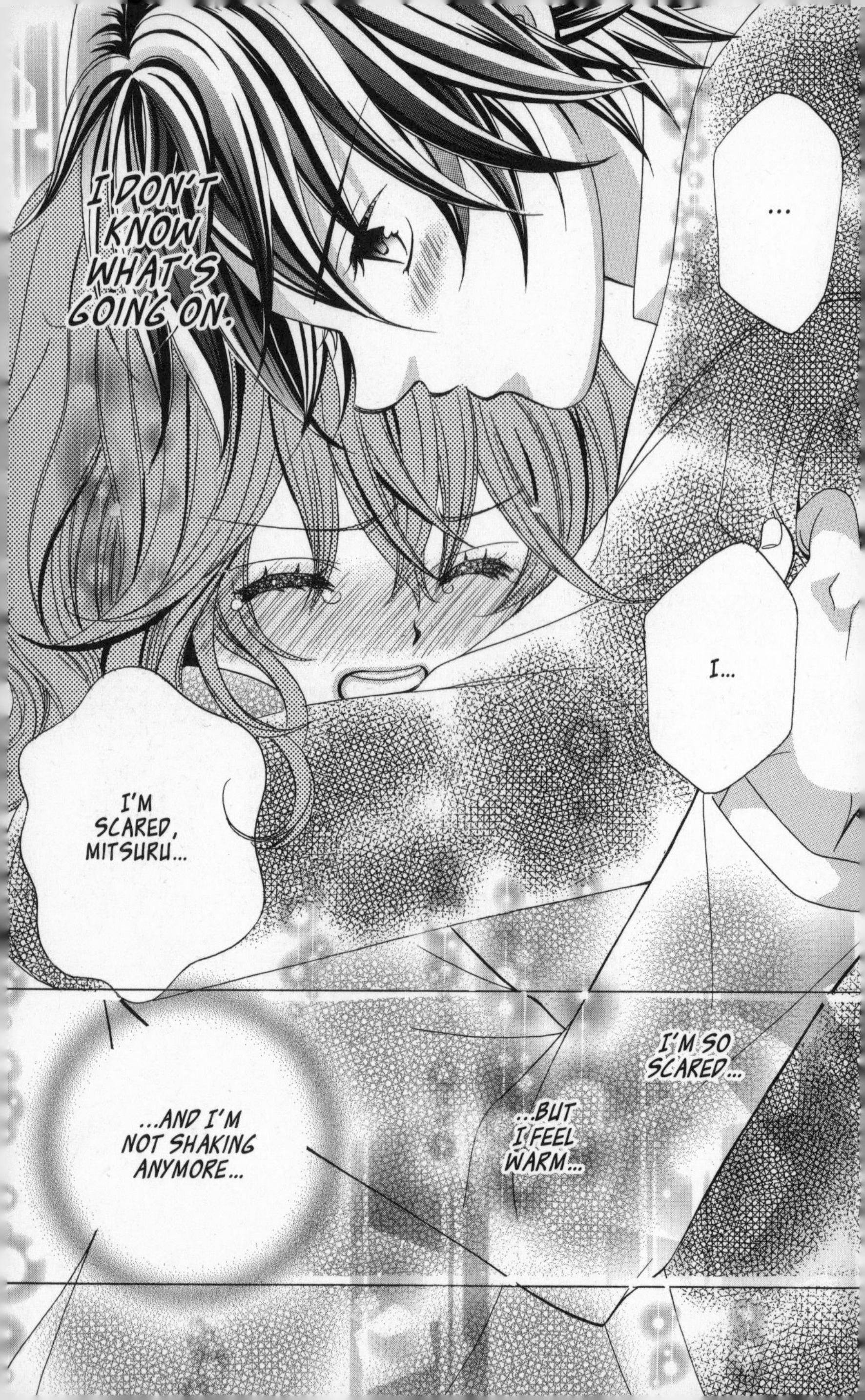
...
I DON'T KNOW WHAT'S GOING ON.
I...
I'M SCARED, MITSURU...
I'M SO SCARED...
...BUT I FEEL WARM...
...AND I'M NOT SHAKING ANYMORE...

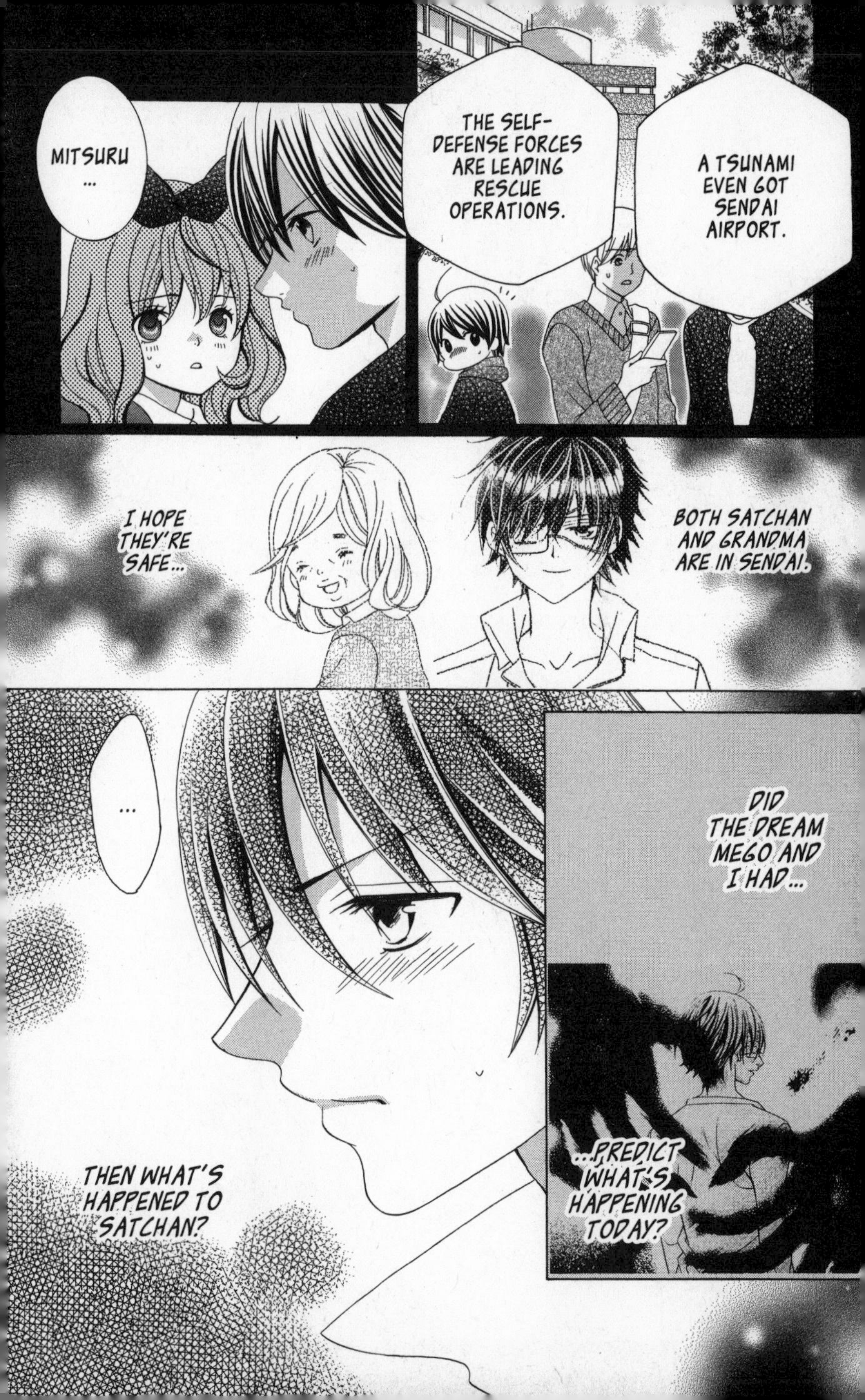
A TSUNAMI EVEN GOT SENDAI AIRPORT.
THE SELF-DEFENSE FORCES ARE LEADING RESCUE OPERATIONS.
MITSURU ...
BOTH SATCHAN AND GRANDMA ARE IN SENDAI.
I HOPE THEY'RE SAFE...
DID THE DREAM MEGO AND I HAD...
...PREDICT WHAT'S HAPPENING TODAY?
...
THEN WHAT'S HAPPENED TO SATCHAN?

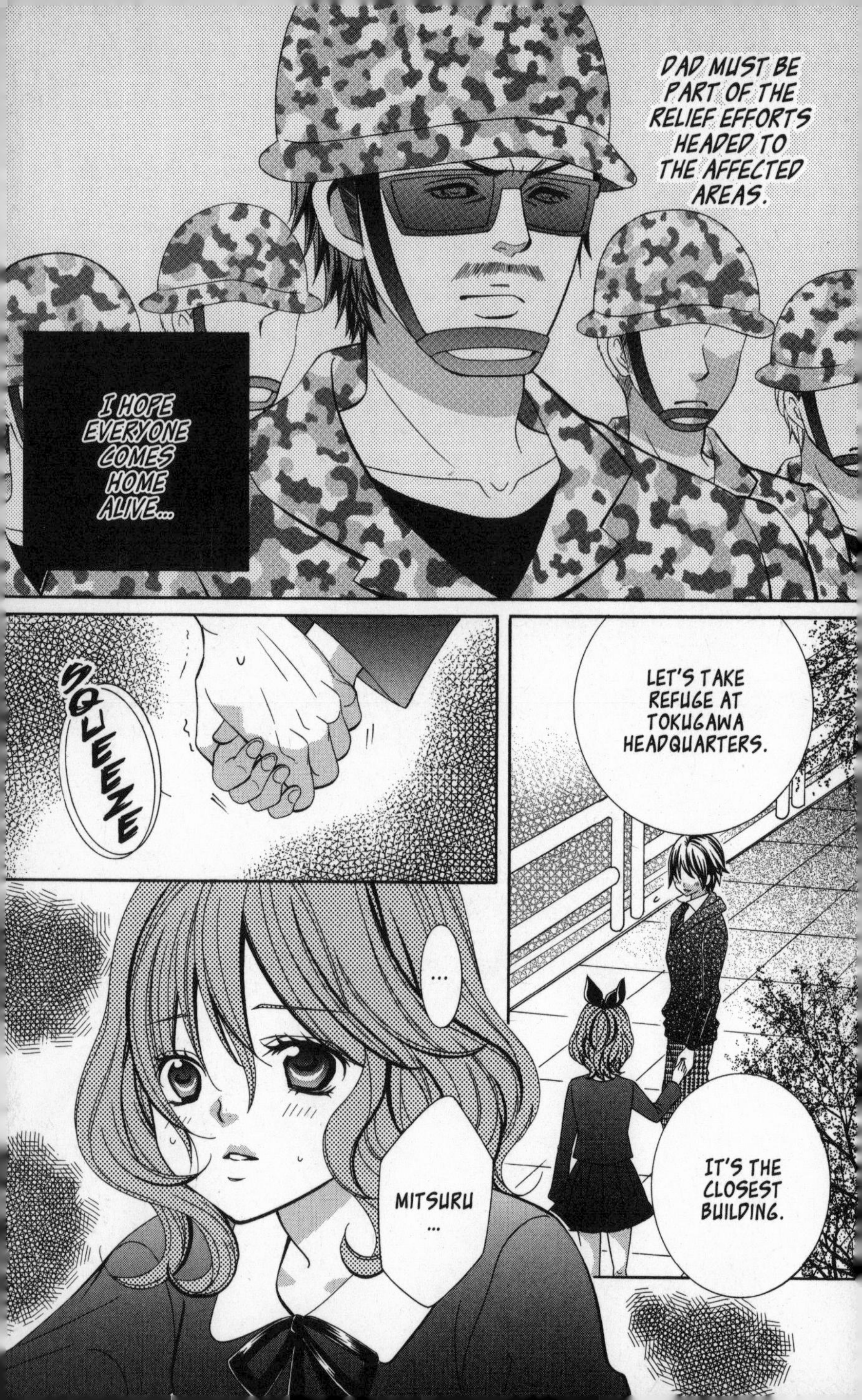
DAD MUST BE PART OF THE RELIEF EFFORTS HEADED TO THE AFFECTED AREAS.
I HOPE EVERYONE COMES HOME ALIVE...
LET'S TAKE REFUGE AT TOKUGAWA HEADQUARTERS.
IT'S THE CLOSEST BUILDING.
SQUEEZE
...
MITSURU ...

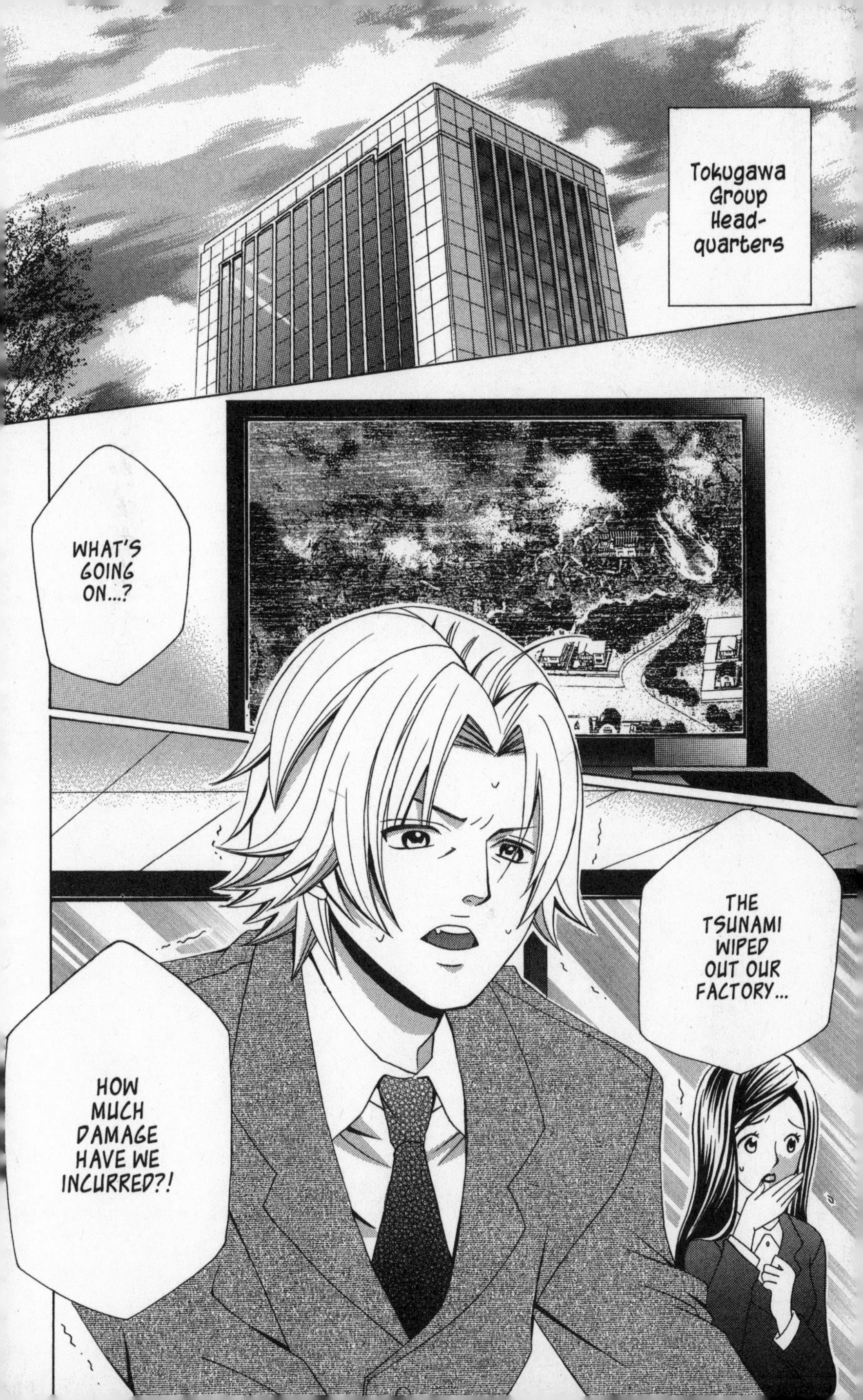
Tokugawa Group Head-quarters
WHAT'S GOING ON...?
THE TSUNAMI WIPED OUT OUR FACTORY...
HOW MUCH DAMAGE HAVE WE INCURRED?!

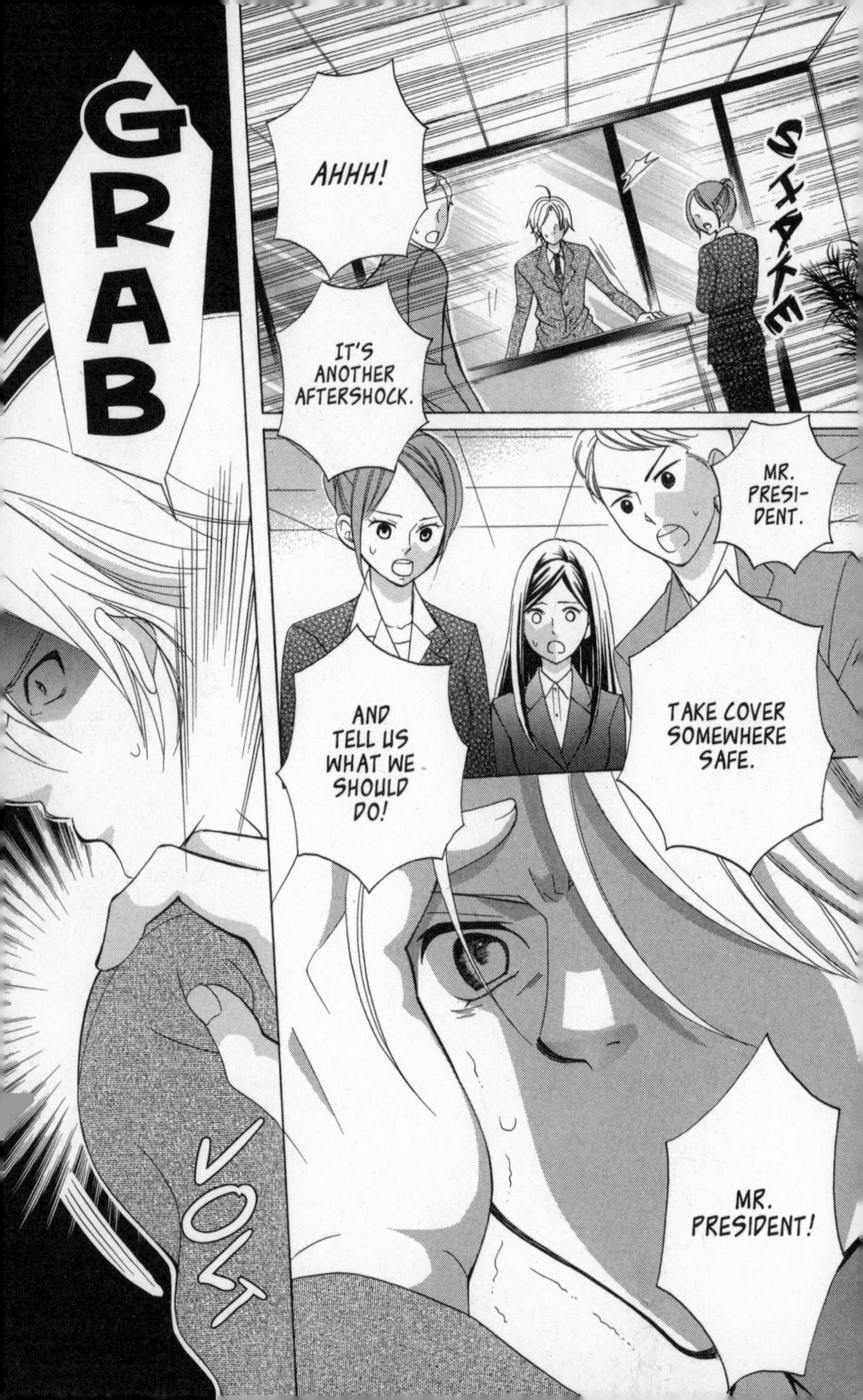
SHAKE
AHHH!
IT'S ANOTHER AFTERSHOCK.
MR. PRESIDENT.
TAKE COVER SOMEWHERE SAFE.
AND TELL US WHAT WE SHOULD DO!
MR. PRESIDENT!
GRAB
JOLT

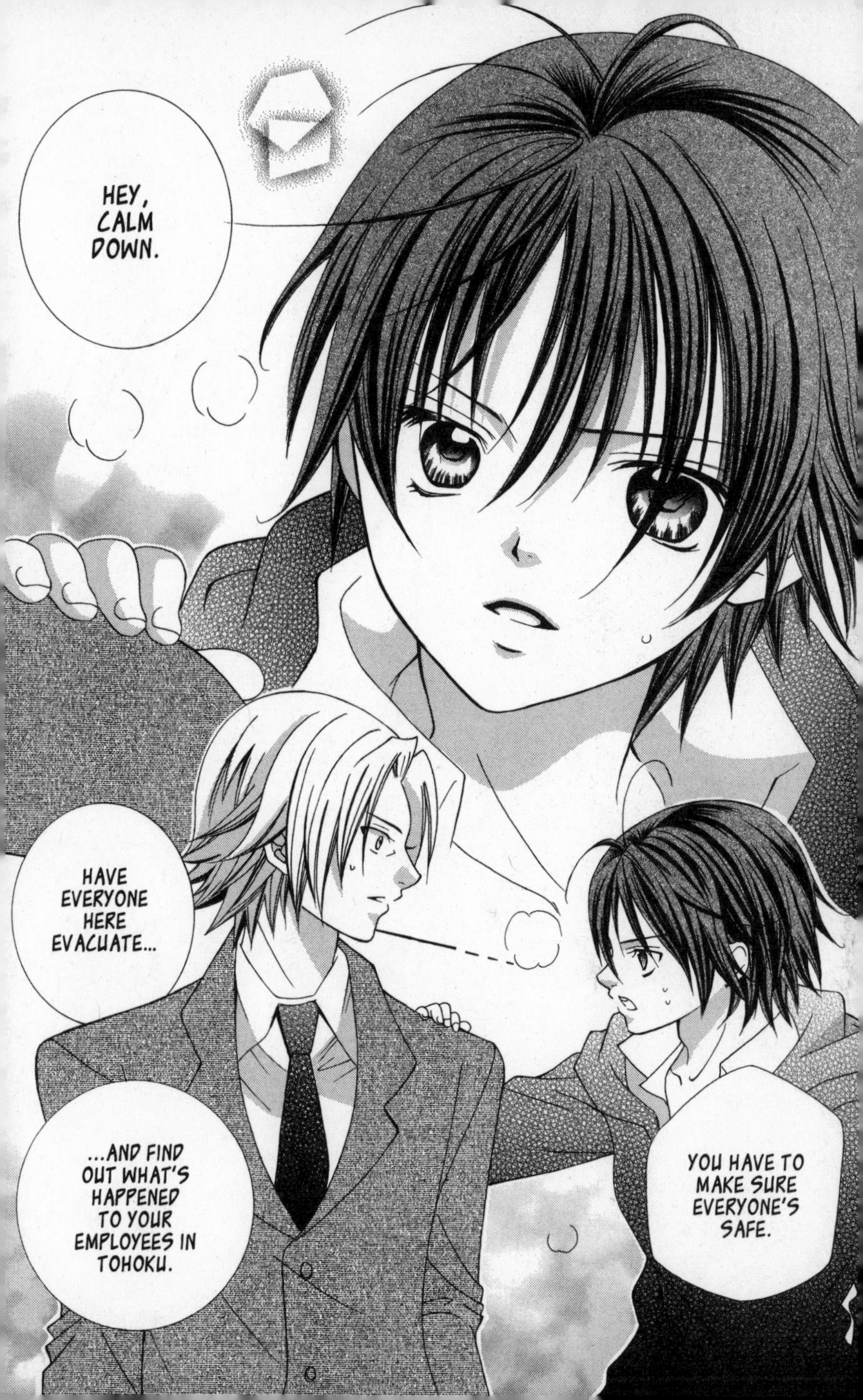
HEY, CALM DOWN.
HAVE EVERYONE HERE EVACUATE...
...AND FIND OUT WHAT'S HAPPENED TO YOUR EMPLOYEES IN TOHOKU.
YOU HAVE TO MAKE SURE EVERYONE'S SAFE.

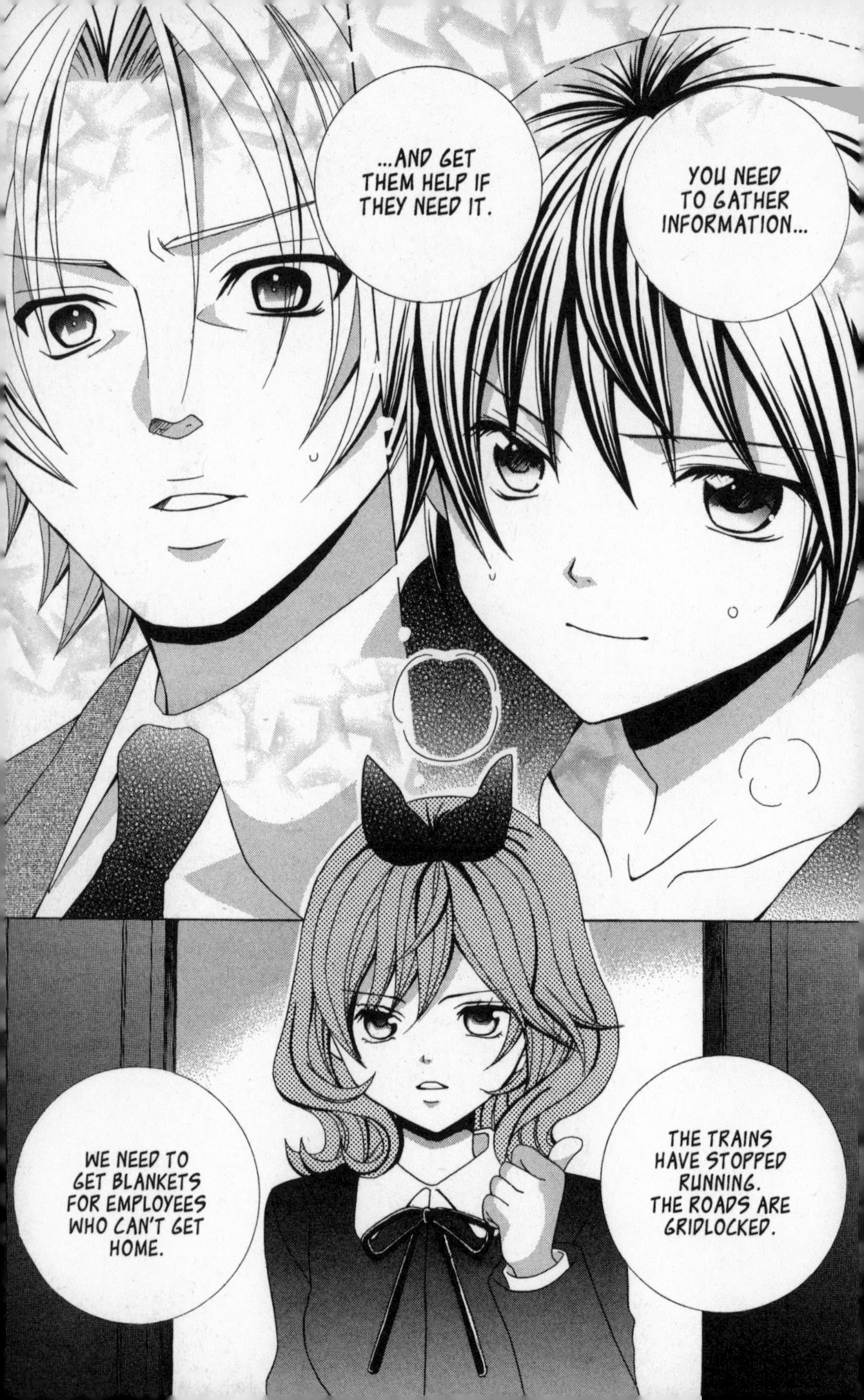
YOU NEED TO GATHER INFORMATION...
...AND GET THEM HELP IF THEY NEED IT.
THE TRAINS HAVE STOPPED RUNNING. THE ROADS ARE GRIDLOCKED.
WE NEED TO GET BLANKETS FOR EMPLOYEES WHO CAN'T GET HOME.

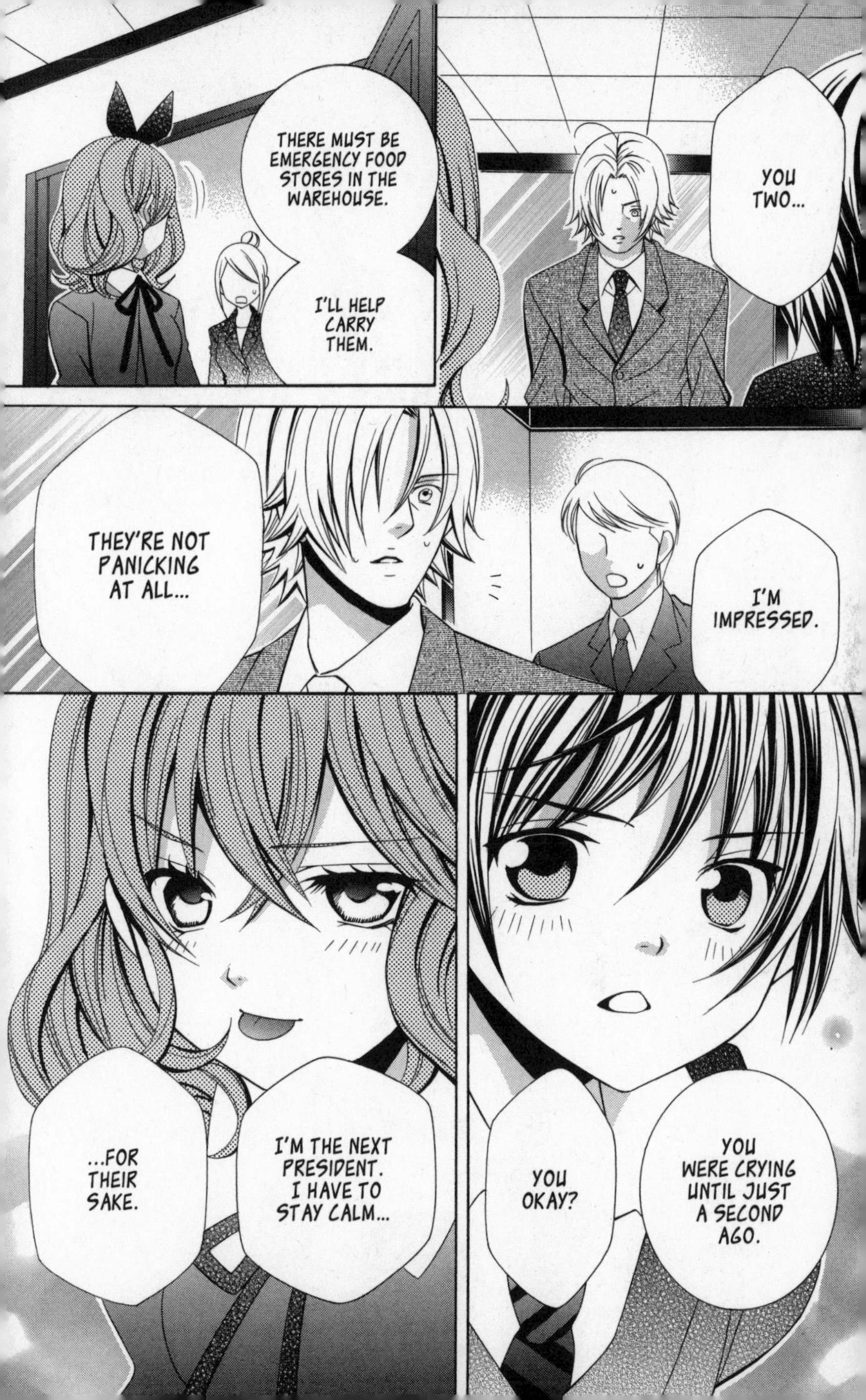
YOU TWO...
THERE MUST BE EMERGENCY FOOD STORES IN THE WAREHOUSE.
I'LL HELP CARRY THEM.
I'M IMPRESSED.
THEY'RE NOT PANICKING AT ALL...
YOU WERE CRYING UNTIL JUST A SECOND AGO.
YOU OKAY?
I'M THE NEXT PRESIDENT. I HAVE TO STAY CALM...
...FOR THEIR SAKE.

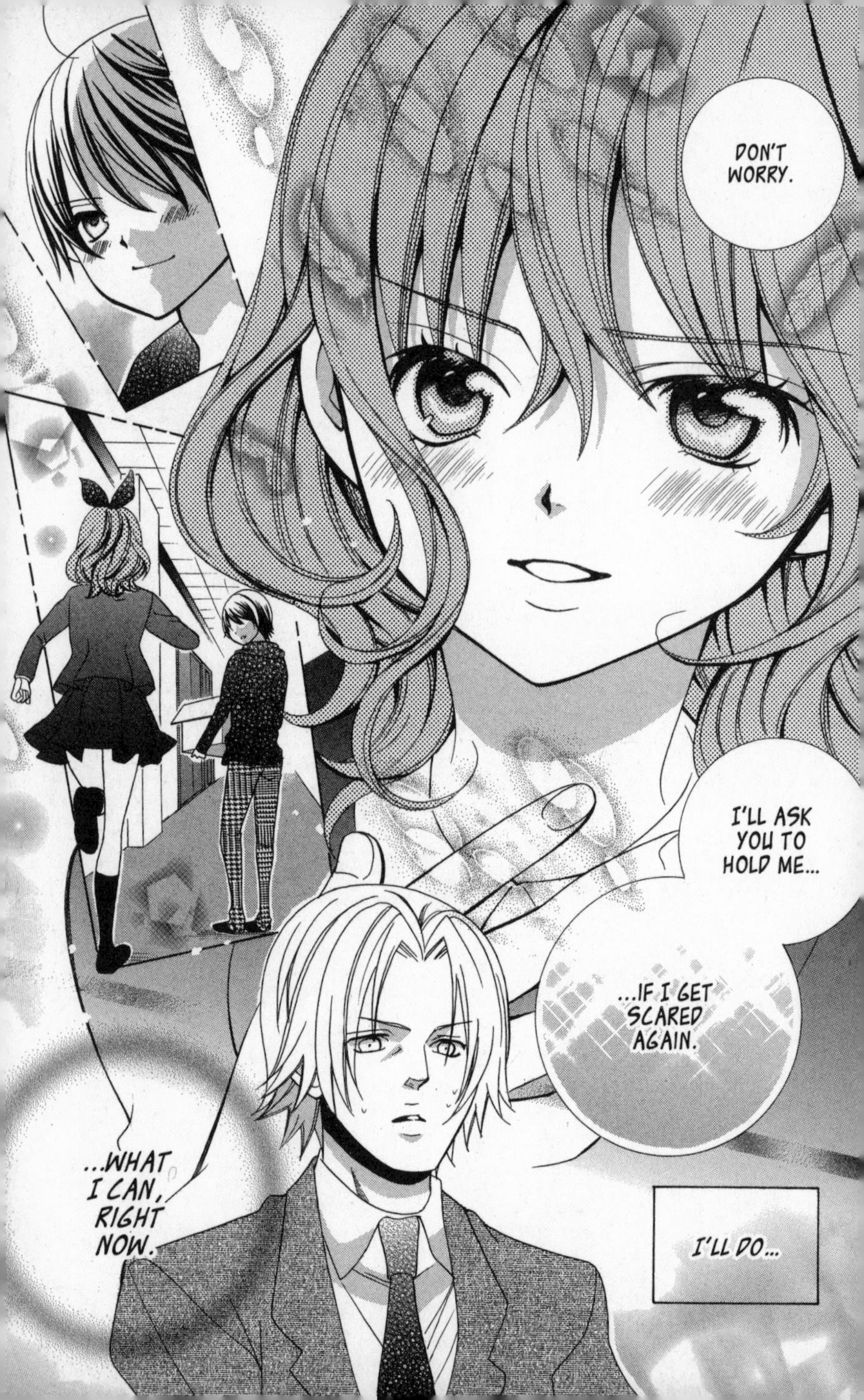
DON'T WORRY.
I'LL ASK YOU TO HOLD ME...
...IF I GET SCARED AGAIN.
I'LL DO...
...WHAT I CAN, RIGHT NOW.

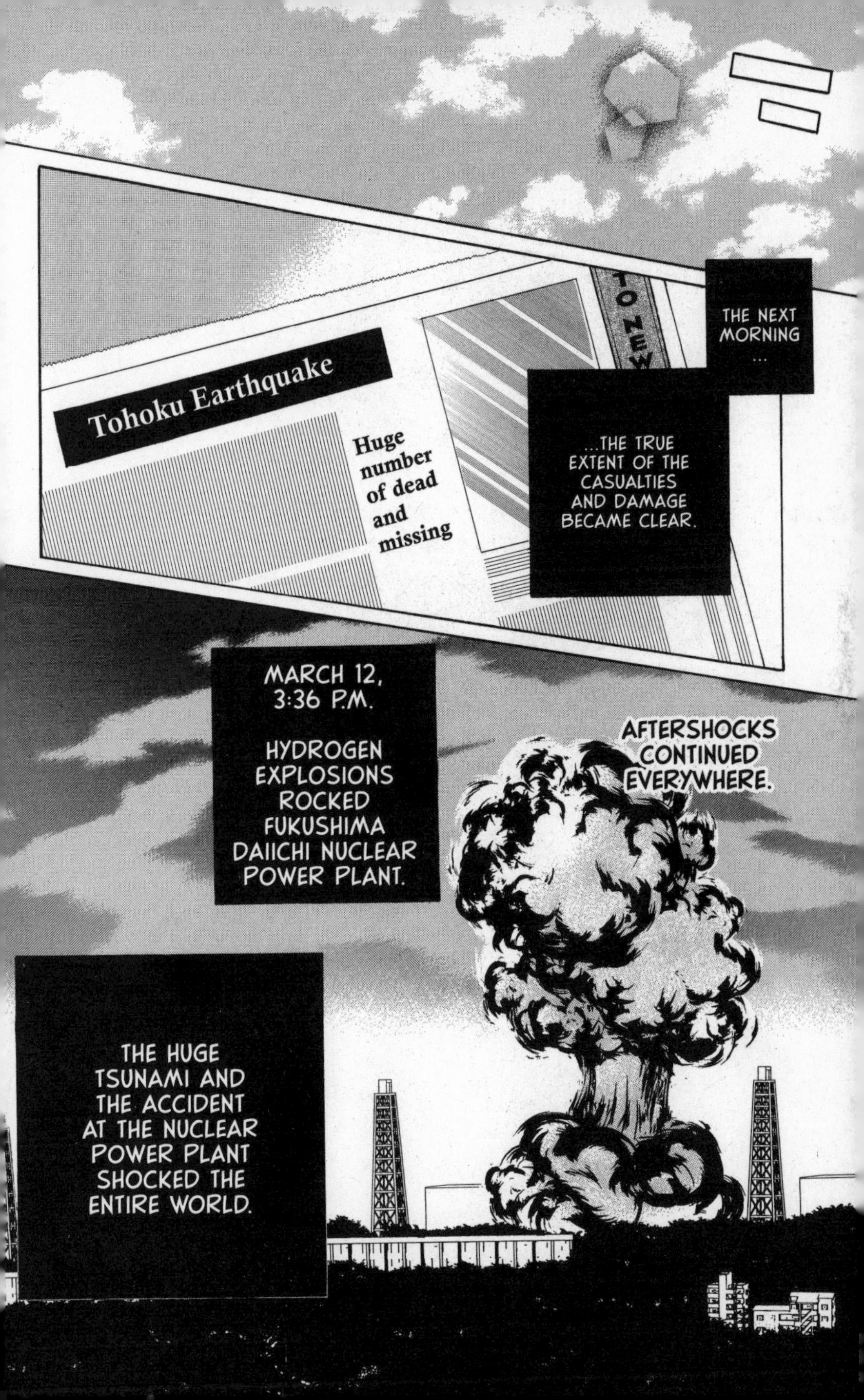
THE NEXT MORNING ...
...THE TRUE EXTENT OF THE CASUALTIES AND DAMAGE BECAME CLEAR.
Tohoku Earthquake
Huge number of dead and missing
AFTERSHOCKS CONTINUED EVERYWHERE.
MARCH 12, 3:36 P.M.
HYDROGEN EXPLOSIONS ROCKED FUKUSHIMA DAIICHI NUCLEAR POWER PLANT.
THE HUGE TSUNAMI AND THE ACCIDENT AT THE NUCLEAR POWER PLANT SHOCKED THE ENTIRE WORLD.

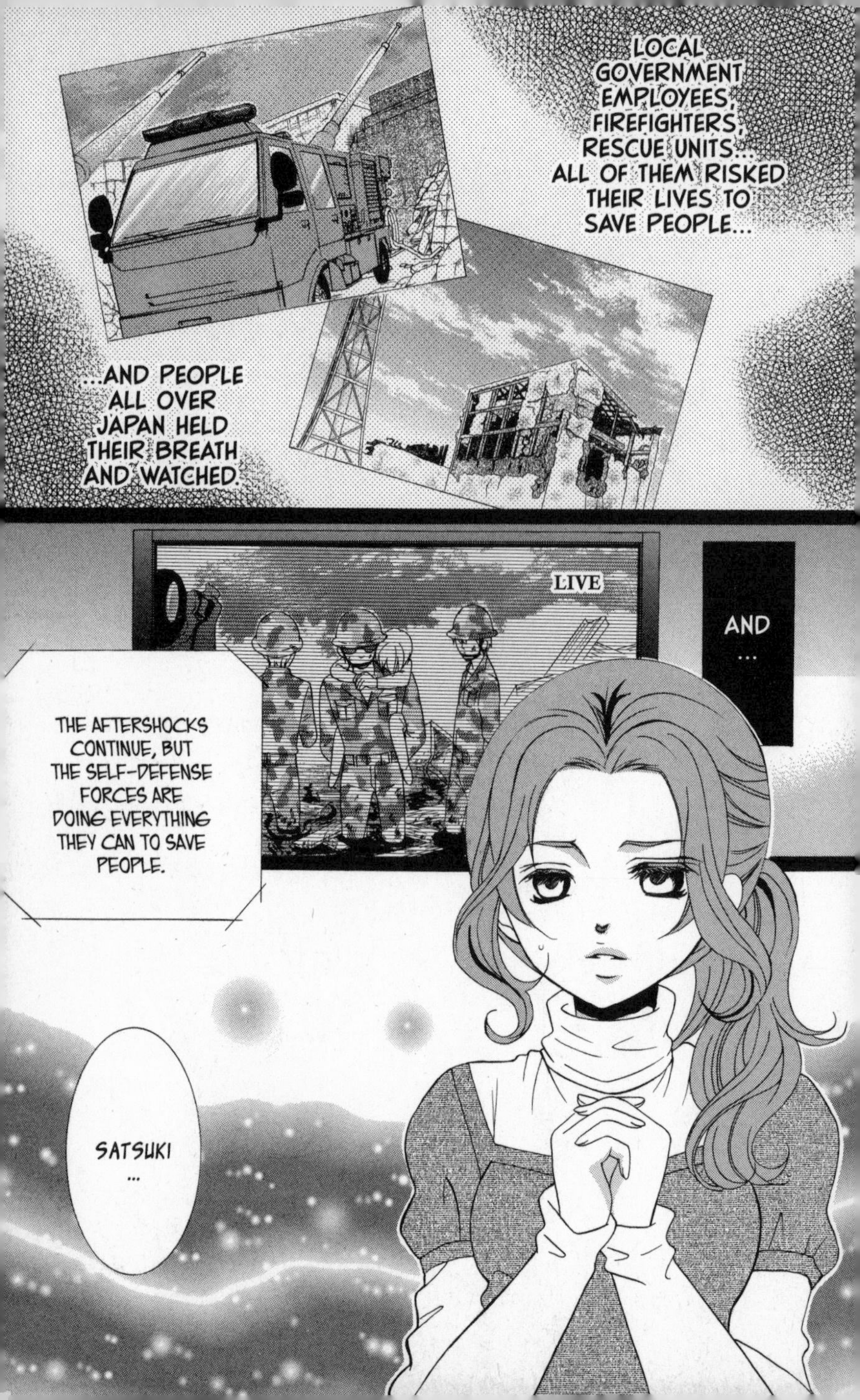
LOCAL GOVERNMENT EMPLOYEES, FIREFIGHTERS, RESCUE UNITS... ALL OF THEM RISKED THEIR LIVES TO SAVE PEOPLE...
...AND PEOPLE ALL OVER JAPAN HELD THEIR BREATH AND WATCHED.
AND ...
LIVE
THE AFTERSHOCKS CONTINUE, BUT THE SELF-DEFENSE FORCES ARE DOING EVERYTHING THEY CAN TO SAVE PEOPLE.
SATSUKI ...

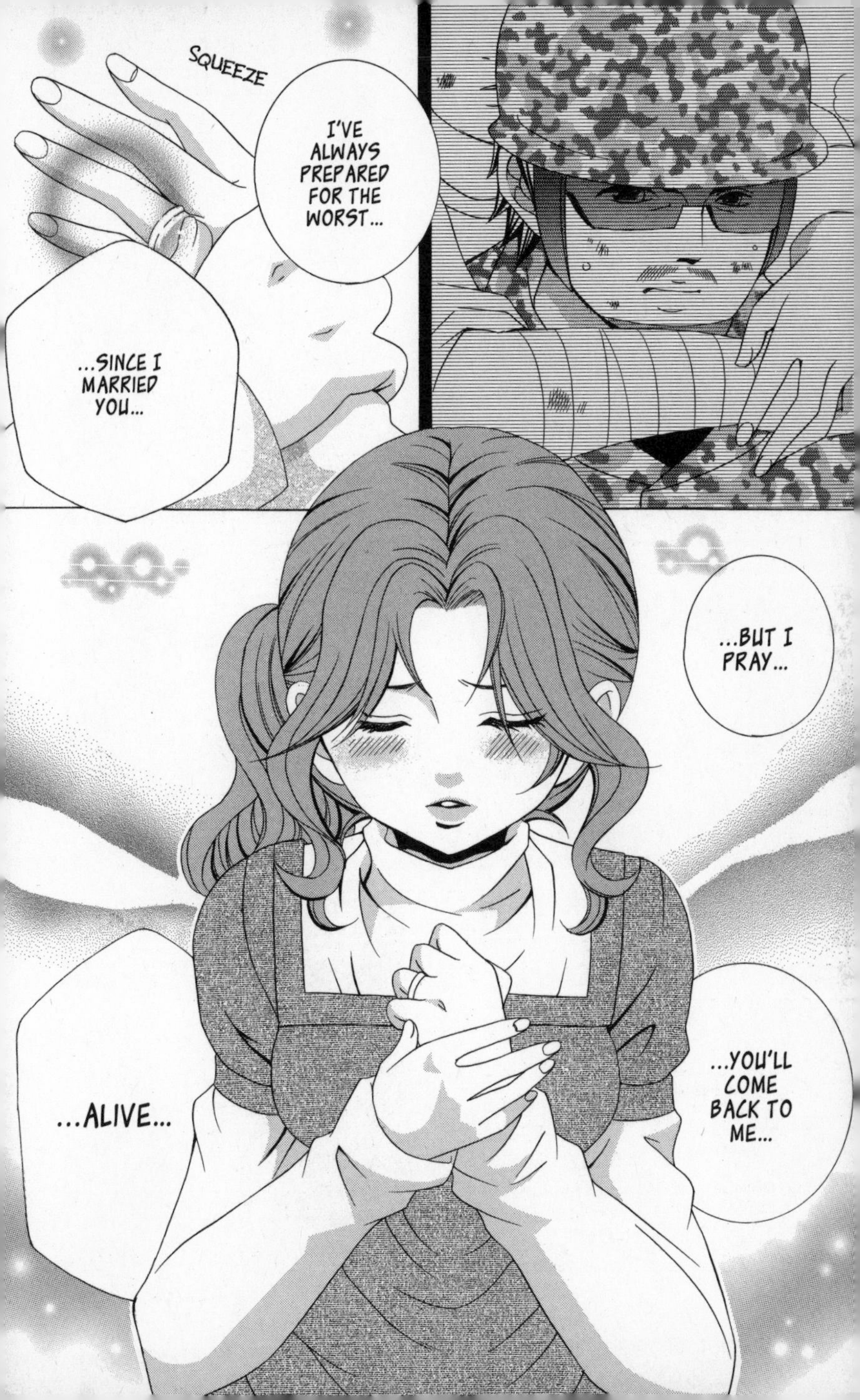
SQUEEZE
I'VE ALWAYS PREPARED FOR THE WORST...
...SINCE I MARRIED YOU...
...BUT I PRAY...
...YOU'LL COME BACK TO ME...
...ALIVE...

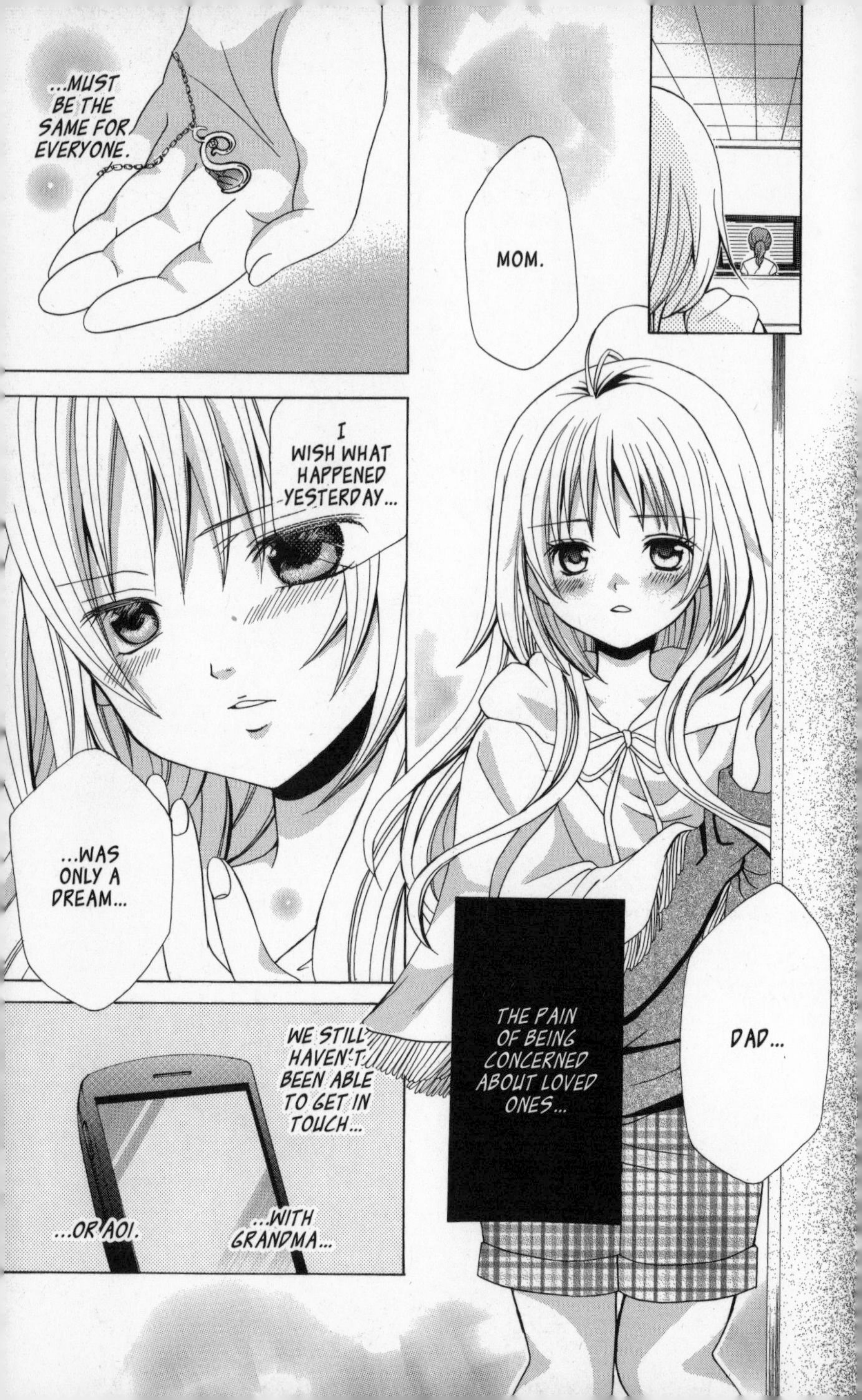
MOM.
DAD...
THE PAIN OF BEING CONCERNED ABOUT LOVED ONES...
...MUST BE THE SAME FOR EVERYONE.
I WISH WHAT HAPPENED YESTERDAY...
...WAS ONLY A DREAM...
WE STILL HAVEN'T BEEN ABLE TO GET IN TOUCH...
...WITH GRANDMA...
...OR AOI.

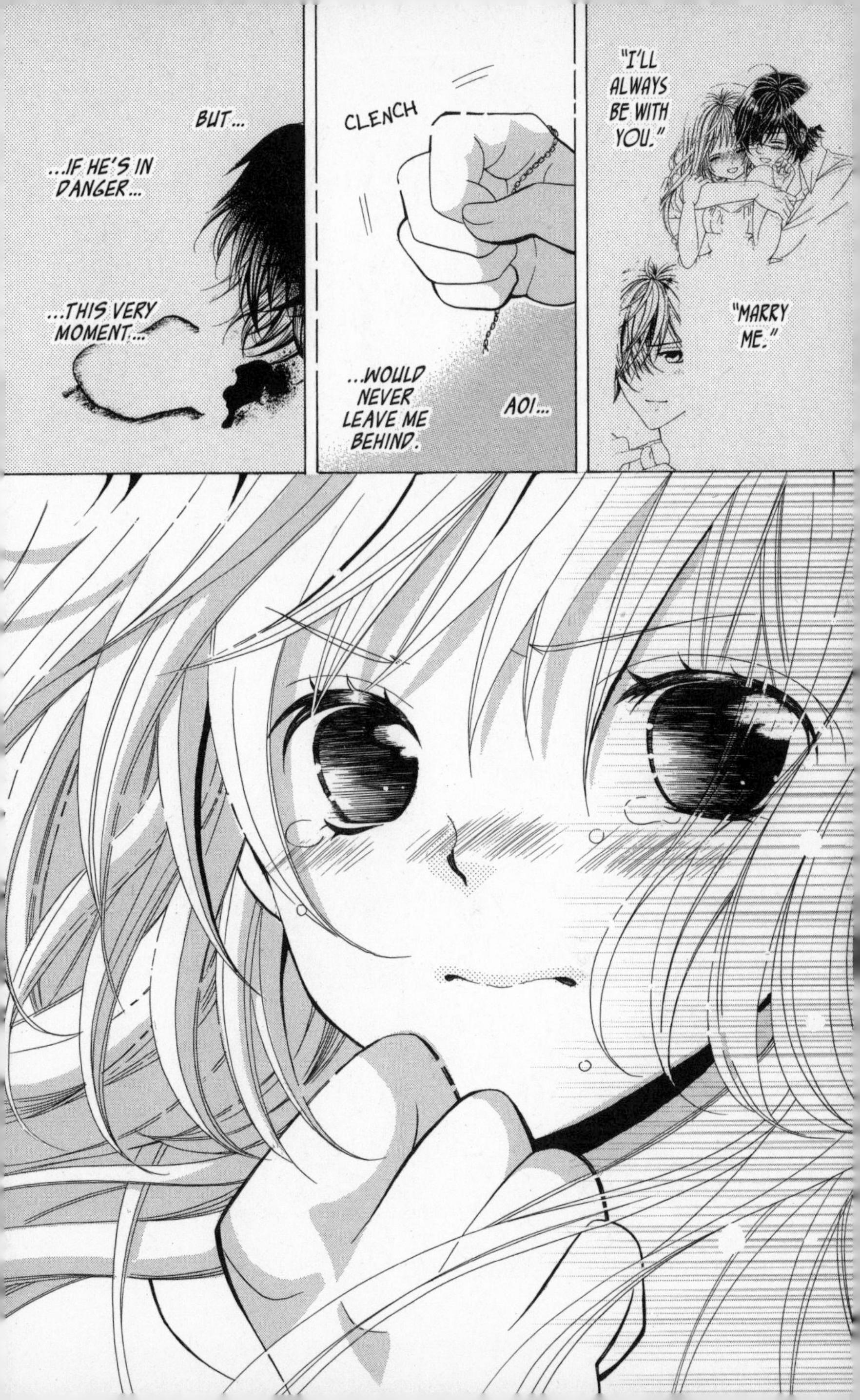
"I'LL ALWAYS BE WITH YOU."
"MARRY ME."
CLENCH
AOI...
...WOULD NEVER LEAVE ME BEHIND.
BUT...
...IF HE'S IN DANGER...
...THIS VERY MOMENT...

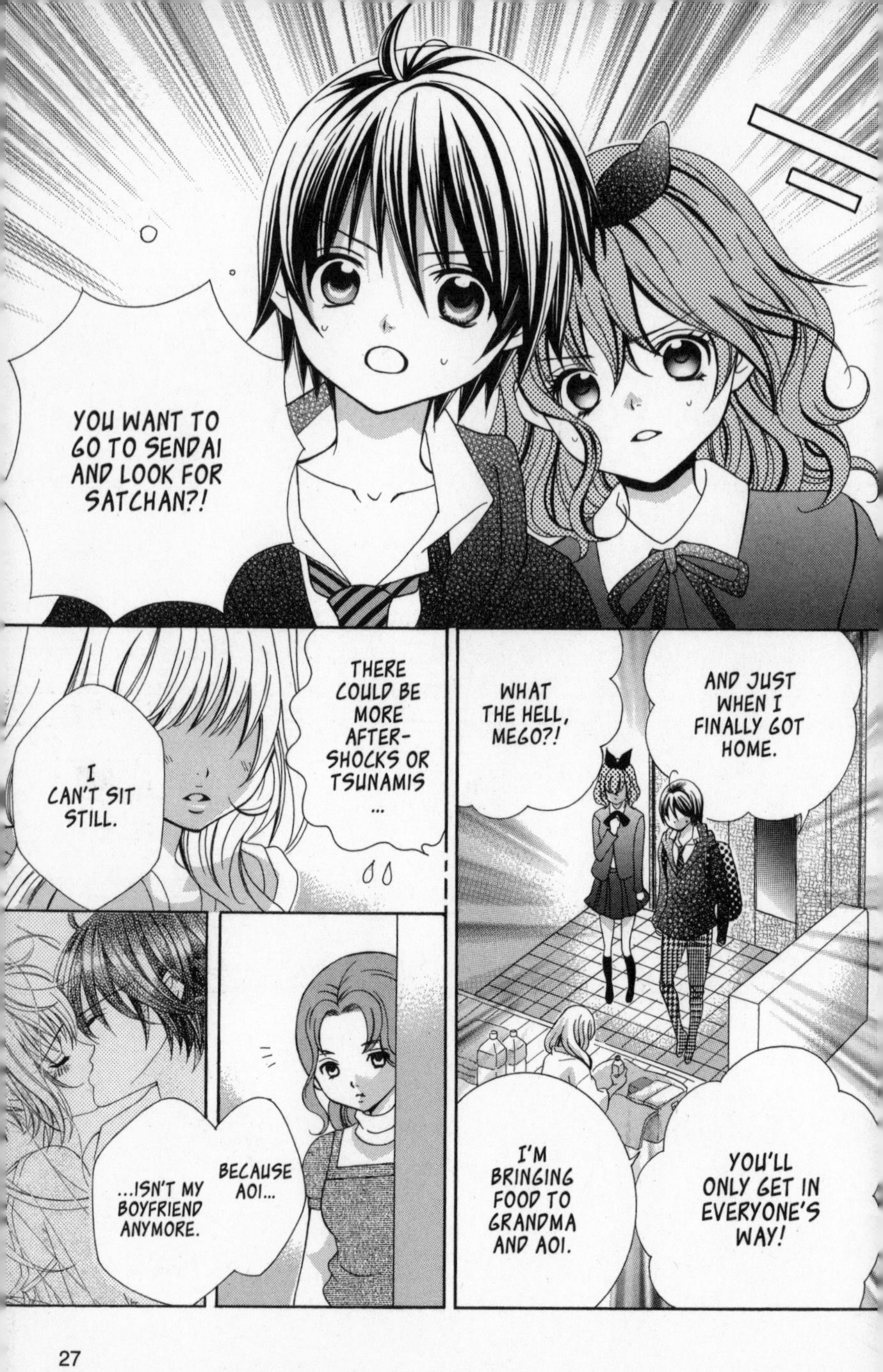
YOU WANT TO GO TO SENDAI AND LOOK FOR SATCHAN?!
AND JUST WHEN I FINALLY GOT HOME.
WHAT THE HELL, MEGO?!
YOU'LL ONLY GET IN EVERYONE'S WAY!
I'M BRINGING FOOD TO GRANDMA AND AOI.
THERE COULD BE MORE AFTER-SHOCKS OR TSUNAMIS ...
I CAN'T SIT STILL.
BECAUSE AOI...
...ISN'T MY BOYFRIEND ANYMORE.

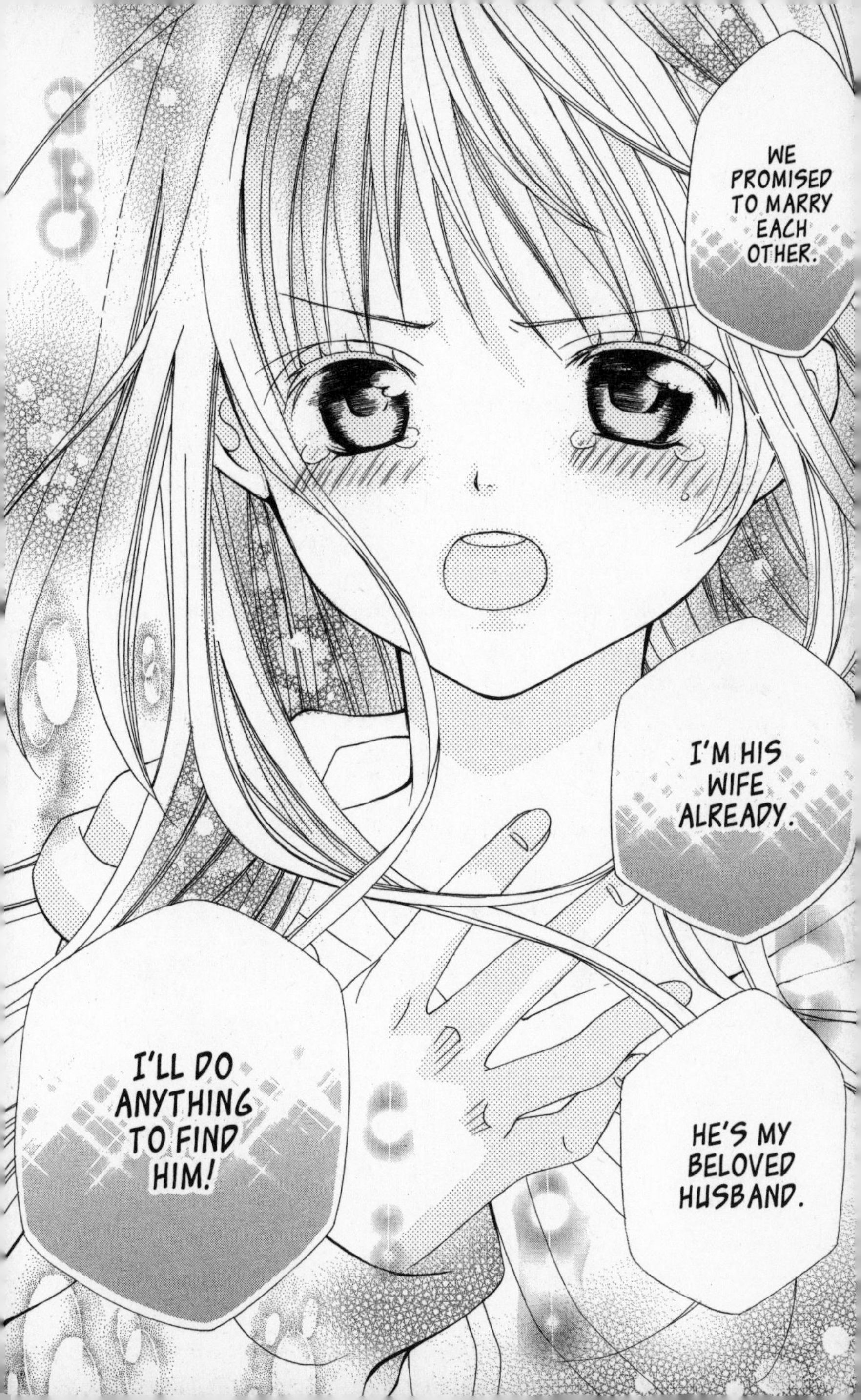
WE PROMISED TO MARRY EACH OTHER.
I'M HIS WIFE ALREADY.
HE'S MY BELOVED HUSBAND.
I'LL DO ANYTHING TO FIND HIM!

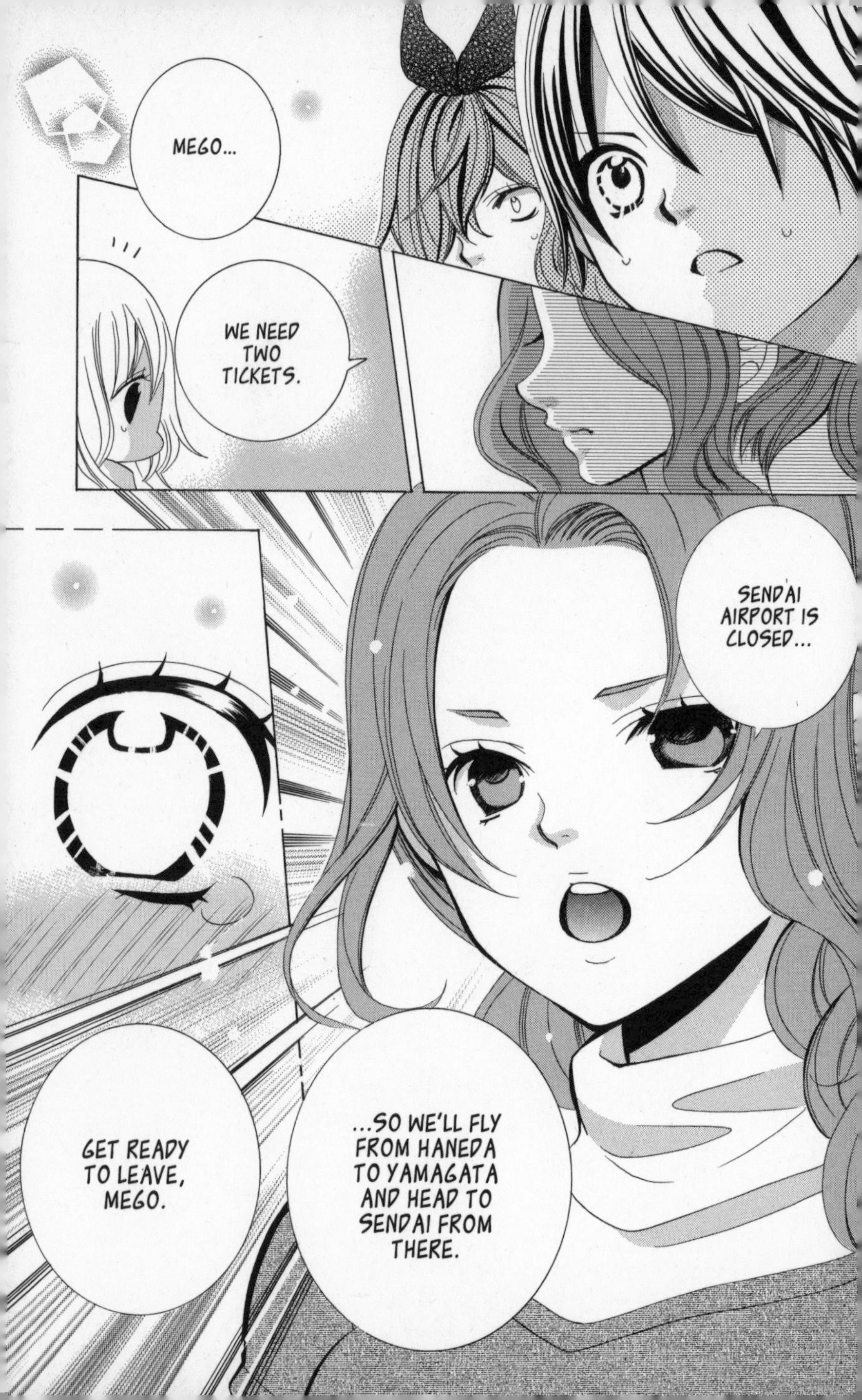
MEGO...
WE NEED TWO TICKETS.
SEND'AI AIRPORT IS CLOSED...
...SO WE'LL FLY FROM HANEDA TO YAMAGATA AND HEAD TO SENDAI FROM THERE.
GET READY TO LEAVE, MEGO.

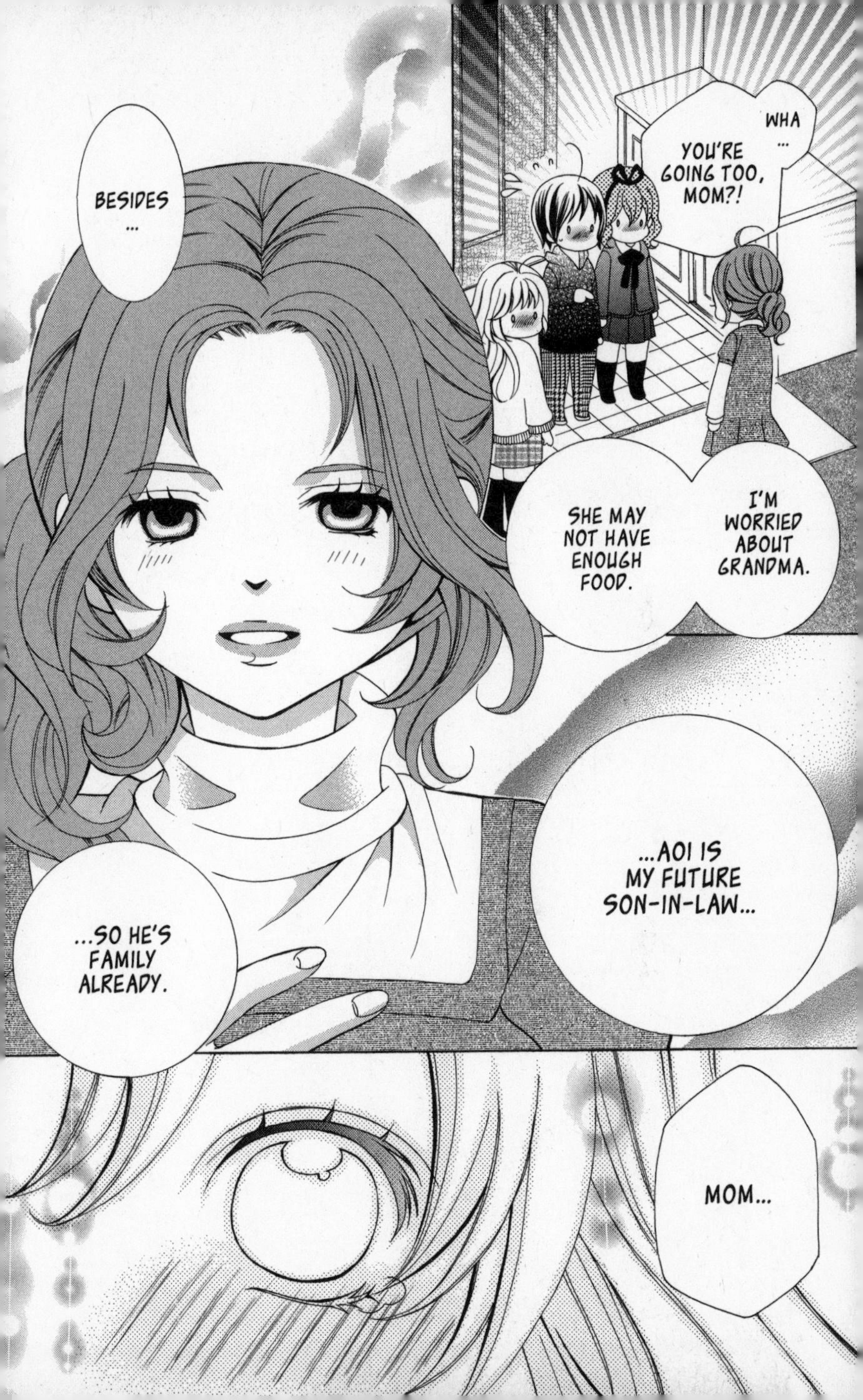
WHA...
YOU'RE GOING TOO, MOM?!
I'M WORRIED ABOUT GRANDMA.
SHE MAY NOT HAVE ENOUGH FOOD.
BESIDES...
...AOI IS MY FUTURE SON-IN-LAW...
...SO HE'S FAMILY ALREADY.
MOM...

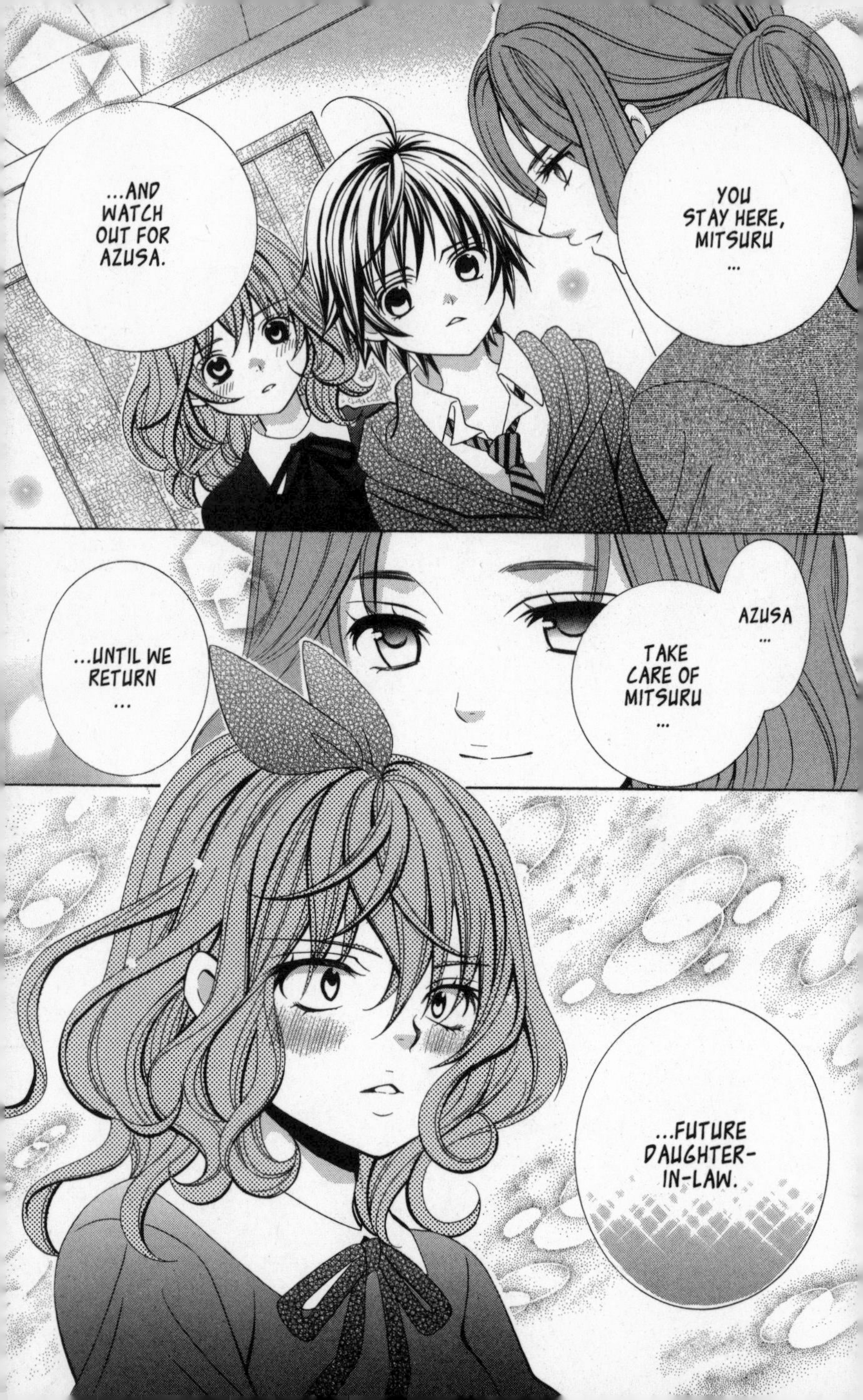
YOU STAY HERE, MITSURU ...
...AND WATCH OUT FOR AZUSA.
AZUSA ...
TAKE CARE OF MITSURU ...
...UNTIL WE RETURN ...
...FUTURE DAUGHTER-IN-LAW.

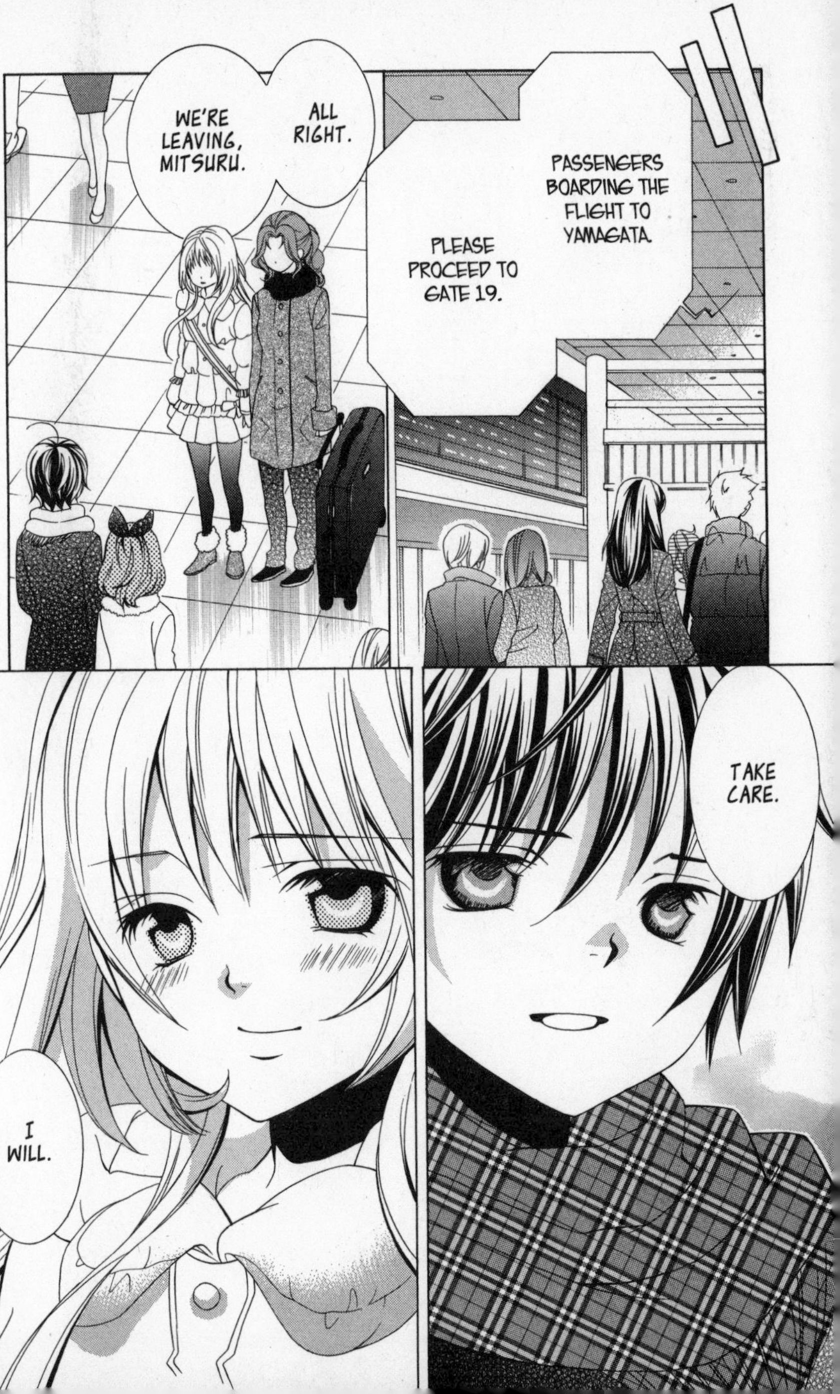
PASSENGERS BOARDING THE FLIGHT TO YAMAGATA.
PLEASE PROCEED TO GATE 19.
ALL RIGHT.
WE'RE LEAVING, MITSURU.
TAKE CARE.
I WILL.

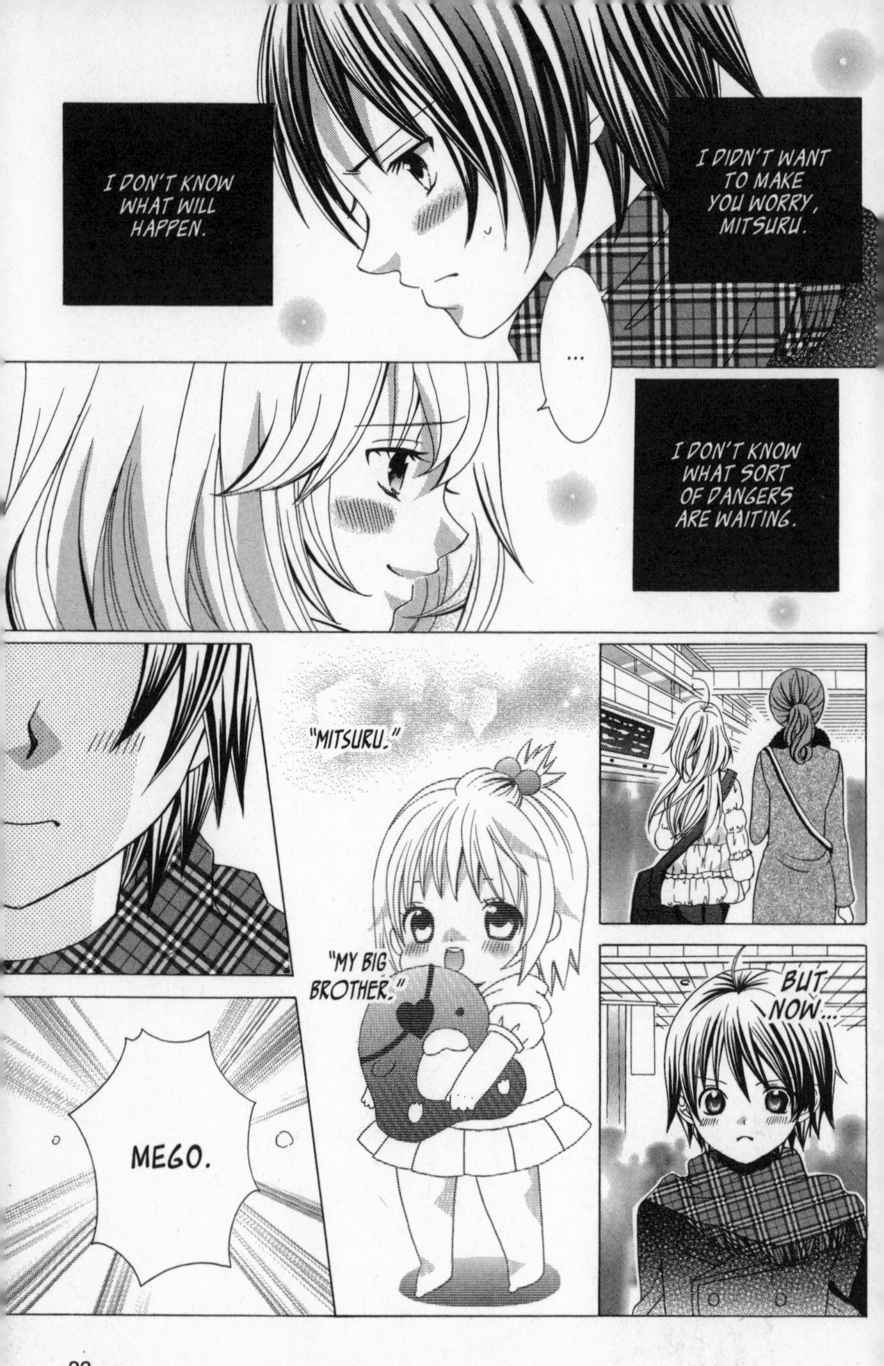

I DIDN'T WANT TO MAKE YOU WORRY, MITSURU.
I DON'T KNOW WHAT WILL HAPPEN.
...
I DON'T KNOW WHAT SORT OF DANGERS ARE WAITING.
BUT NOW...
"MITSURU."
"MY BIG BROTHER."
MEGO.

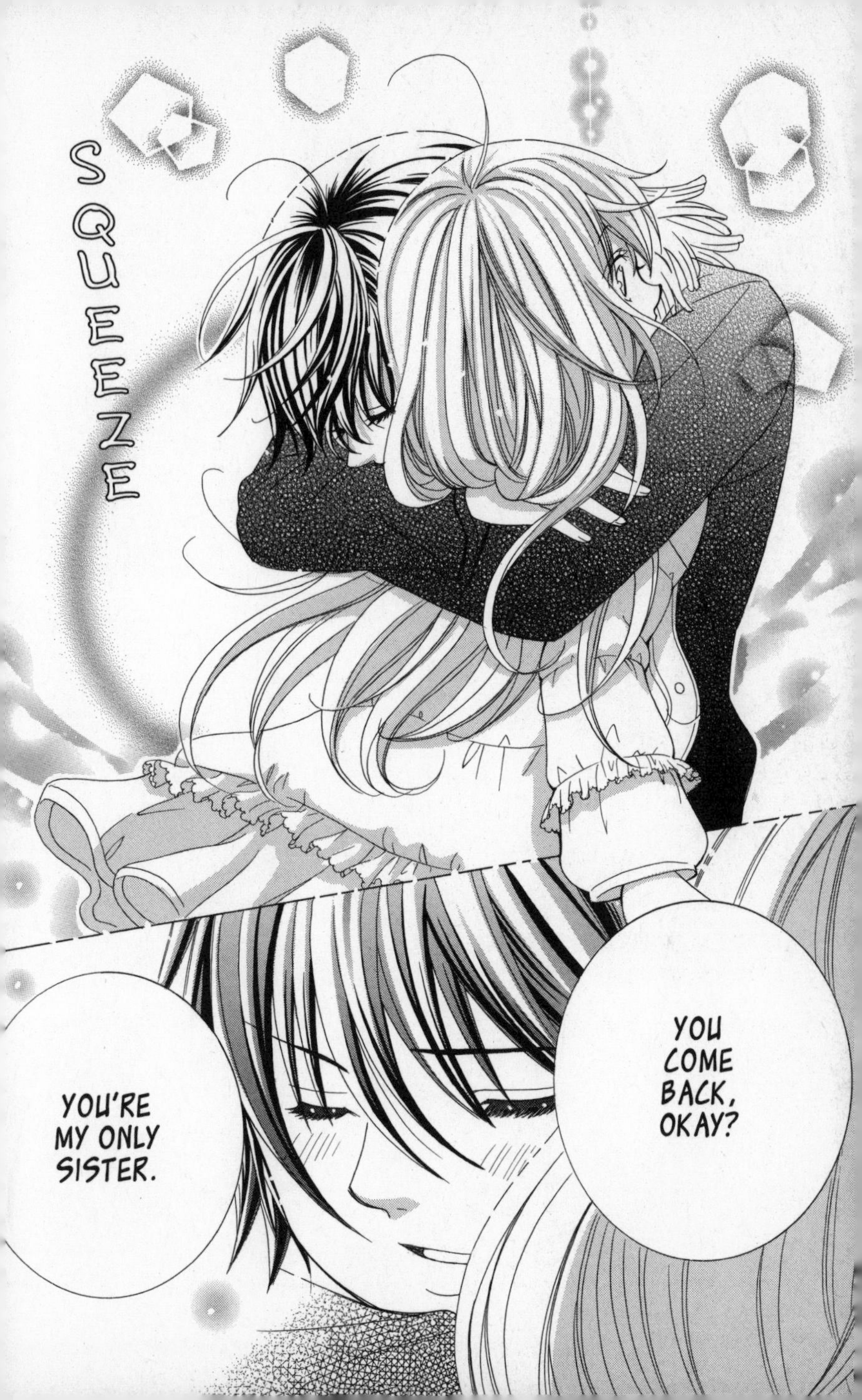
SQUEEZE
YOU COME BACK, OKAY?
YOU'RE MY ONLY SISTER.

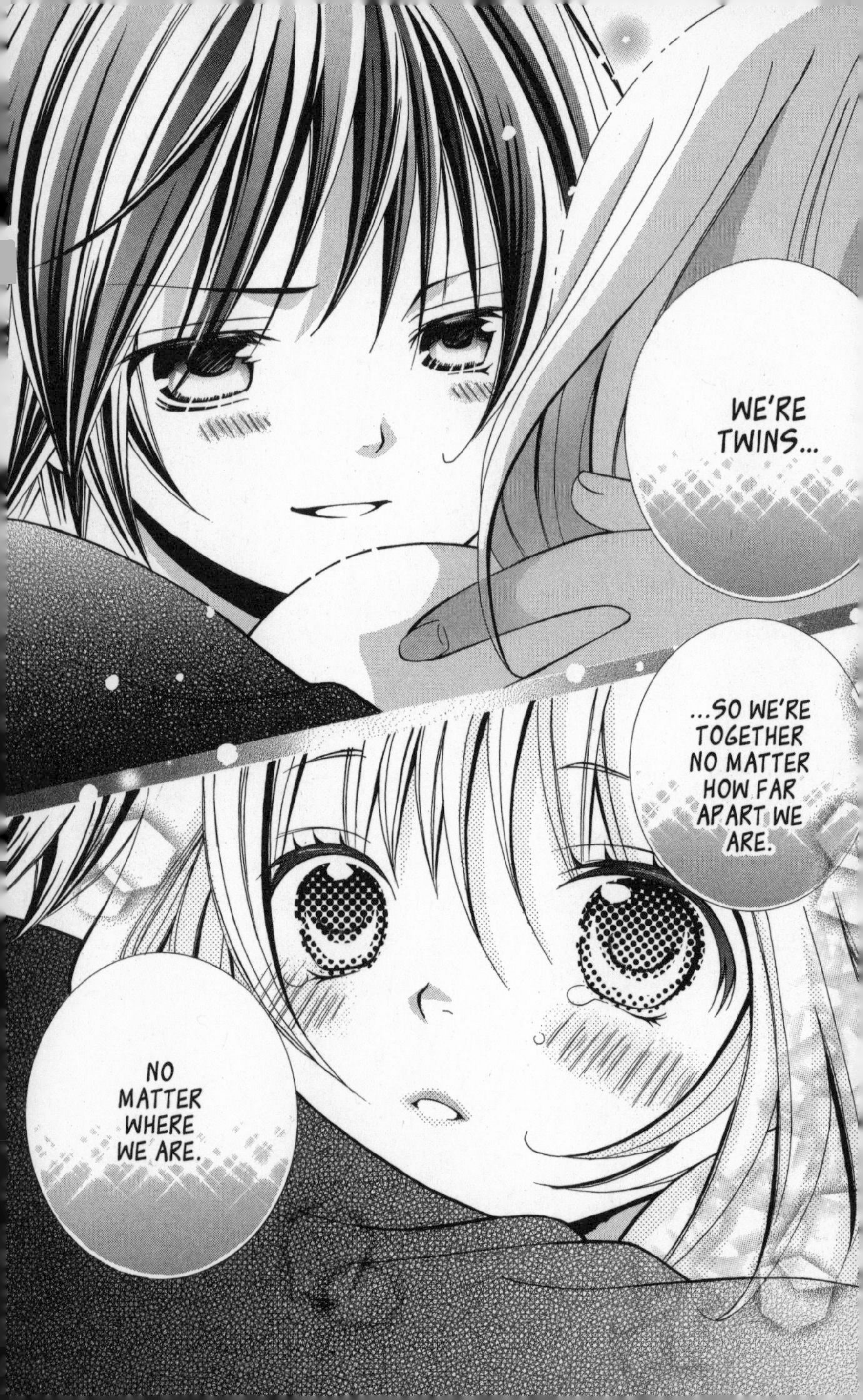
WE'RE TWINS...
...SO WE'RE TOGETHER NO MATTER HOW FAR APART WE ARE.
NO MATTER WHERE WE ARE.

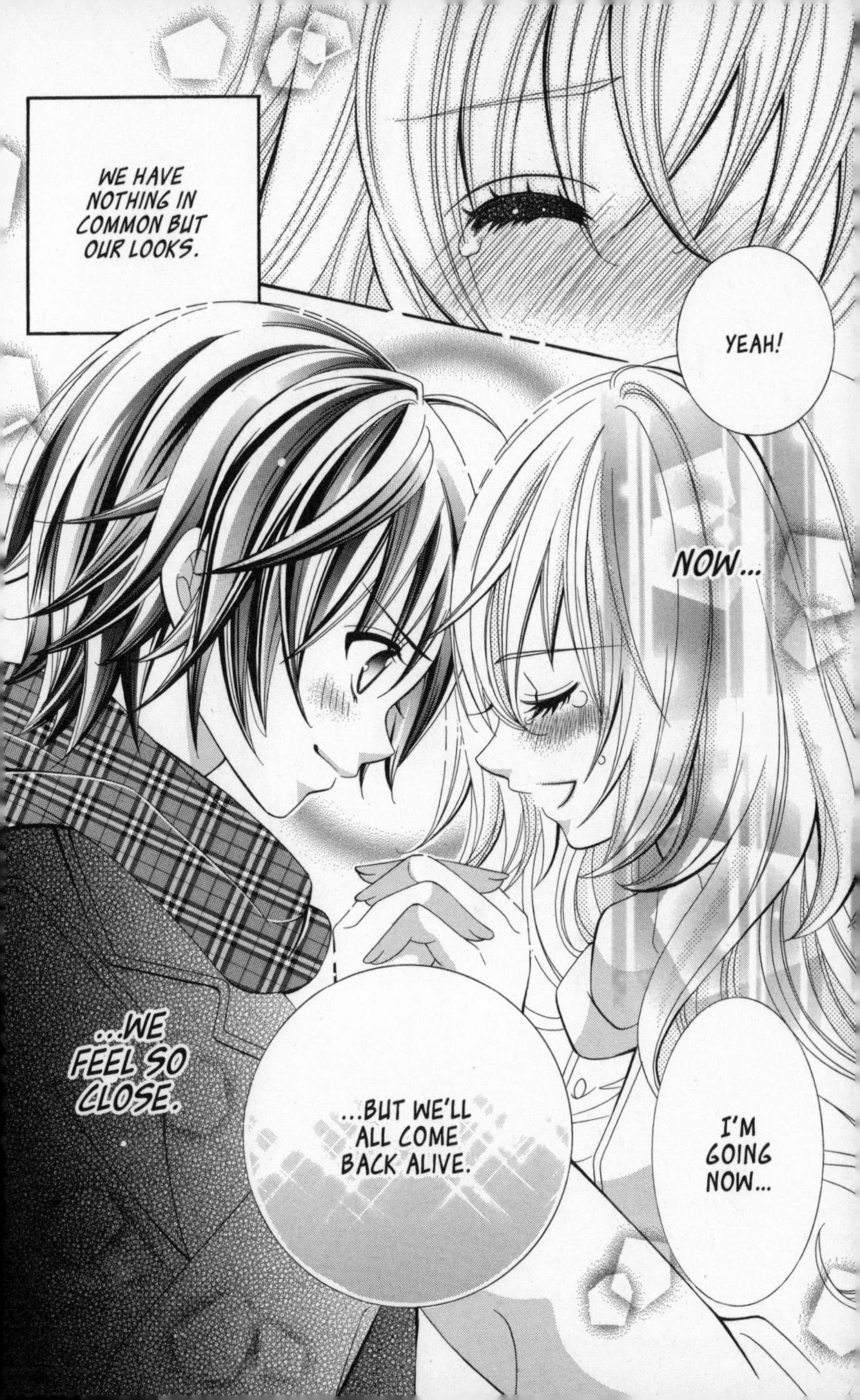
WE HAVE NOTHING IN COMMON BUT OUR LOOKS.
YEAH!
NOW...
...WE FEEL SO CLOSE.
I'M GOING NOW...
...BUT WE'LL ALL COME BACK ALIVE.

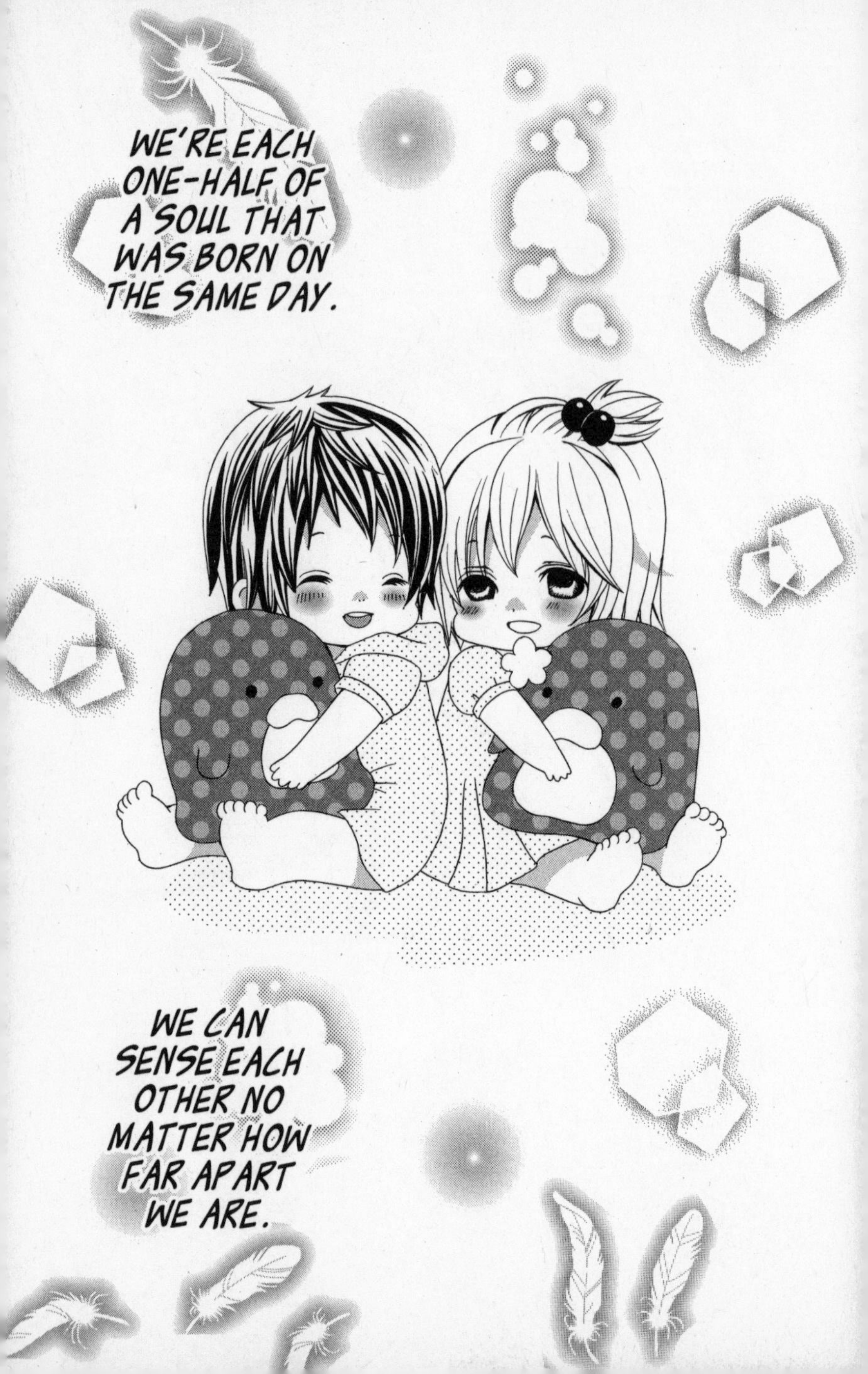
WE'RE EACH ONE-HALF OF A SOUL THAT WAS BORN ON THE SAME DAY.
WE CAN SENSE EACH OTHER NO MATTER HOW FAR APART WE ARE.

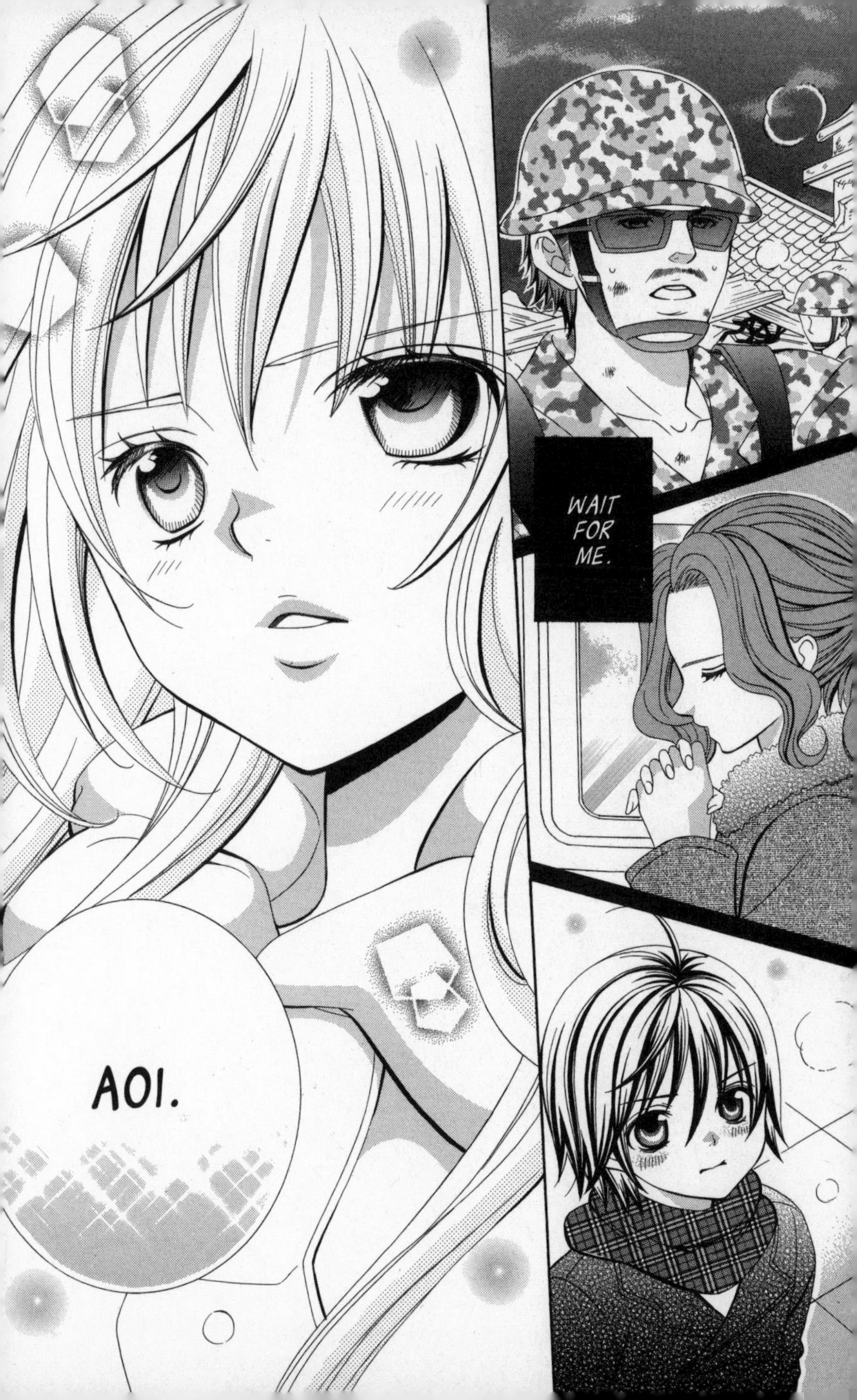
WAIT FOR ME.
AOI.

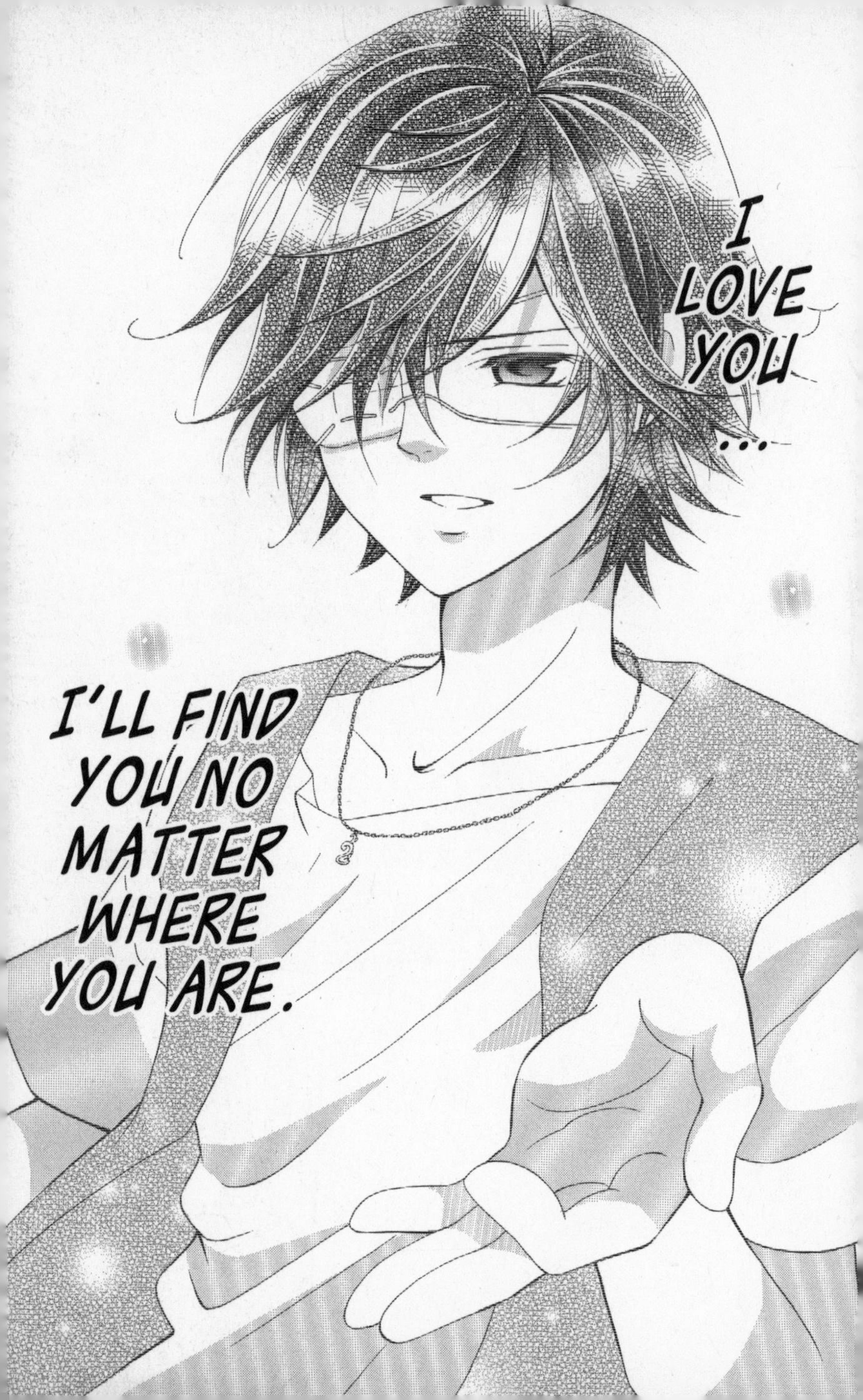
I LOVE YOU...
I'LL FIND YOU NO MATTER WHERE YOU ARE.

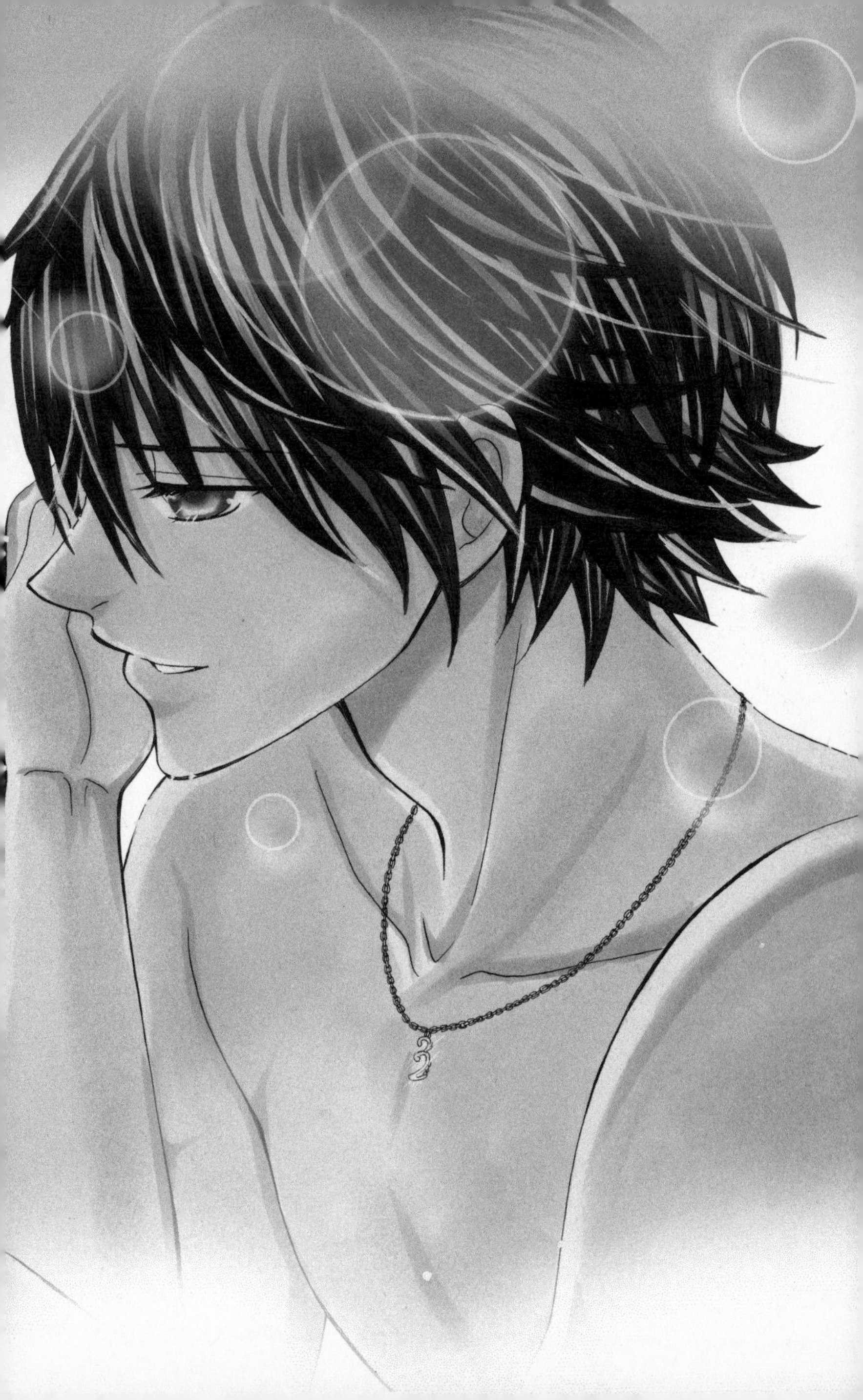

Chapter 68

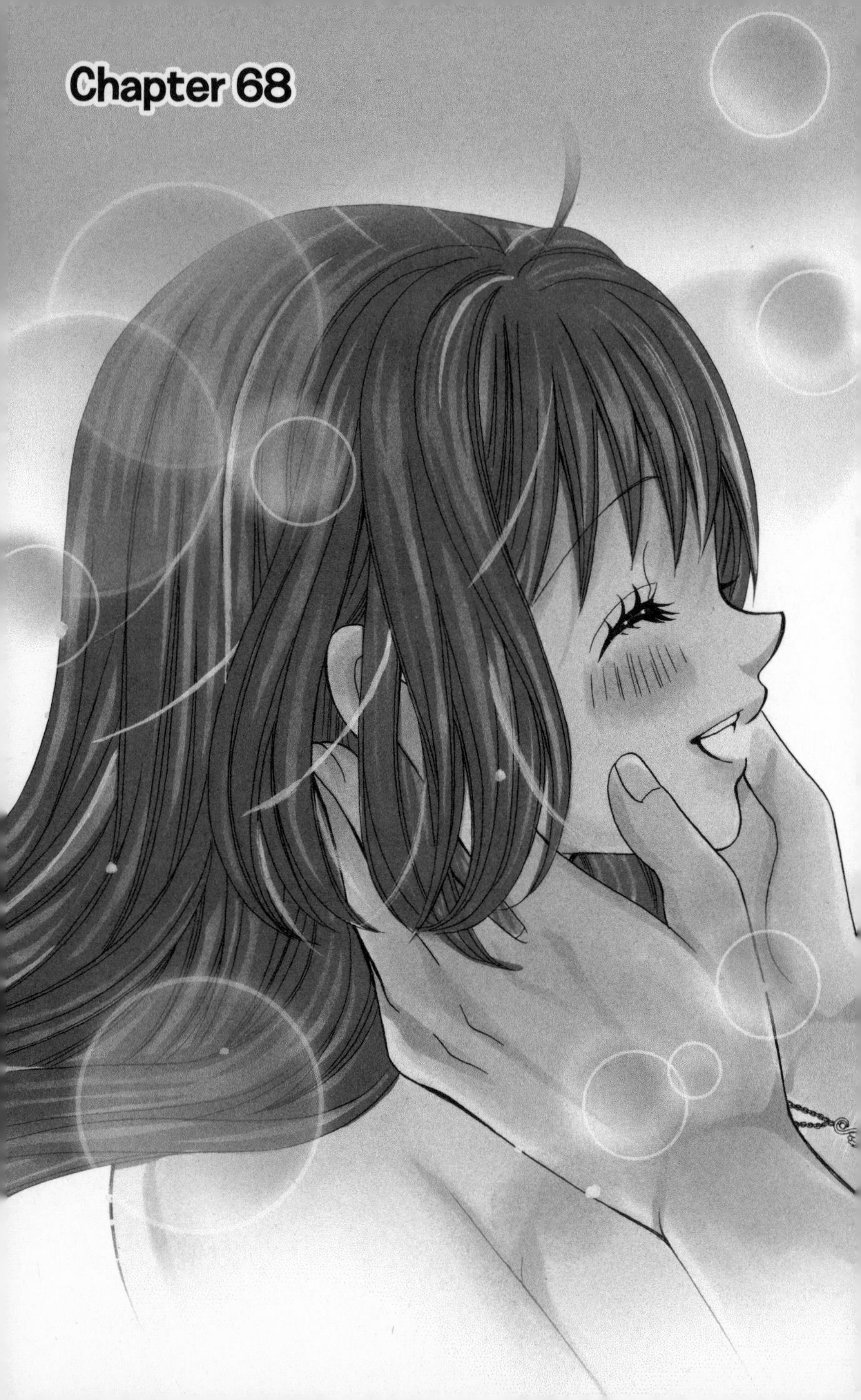

So Cute! Fan Art Feature ♥

EVERYONE'S DRAWINGS ARE SO CUTE, THEY HURT!!

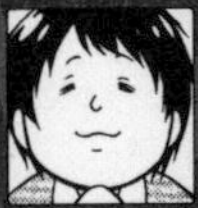

Utaro

Editor Utaro has commented on each one this time!!♪

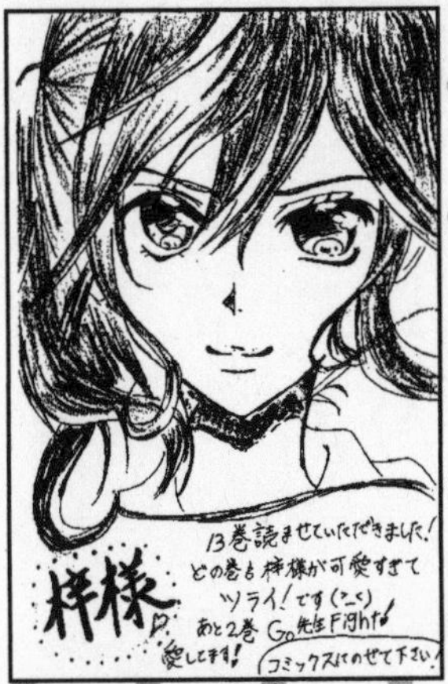
梓様
13巻読ませていただきました!
どの巻も梓様が可愛すぎて
ツライ!です(>_<)
あと2巻 Go 先生 Fight!
愛してます!
コミックスにのせて下さい!

Haruka Suzuki (Iwate) ↑

Ed.: This Azusa is so beautiful it hurts!!

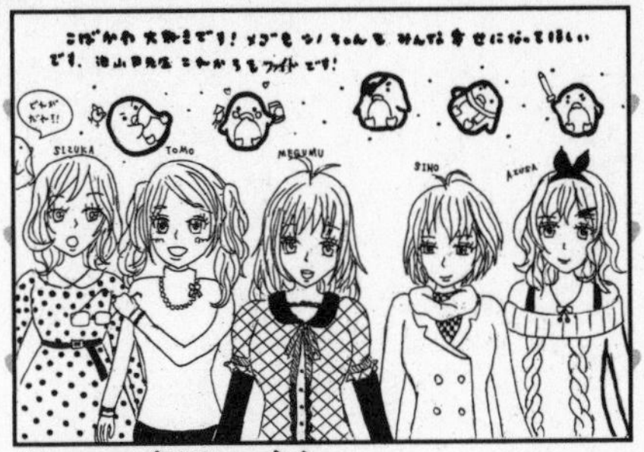
SIZUKA
TOMO
MEGUMU
SINO
AZUSA

Miya-chan (Ishikawa) ↑

Ed.: All the girls! Gorgeous!!

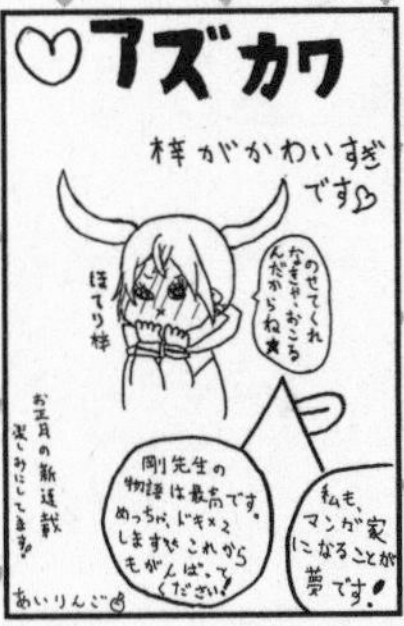
♡アズカワ
梓がかわいすぎです♡
のせてくれなきゃ、おこるんだからね★
ほてり梓
剛先生の物語は最高です。めっちゃドキドキしますっ これからもがんばってください!
私も、マンガ家になることが夢です!
あいりんご

Airingo (Akita) ←

Ed.: She looks cute even when she's angry. ♥

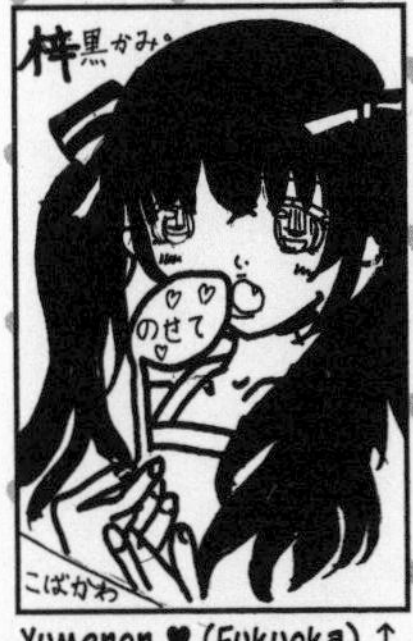
梓黒かみ
のせて
こばかわ

Yumenon ♥ (Fukuoka) ↑

Ed.: Azusa looks great with black hair too!!

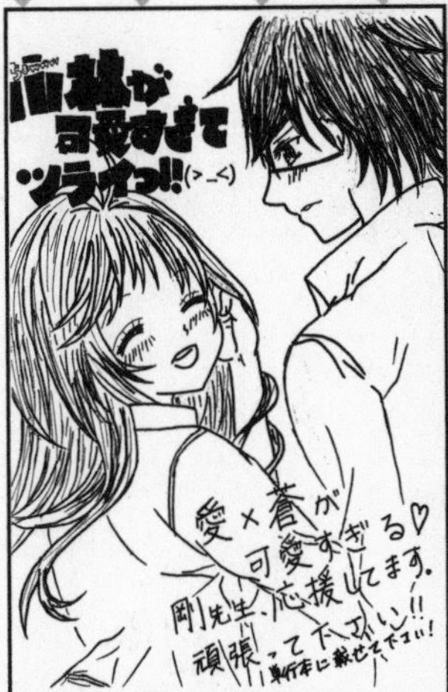
小林が可愛すぎてツライっ!!(>_<)
愛×蒼が可愛すぎる♡
応援してます。
剛先生、頑張って下さい!!
単行本に載せて下さい

Mayu Yamada ↑

Ed.: You can tell they're so in love. (^^)

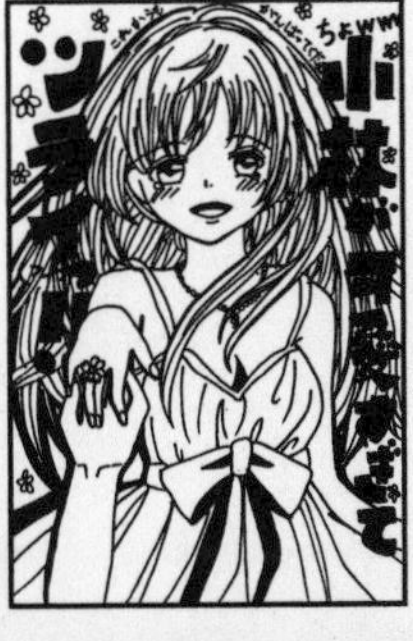

Shion Kai (Aichi) →

Ed.: I can't help but cry seeing the happy Mego!

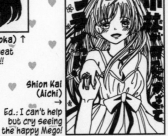

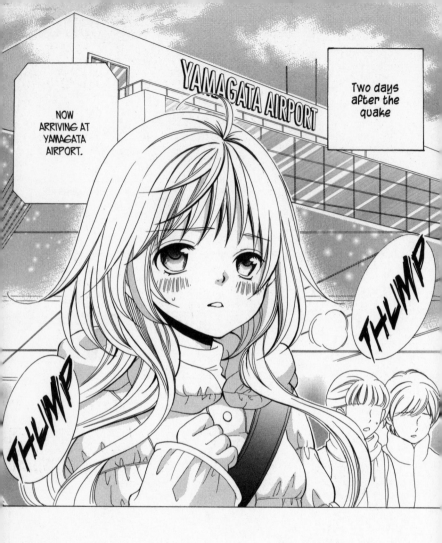

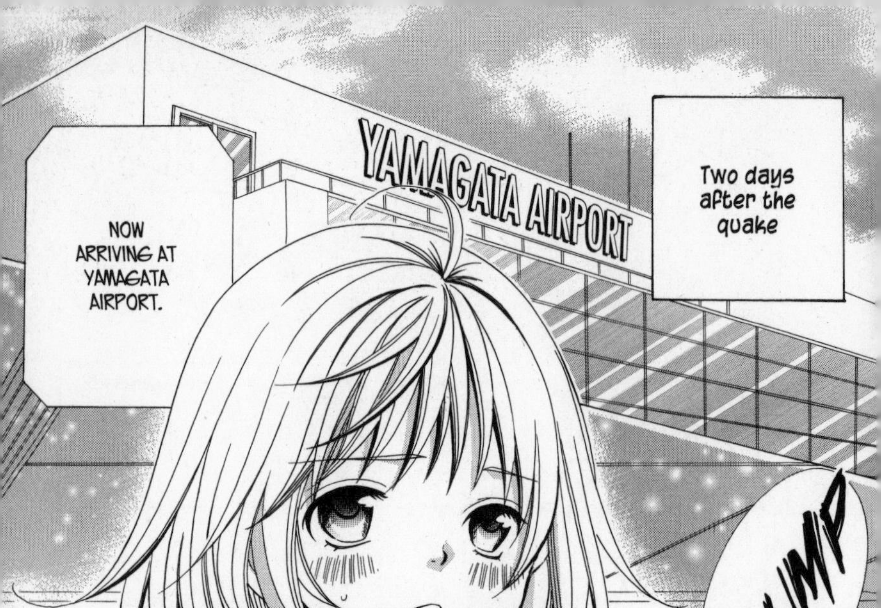
Two days after the quake
YAMAGATA AIRPORT
NOW ARRIVING AT YAMAGATA AIRPORT.
THUMP
THUMP

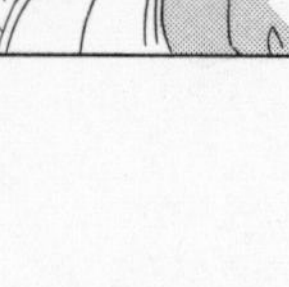

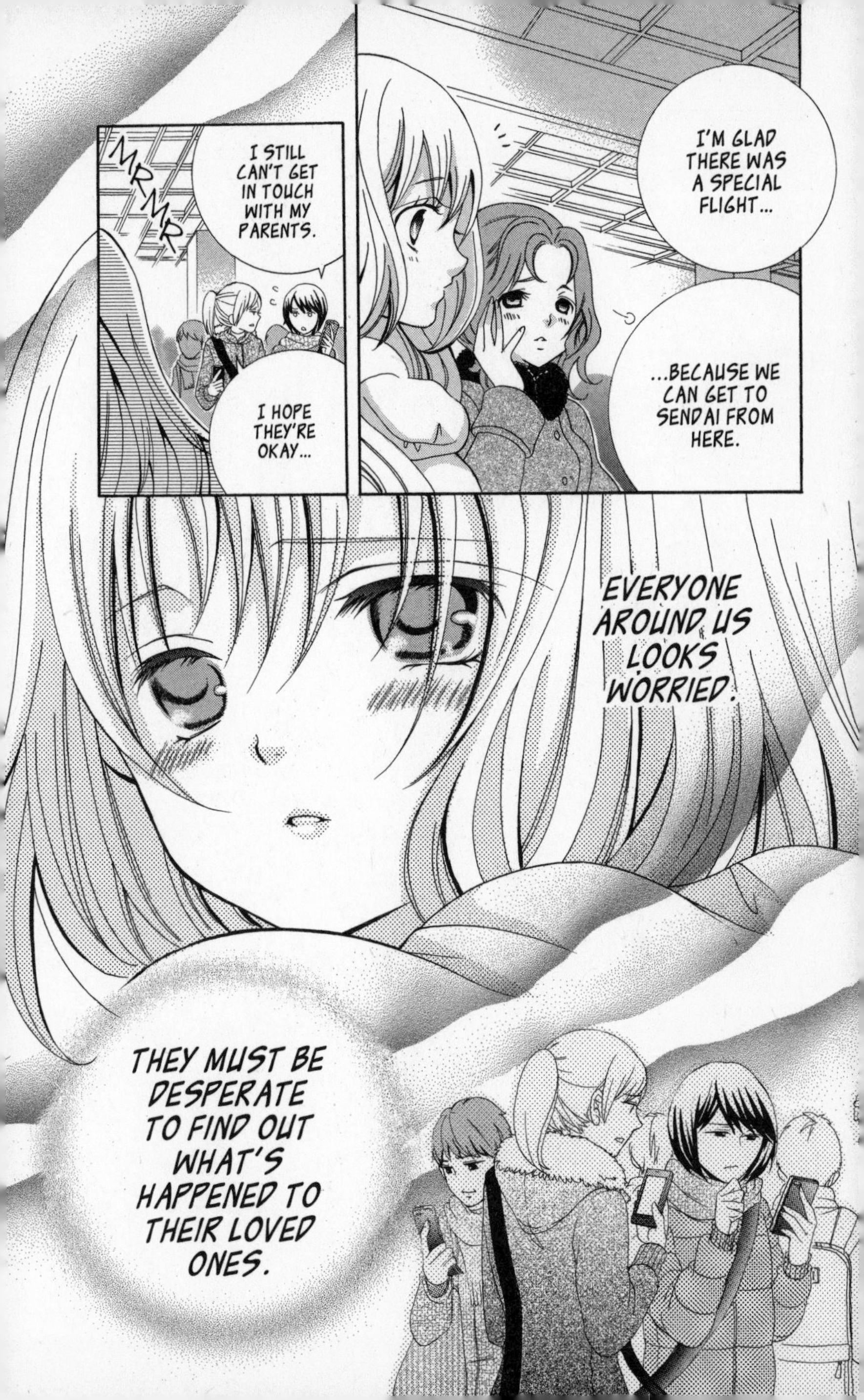
I'M GLAD THERE WAS A SPECIAL FLIGHT...
...BECAUSE WE CAN GET TO SENDAI FROM HERE.
MRMR
I STILL CAN'T GET IN TOUCH WITH MY PARENTS.
I HOPE THEY'RE OKAY...
EVERYONE AROUND US LOOKS WORRIED.
THEY MUST BE DESPERATE TO FIND OUT WHAT'S HAPPENED TO THEIR LOVED ONES.

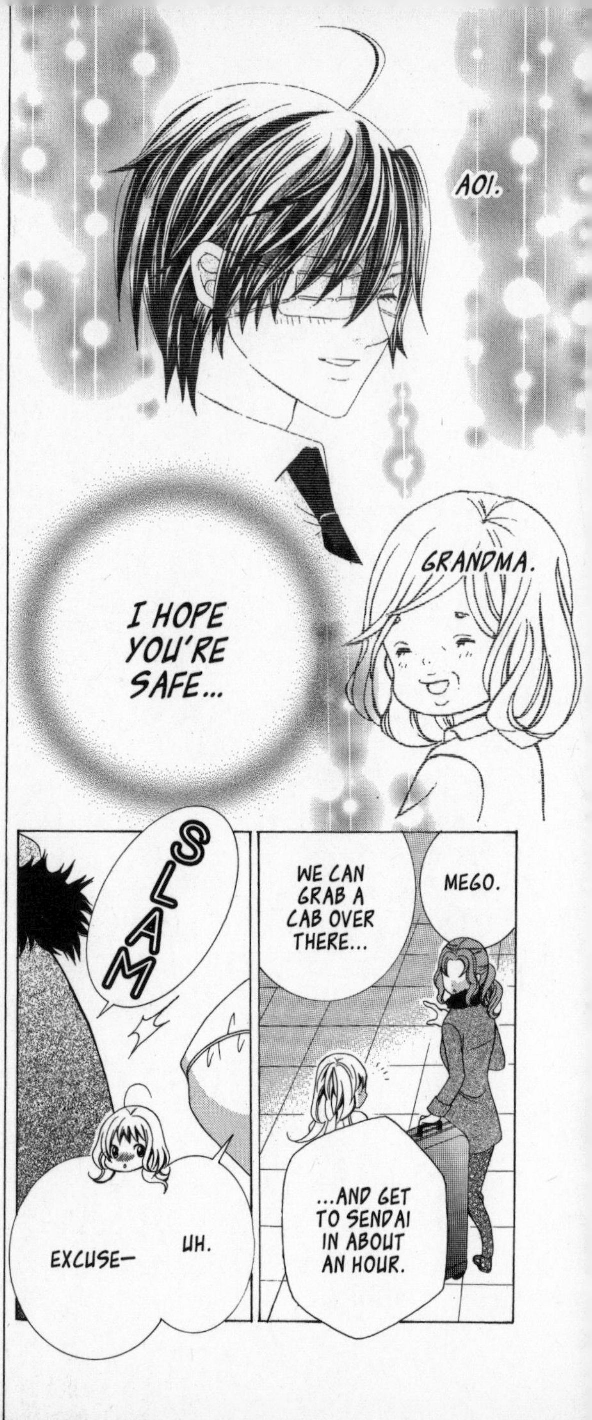
AOI.
GRANDMA.
I HOPE YOU'RE SAFE...
MEGO.
WE CAN GRAB A CAB OVER THERE...
...AND GET TO SENDAI IN ABOUT AN HOUR.
SLAM
UH.
EXCUSE—

SPECIAL THANKS

Yuka Ito-sama,
Rieko Hirai-sama,
Kayoko Takahashi-sama,
Kawasaki-sama,
Nagisa Sato Sensei.

Rei Nanase Sensei,
Arisu Fujishiro Sensei,
Mumi Mimura Sensei,
Masayo Nagata-sama,
Naochan-sama,
Asuka Sakura Sensei
and many others.

Bookstore Dan Kinshicho Branch, Kinokuniya Shinjuku Branch, LIBRO Ikebukuro Branch, Kinokuniya Hankyu 32-Bangai Branch.

Sendai Hachimonjiya Bookstore, Books HOSHINO Kintetsu Pass'e Branch, Asahiya Tennoji MiO Branch, Kurashiki Kikuya Bookstore.

Salesperson:
Mizusawa-sama

Previous salesperson:
Honma-sama

Previous editor:
Shoji-sama

Current editor:
Utaro-sama

I also sincerely express my gratitude to everyone who picked up this volume.

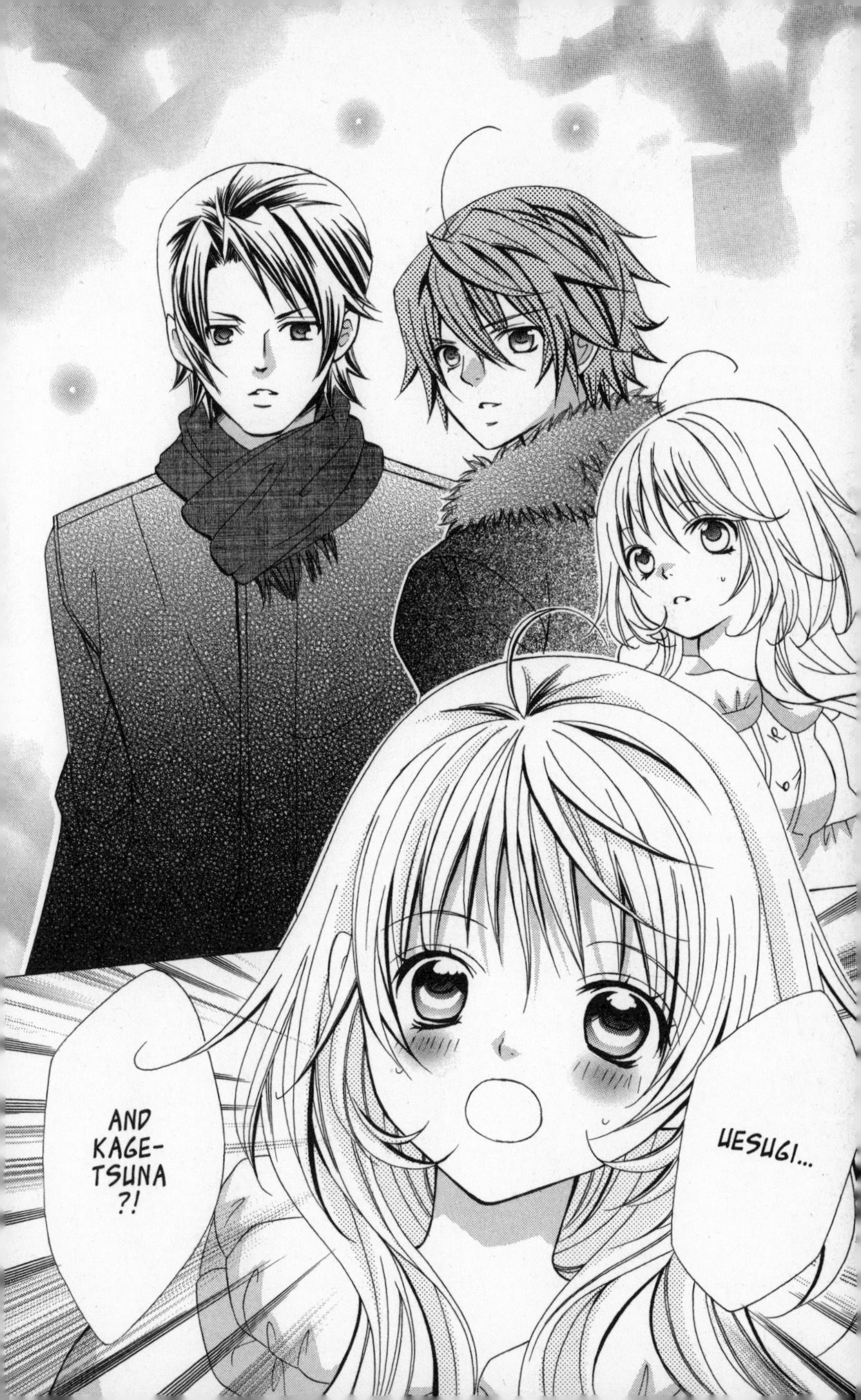
UESUGI...
AND KAGE-TSUNA ?!

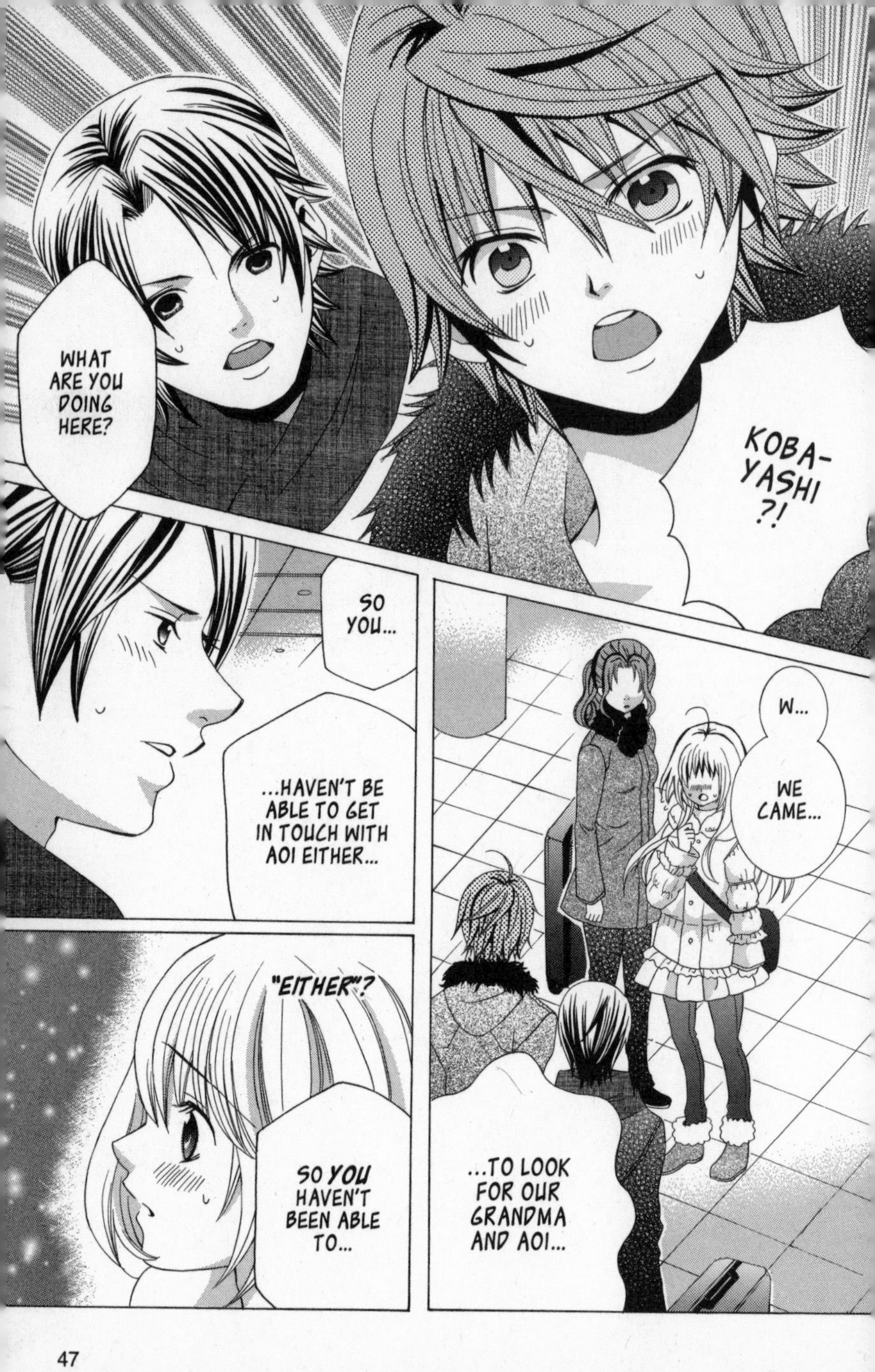
KOBA-YASHI?!
WHAT ARE YOU DOING HERE?
W...
WE CAME...
...TO LOOK FOR OUR GRANDMA AND AOI...
SO YOU...
...HAVEN'T BE ABLE TO GET IN TOUCH WITH AOI EITHER...
"EITHER"?
SO *YOU* HAVEN'T BEEN ABLE TO...

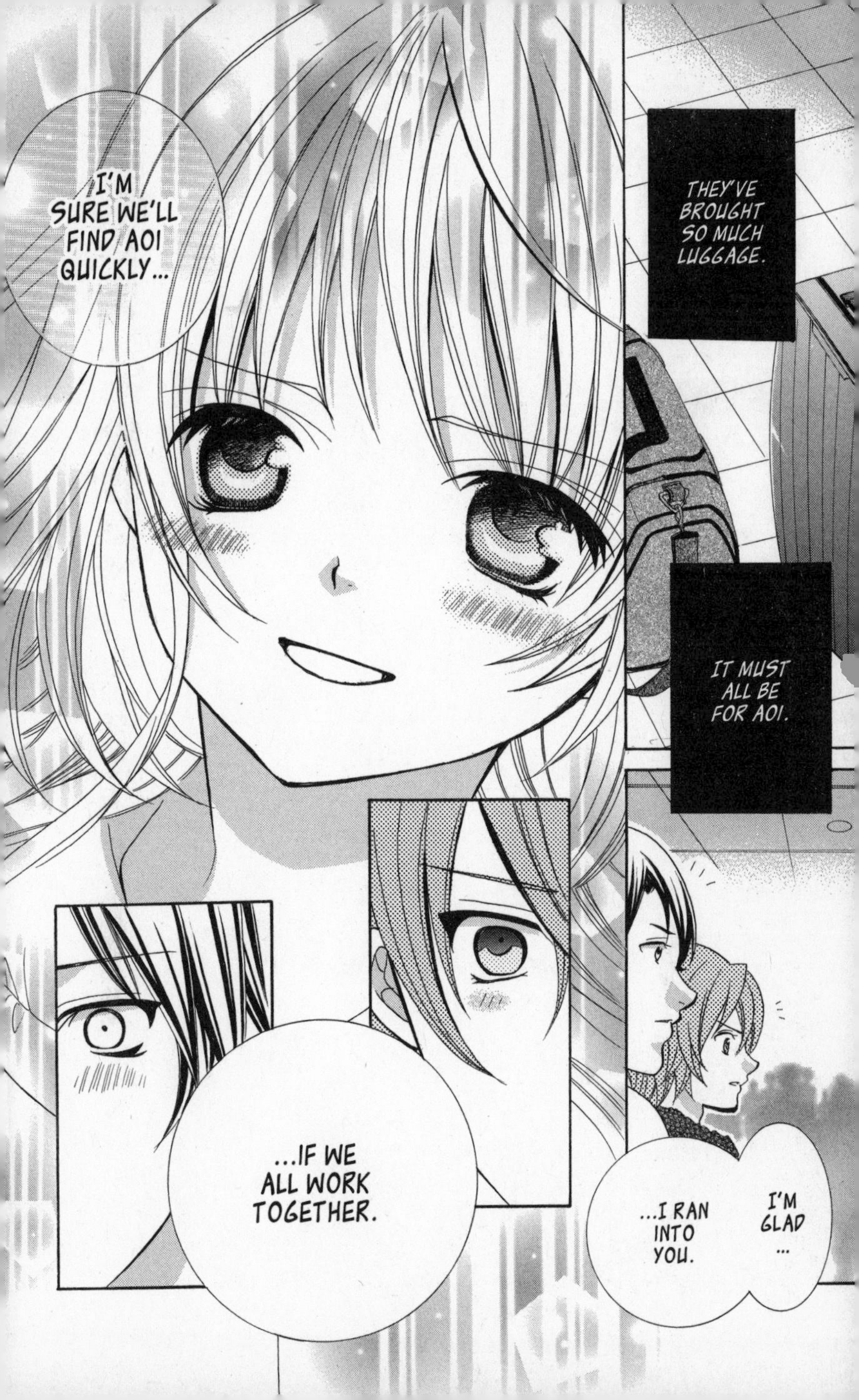
THEY'VE BROUGHT SO MUCH LUGGAGE.
IT MUST ALL BE FOR AOI.
I'M GLAD...
...I RAN INTO YOU.
I'M SURE WE'LL FIND AOI QUICKLY...
...IF WE ALL WORK TOGETHER.

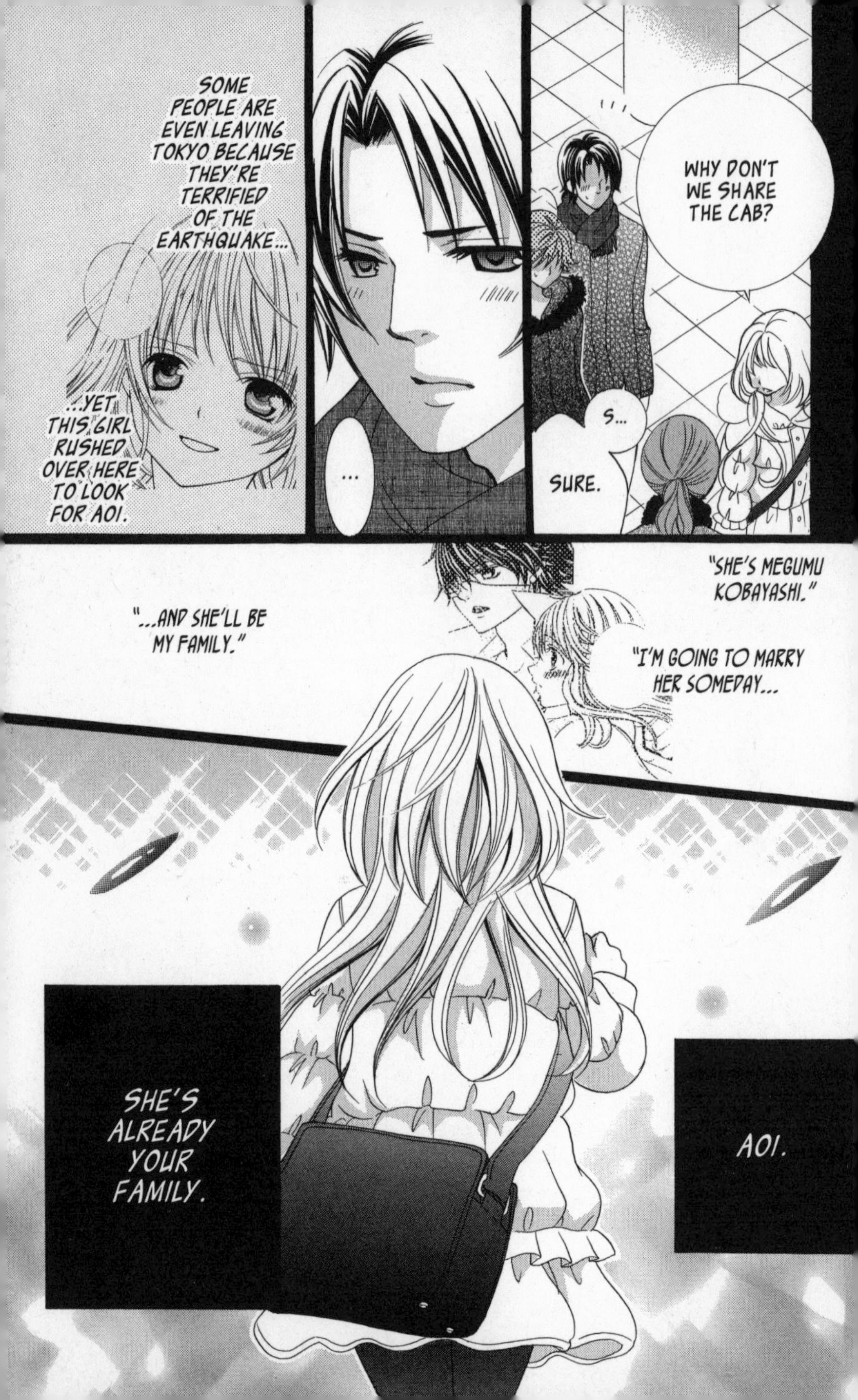
WHY DON'T WE SHARE THE CAB?
S...
SURE.
...
SOME PEOPLE ARE EVEN LEAVING TOKYO BECAUSE THEY'RE TERRIFIED OF THE EARTHQUAKE...
...YET THIS GIRL RUSHED OVER HERE TO LOOK FOR AOI.
"SHE'S MEGUMU KOBAYASHI."
"I'M GOING TO MARRY HER SOMEDAY...
"...AND SHE'LL BE MY FAMILY."
AOI.
SHE'S ALREADY YOUR FAMILY.

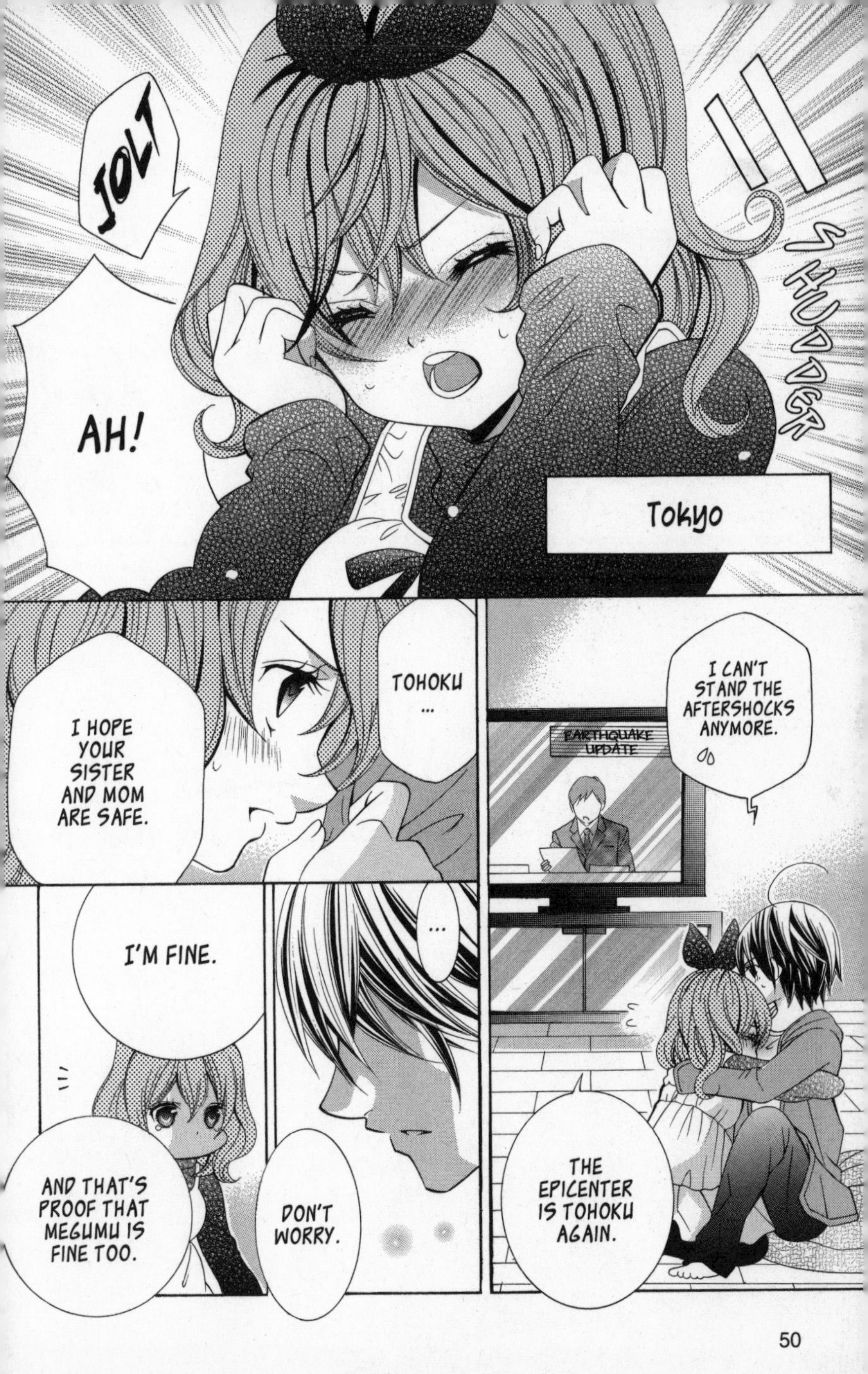
SHUDDER
JOLT
AH!
Tokyo
I CAN'T STAND THE AFTERSHOCKS ANYMORE.
EARTHQUAKE UPDATE
THE EPICENTER IS TOHOKU AGAIN.
TOHOKU ...
I HOPE YOUR SISTER AND MOM ARE SAFE.
...
DON'T WORRY.
I'M FINE.
AND THAT'S PROOF THAT MEGUMU IS FINE TOO.

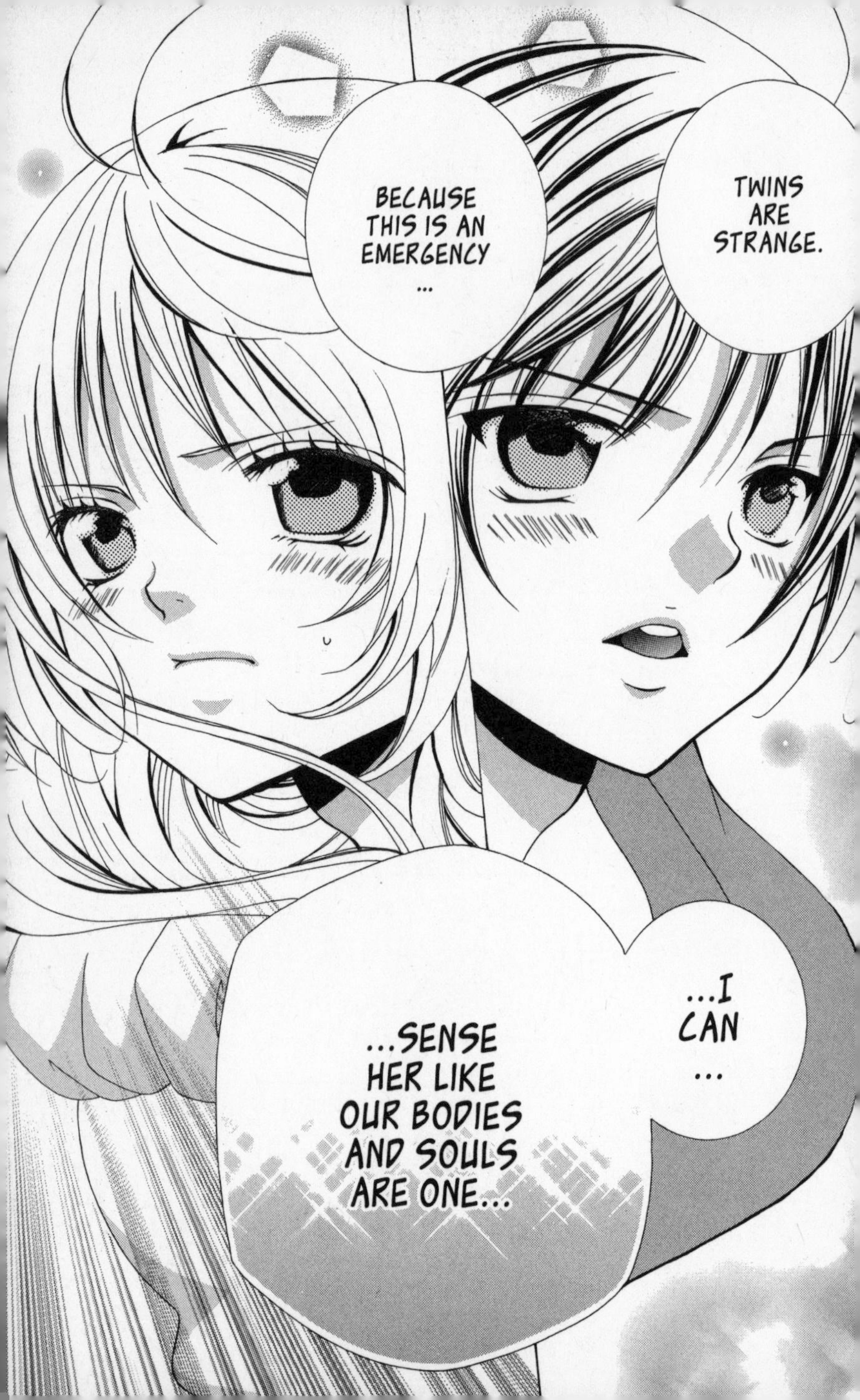
TWINS ARE STRANGE.
BECAUSE THIS IS AN EMERGENCY ...
...I CAN ...
...SENSE HER LIKE OUR BODIES AND SOULS ARE ONE...

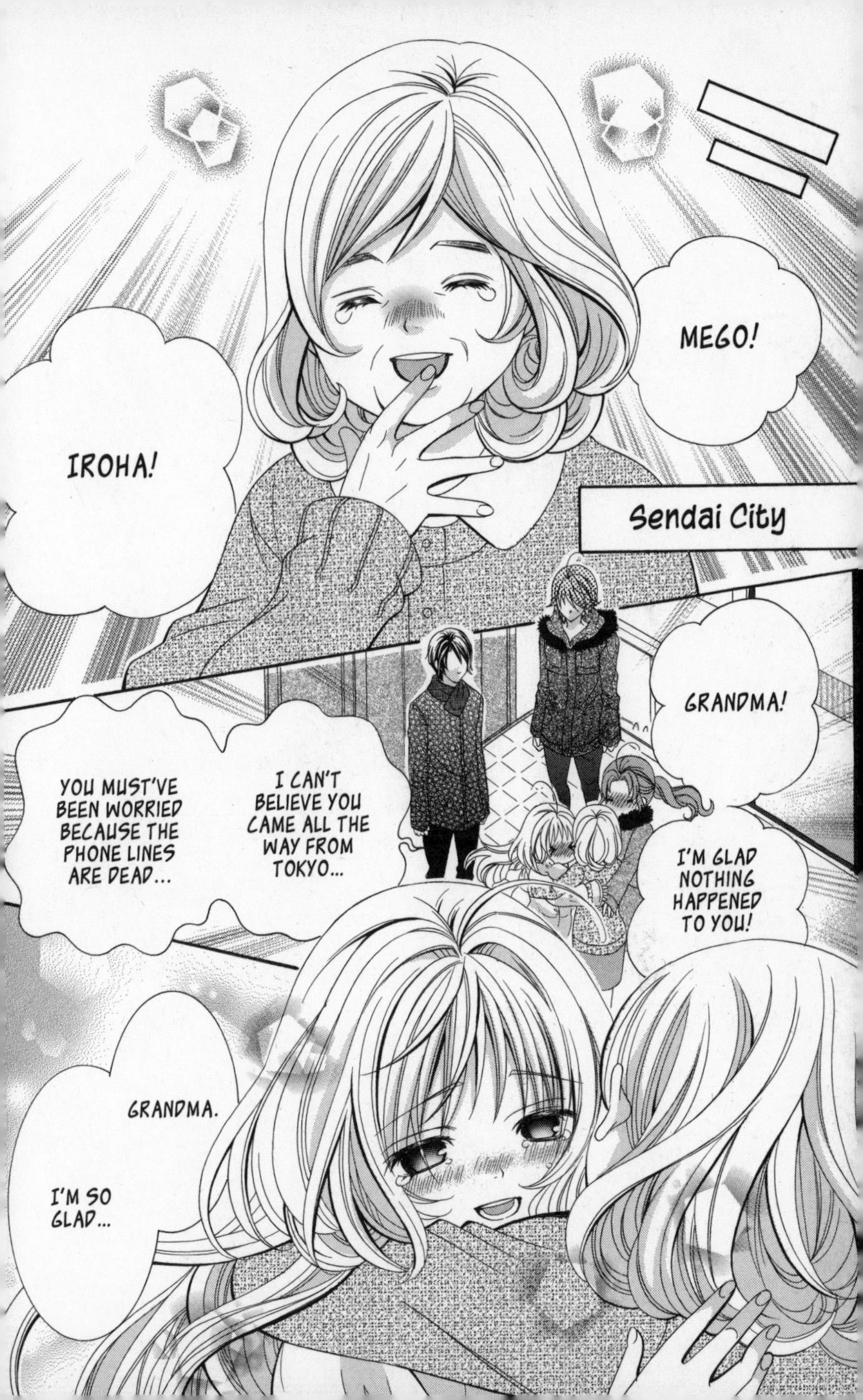
MEGO!
IROHA!
Sendai City
GRANDMA!
I'M GLAD NOTHING HAPPENED TO YOU!
I CAN'T BELIEVE YOU CAME ALL THE WAY FROM TOKYO...
YOU MUST'VE BEEN WORRIED BECAUSE THE PHONE LINES ARE DEAD...
GRANDMA.
I'M SO GLAD...

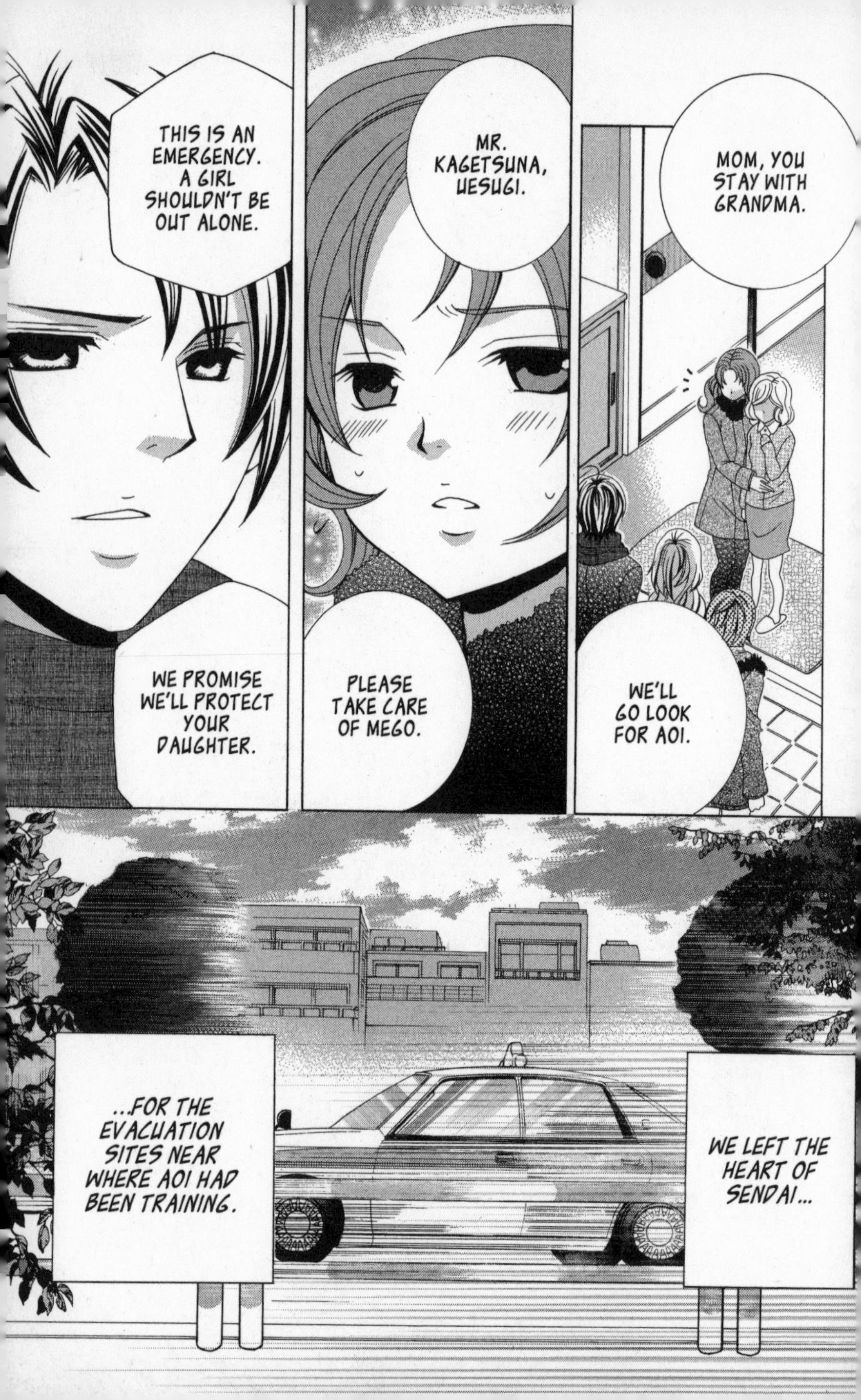
MOM, YOU STAY WITH GRANDMA.
WE'LL GO LOOK FOR AOI.
MR. KAGETSUNA, UESUGI.
PLEASE TAKE CARE OF MEGO.
THIS IS AN EMERGENCY. A GIRL SHOULDN'T BE OUT ALONE.
WE PROMISE WE'LL PROTECT YOUR DAUGHTER.
WE LEFT THE HEART OF SENDAI...
...FOR THE EVACUATION SITES NEAR WHERE AOI HAD BEEN TRAINING.

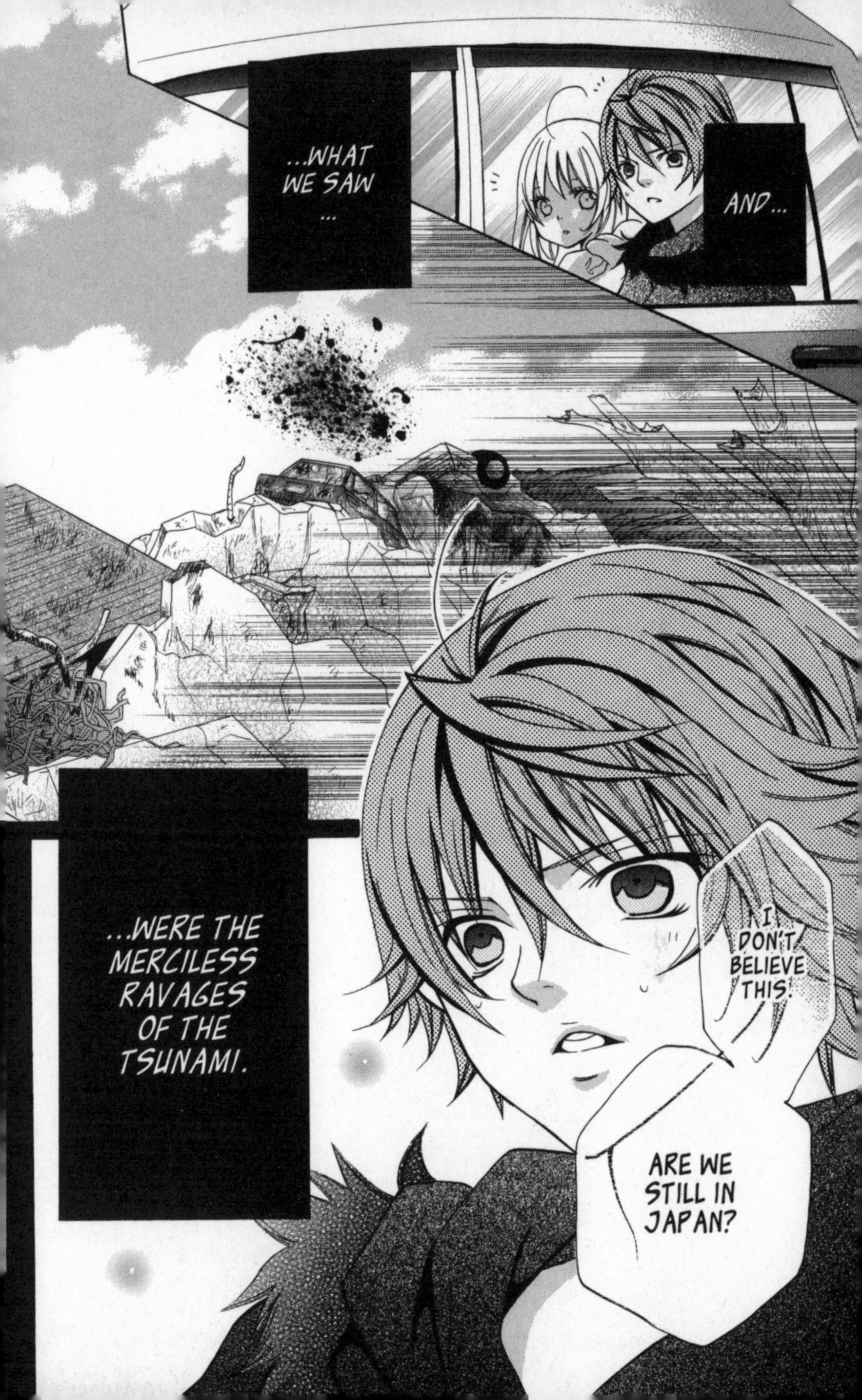
AND...
...WHAT WE SAW ...
...WERE THE MERCILESS RAVAGES OF THE TSUNAMI.
I DON'T BELIEVE THIS.
ARE WE STILL IN JAPAN?

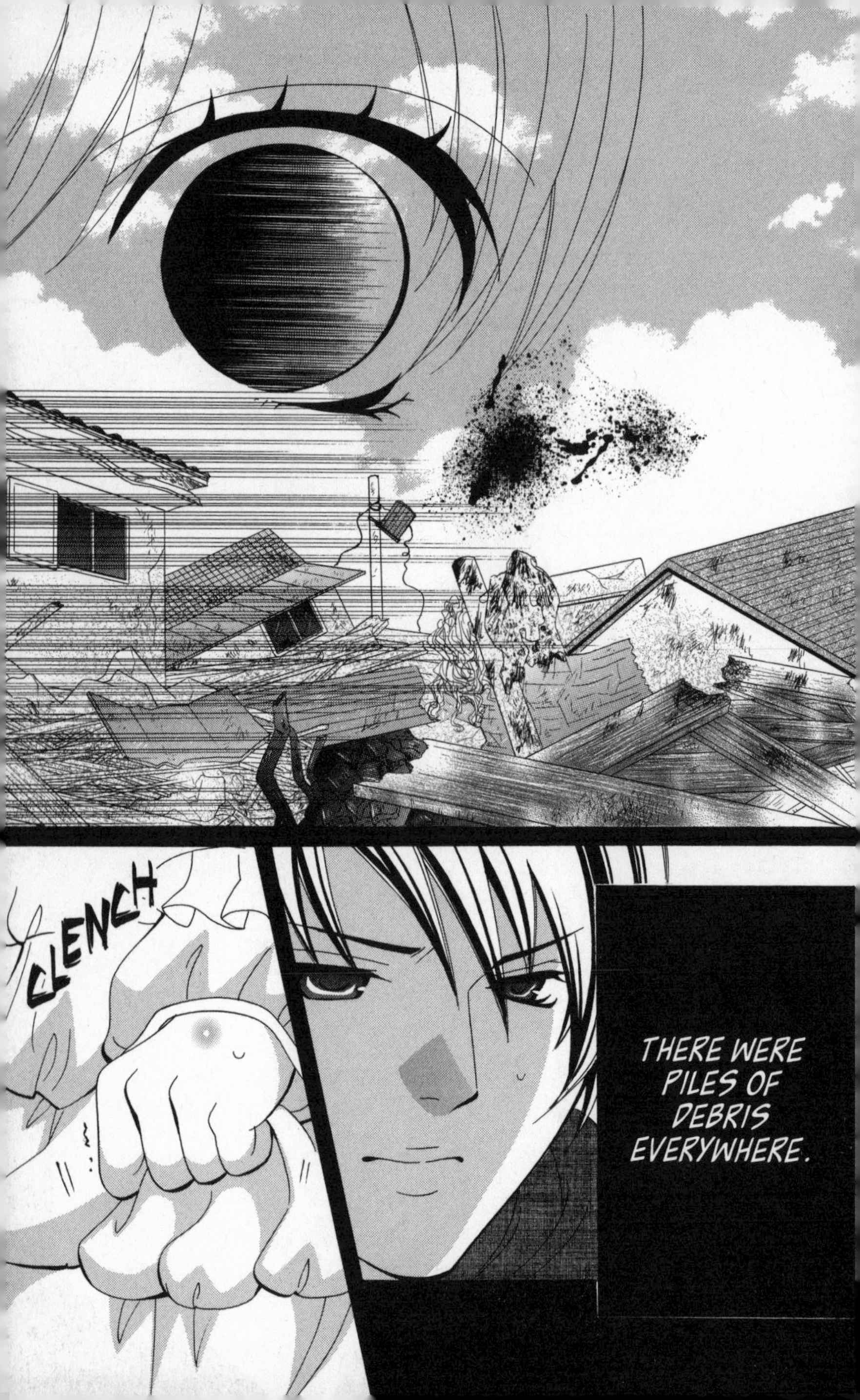
THERE WERE PILES OF DEBRIS EVERYWHERE.
CLENCH

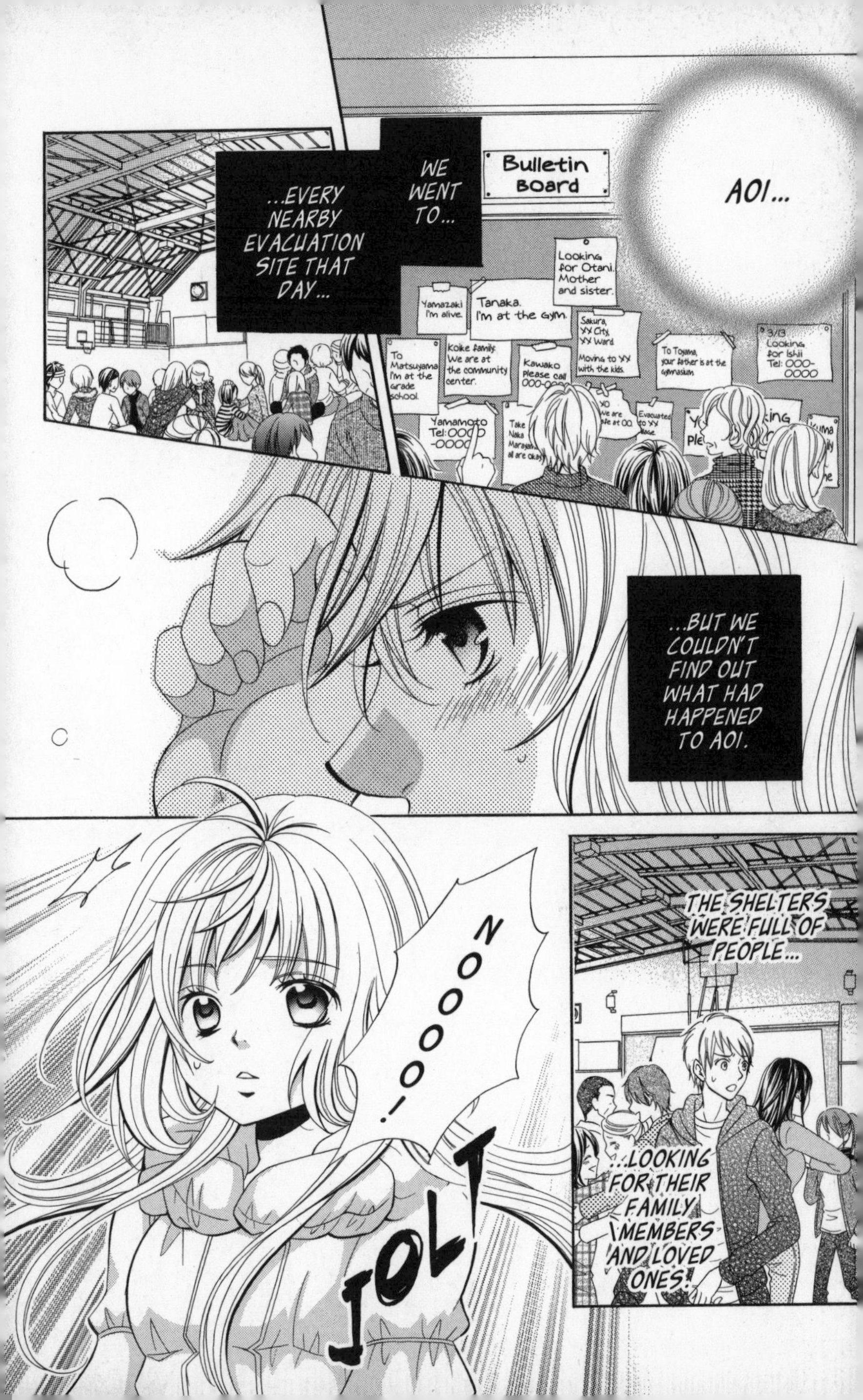
AOI...
Bulletin Board
Looking for Otani. Mother and sister.
3/13 Looking for Ishii Tel: 000-0000
To Toyama, your father is at the gymnasium.
Sakura, XX City, XX Ward Moving to XX with the kids.
Tanaka. I'm at the gym.
Yamazaki I'm alive.
Kawako please call 000-000
Koike family: We are at the community center.
To Matsuyama I'm at the grade school.
Yamamoto Tel: 0000-0000
WE WENT TO...
...EVERY NEARBY EVACUATION SITE THAT DAY...
...BUT WE COULDN'T FIND OUT WHAT HAD HAPPENED TO AOI.
THE SHELTERS WERE FULL OF PEOPLE...
...LOOKING FOR THEIR FAMILY MEMBERS AND LOVED ONES!
NOOOOO-!
JOLT

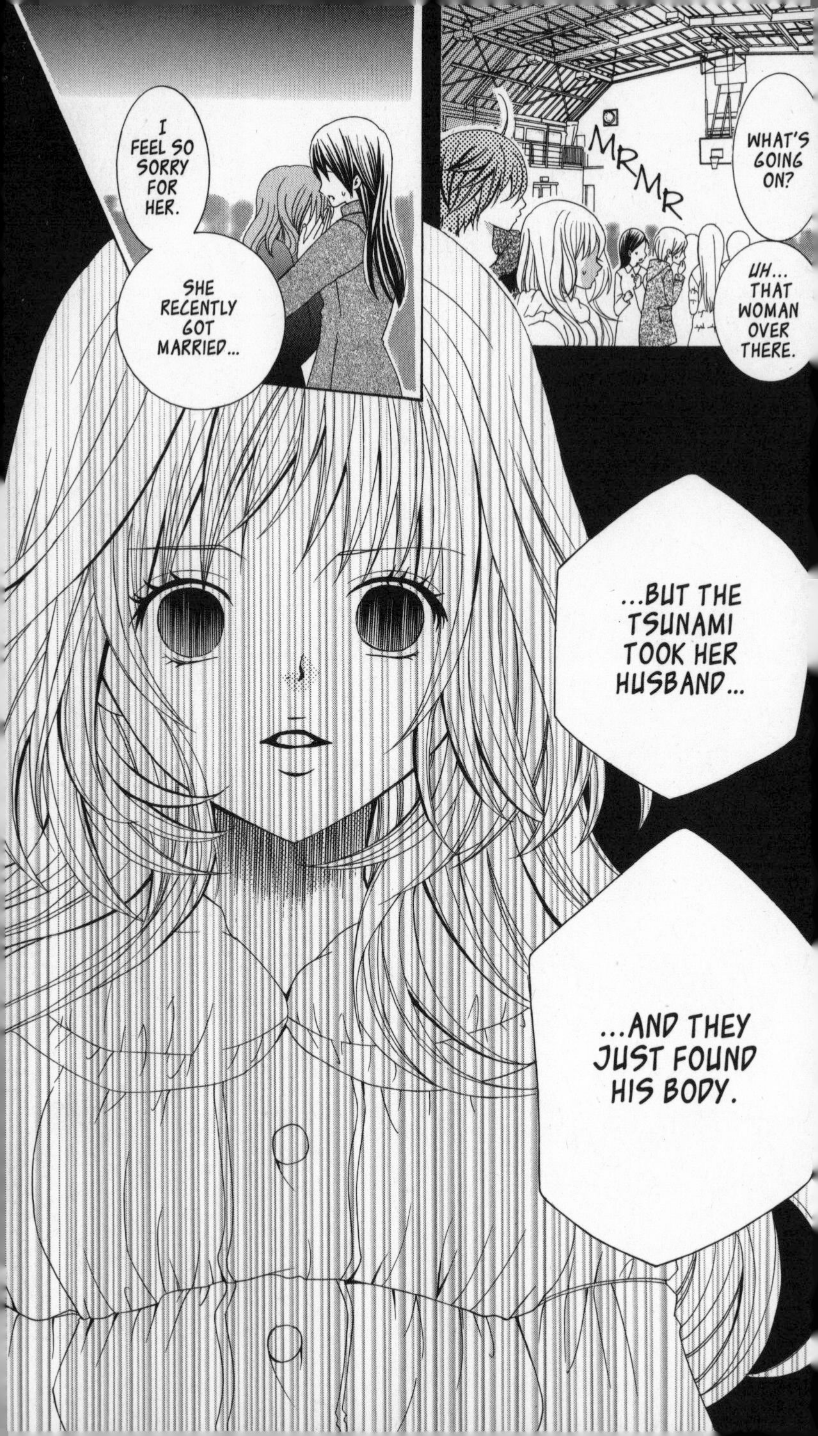
MRMR
WHAT'S GOING ON?
UH... THAT WOMAN OVER THERE.
I FEEL SO SORRY FOR HER.
SHE RECENTLY GOT MARRIED...
...BUT THE TSUNAMI TOOK HER HUSBAND...
...AND THEY JUST FOUND HIS BODY.

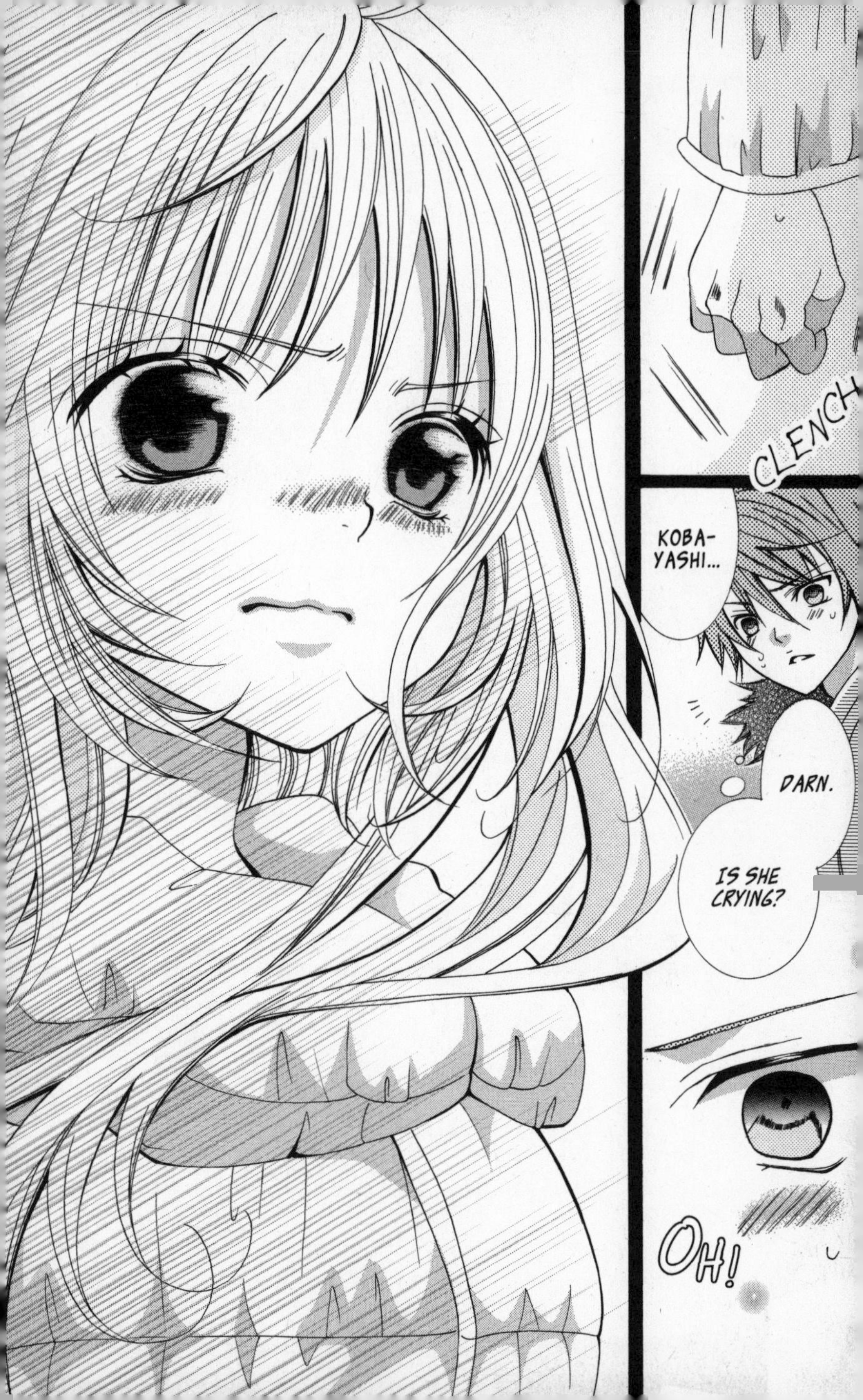
CLENCH
KOBA-YASHI...
DARN.
IS SHE CRYING?
OH!

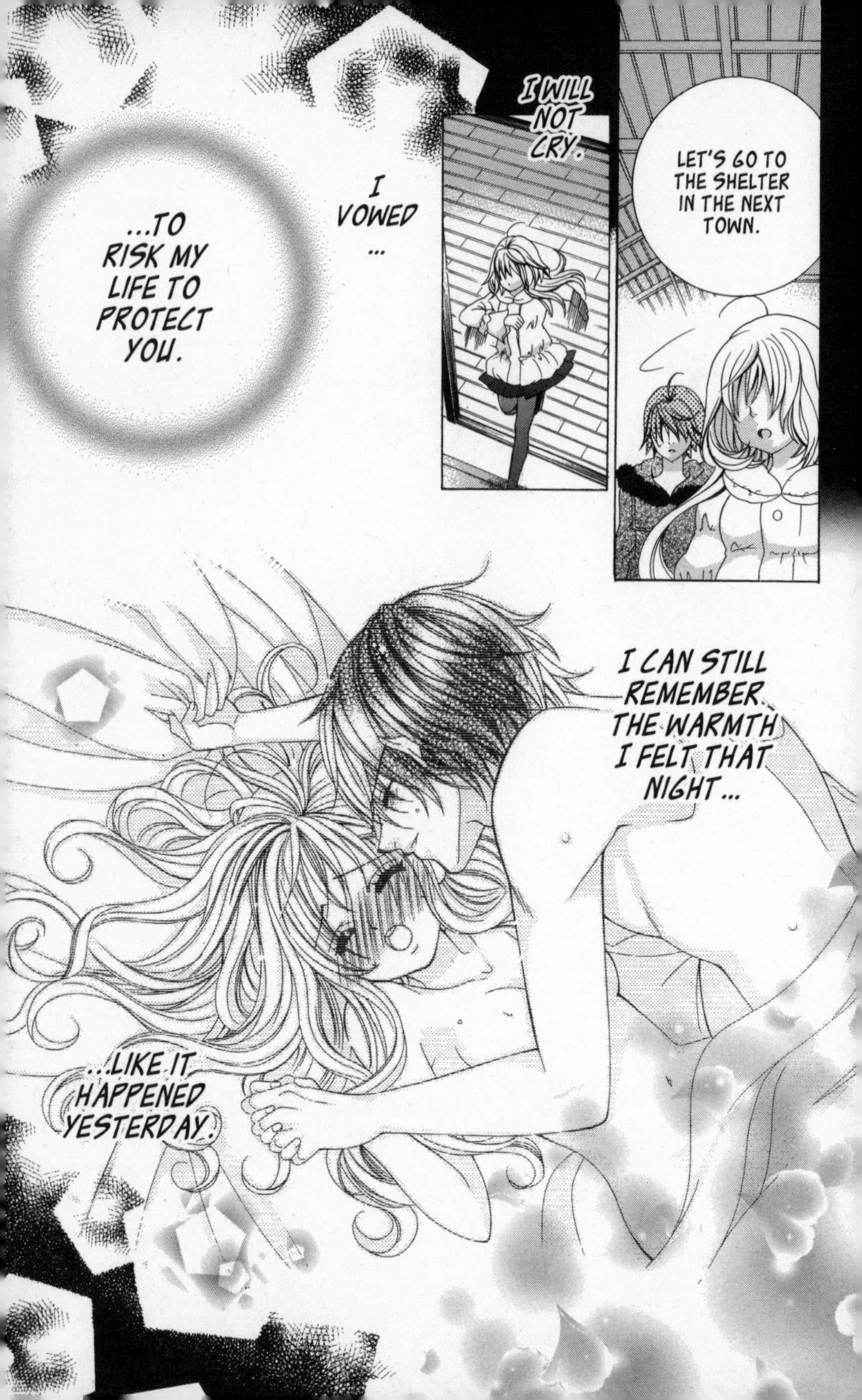
LET'S GO TO THE SHELTER IN THE NEXT TOWN.
I WILL NOT CRY.
I VOWED ...
...TO RISK MY LIFE TO PROTECT YOU.
I CAN STILL REMEMBER THE WARMTH I FELT THAT NIGHT...
...LIKE IT HAPPENED YESTERDAY.

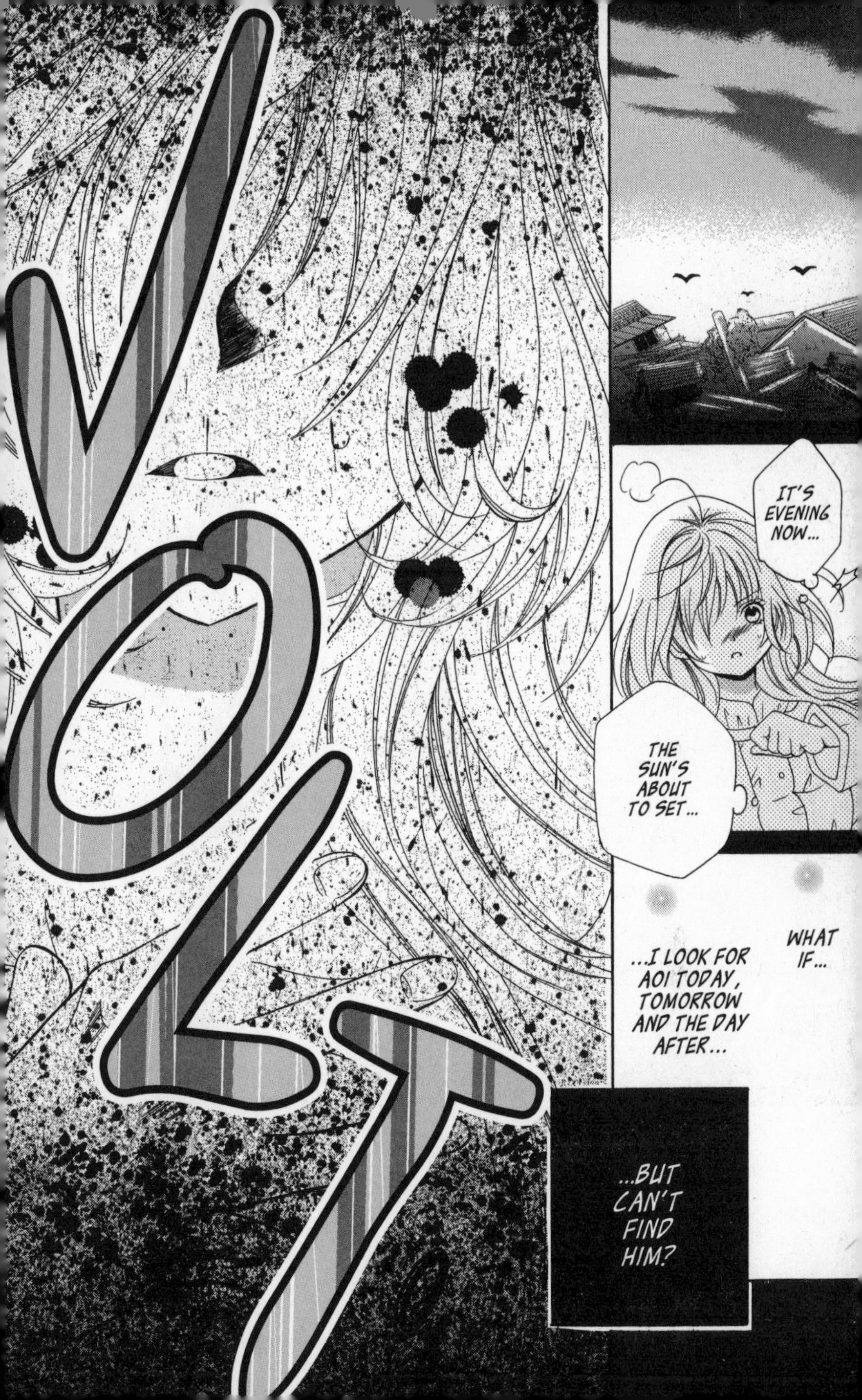
IT'S EVENING NOW...
THE SUN'S ABOUT TO SET...
WHAT IF...
...I LOOK FOR AOI TODAY, TOMORROW AND THE DAY AFTER...
...BUT CAN'T FIND HIM?
JOLT

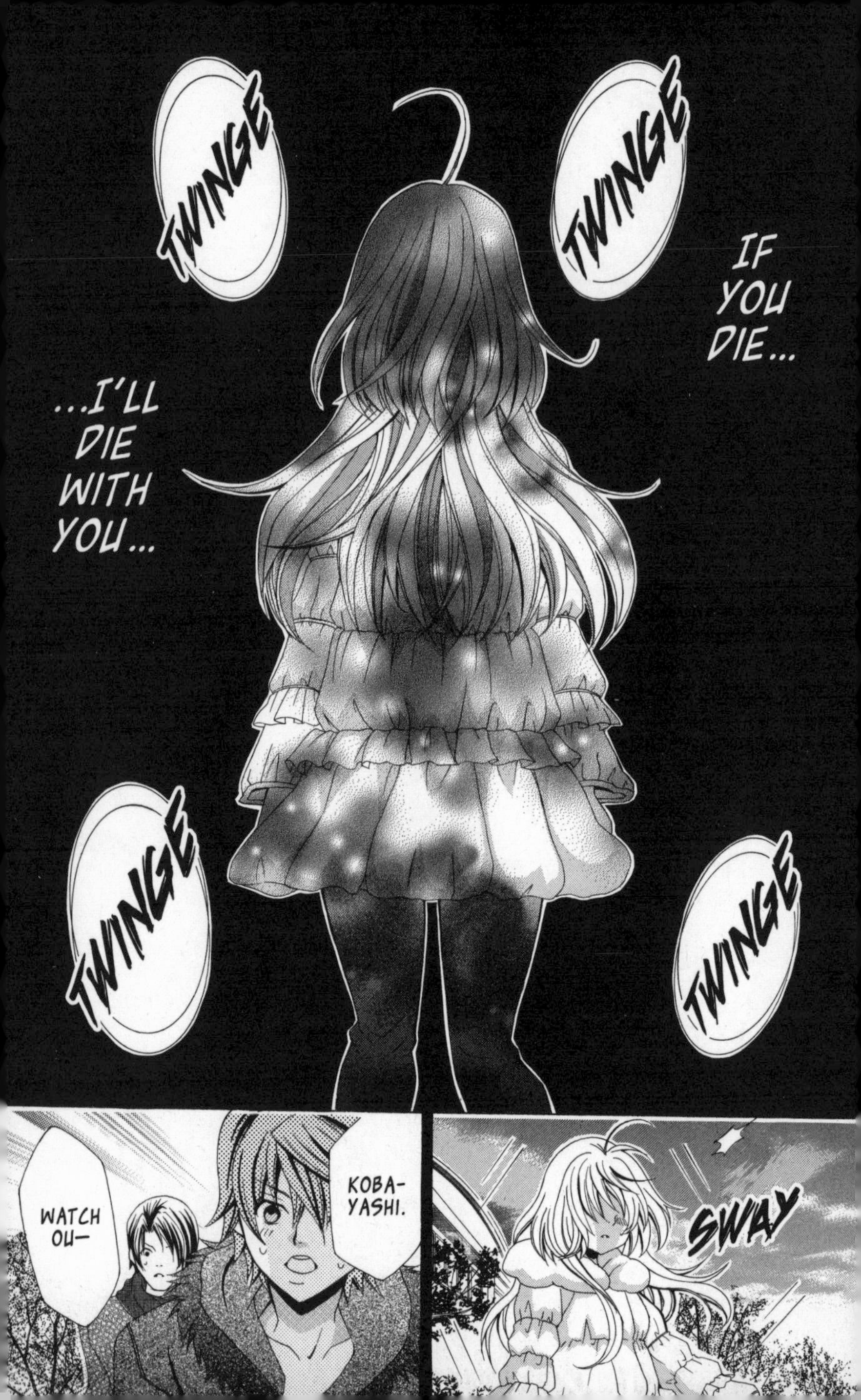
TWINGE
IF YOU DIE...
TWINGE
...I'LL DIE WITH YOU...
TWINGE
TWINGE
SWAY
KOBA-YASHI.
WATCH OU—

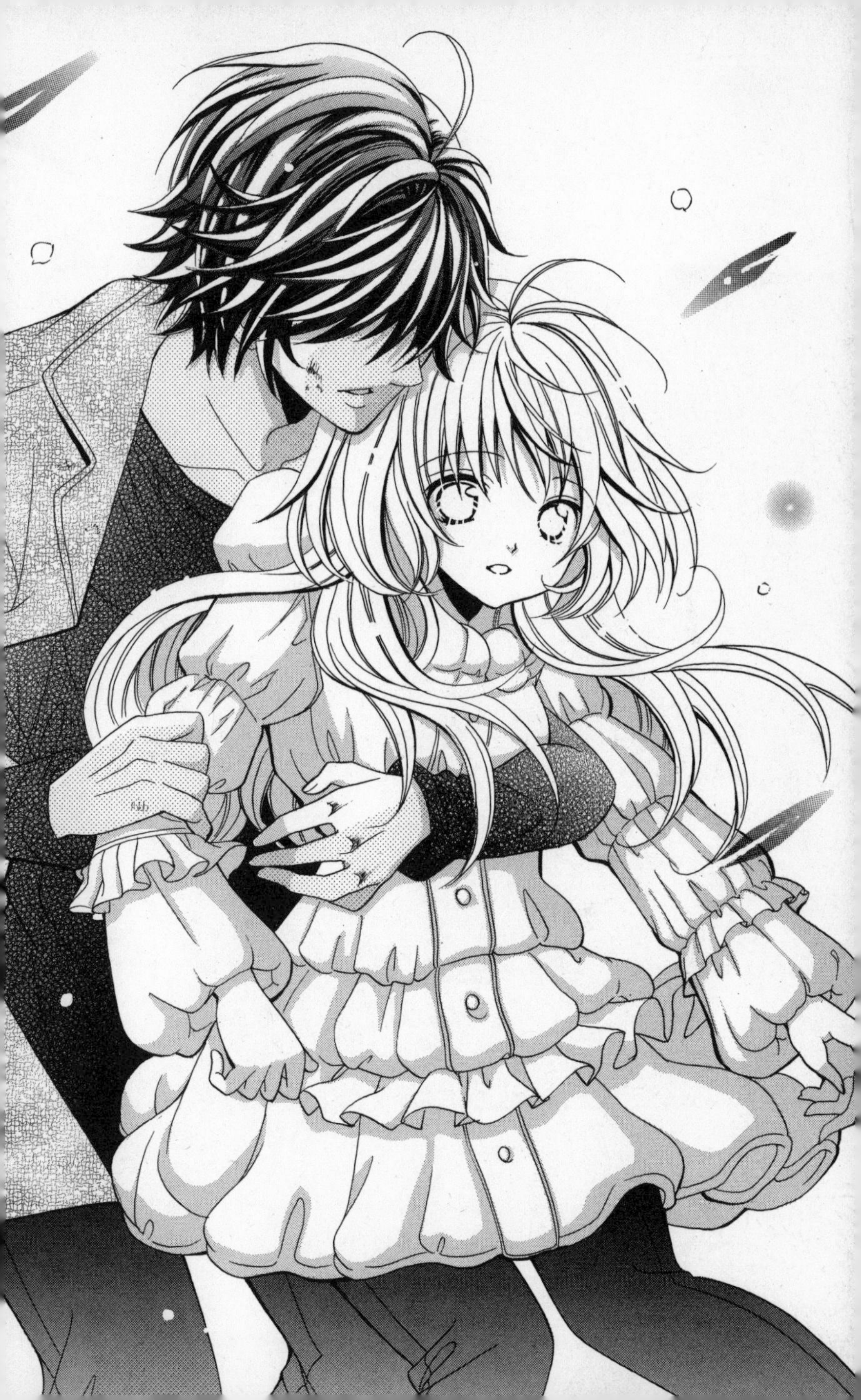

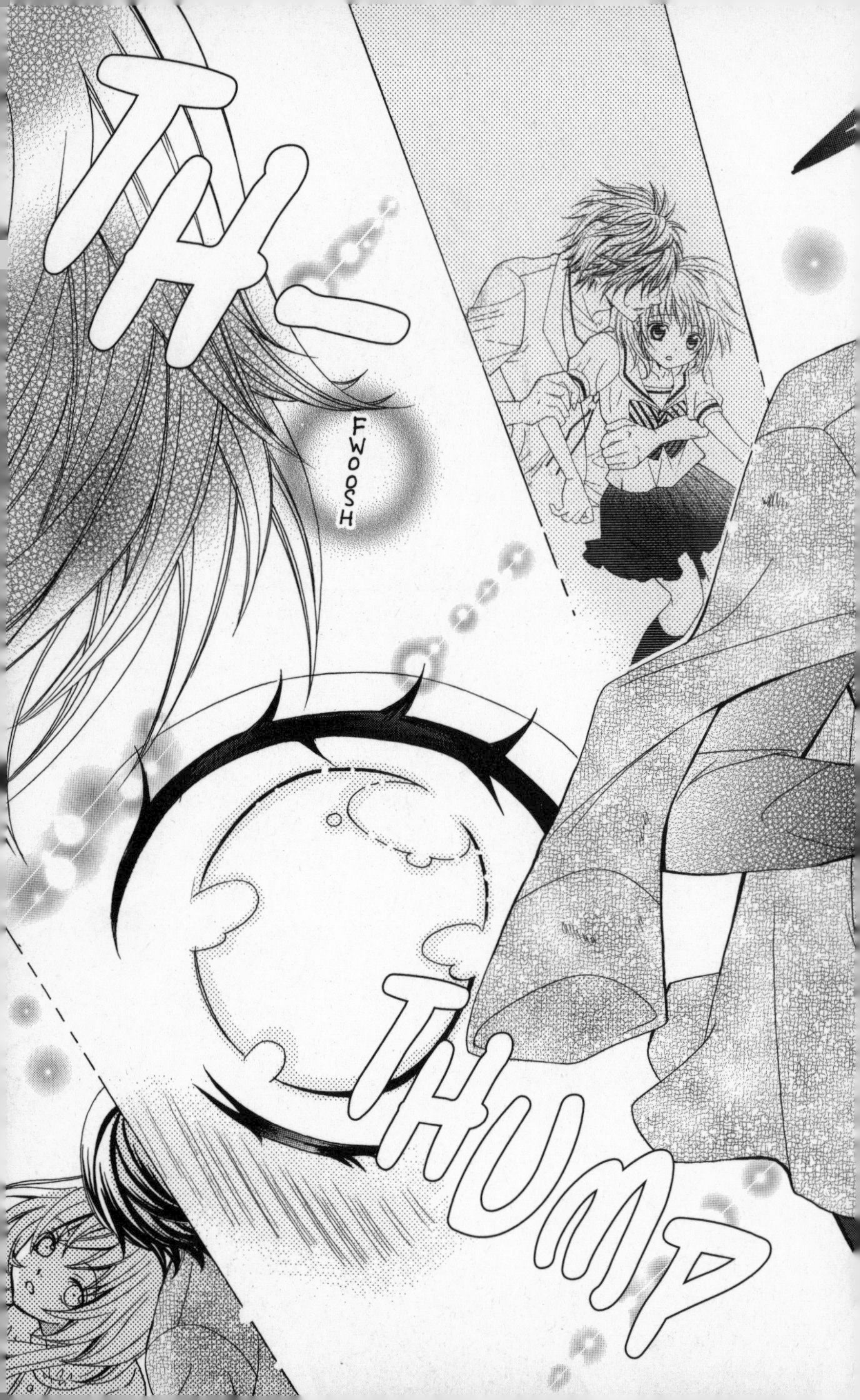
TH-
FWOOSH
THUMP

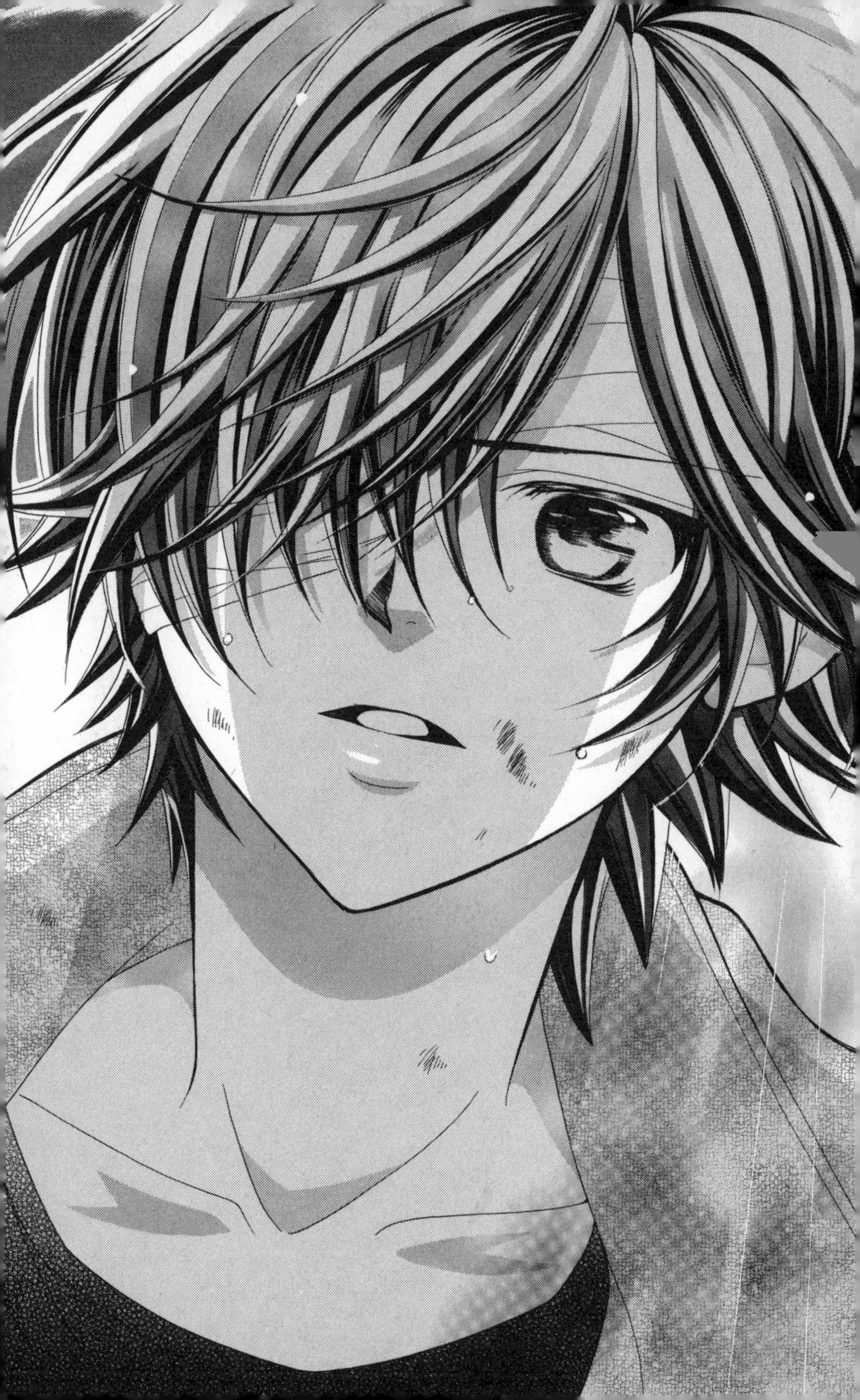

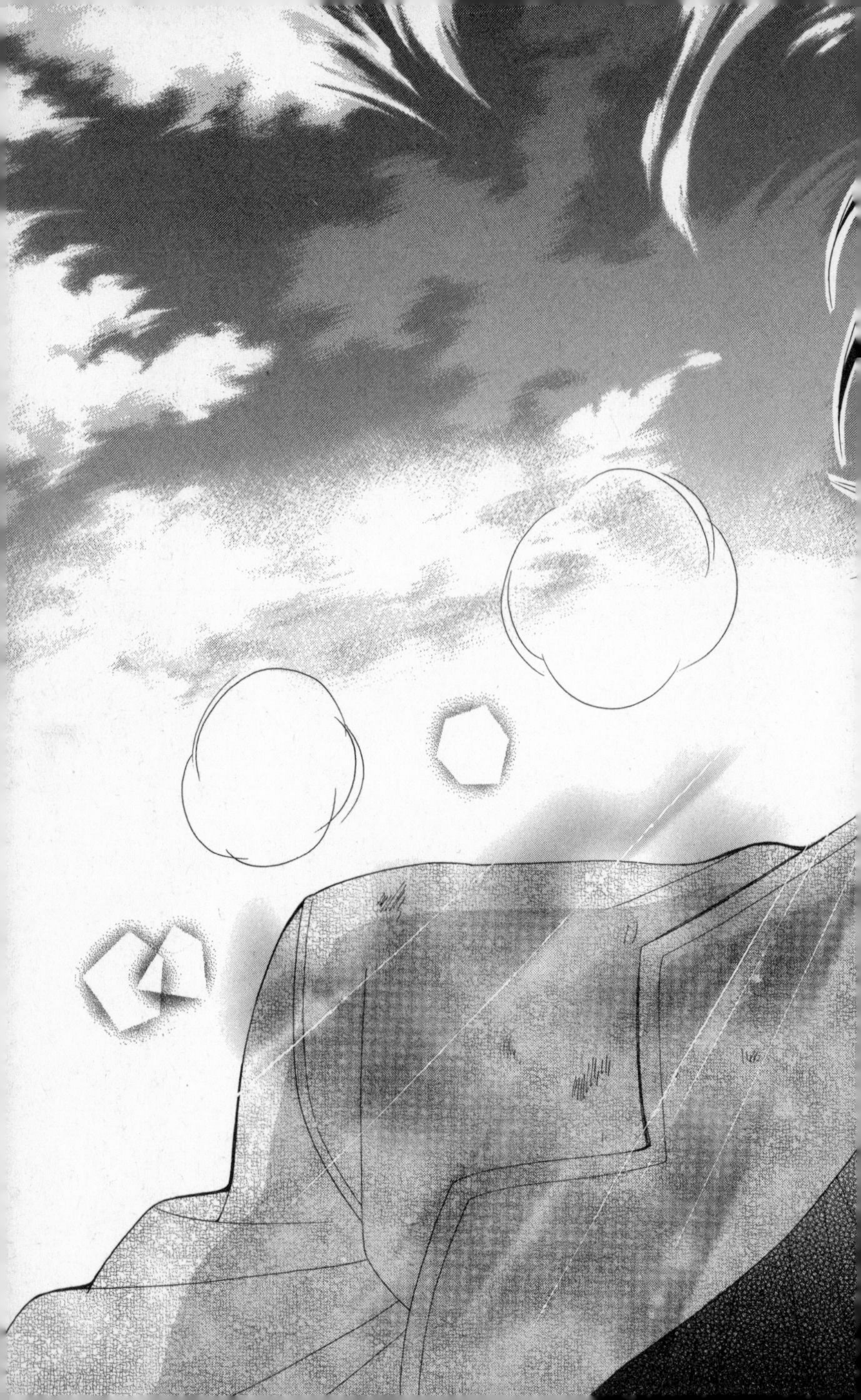

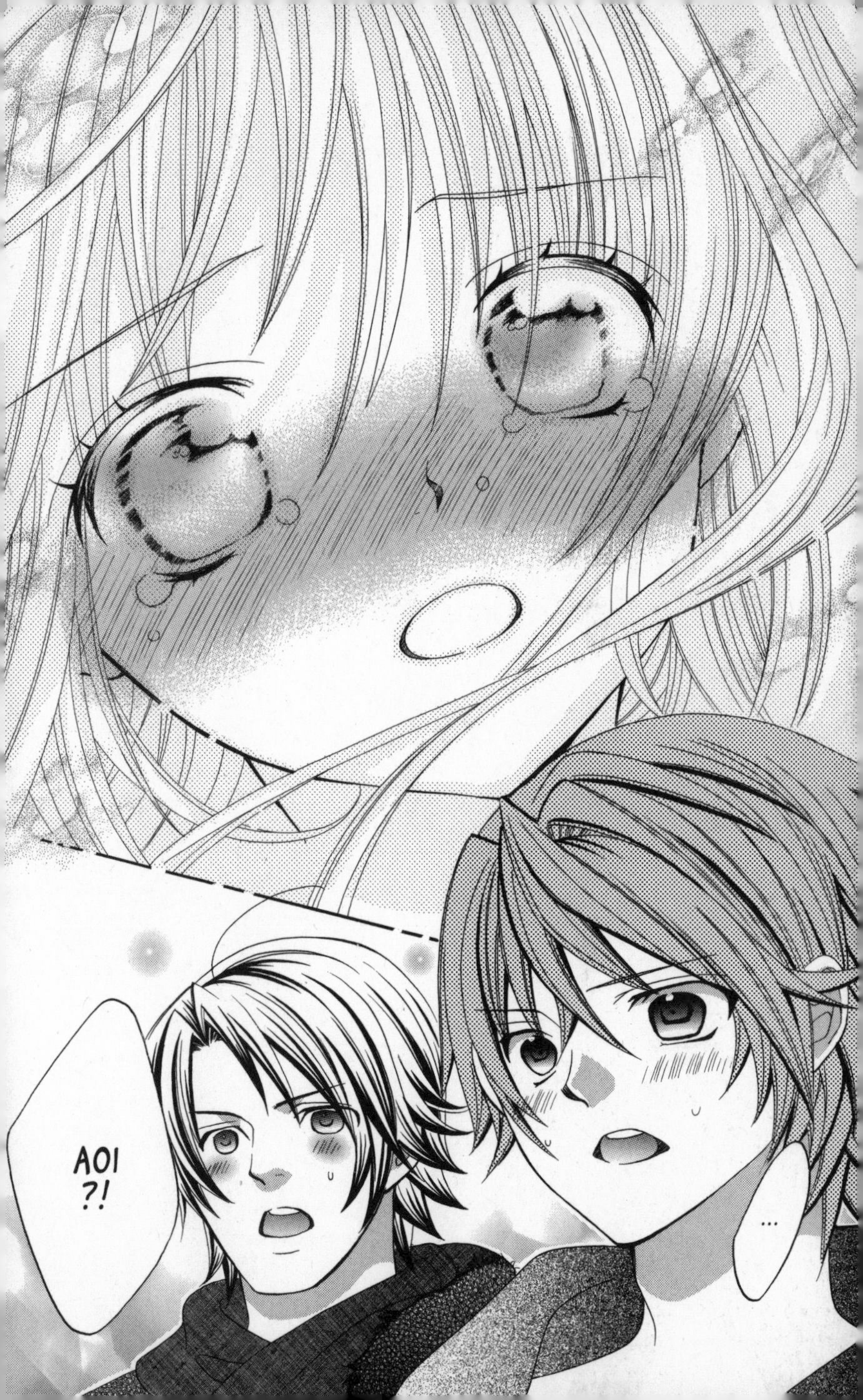
...
AOI ?!

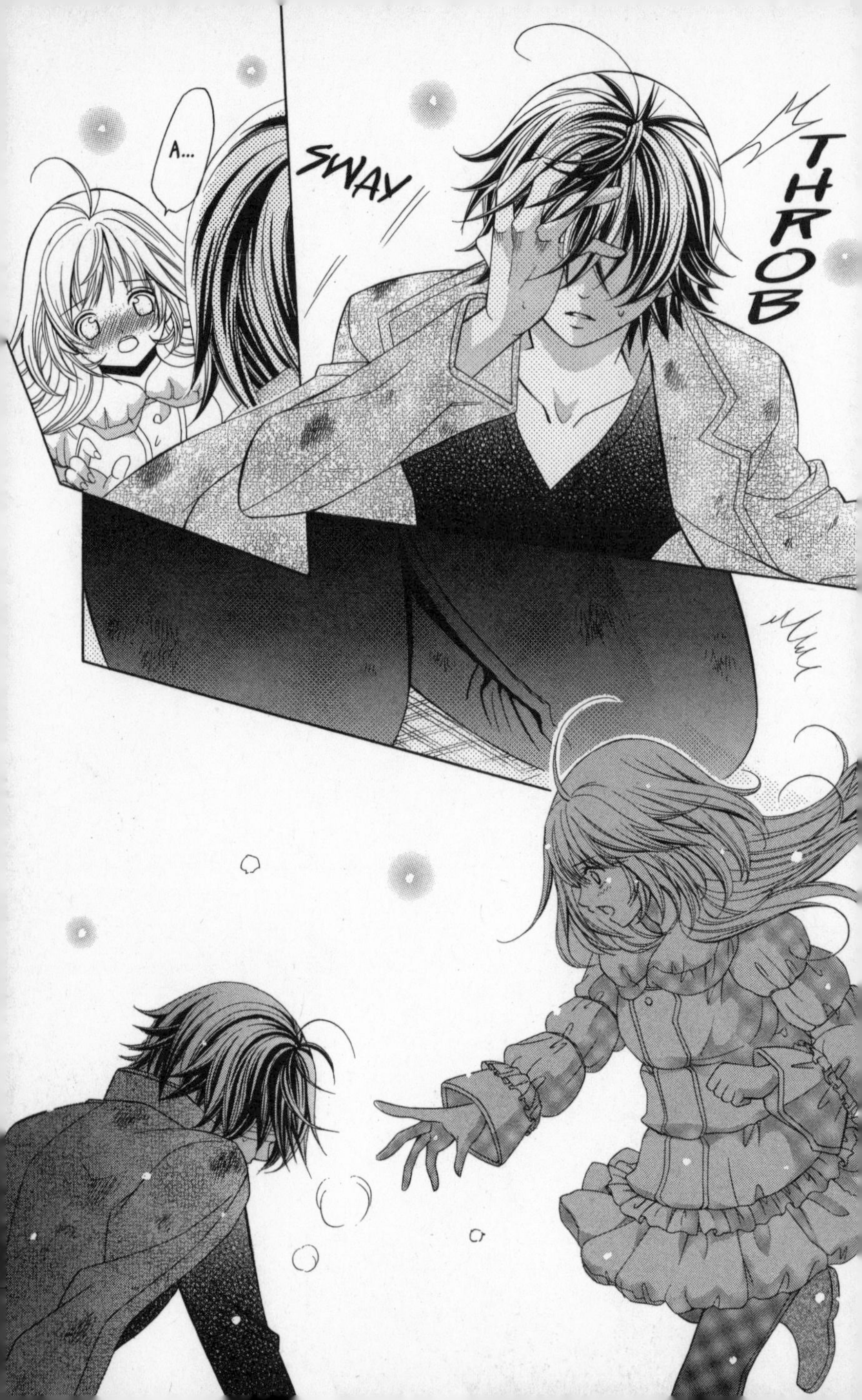
THROB
SWAY
A...

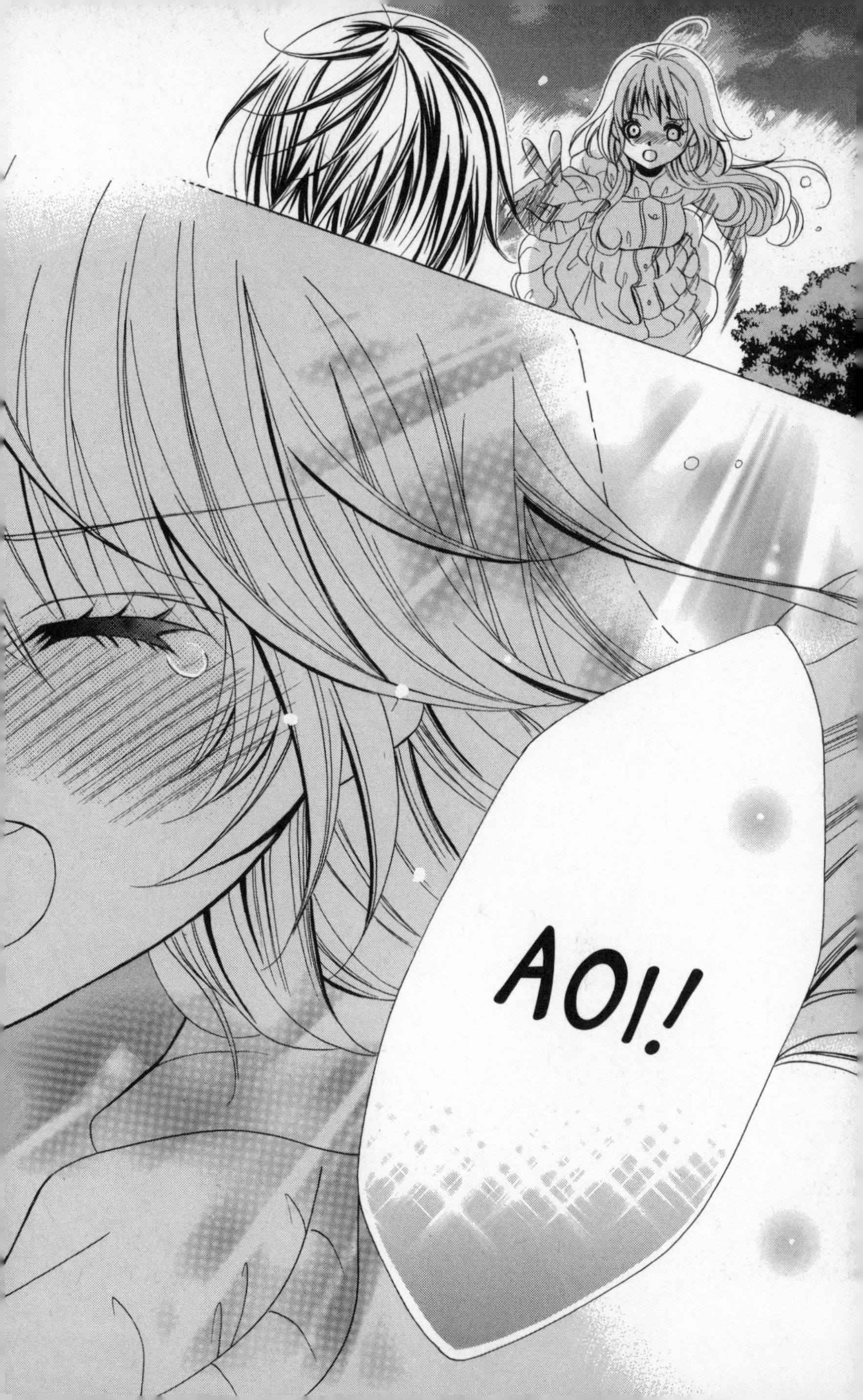
AOI!

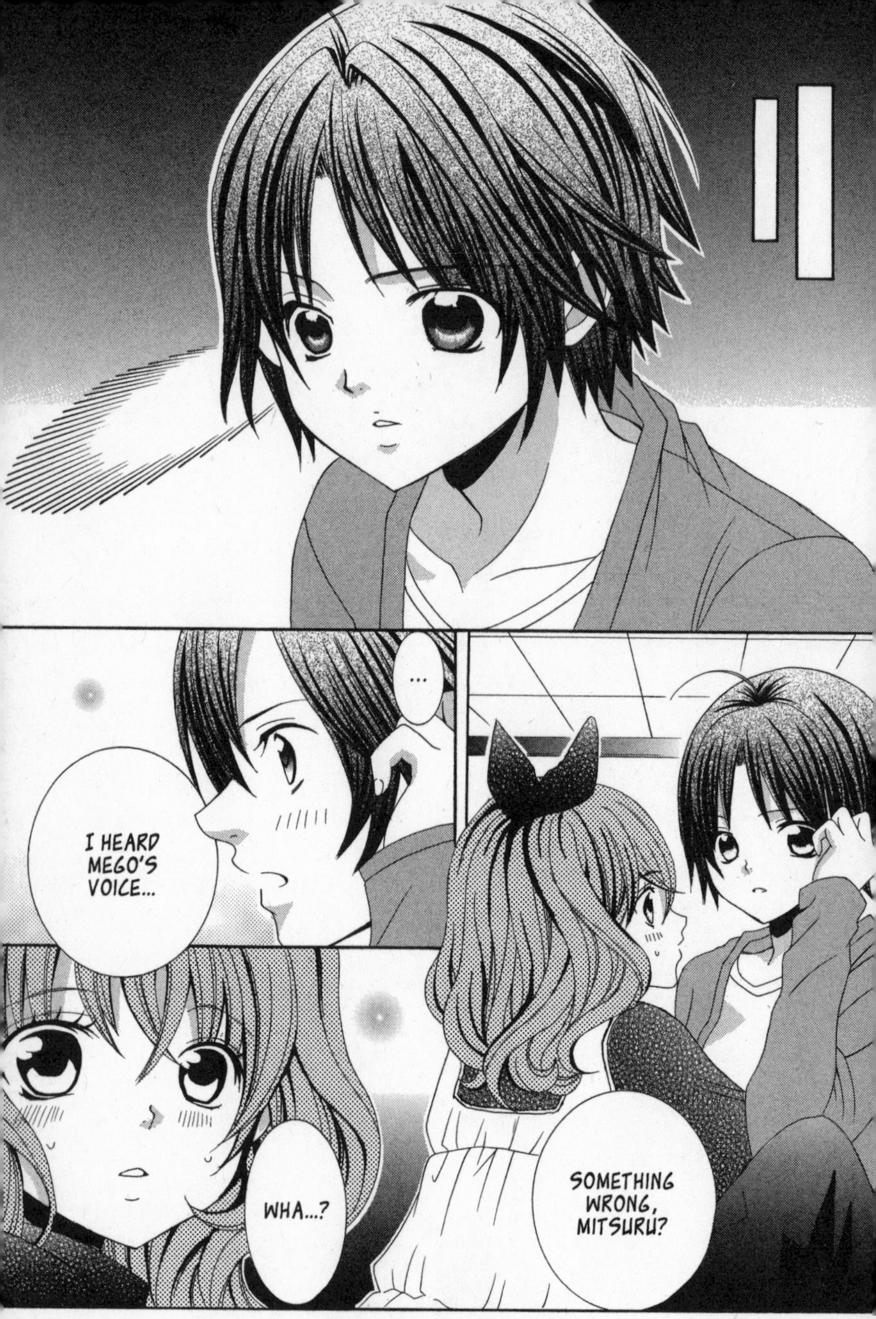
SOMETHING WRONG, MITSURU?
...
I HEARD MEGO'S VOICE...
WHA...?

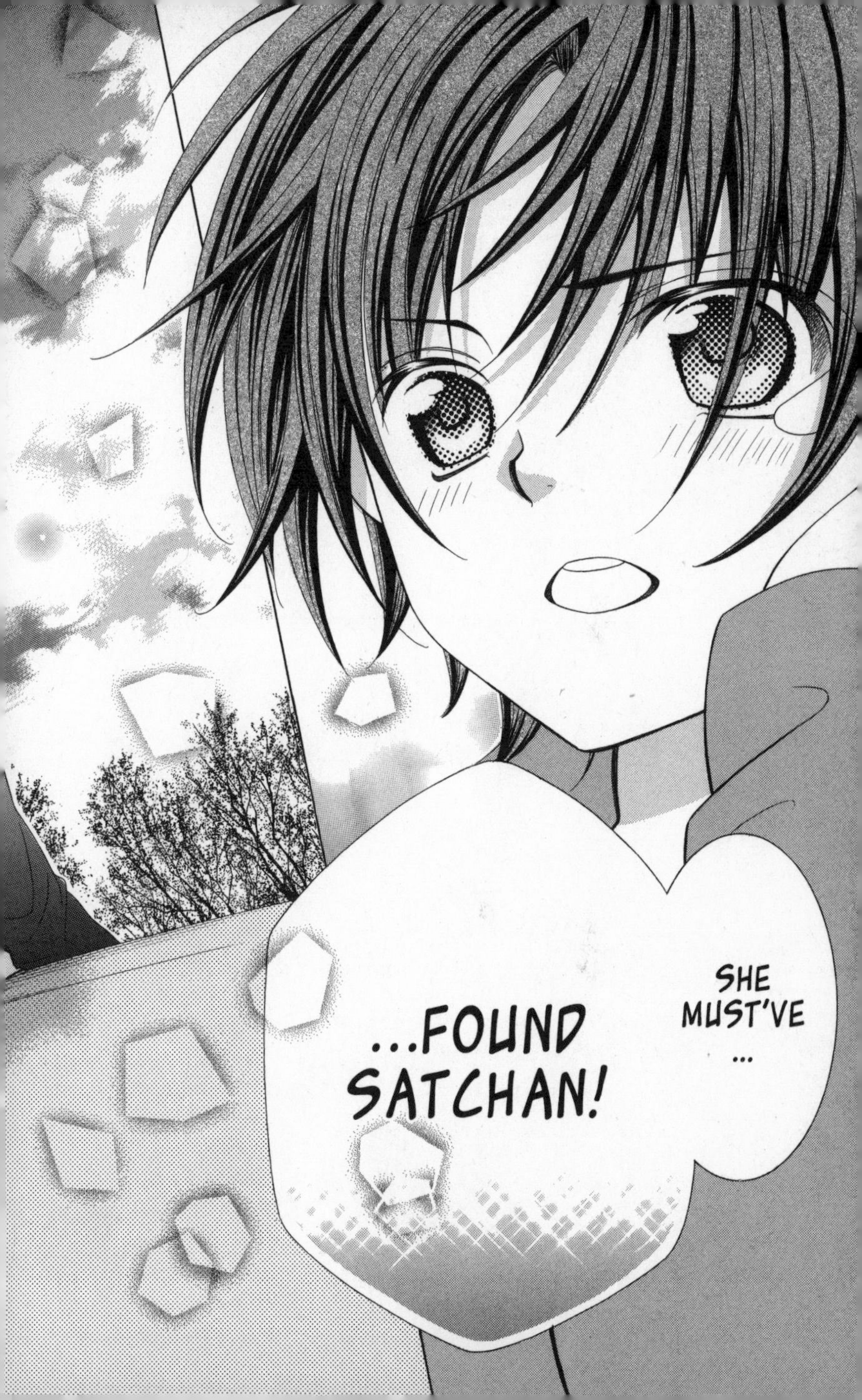
SHE MUST'VE ...
...FOUND SATCHAN!

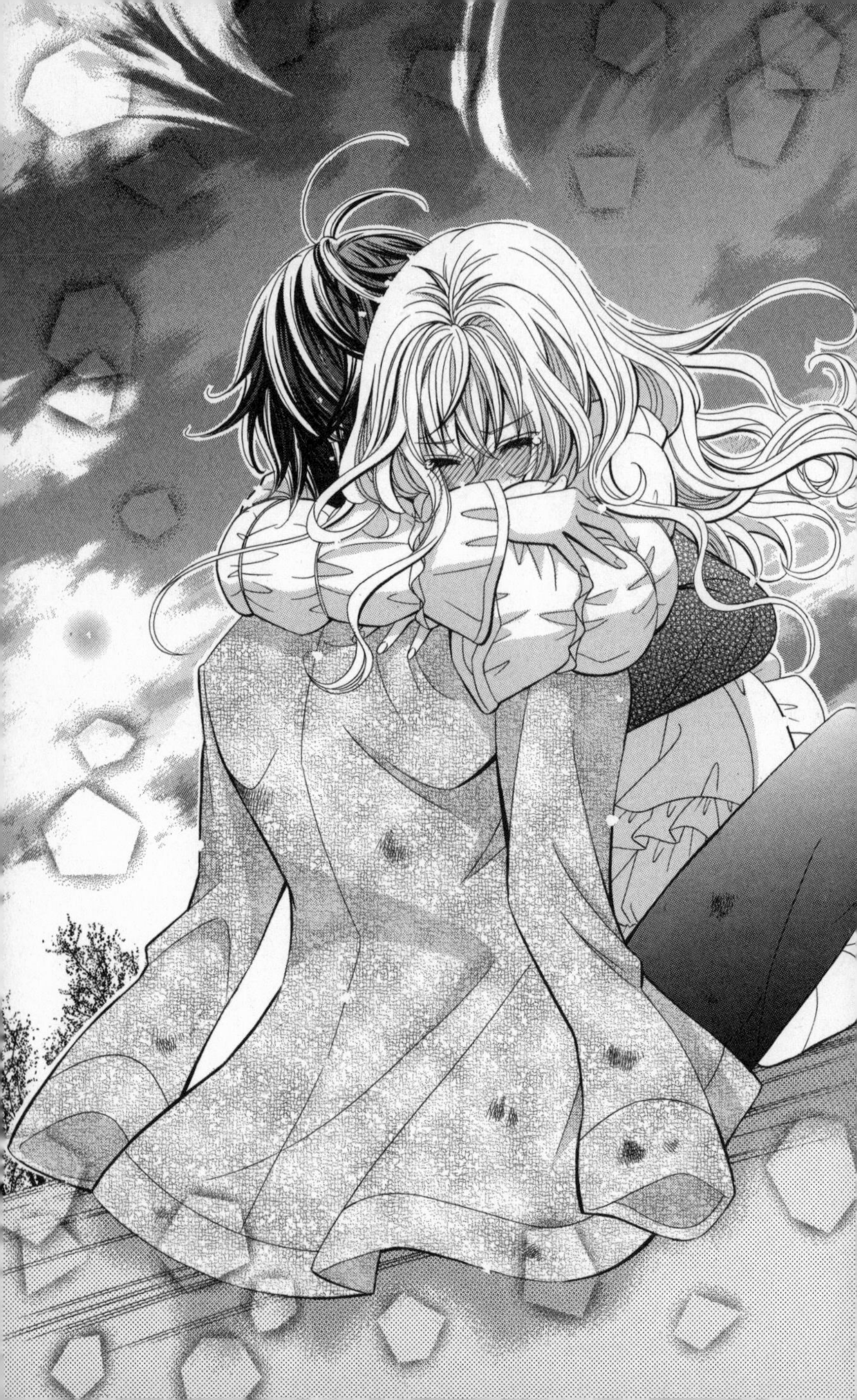

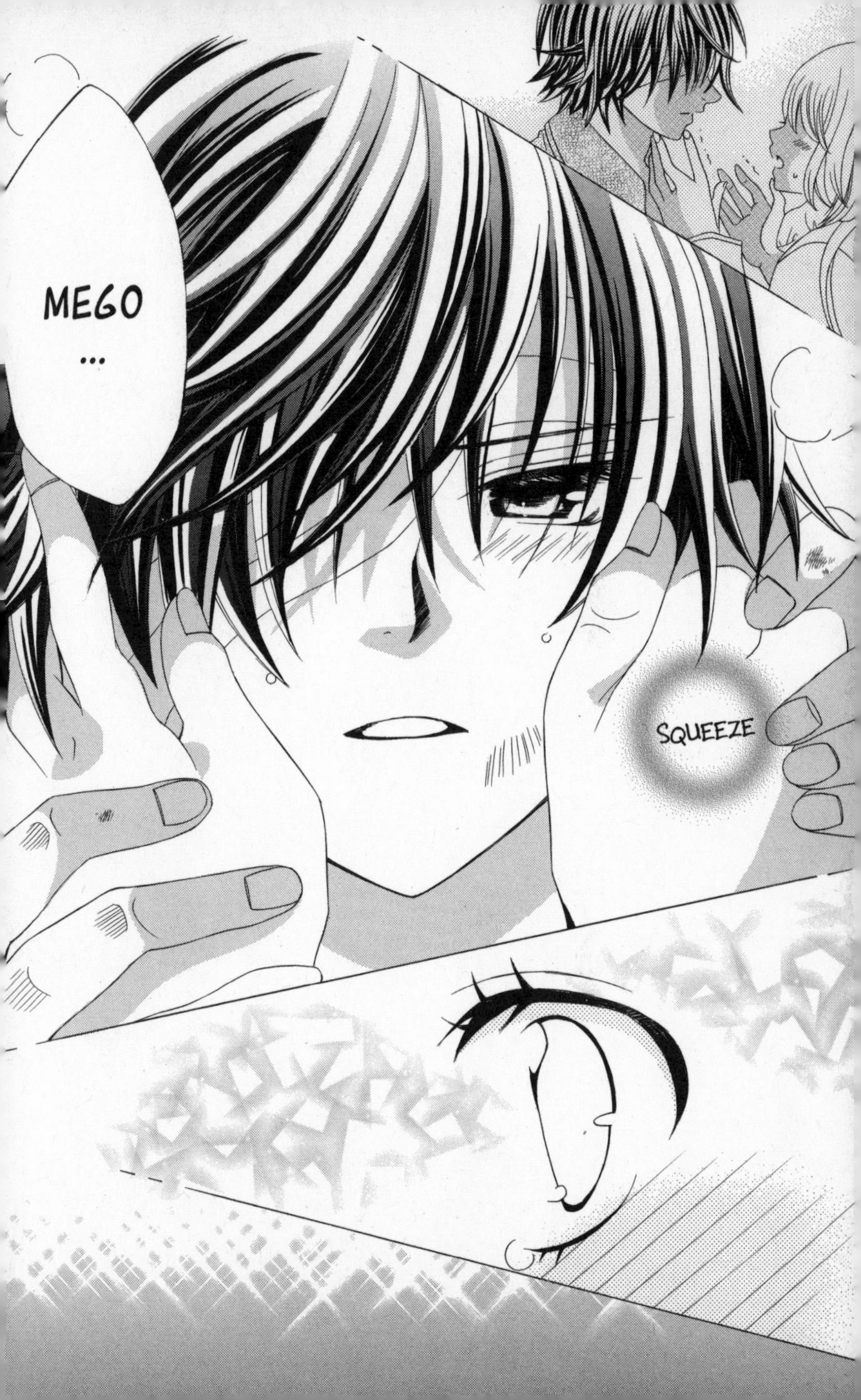
MEGO
...
SQUEEZE

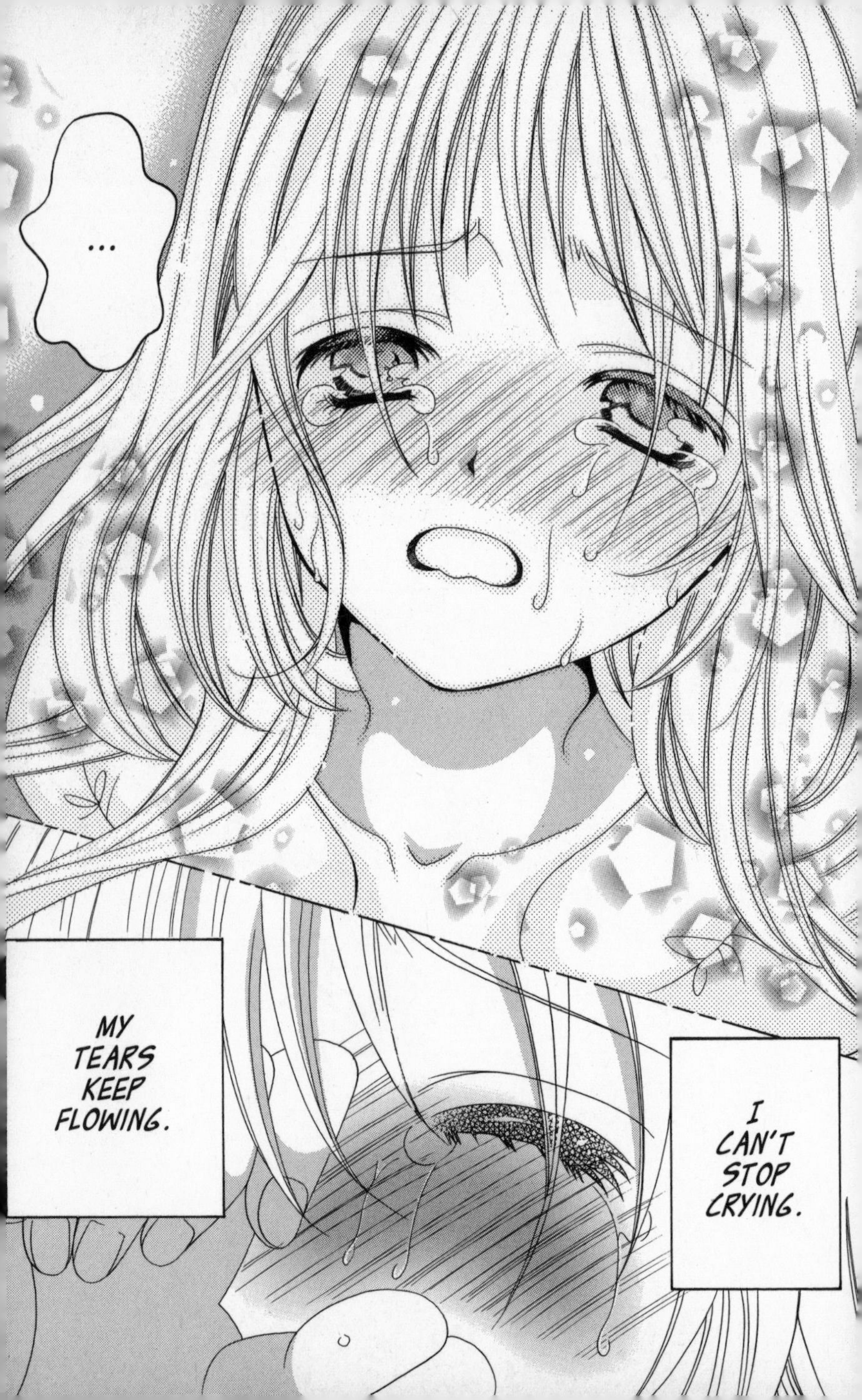
...
I CAN'T STOP CRYING.
MY TEARS KEEP FLOWING.

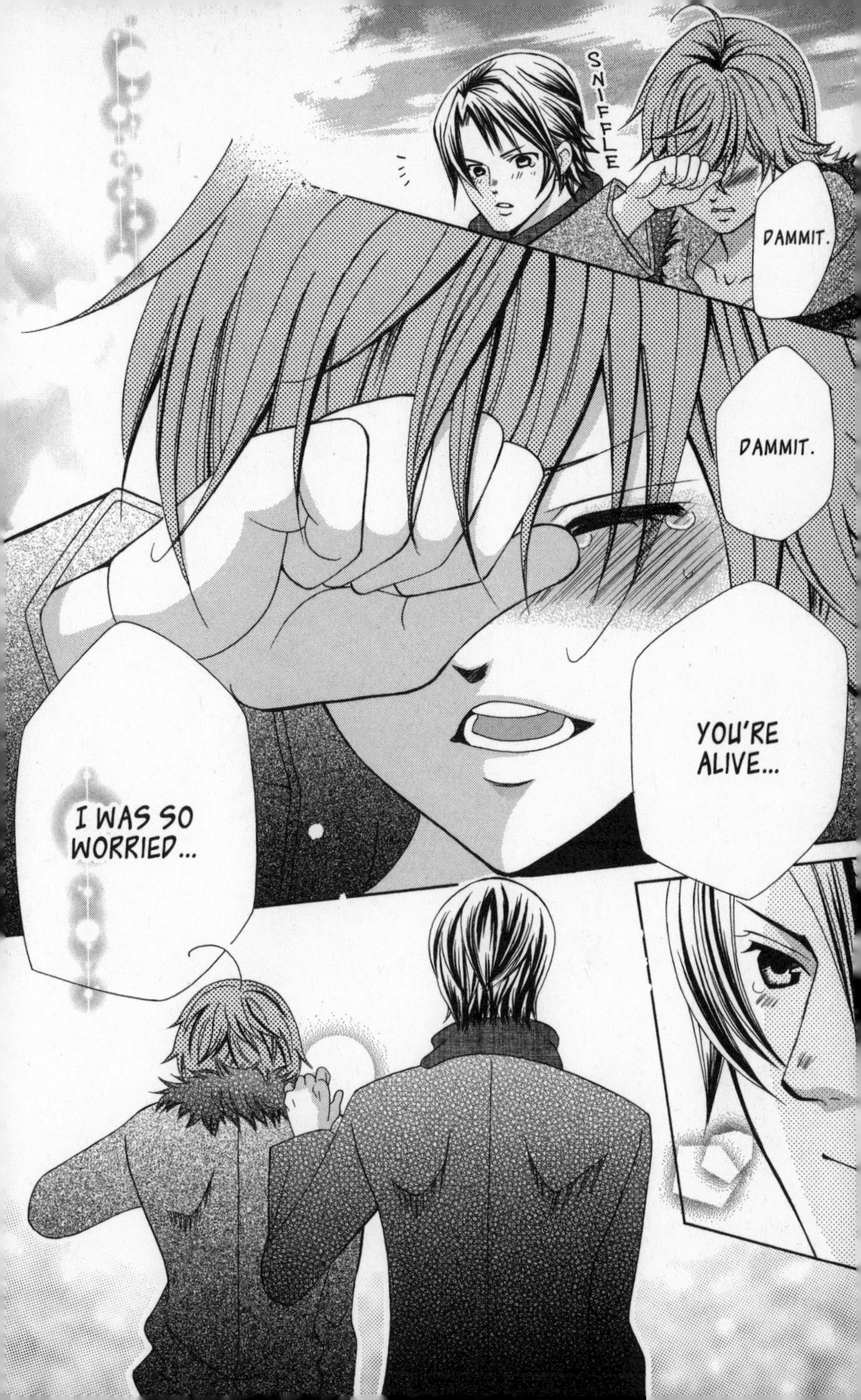
SNIFFLE
DAMMIT.
DAMMIT.
YOU'RE ALIVE...
I WAS SO WORRIED...

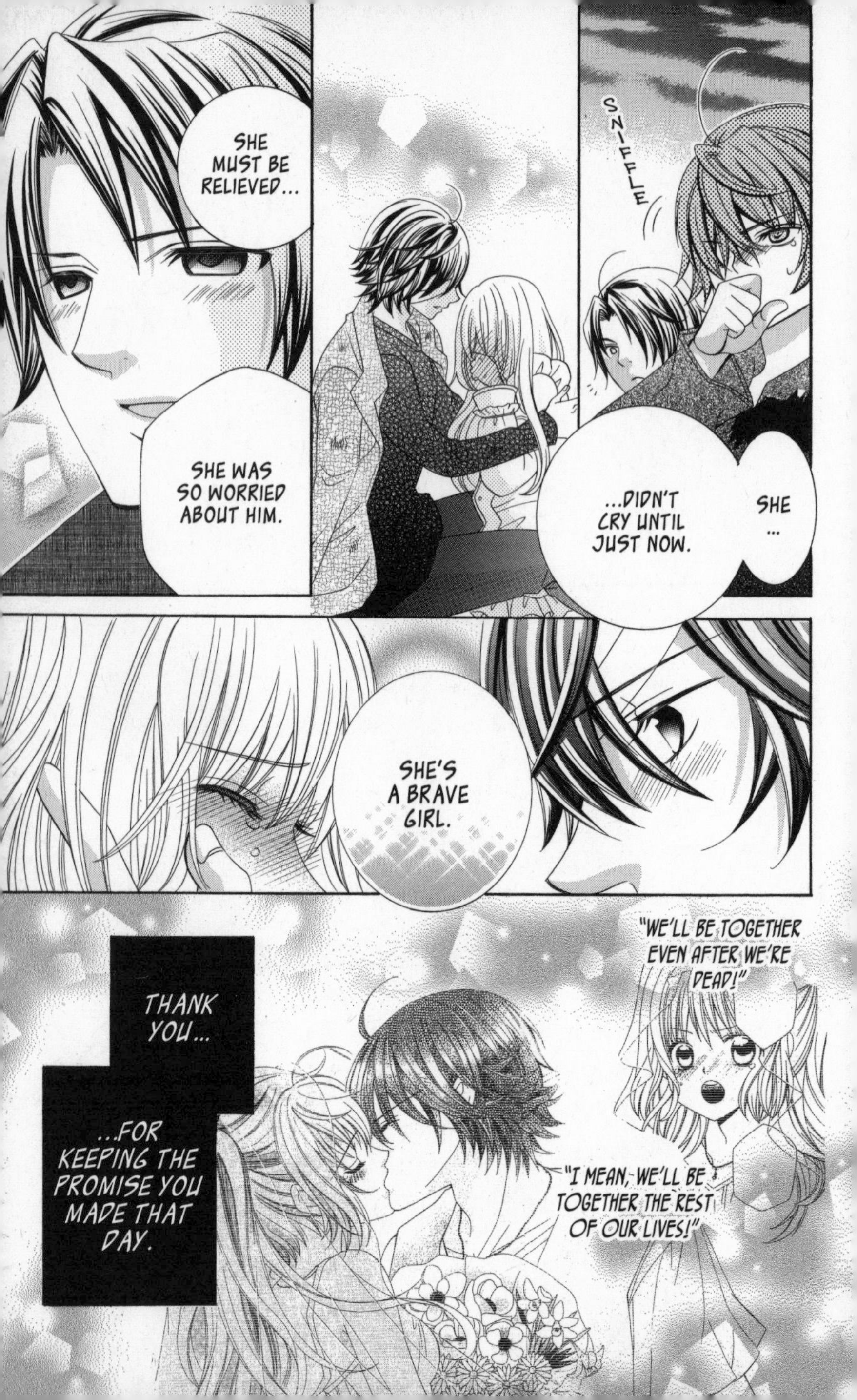
SNIFFLE
SHE ...
...DIDN'T CRY UNTIL JUST NOW.
SHE MUST BE RELIEVED...
SHE WAS SO WORRIED ABOUT HIM.
SHE'S A BRAVE GIRL.
"WE'LL BE TOGETHER EVEN AFTER WE'RE DEAD!"
"I MEAN, WE'LL BE TOGETHER THE REST OF OUR LIVES!"
THANK YOU...
...FOR KEEPING THE PROMISE YOU MADE THAT DAY.

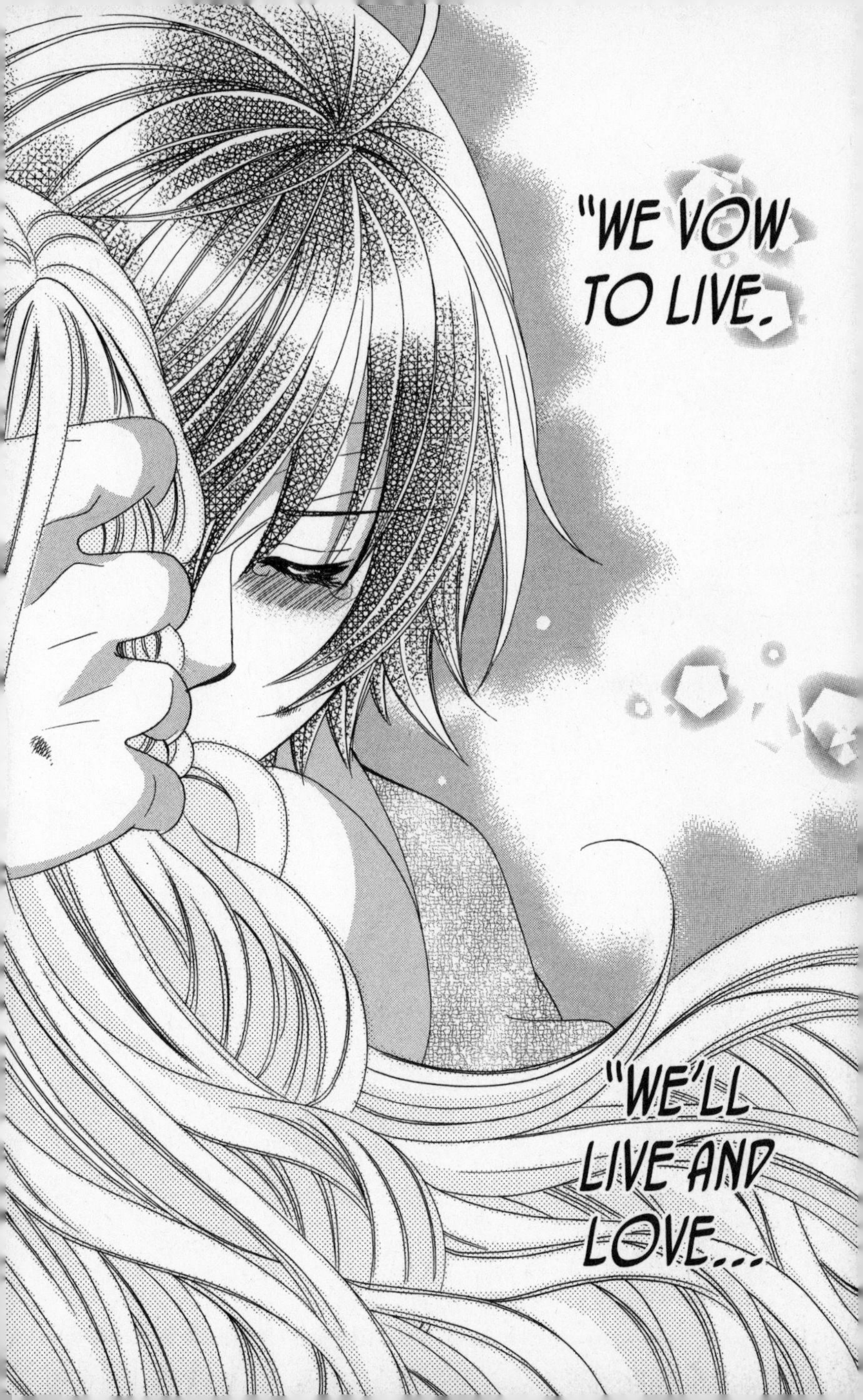
"WE VOW TO LIVE.
"WE'LL LIVE AND LOVE...

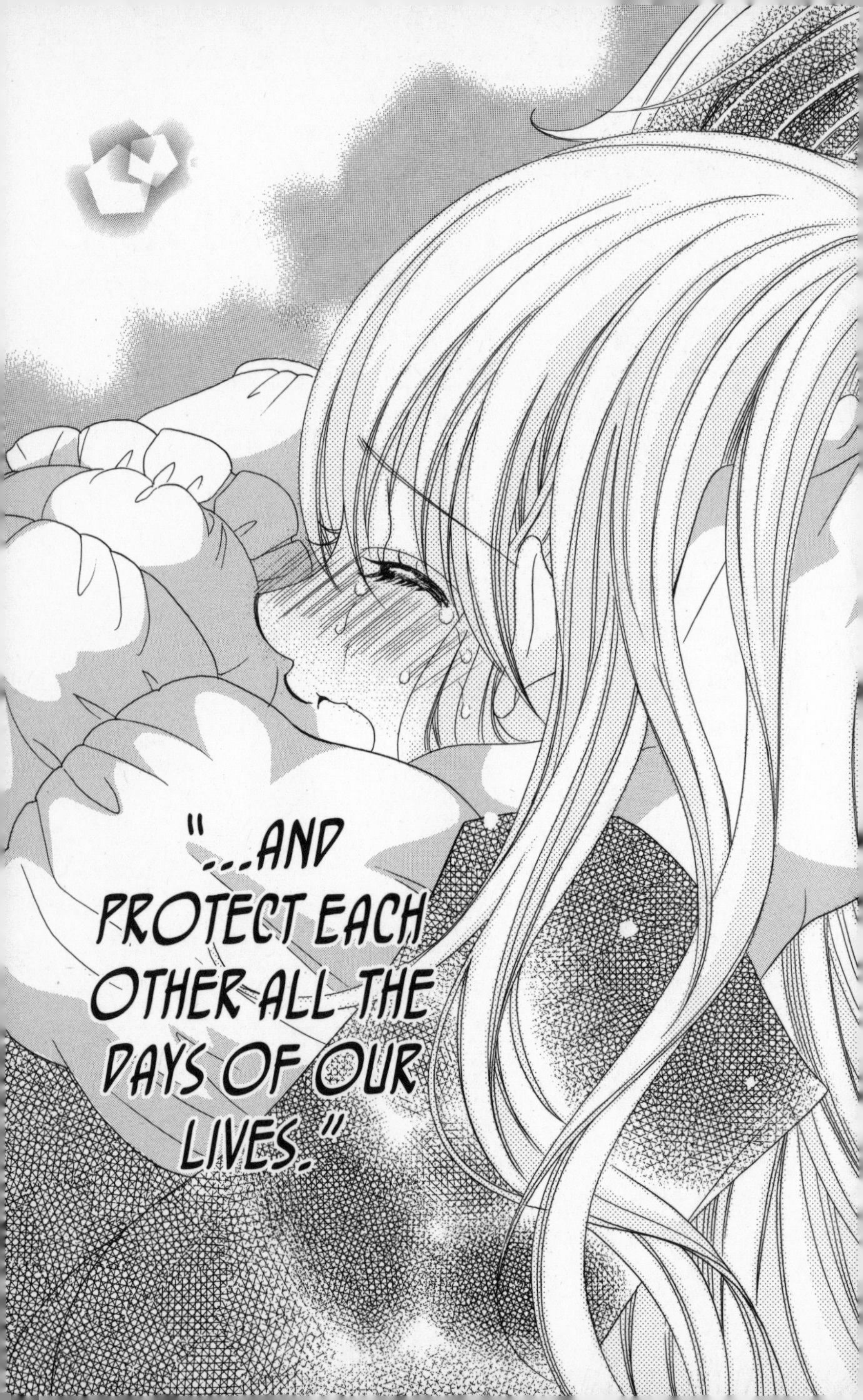
"...AND PROTECT EACH OTHER ALL THE DAYS OF OUR LIVES."

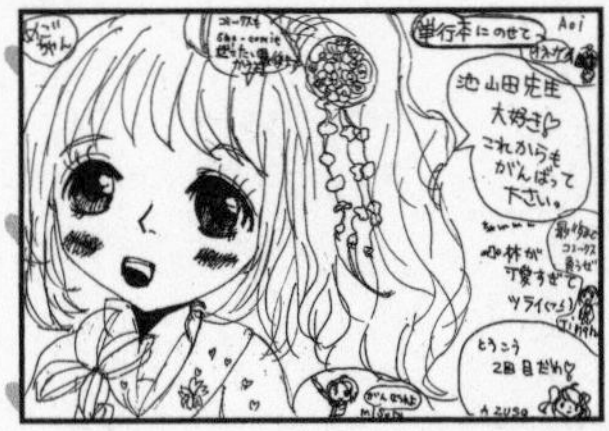
単行本にのせて
池山田先生大好き♡
これからもがんばって下さい。

Sakurako Iwasaki (Kanagawa) ←

Ed.: Please support the series until the end!!

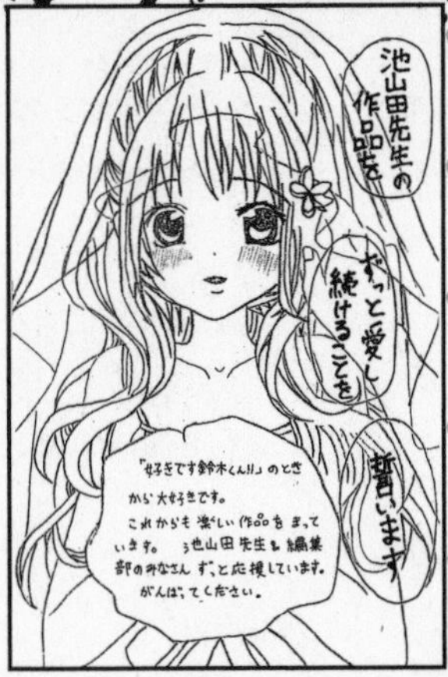
池山田先生の作品を
ずっと愛し続けることを
誓います
「好きです鈴木くん!!」のときから大好きです。これからも楽しい作品を待っています。池山田先生&編集部のみなさん ずっと応援しています。がんばってください。

Hizuna (Miyagi) ←

Ed.: I... I vow too!

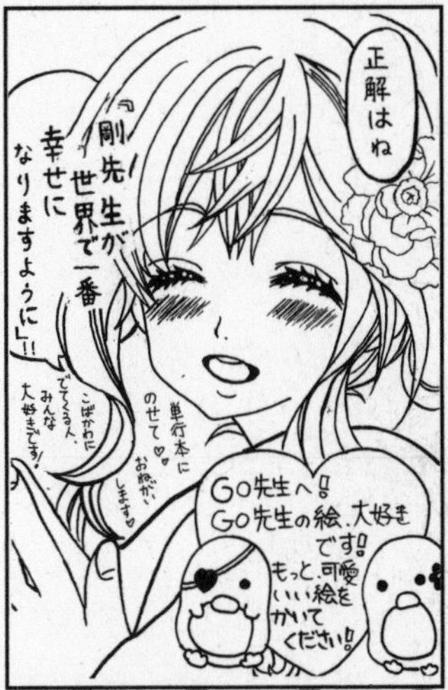
正解はね
「剛先生が世界で一番幸せになりますように」!!
単行本にのせてお願いします
こばかわにでてくるみんな大好きです!
GO先生へ!!
GO先生の絵、大好きです!!
もっと、可愛いい絵をかいてください!!

Kumarin (Kanagawa) ↑

Ed.: I hope everyone ends up happy!!

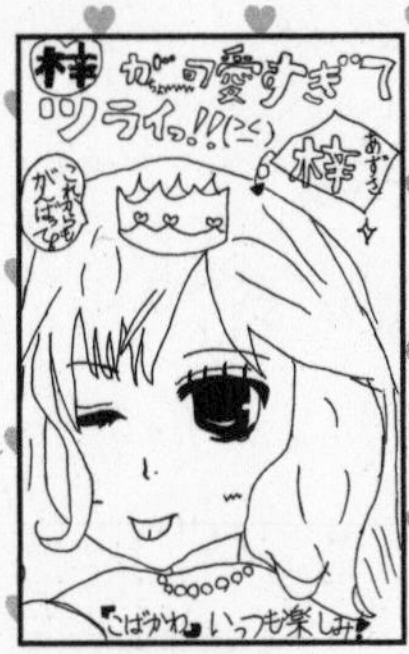
梓が愛すぎてツライっ!!
梓
これからもがんばって
「こばかわ」いつも楽しみ!

Kokokko Gurashi ↑ (Aomori)

Ed.: I love Azusa's "my bad." ♥

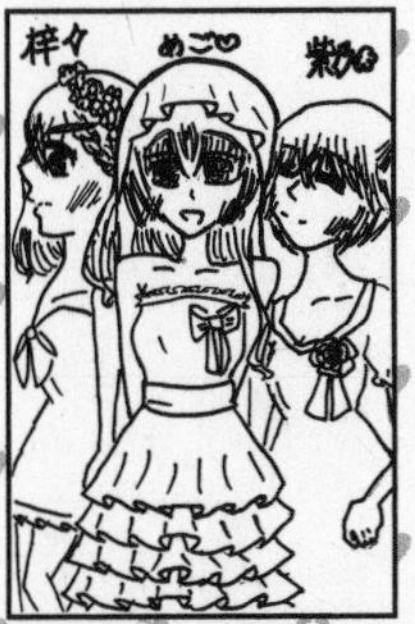
梓々
めご♡

Moririn (Kanagawa) ↑

Ed.: The beautiful dresses knocked me out!!

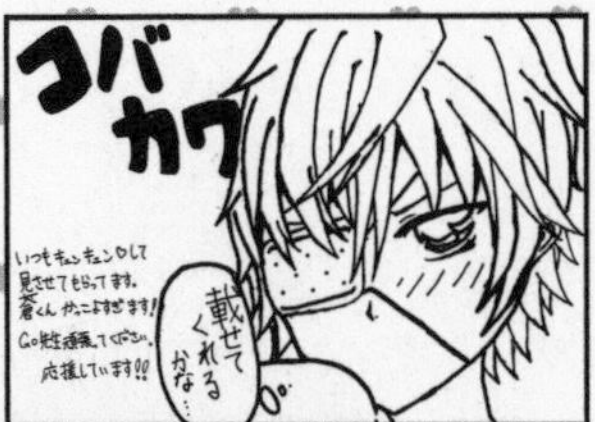
コバカワ
いつもキュンキュンして見させてもらってます。
蒼くんかっこよすぎます!
GO先生頑張ってください。
応援してます!!
載せてくれるかな…

Ayaka Date (Fukuoka) ↑

Ed.: Bored Aoi's cool too!!

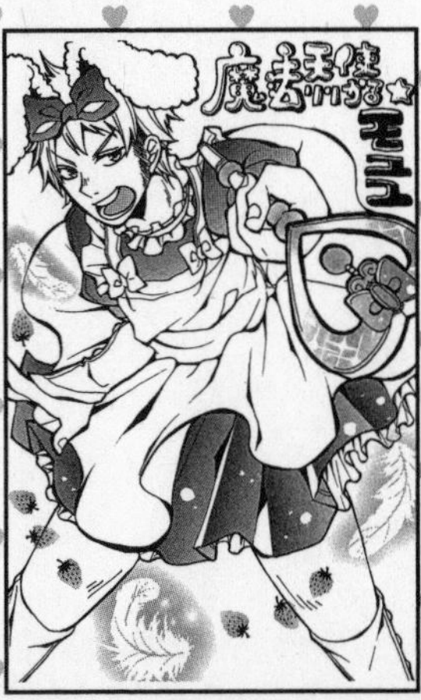

←

Edao (Chiba) ←

Ed.: A-all I can do is laugh!!

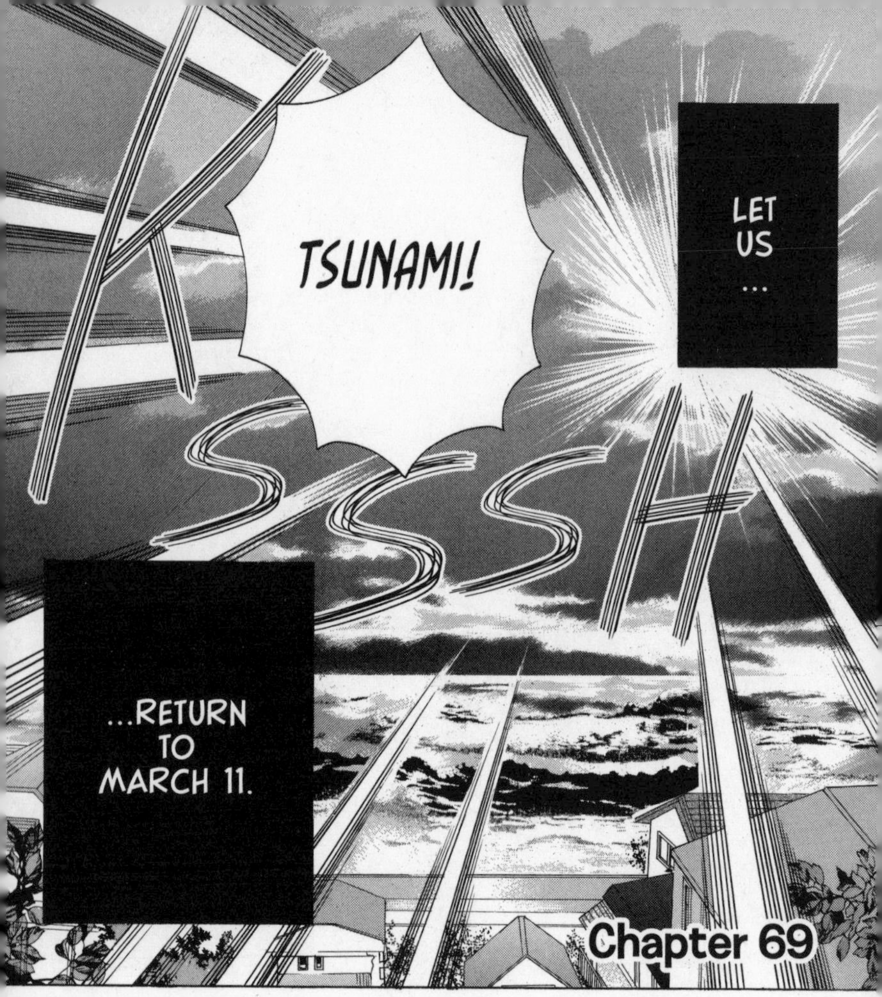
LET US ...
TSUNAMI!
SSSH
...RETURN TO MARCH 11.
Chapter 69

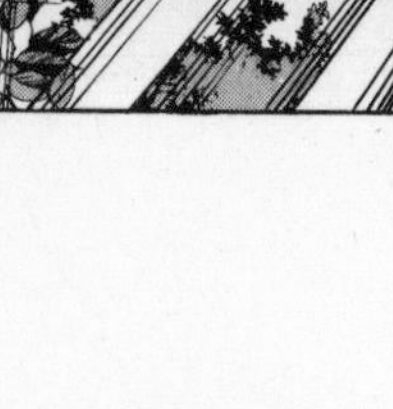
WHISPER

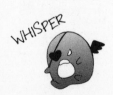

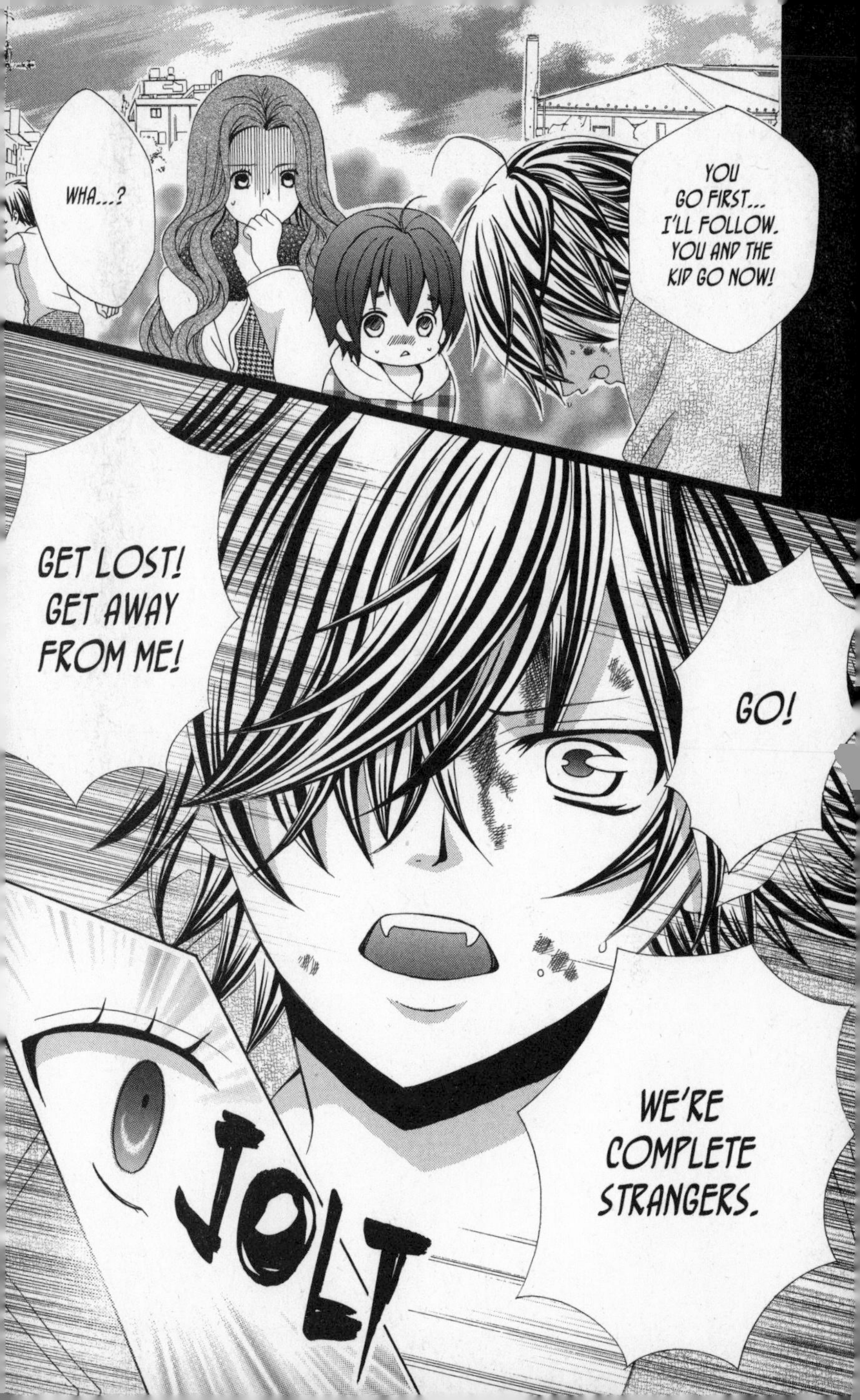
YOU GO FIRST... I'LL FOLLOW. YOU AND THE KID GO NOW!
WHA...?
GO!
GET LOST! GET AWAY FROM ME!
WE'RE COMPLETE STRANGERS.
JOLT

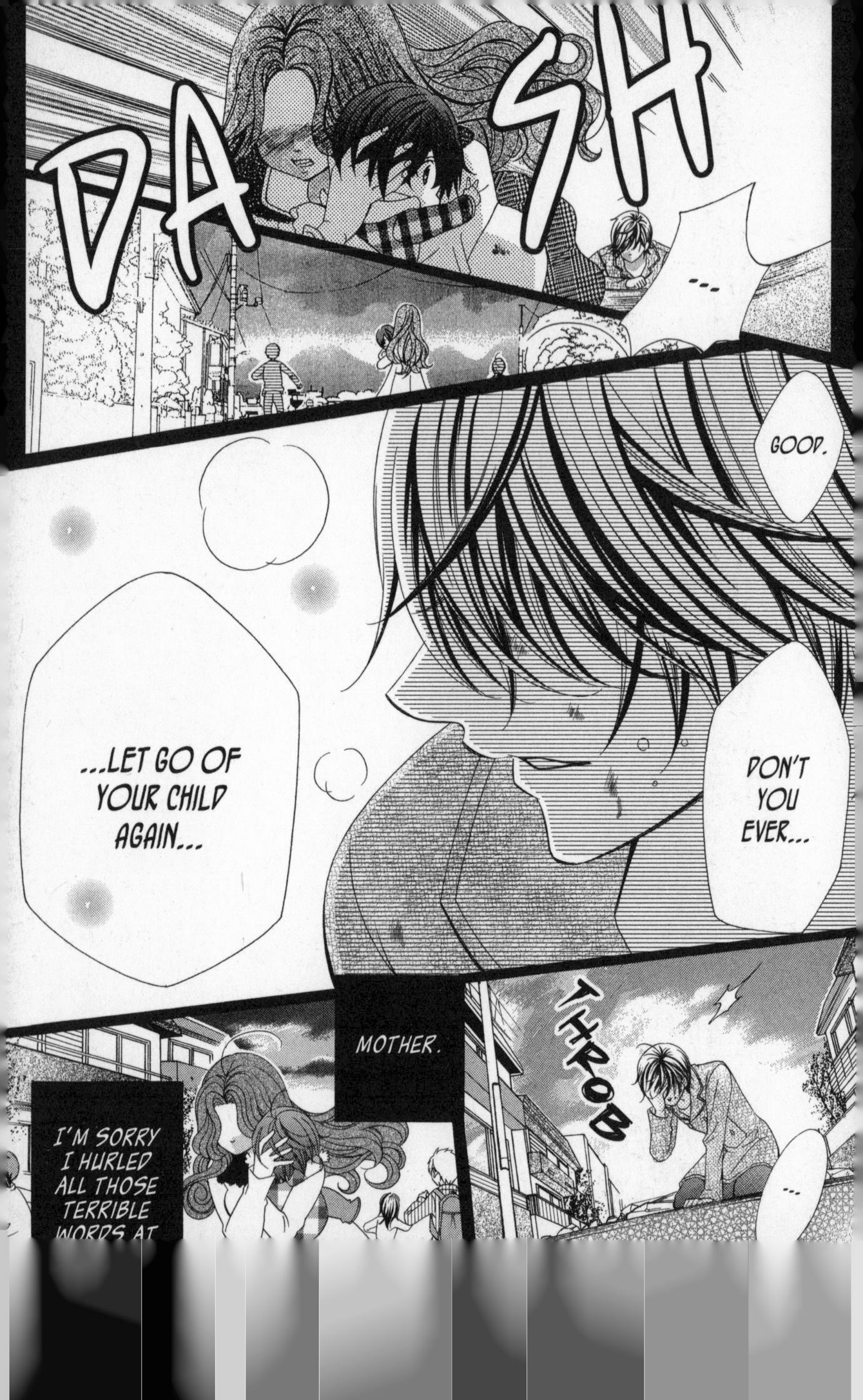
DASH
...
GOOD.
DON'T YOU EVER...
...LET GO OF YOUR CHILD AGAIN...
THROB
...
MOTHER.
I'M SORRY I HURLED ALL THOSE TERRIBLE WORDS AT

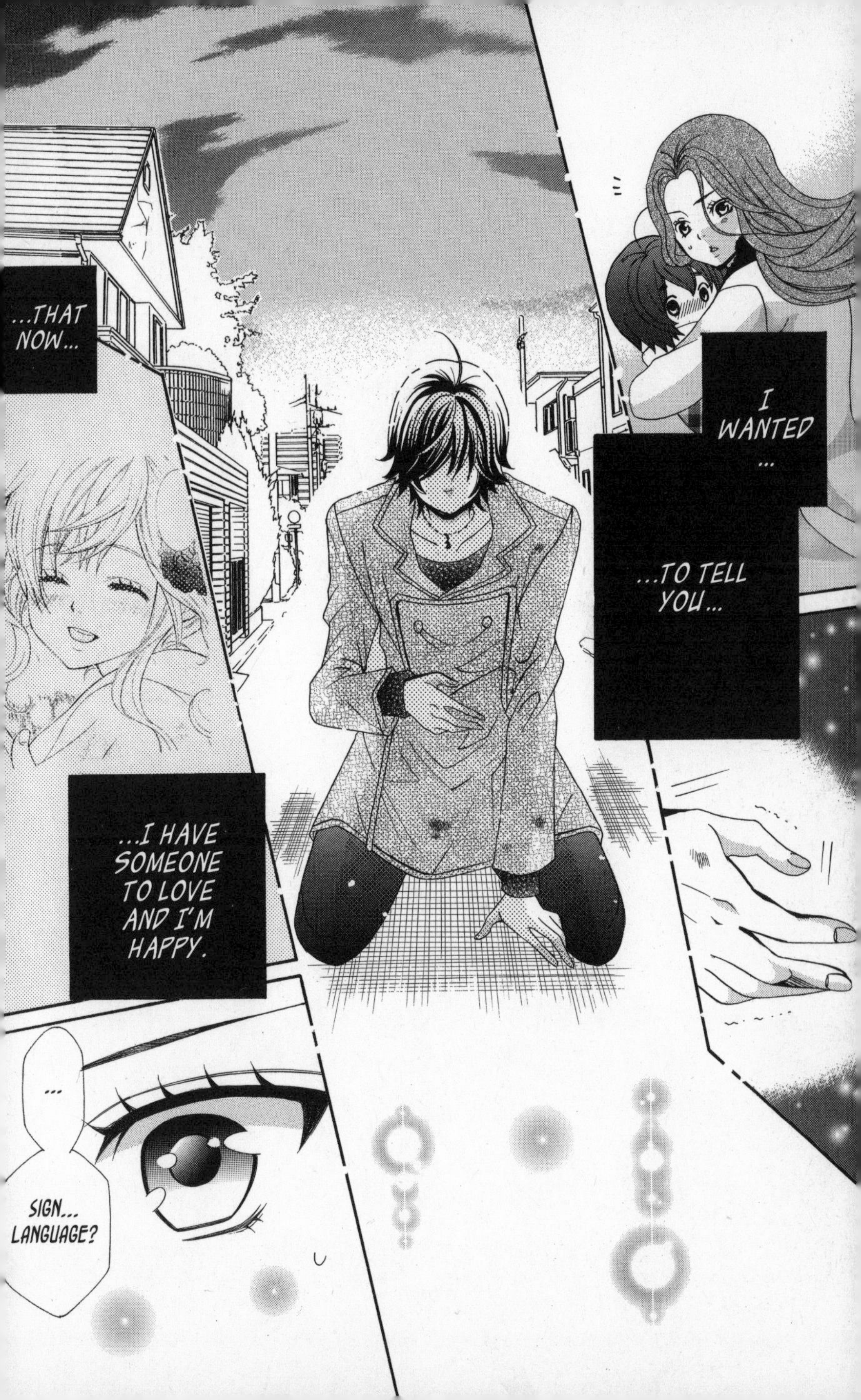
I WANTED ...
...TO TELL YOU...
...THAT NOW...
...I HAVE SOMEONE TO LOVE AND I'M HAPPY.
...
SIGN... LANGUAGE?

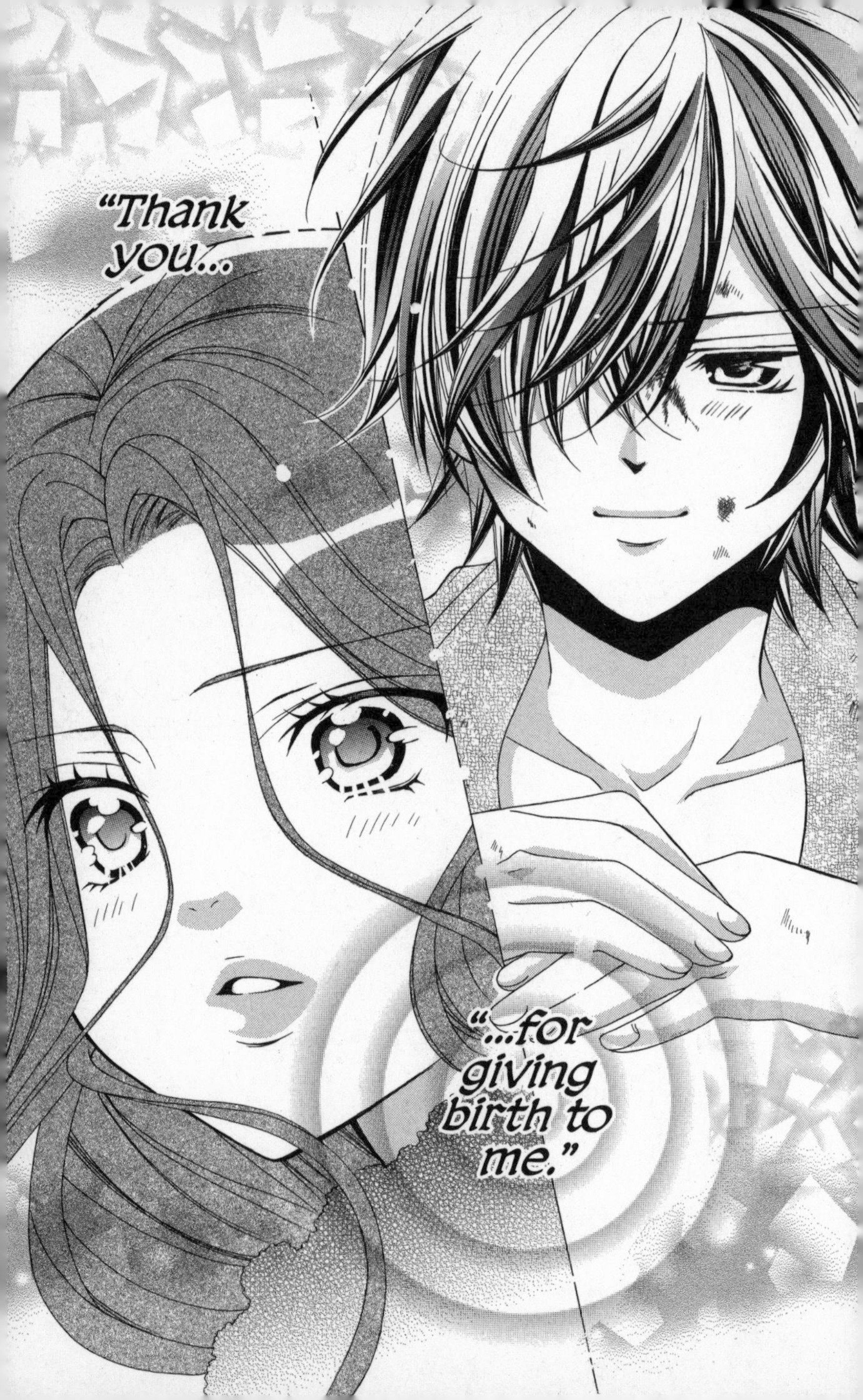
"Thank you...
"...for giving birth to me."

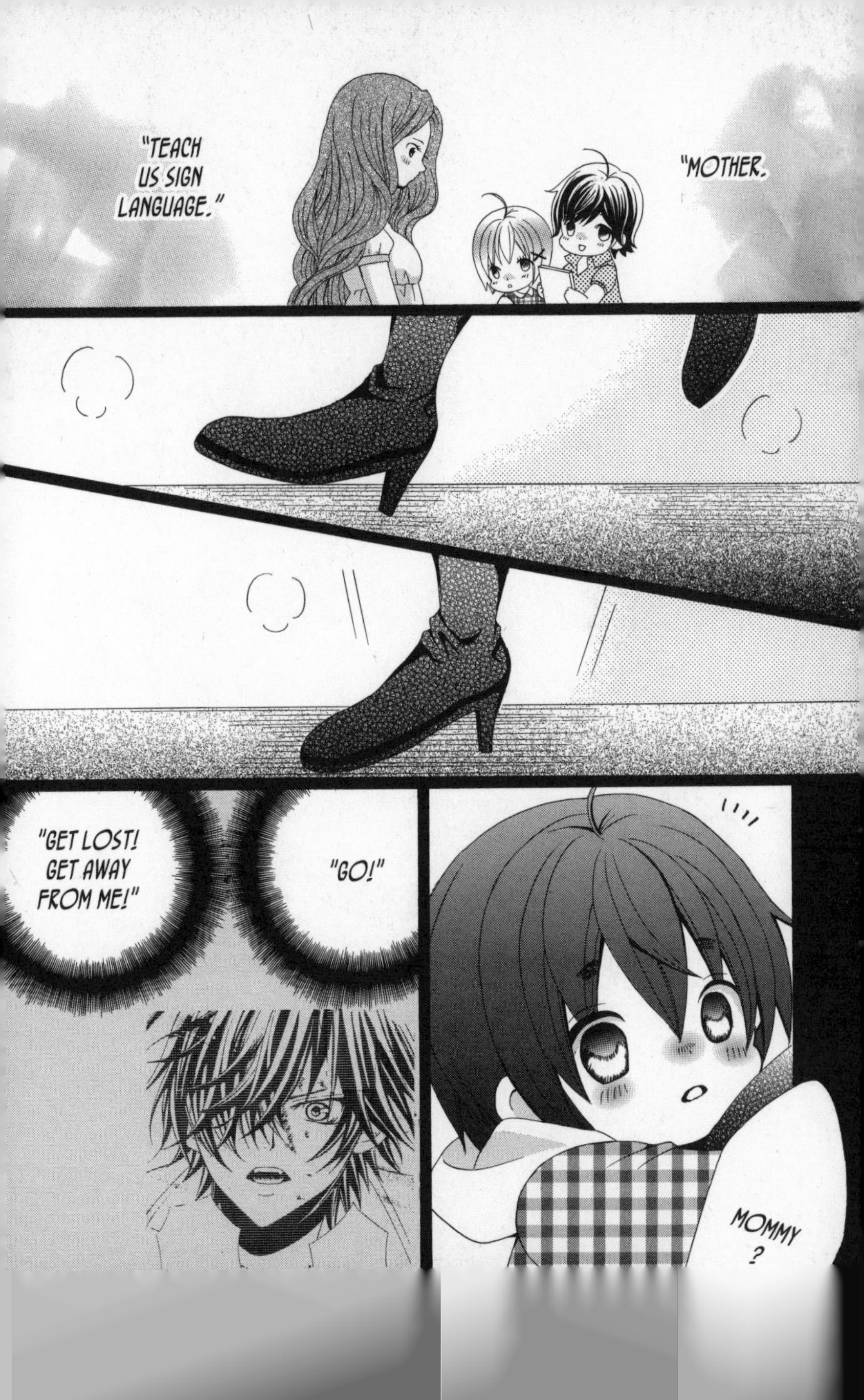
"MOTHER.
"TEACH US SIGN LANGUAGE."
MOMMY ?
"GO!"
"GET LOST! GET AWAY FROM ME!"

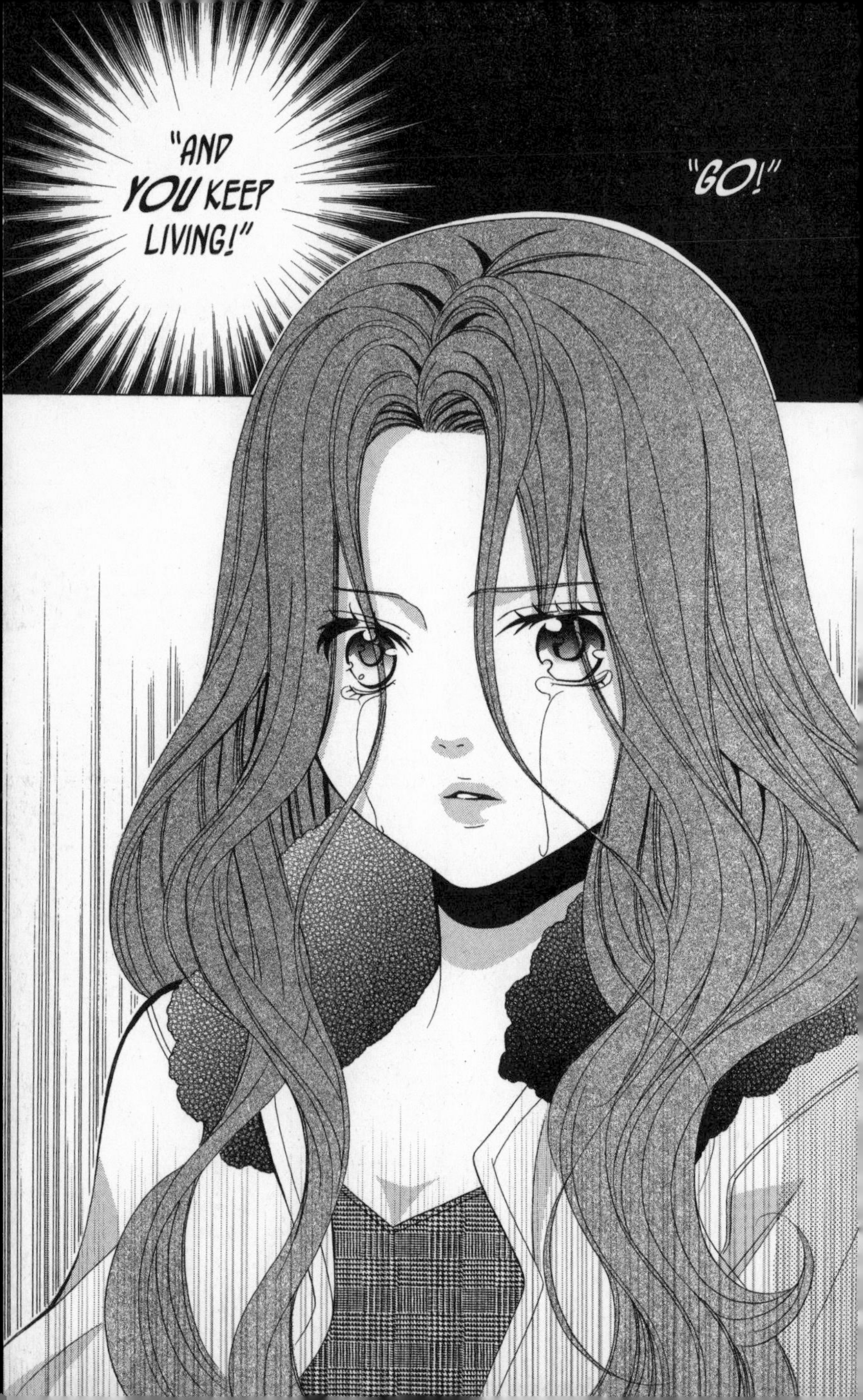
"GO!"
"AND YOU KEEP LIVING!"

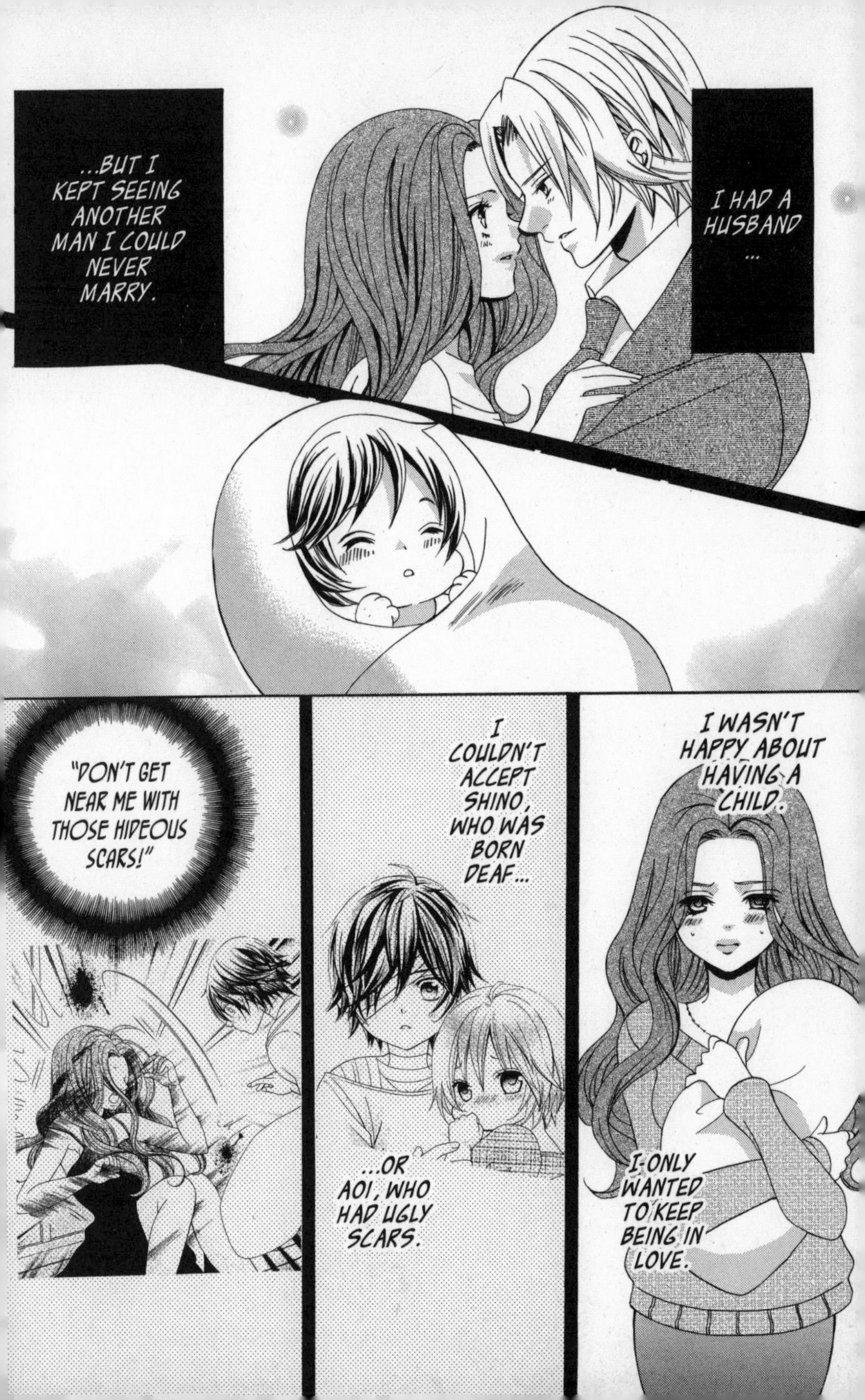
I HAD A HUSBAND...
...BUT I KEPT SEEING ANOTHER MAN I COULD NEVER MARRY.
I WASN'T HAPPY ABOUT HAVING A CHILD.
I ONLY WANTED TO KEEP BEING IN LOVE.
I COULDN'T ACCEPT SHINO, WHO WAS BORN DEAF...
...OR AOI, WHO HAD UGLY SCARS.
"DON'T GET NEAR ME WITH THOSE HIDEOUS SCARS!"

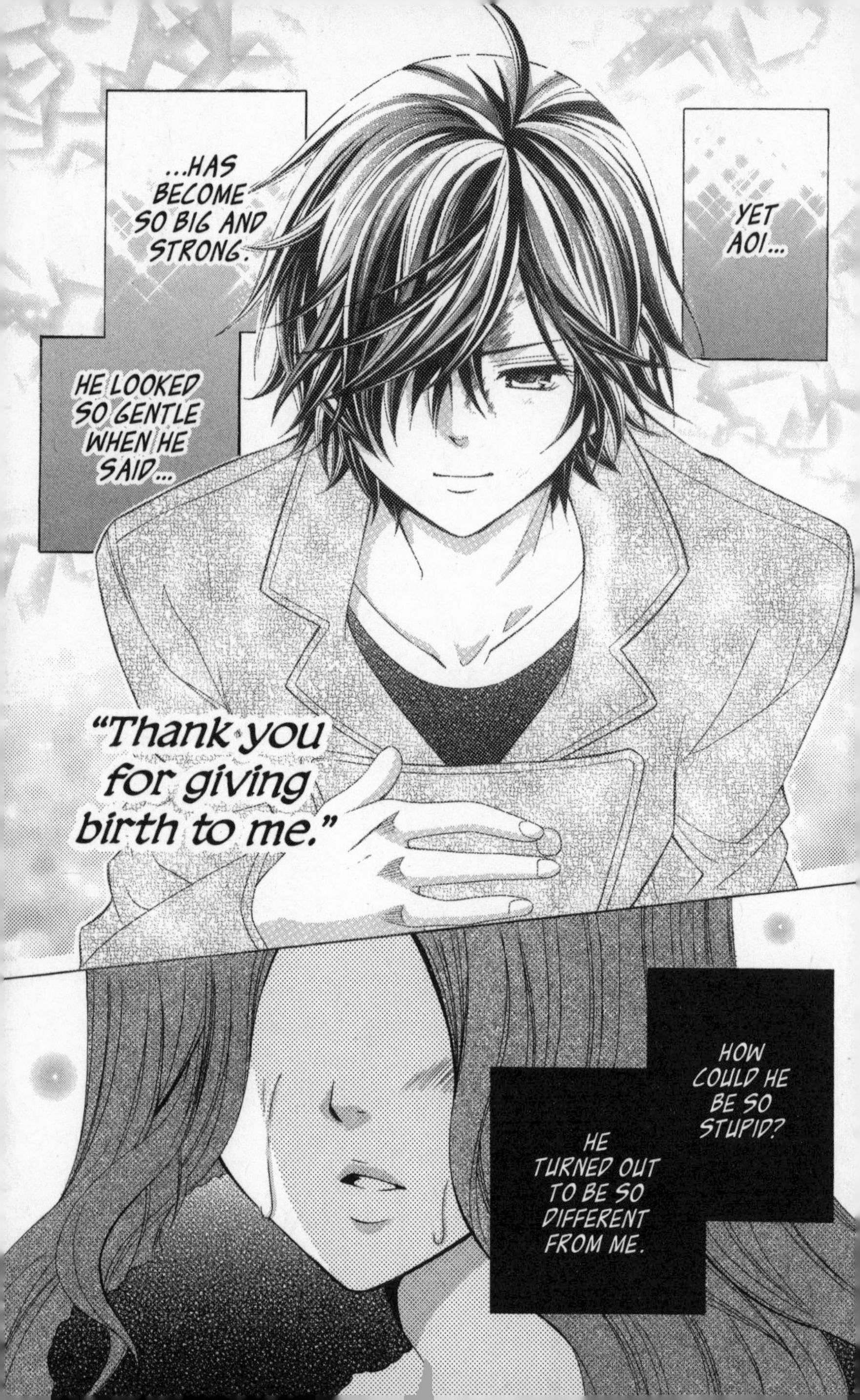
YET AOI...
...HAS BECOME SO BIG AND STRONG.
HE LOOKED SO GENTLE WHEN HE SAID...
"Thank you for giving birth to me."
HOW COULD HE BE SO STUPID?
HE TURNED OUT TO BE SO DIFFERENT FROM ME.

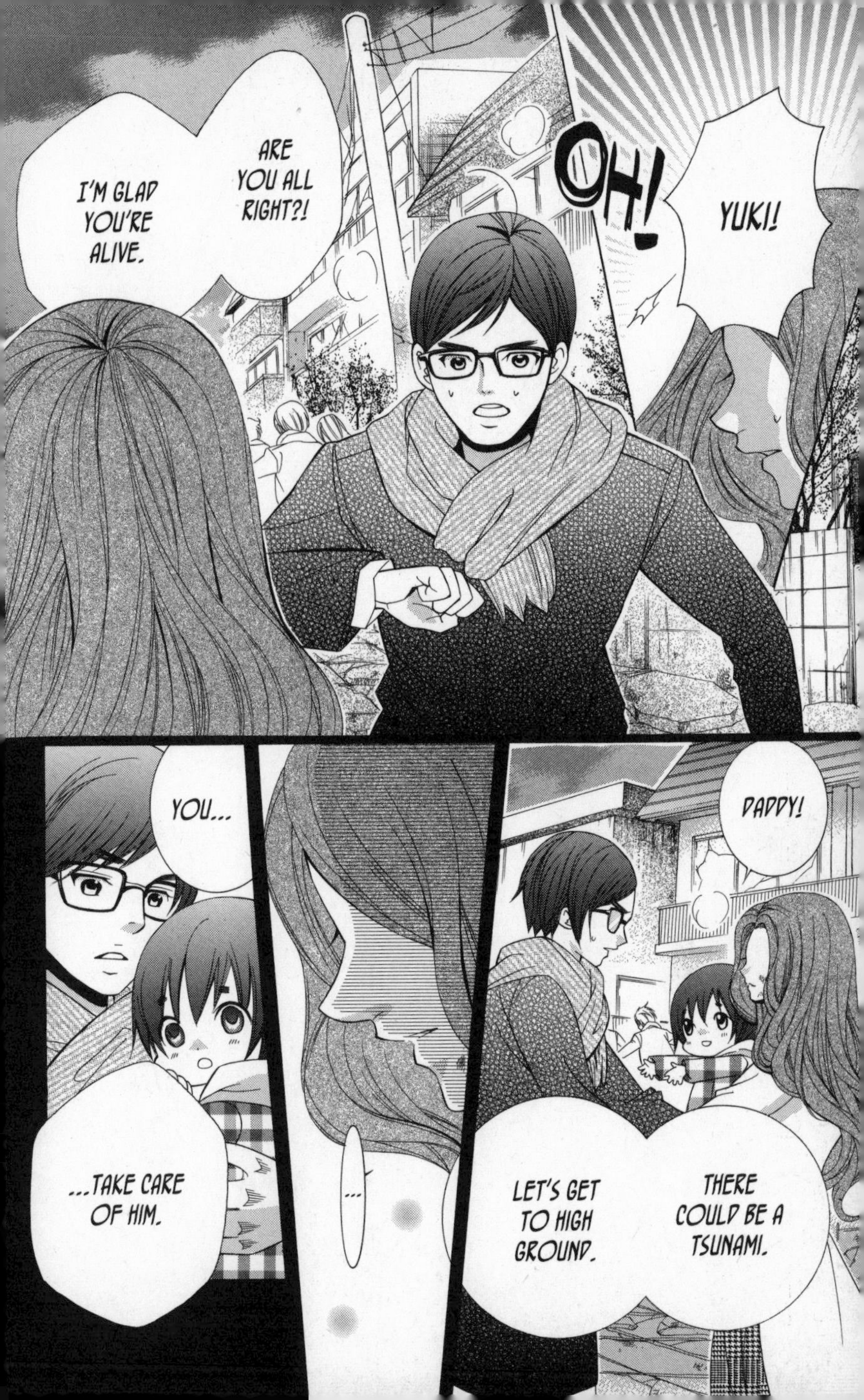
YUKI!
OH!
ARE YOU ALL RIGHT?!
I'M GLAD YOU'RE ALIVE.
DADDY!
THERE COULD BE A TSUNAMI.
LET'S GET TO HIGH GROUND.
...
YOU...
...TAKE CARE OF HIM.

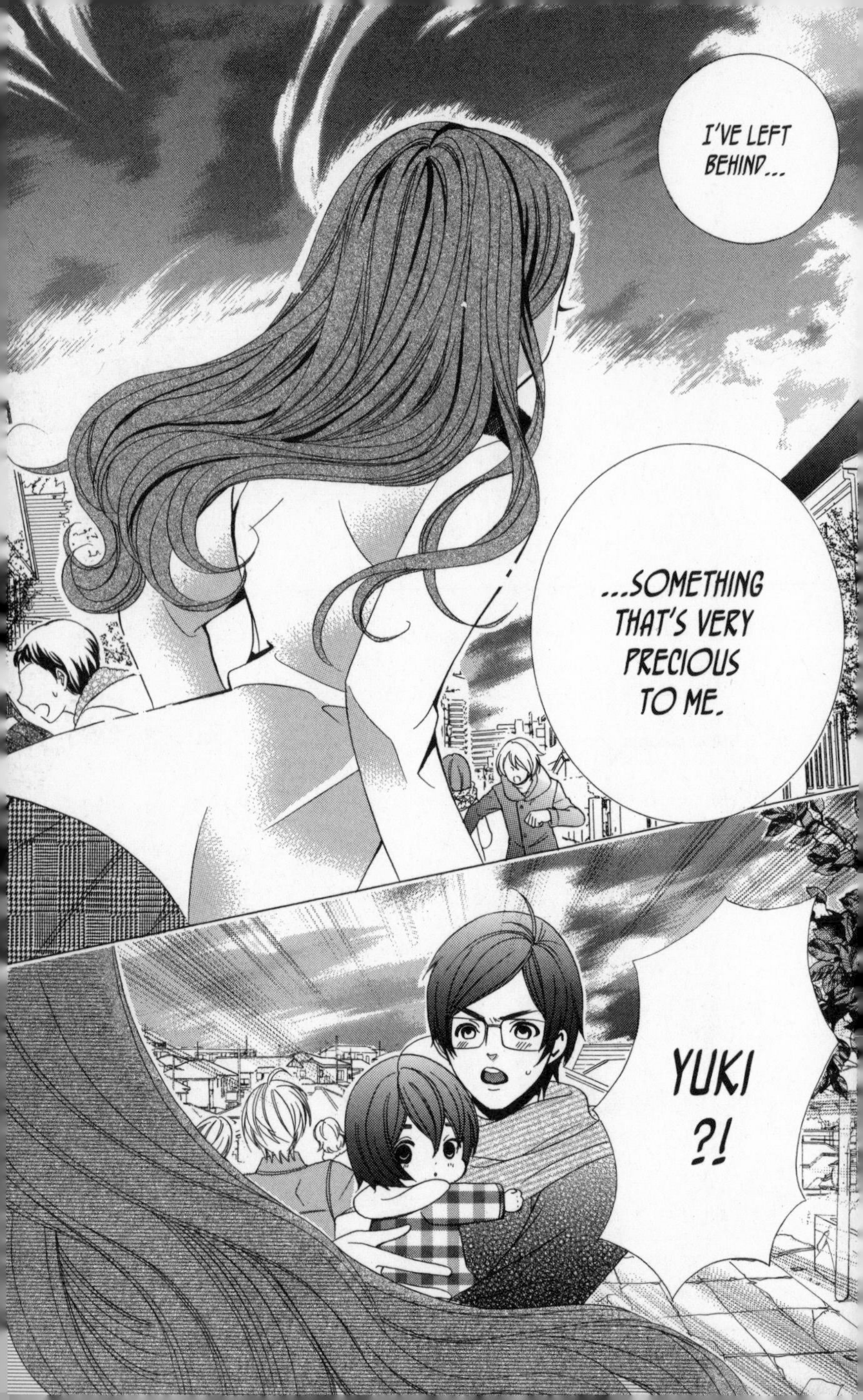
I'VE LEFT BEHIND...
...SOMETHING THAT'S VERY PRECIOUS TO ME.
YUKI ?!

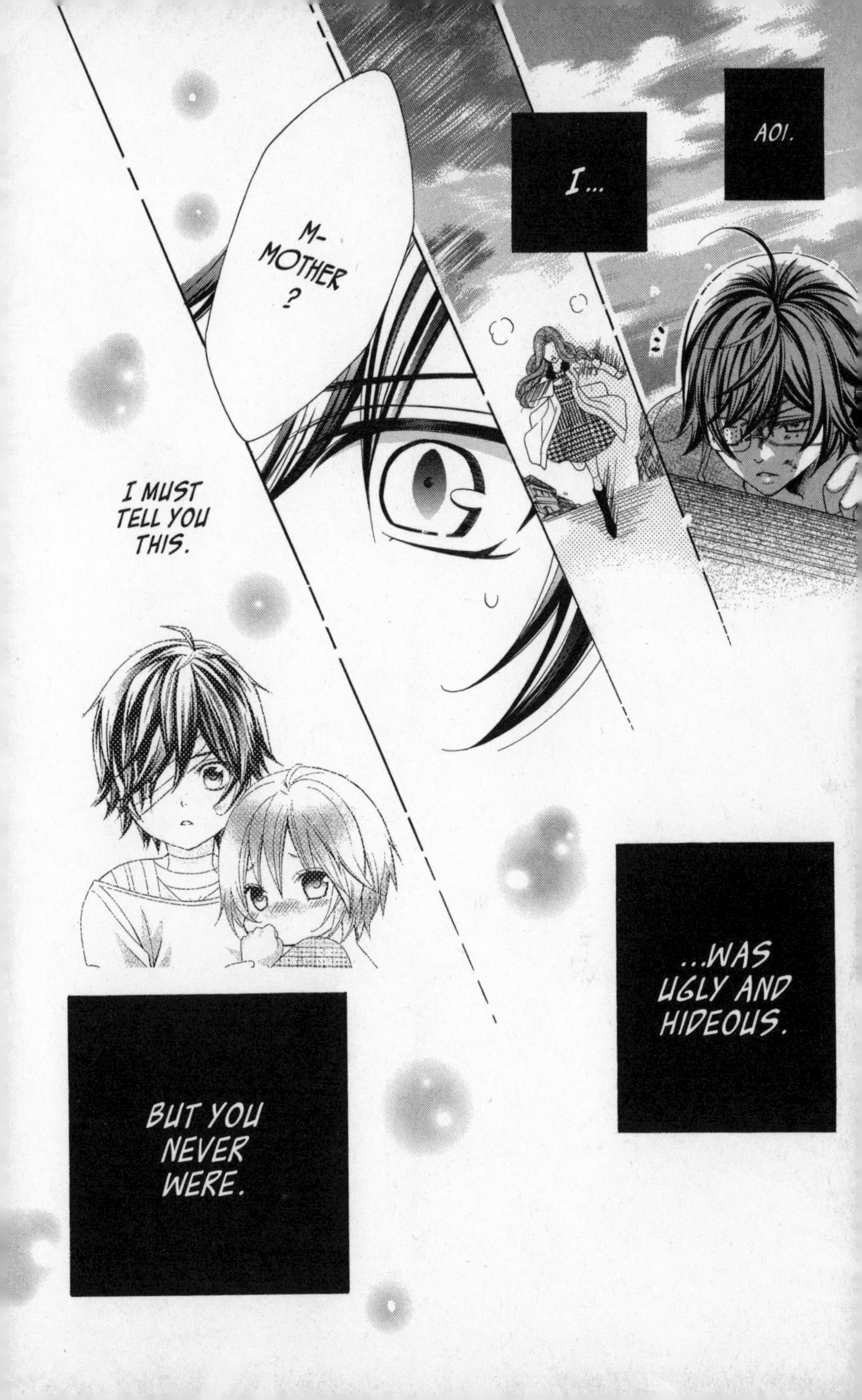
AOI.
I...
M-MOTHER?
I MUST TELL YOU THIS.
...WAS UGLY AND HIDEOUS.
BUT YOU NEVER WERE.

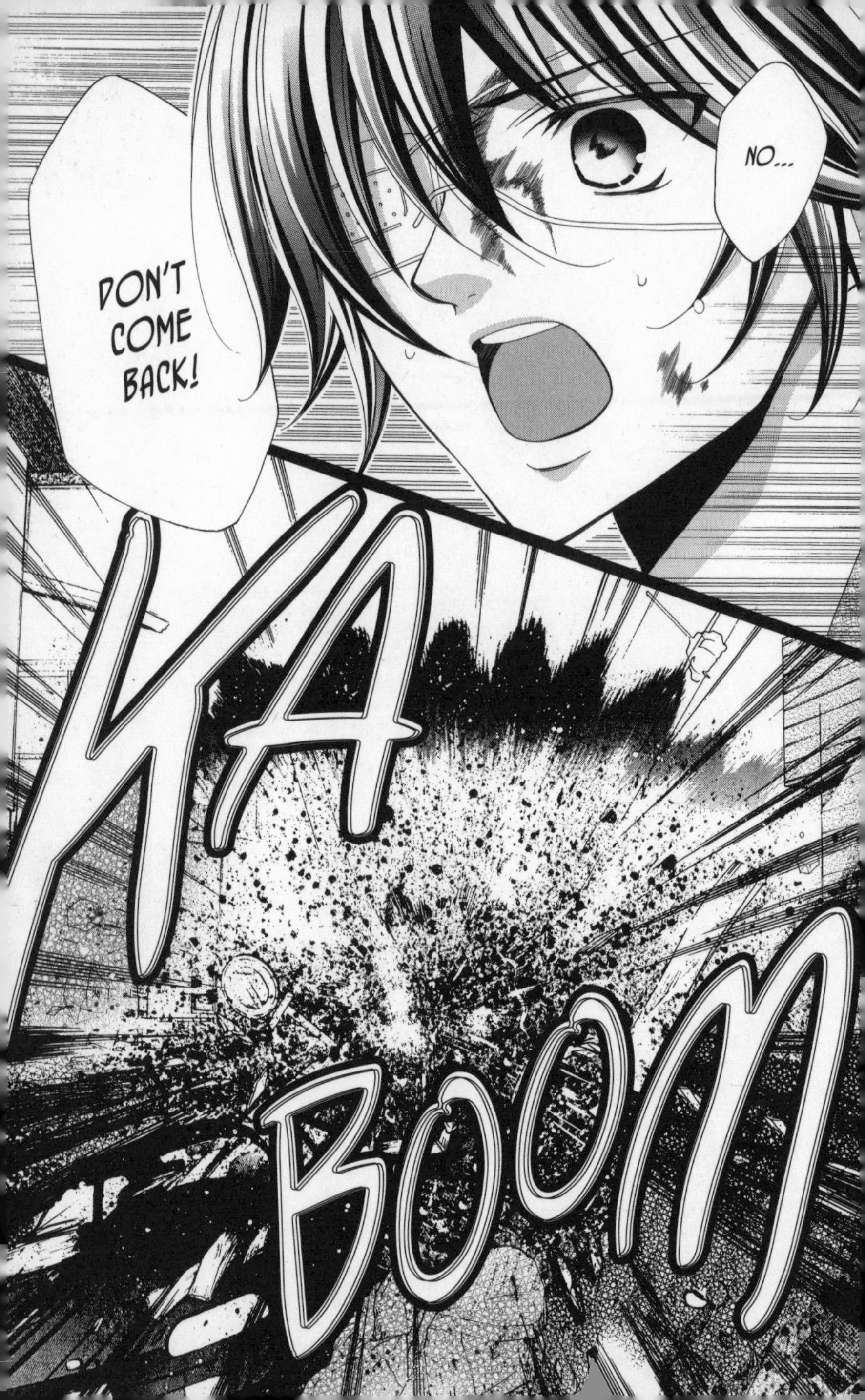
NO...
DON'T COME BACK!
KA
BOOM

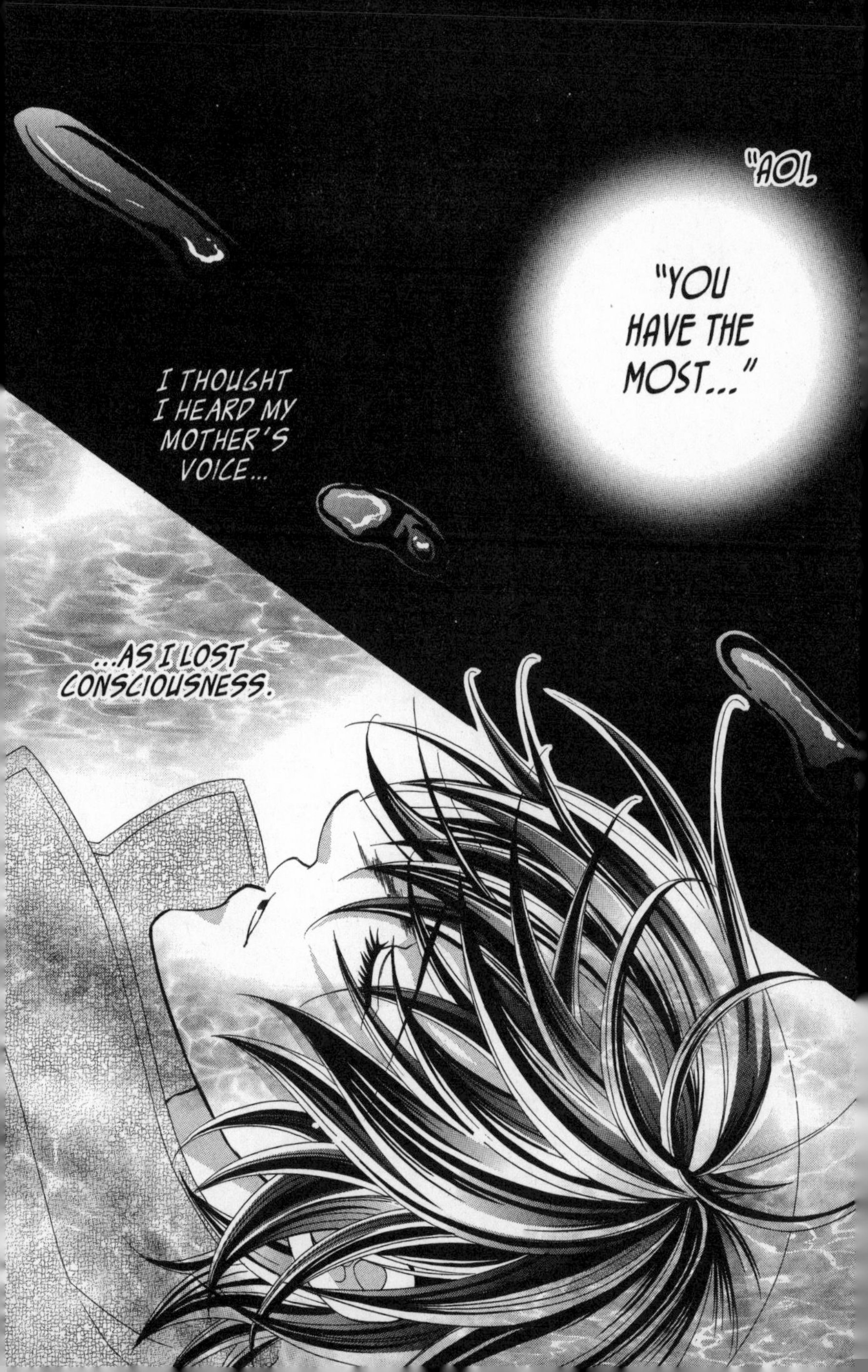
"AOI.
"YOU HAVE THE MOST..."
I THOUGHT I HEARD MY MOTHER'S VOICE...
...AS I LOST CONSCIOUSNESS.

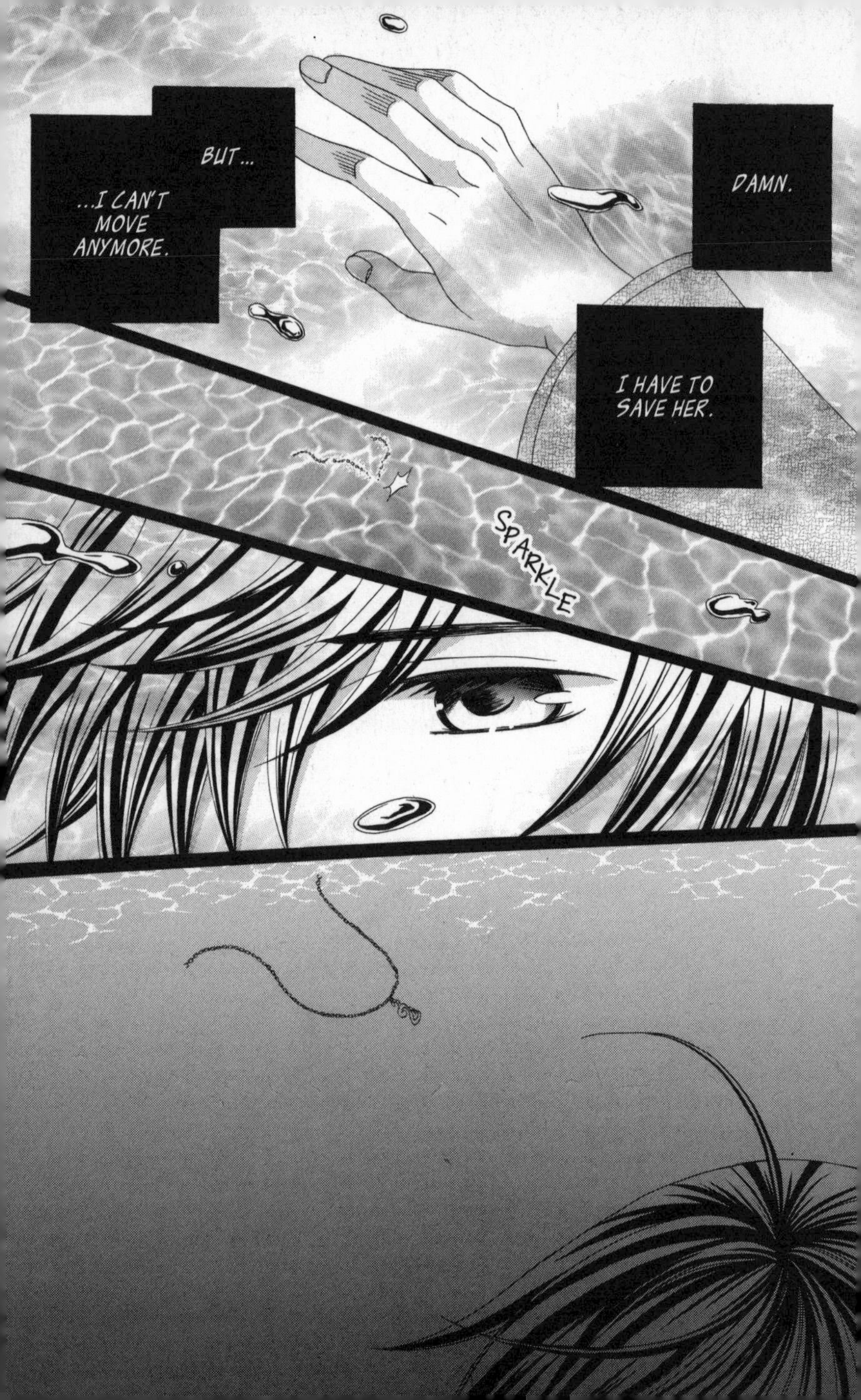
DAMN.
BUT...
...I CAN'T MOVE ANYMORE.
I HAVE TO SAVE HER.
SPARKLE

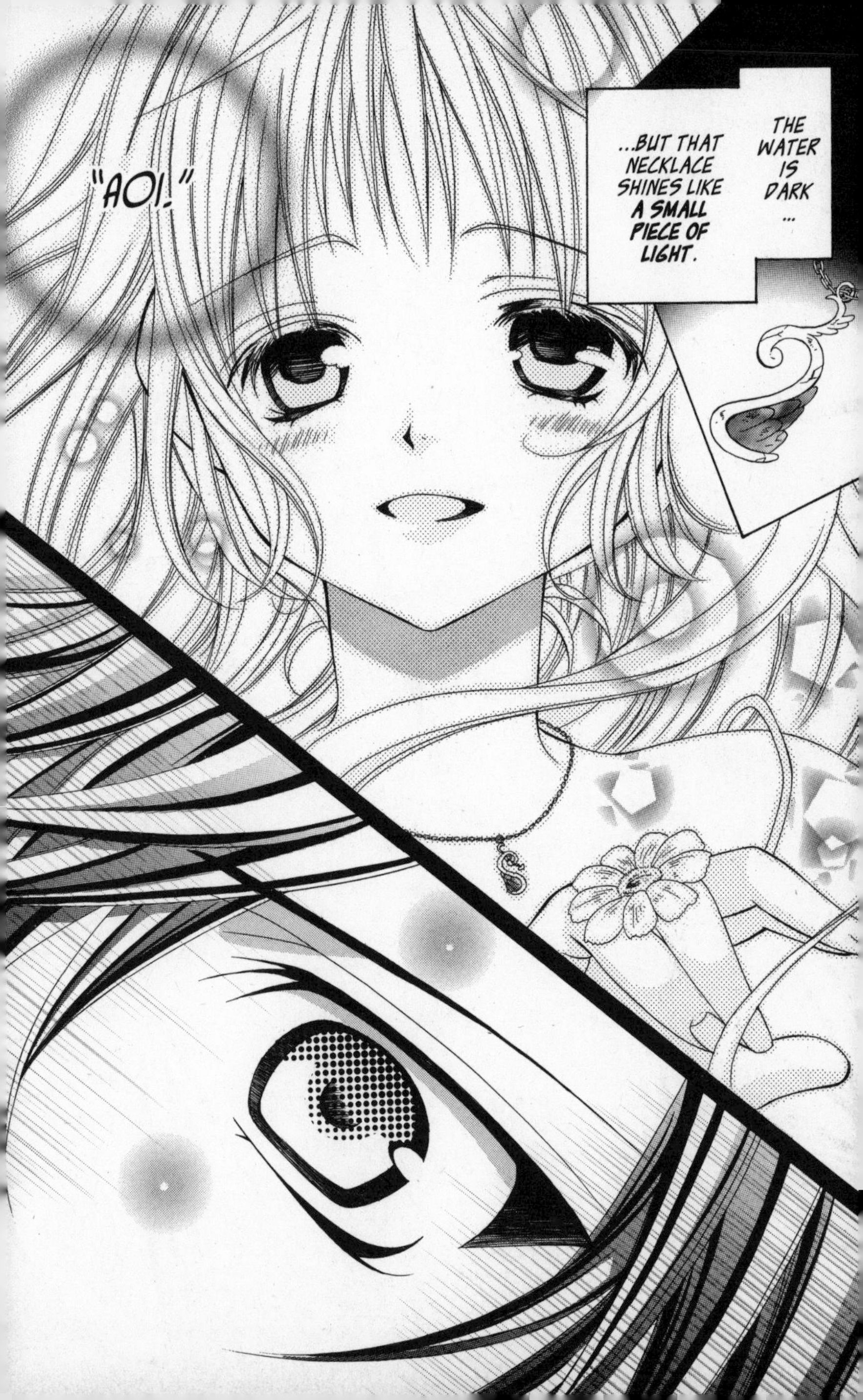
THE WATER IS DARK...
...BUT THAT NECKLACE SHINES LIKE A SMALL PIECE OF LIGHT.
"AOI."

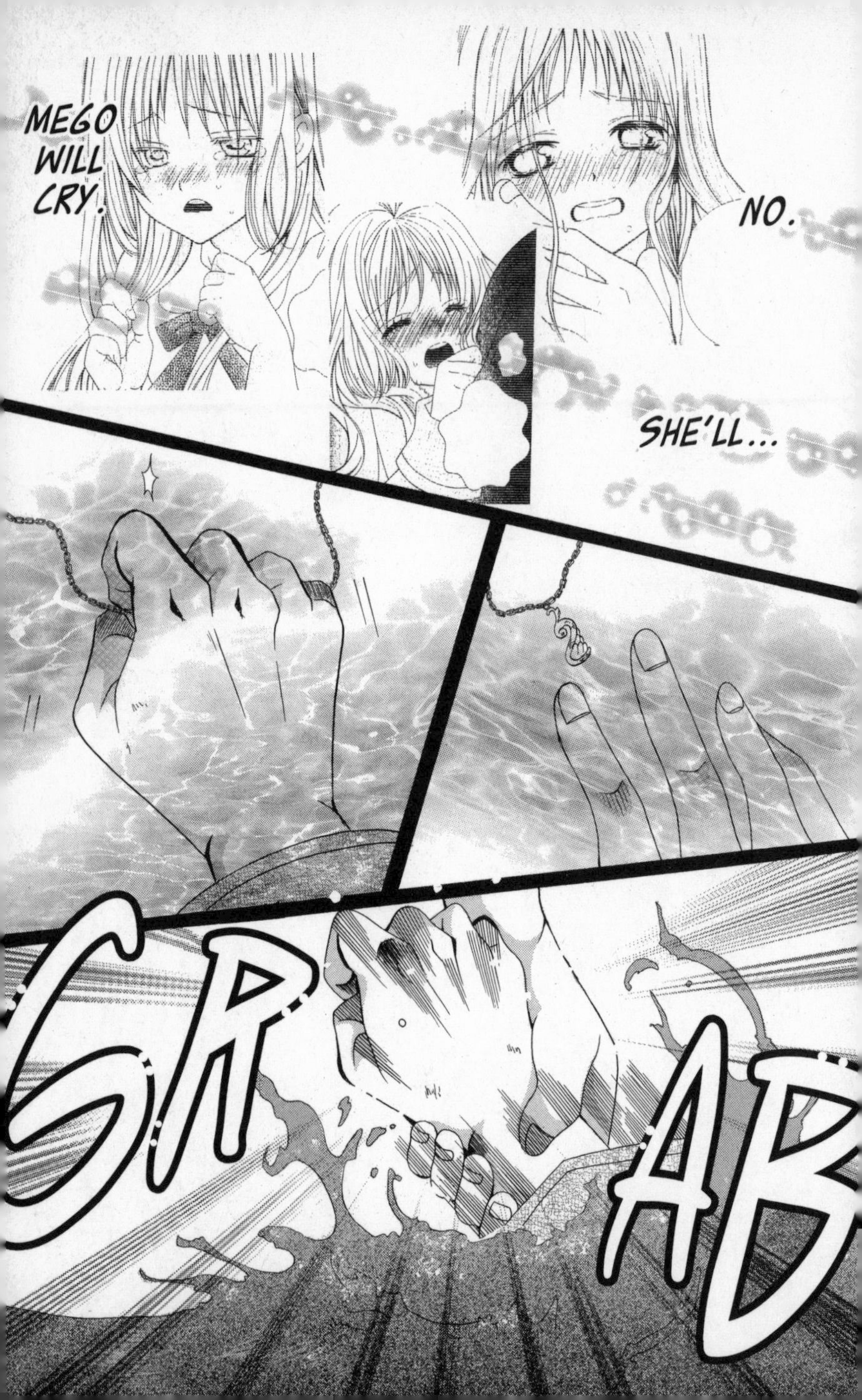
NO.
SHE'LL...
MEGO WILL CRY.
SRAB

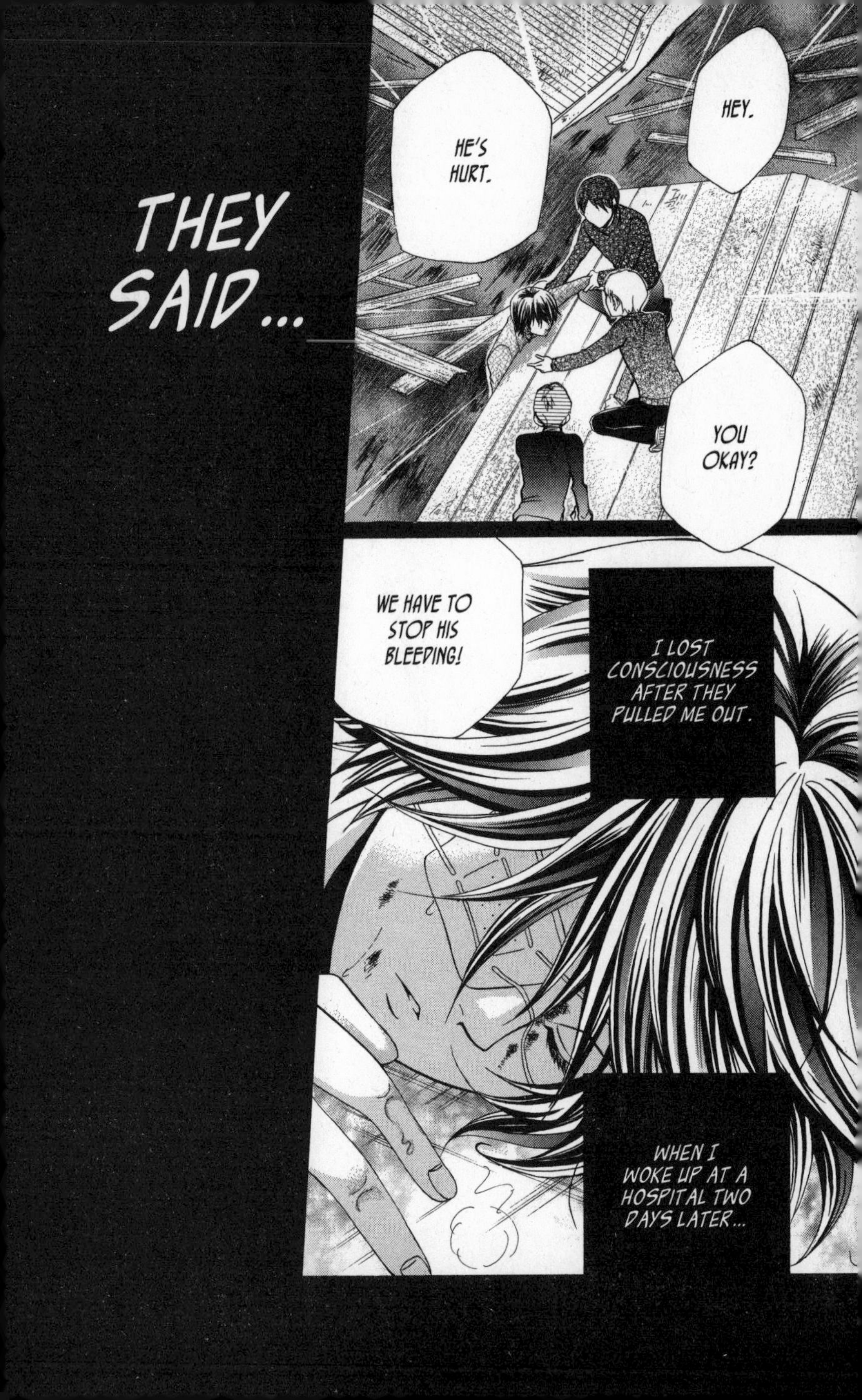
HEY.
YOU OKAY?
HE'S HURT.
THEY SAID...
WE HAVE TO STOP HIS BLEEDING!
I LOST CONSCIOUSNESS AFTER THEY PULLED ME OUT.
WHEN I WOKE UP AT A HOSPITAL TWO DAYS LATER...

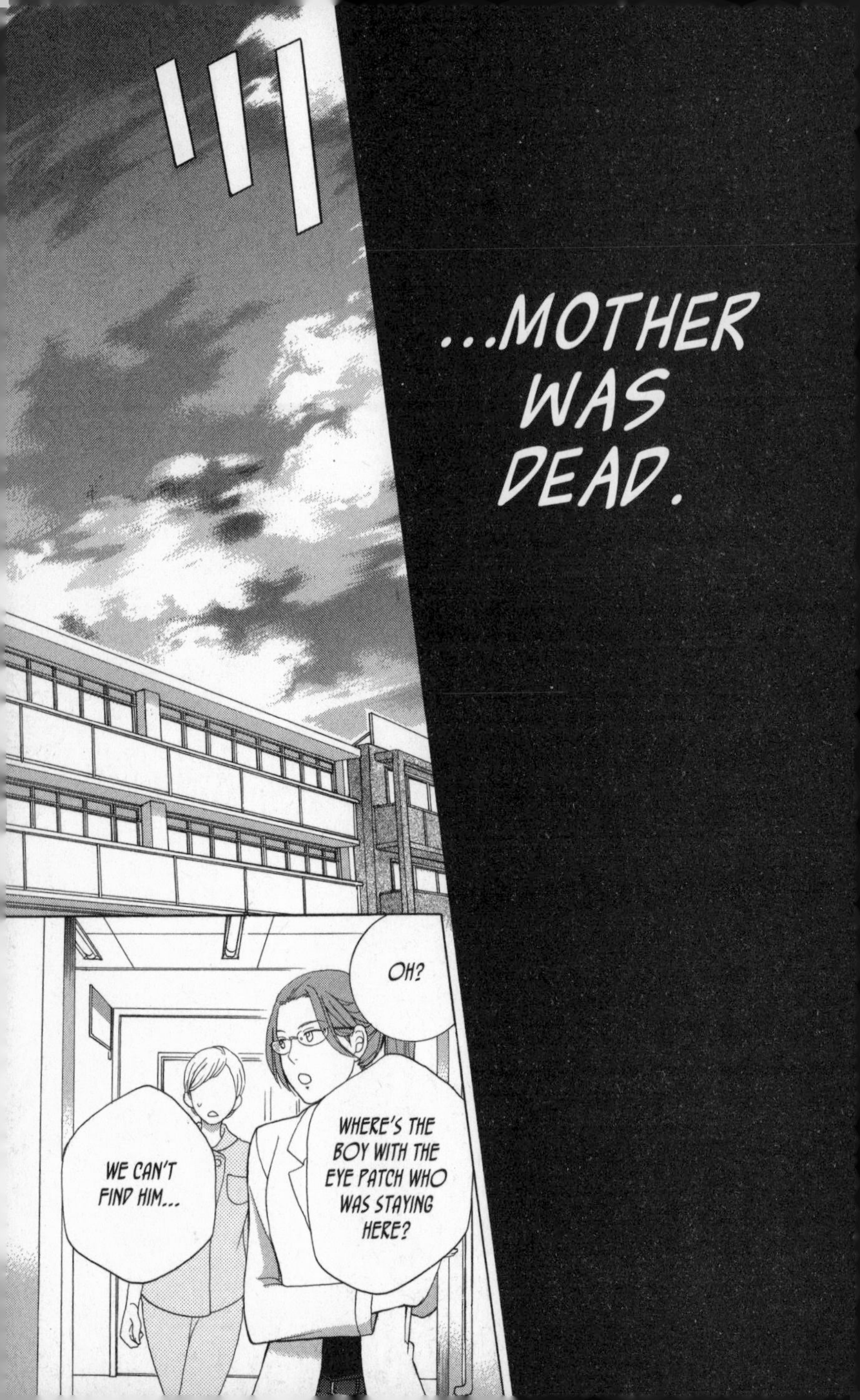
...MOTHER WAS DEAD.
OH?
WHERE'S THE BOY WITH THE EYE PATCH WHO WAS STAYING HERE?
WE CAN'T FIND HIM...

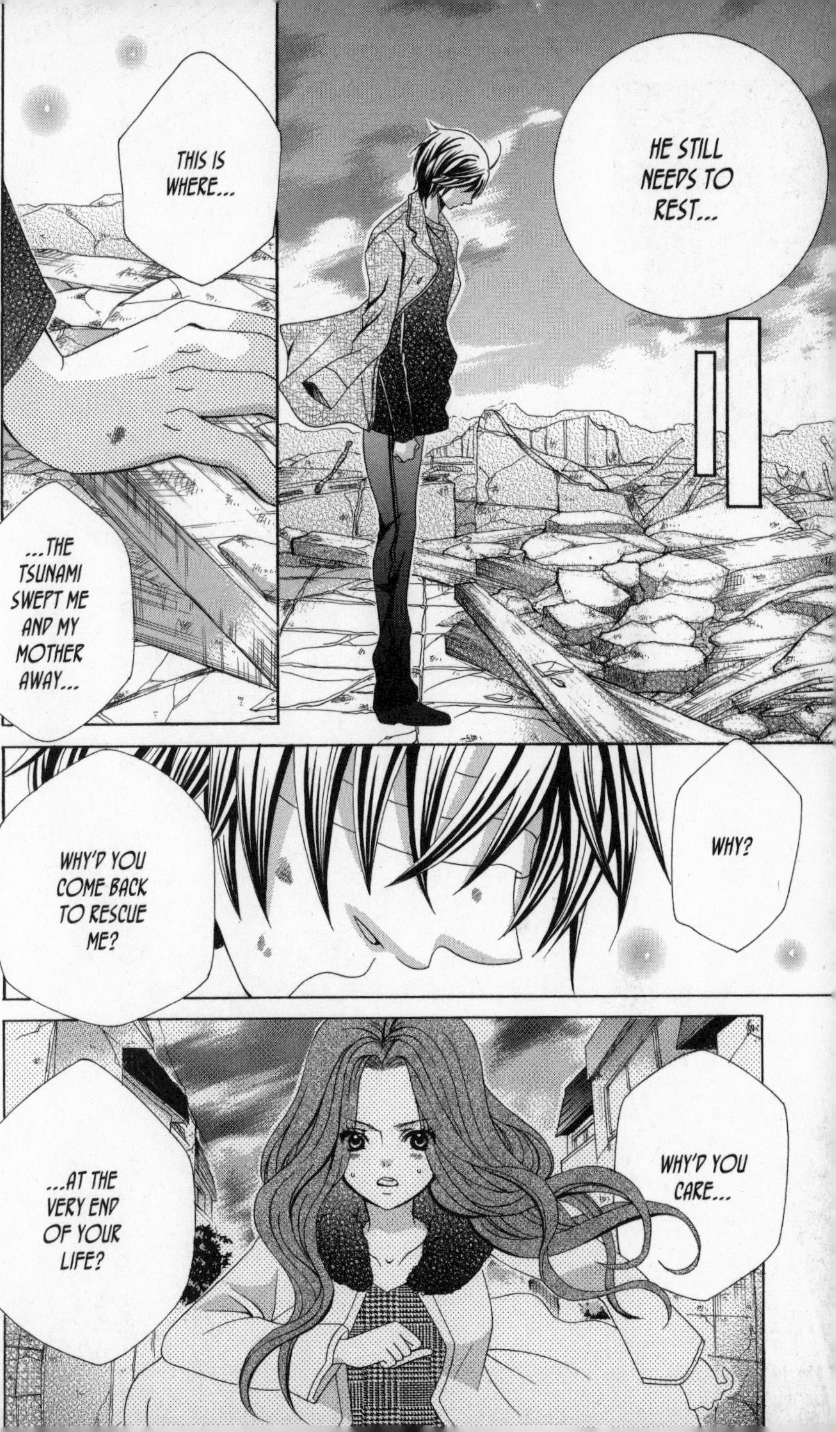
HE STILL NEEDS TO REST...
THIS IS WHERE...
...THE TSUNAMI SWEPT ME AND MY MOTHER AWAY...
WHY?
WHY'D YOU COME BACK TO RESCUE ME?
WHY'D YOU CARE...
...AT THE VERY END OF YOUR LIFE?

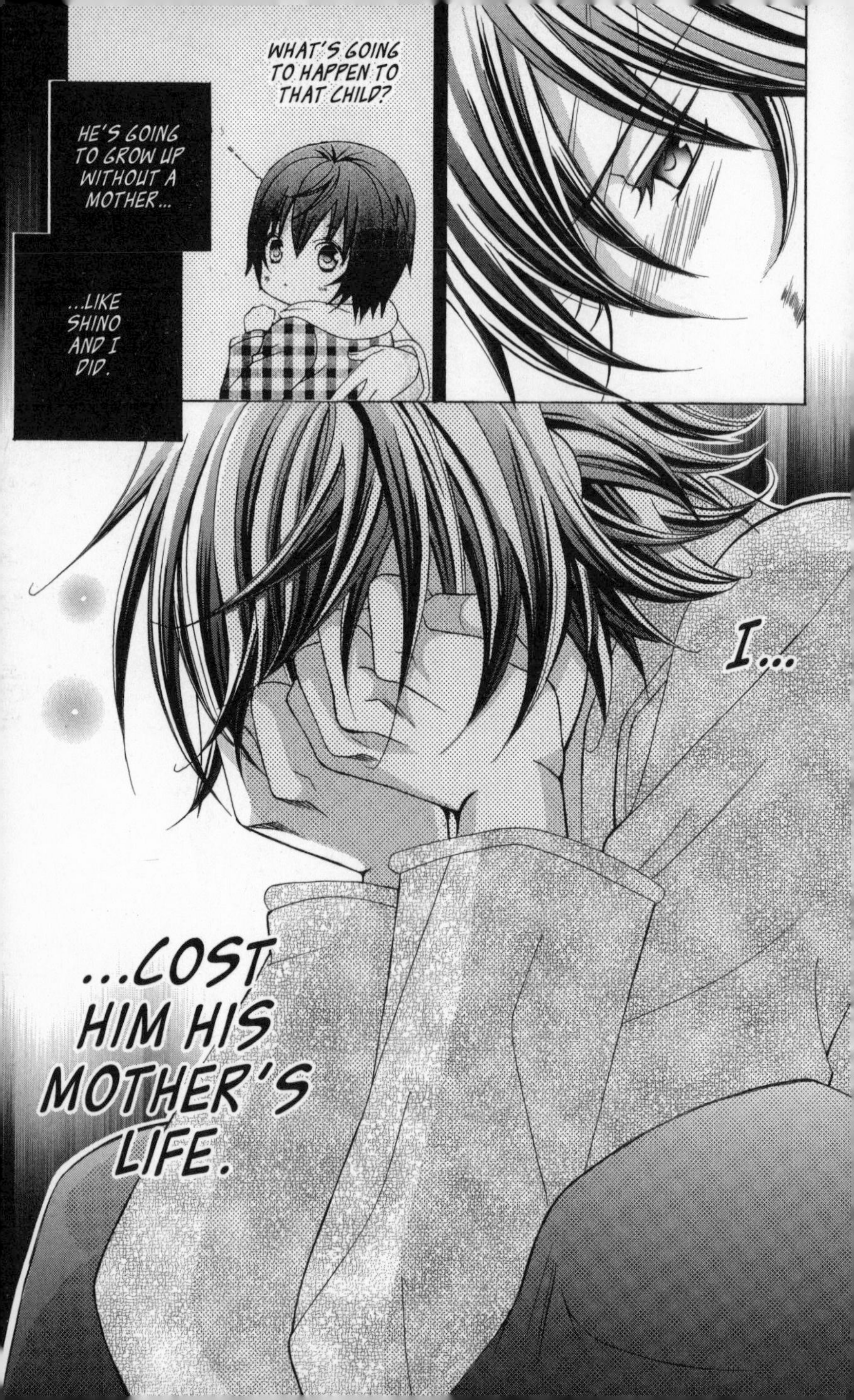
WHAT'S GOING TO HAPPEN TO THAT CHILD?
HE'S GOING TO GROW UP WITHOUT A MOTHER...
...LIKE SHINO AND I DID.
I...
...COST HIM HIS MOTHER'S LIFE.

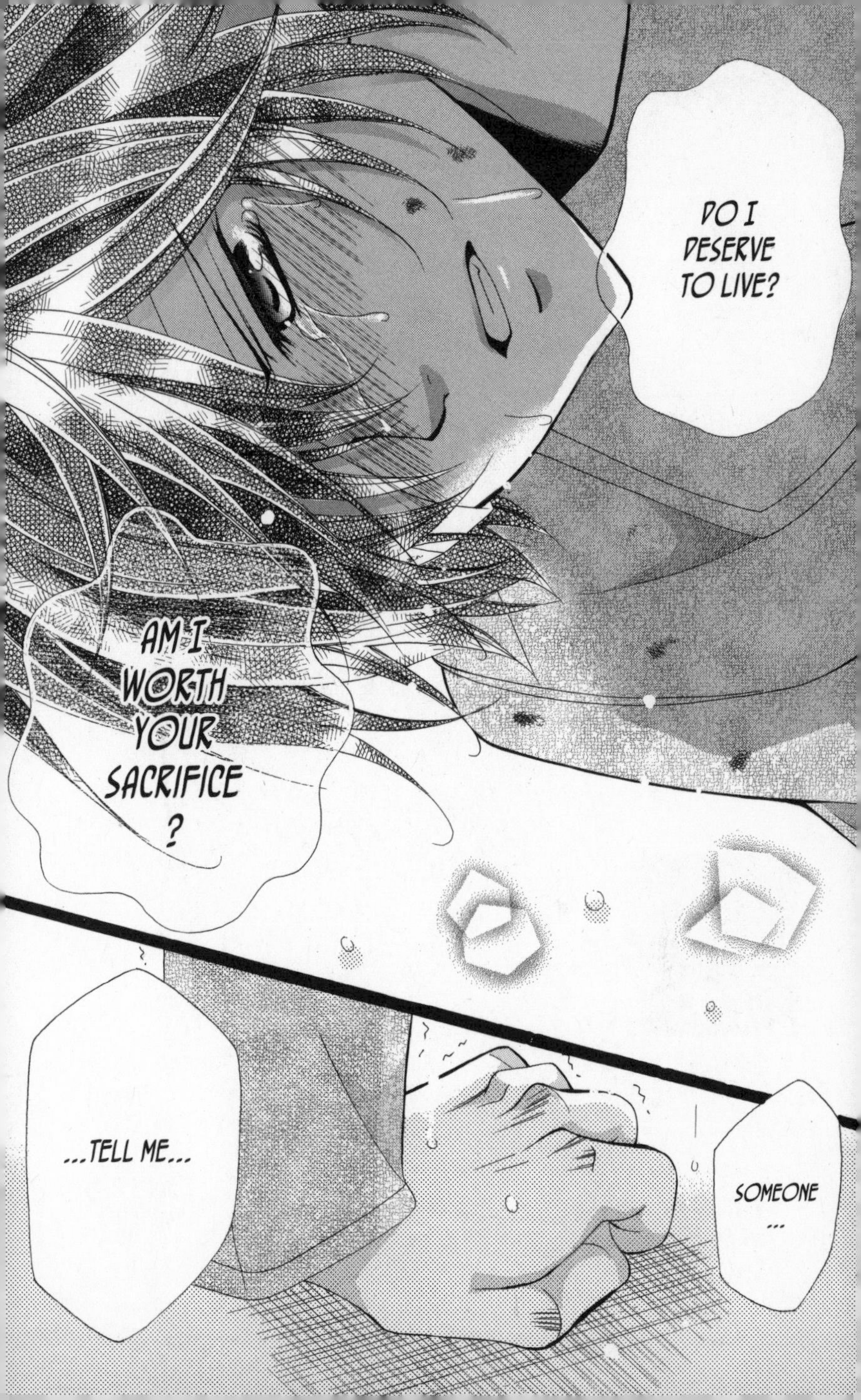
DO I DESERVE TO LIVE?
AM I WORTH YOUR SACRIFICE ?
SOMEONE ...
...TELL ME...

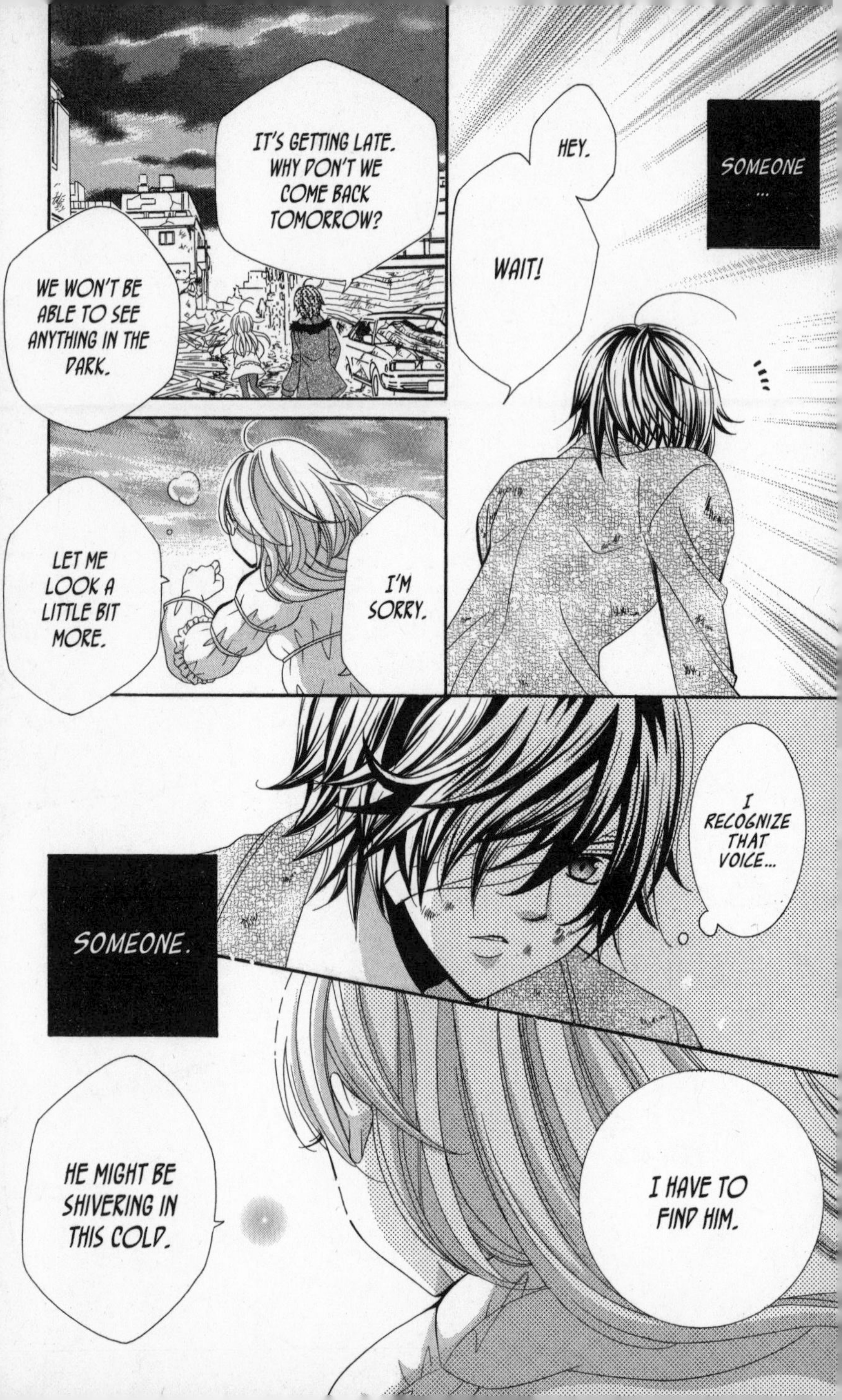
SOMEONE ...
HEY. WAIT!
IT'S GETTING LATE. WHY DON'T WE COME BACK TOMORROW?
WE WON'T BE ABLE TO SEE ANYTHING IN THE DARK.
I'M SORRY.
LET ME LOOK A LITTLE BIT MORE.
I RECOGNIZE THAT VOICE...
SOMEONE.
I HAVE TO FIND HIM.
HE MIGHT BE SHIVERING IN THIS COLD.

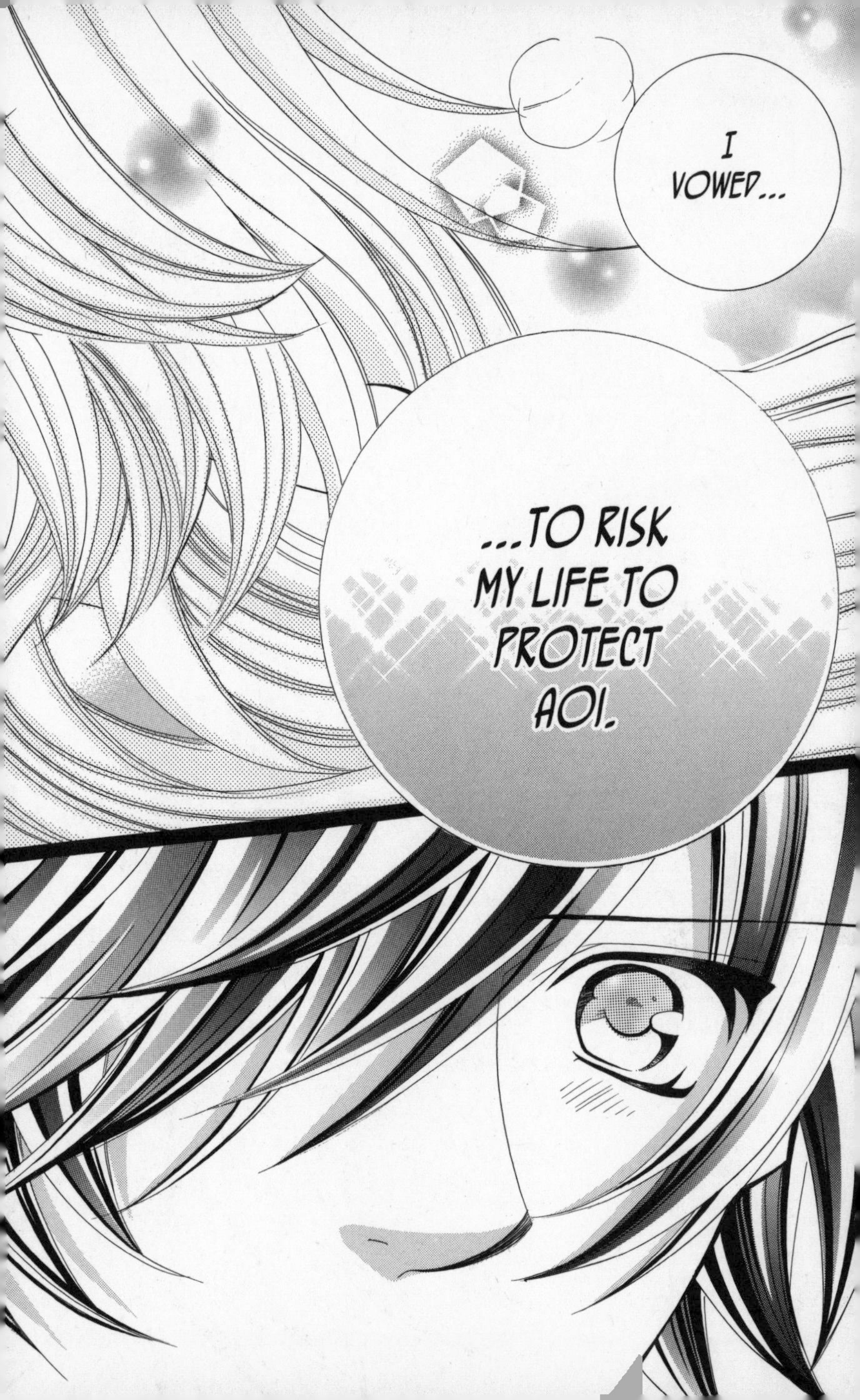
I VOWED...
...TO RISK MY LIFE TO PROTECT AOI.

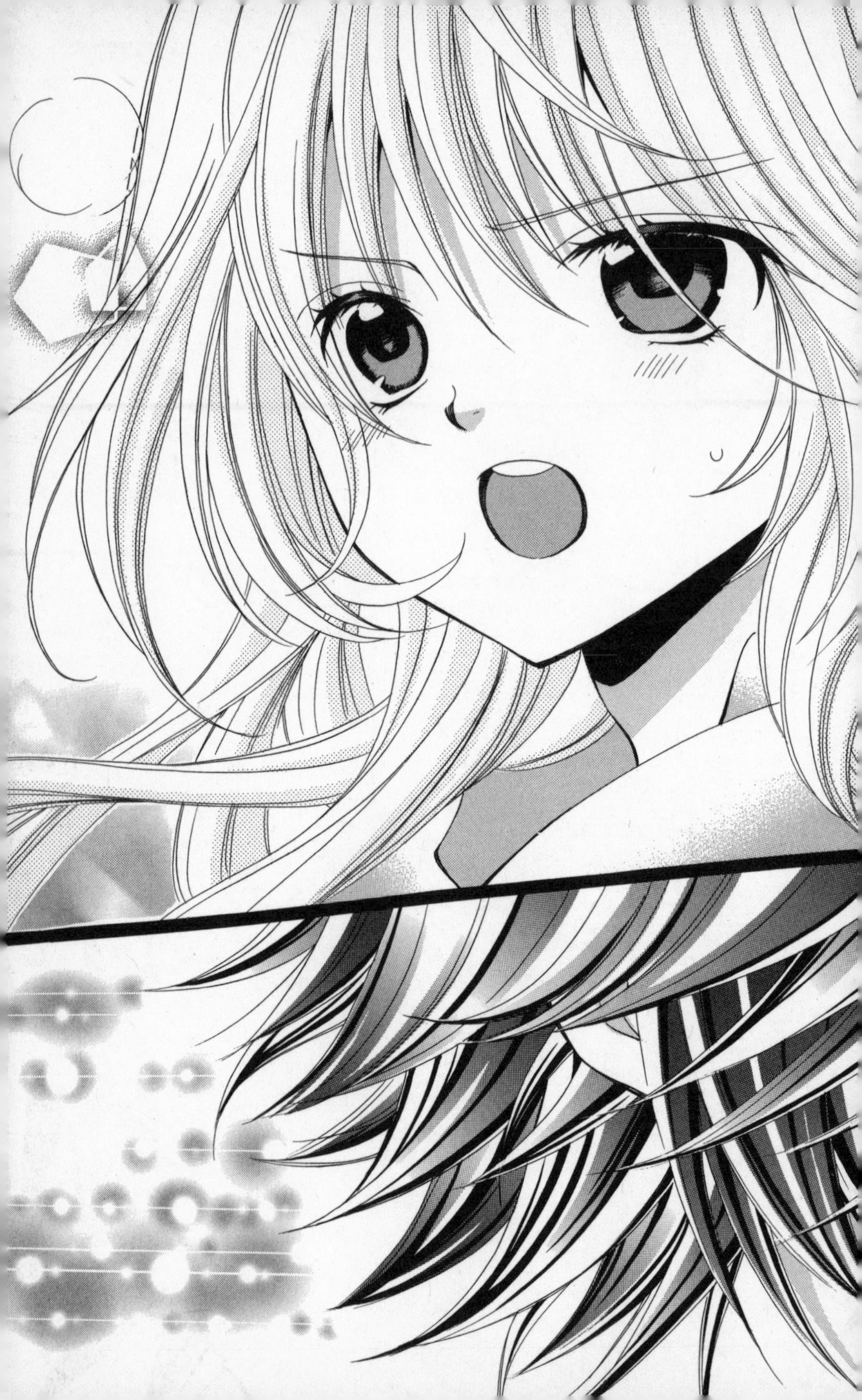

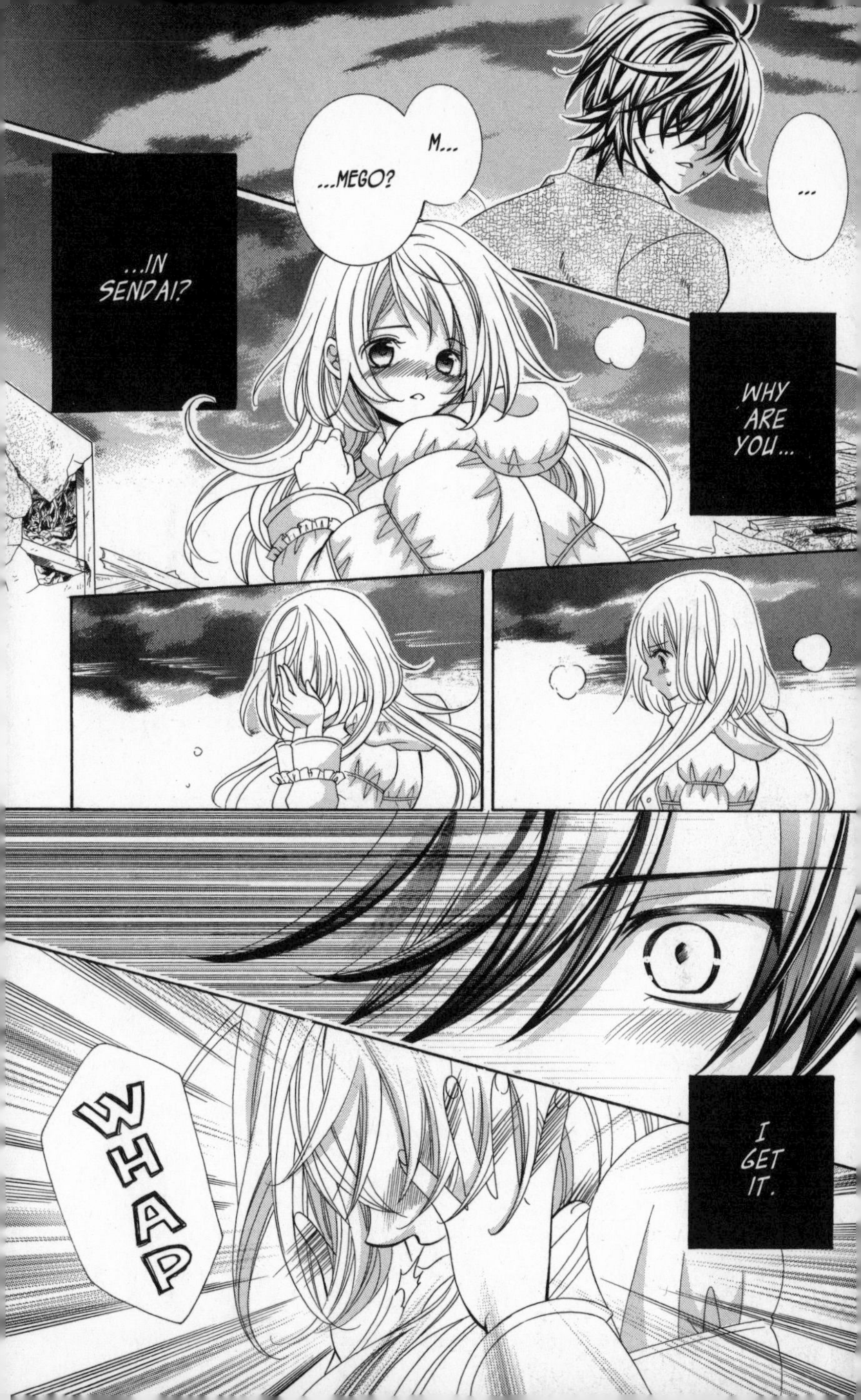
...
M... ...MEGO?
WHY ARE YOU...
...IN SENDAI?
I GET IT.
WHAP

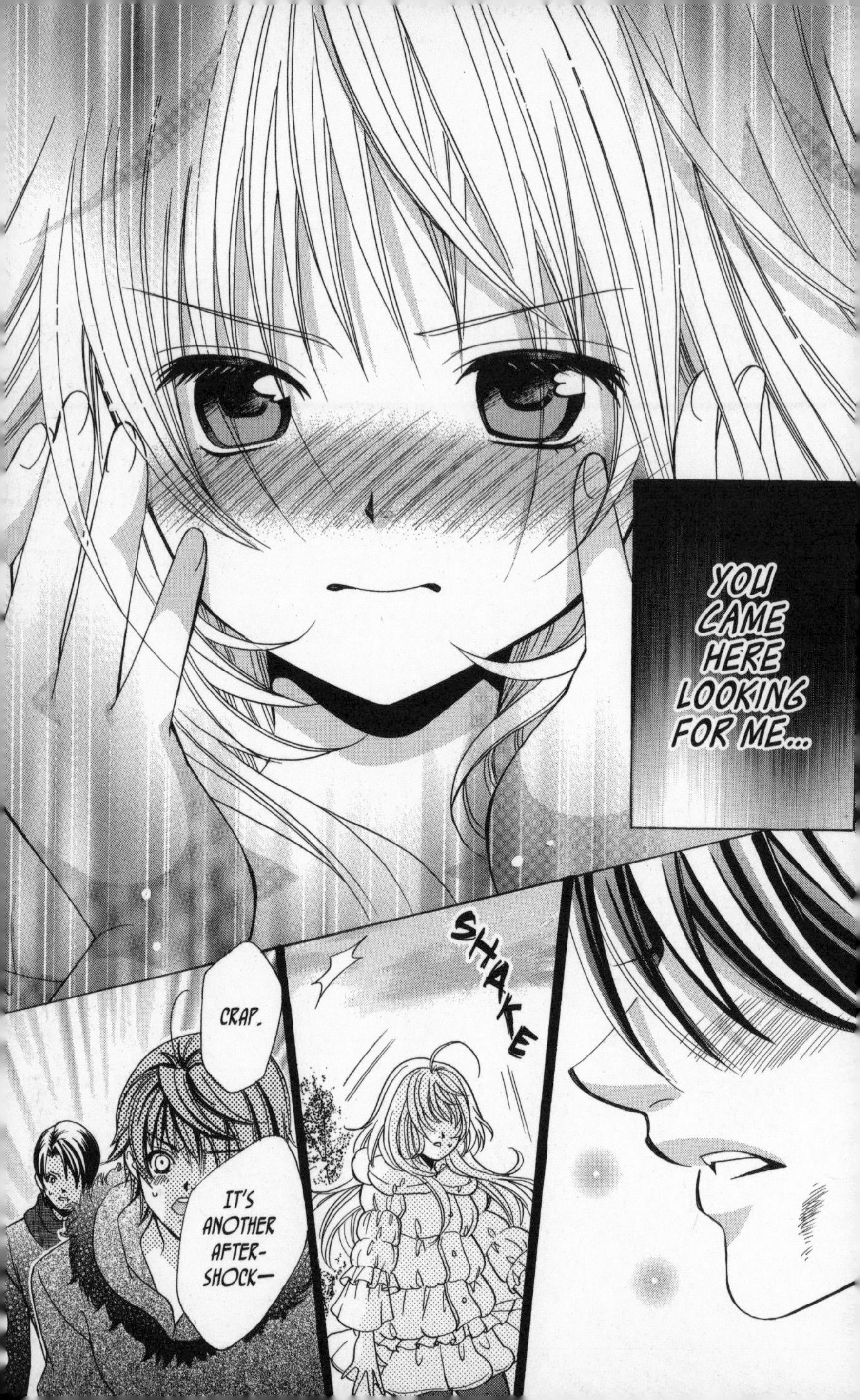
YOU CAME HERE LOOKING FOR ME...
SHAKE
CRAP.
IT'S ANOTHER AFTER-SHOCK—

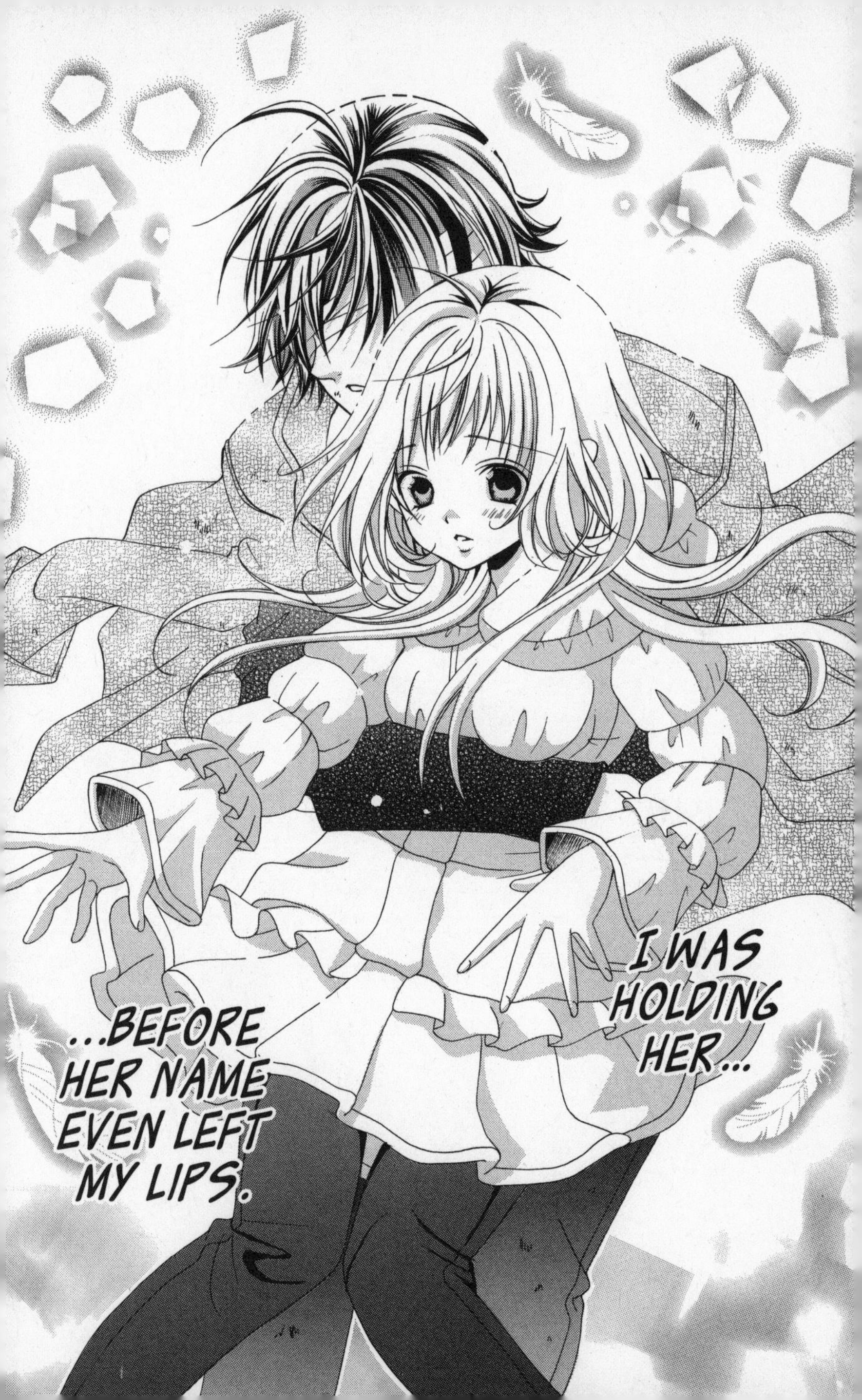
I WAS HOLDING HER...
...BEFORE HER NAME EVEN LEFT MY LIPS.

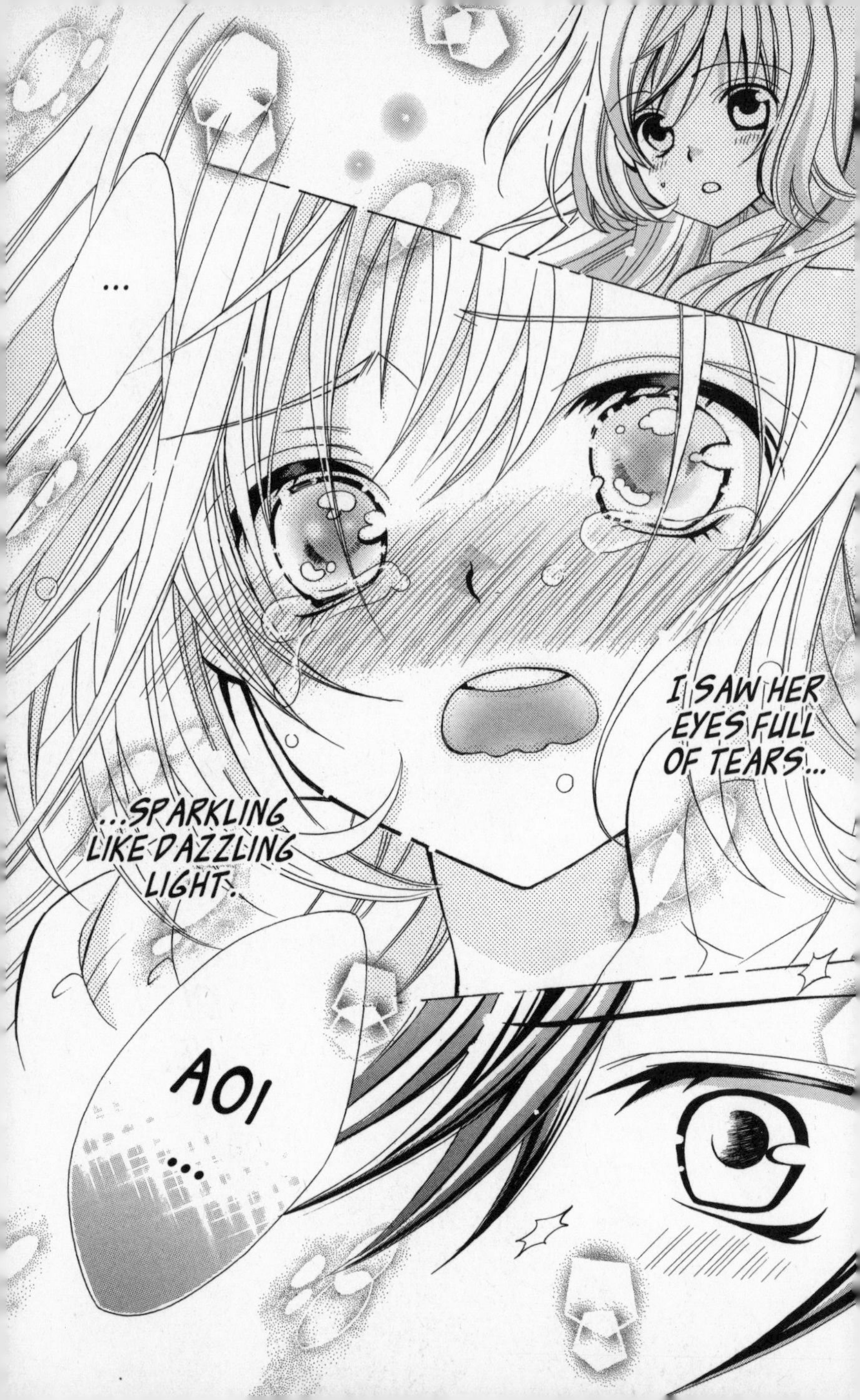
...
I SAW HER EYES FULL OF TEARS...
...SPARKLING LIKE DAZZLING LIGHT.
AOI ...

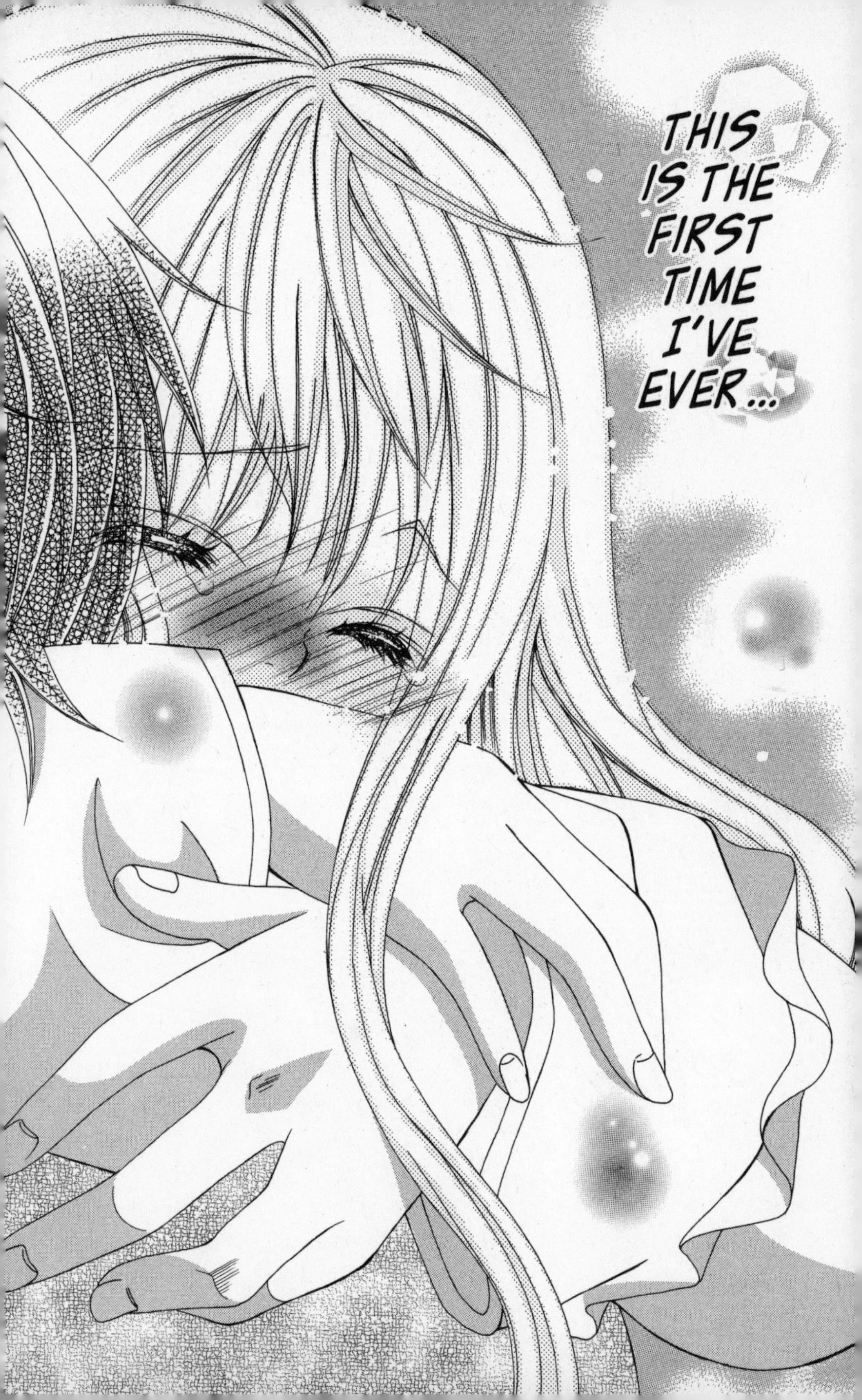
THIS IS THE FIRST TIME I'VE EVER...

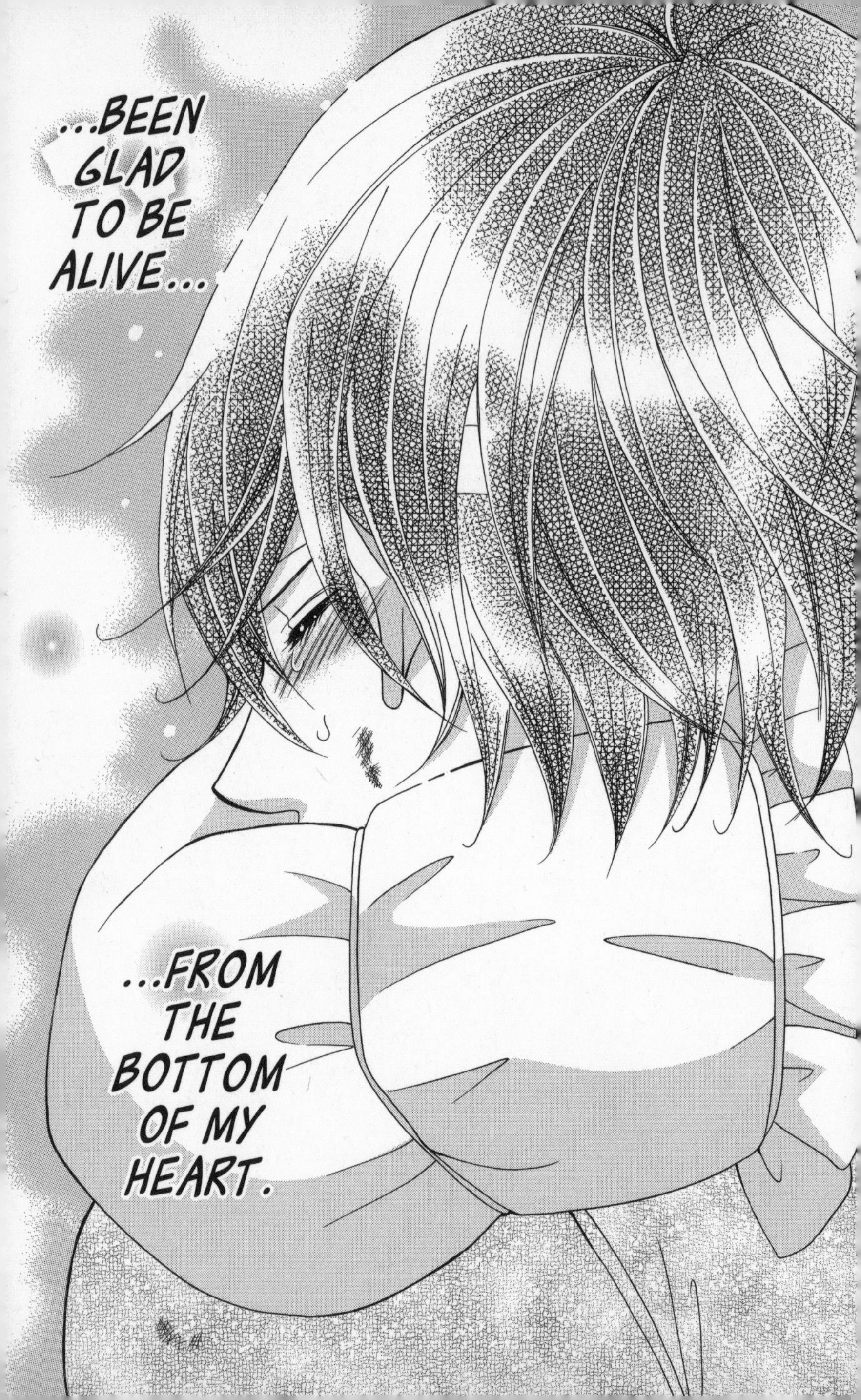
...BEEN GLAD TO BE ALIVE...
...FROM THE BOTTOM OF MY HEART.

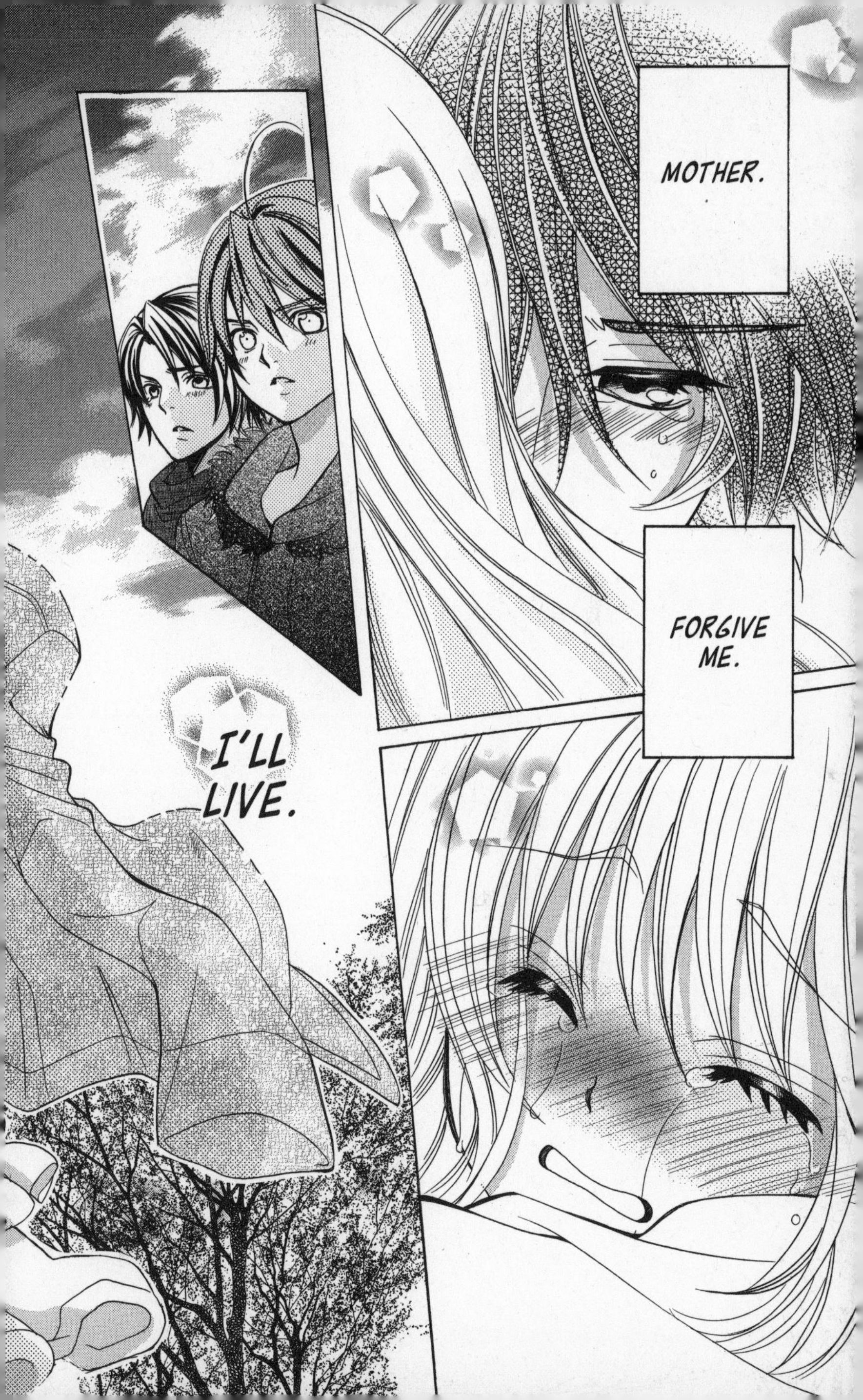
MOTHER.
FORGIVE ME.
I'LL LIVE.

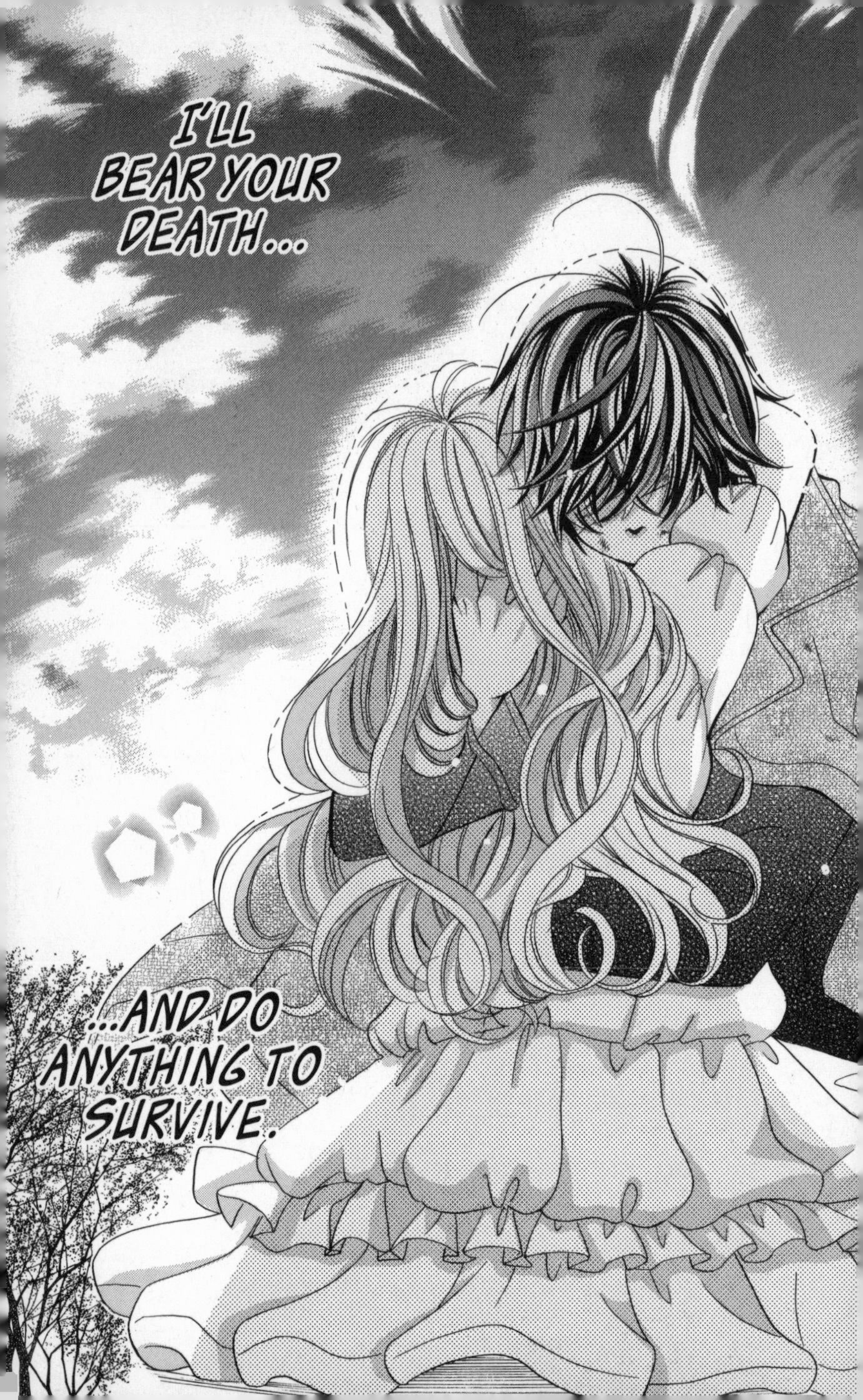
I'LL BEAR YOUR DEATH...
...AND DO ANYTHING TO SURVIVE.

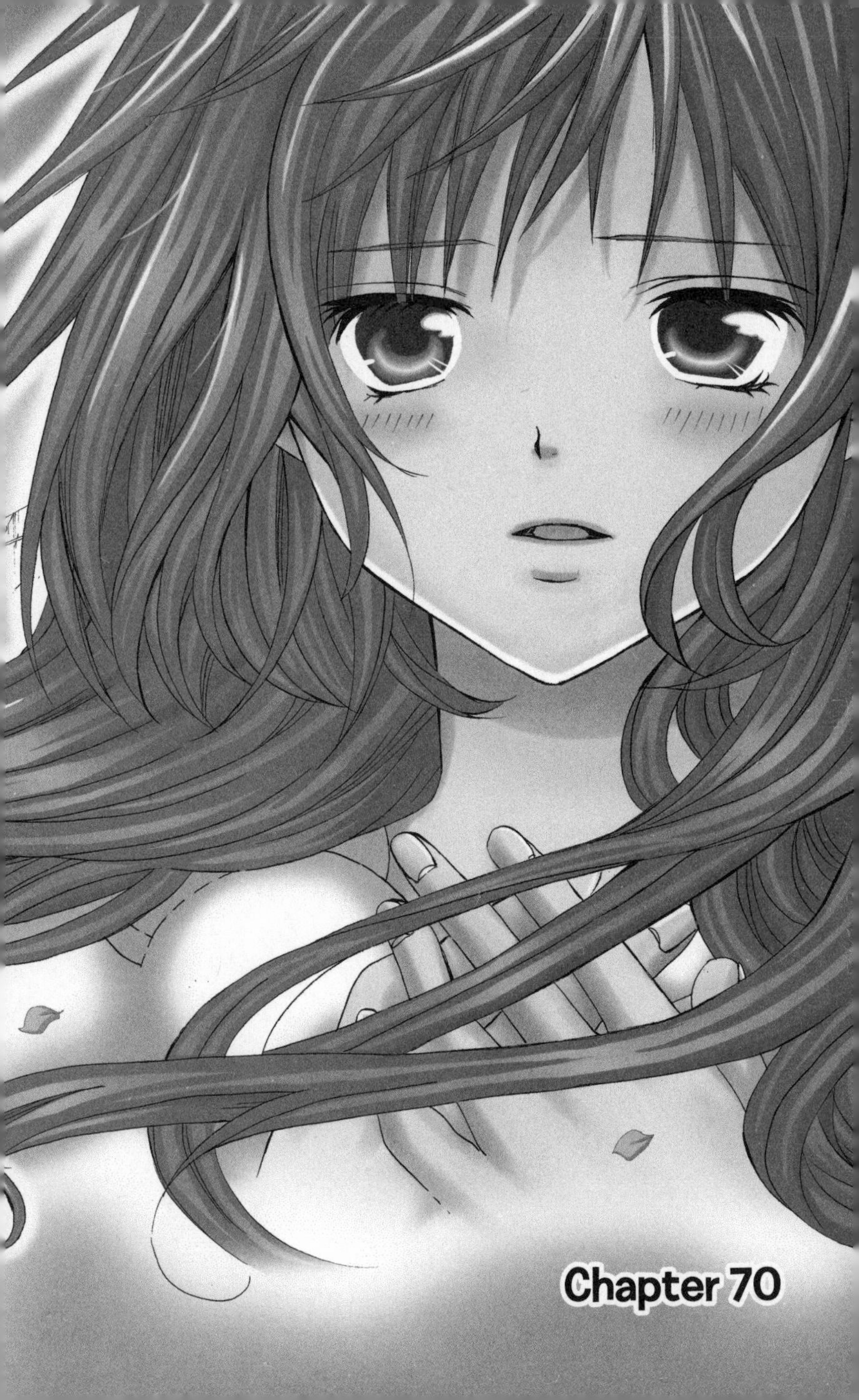
Chapter 70

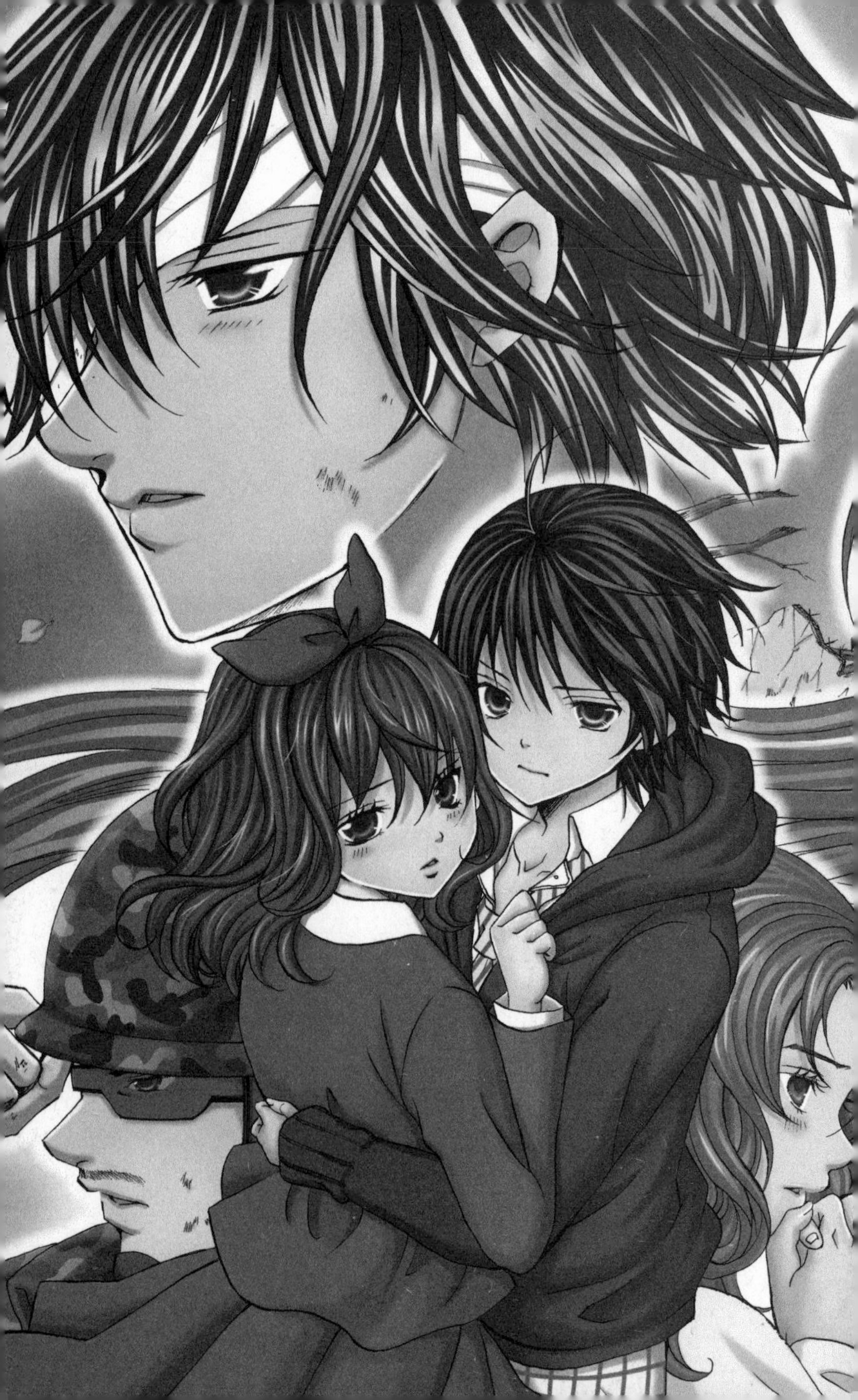

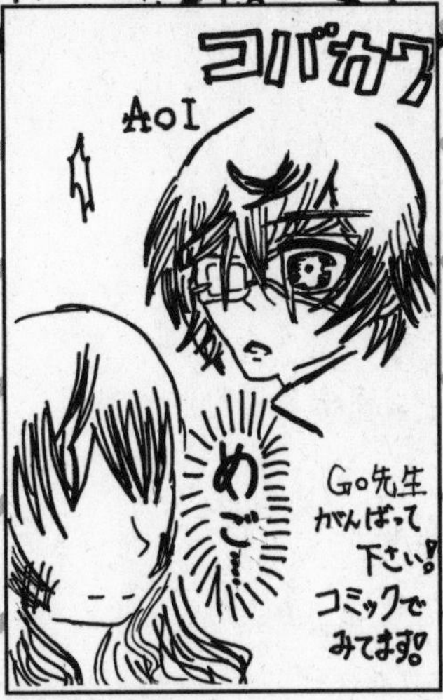
コバカワ
AOI
めご
GO先生
がんばって
下さい!
コミックで
みてます!

MANON (Kanagawa) ↑
Ed.: Witnessing the moment they fell in love!!

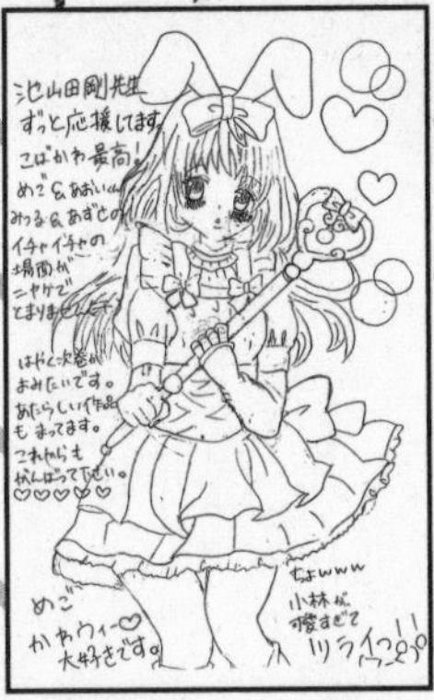
池山田剛先生
ずっと応援してます。
こばかわ最高!
はやく次巻が
よみたいです。
あたらしい作品
もまってます。
これからも
がんばって下さい。
めご
かわウィー♡
大好きです。
小林が
可愛すぎて
ツライっ

Lunaluna (Nagano) ←
Ed.: Rabbit ears are justice!!

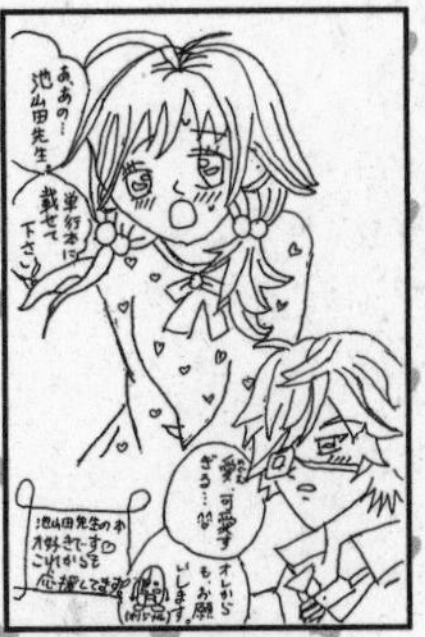
あ あの…
池山田先生
単行本に
載せて
下さい

Ena Kitagawa (Gifu) ↑
Ed.: I asked too.

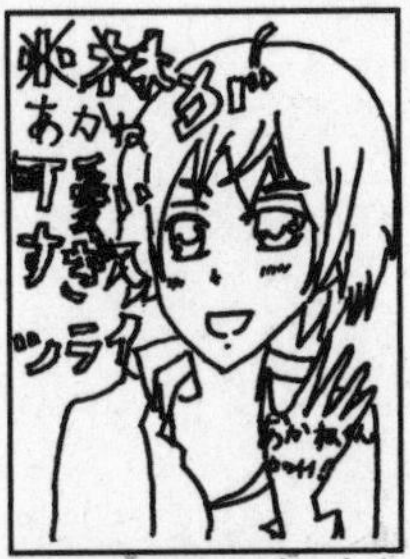
あかね
ツライ

Momoka Yoshida (Mie) ↑
Ed.: Akane's first appearance!!

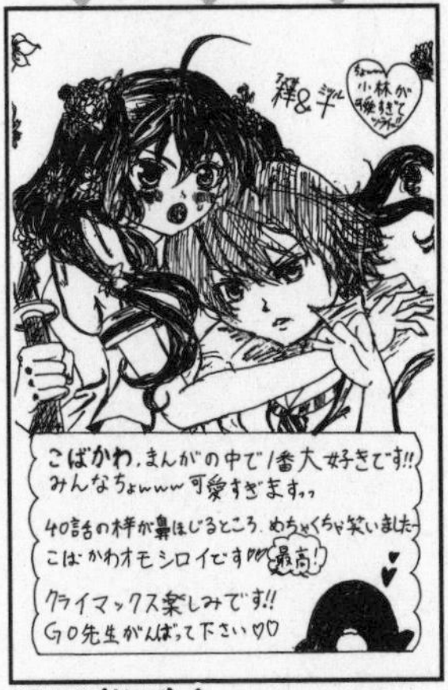
こばかわ、まんがの中で1番大好きです!!
みんなちょwww 可愛すぎますっ
40話の梓が鼻ほじるところ、めちゃくちゃ笑いました～
こばかわオモシロイです 最高!
クライマックス楽しみです!!
GO先生がんばって下さい♡

Mikitii (Aichi) ↑
Ed.: They both look gallant!!

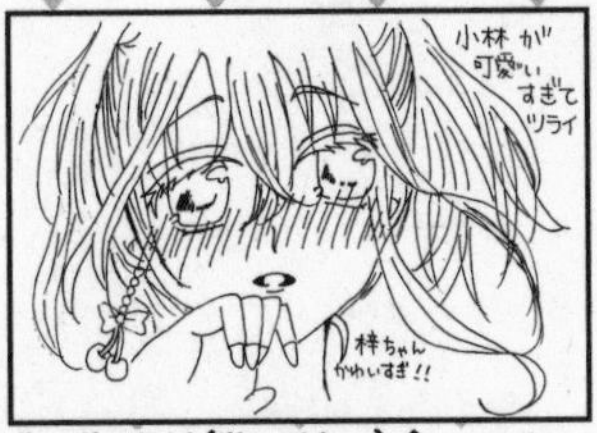
小林が
可愛い
すぎて
ツライ
梓ちゃん
かわいすぎ!!

Noa Konishi (Hiroshima) ↑
Ed.: A sweet Azusa is delicious. ♥

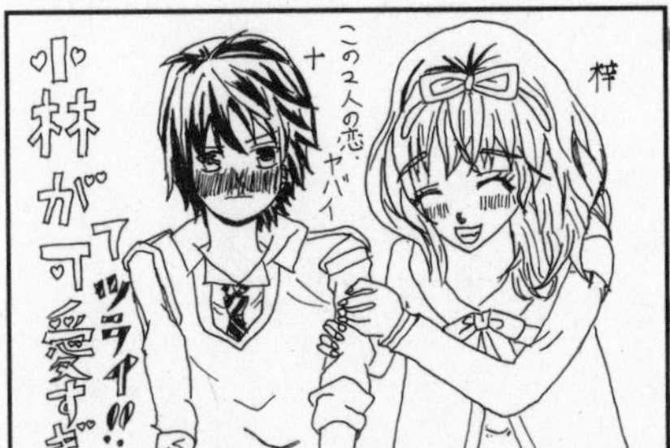
小林が可愛すぎてツライ!!
この2人の恋ヤバイ
梓

Yumi Aoki (Saitama) ↑
Ed.: You can't help but root for them. ♥

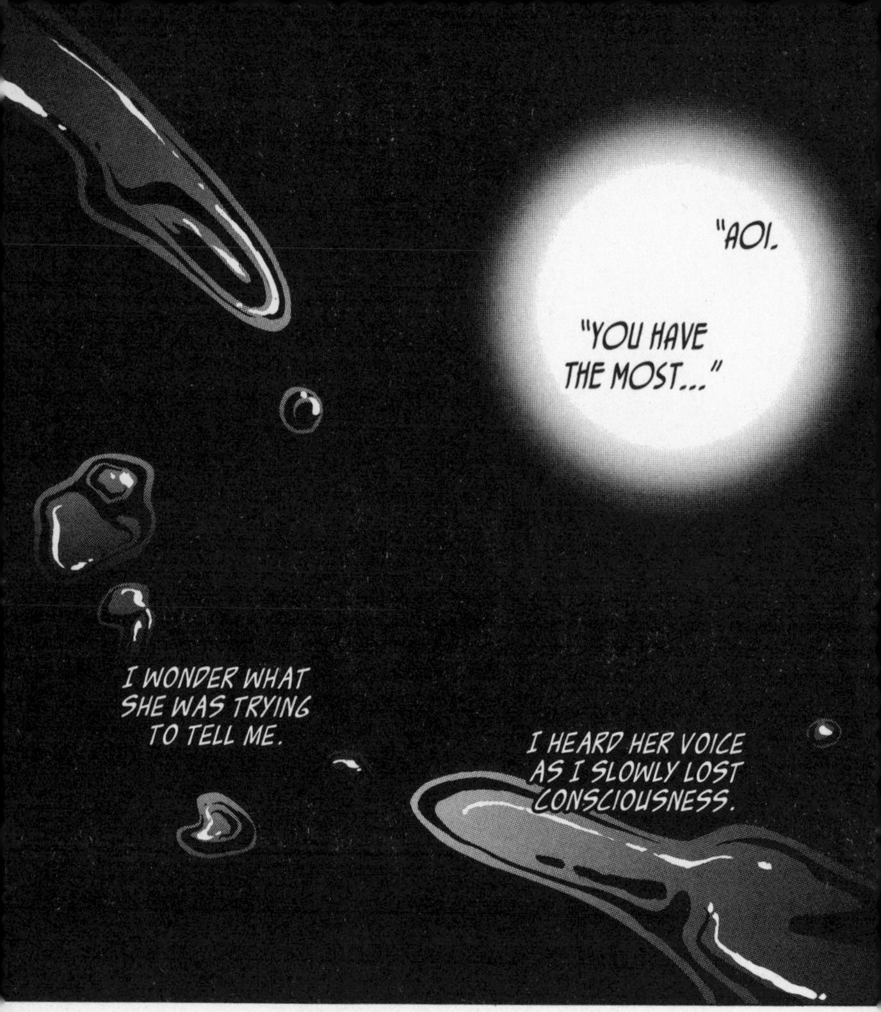
"AOI.
"YOU HAVE THE MOST..."
I HEARD HER VOICE AS I SLOWLY LOST CONSCIOUSNESS.
I WONDER WHAT SHE WAS TRYING TO TELL ME.

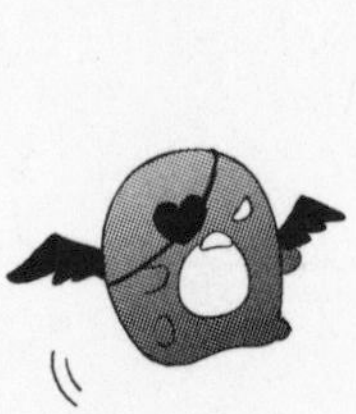

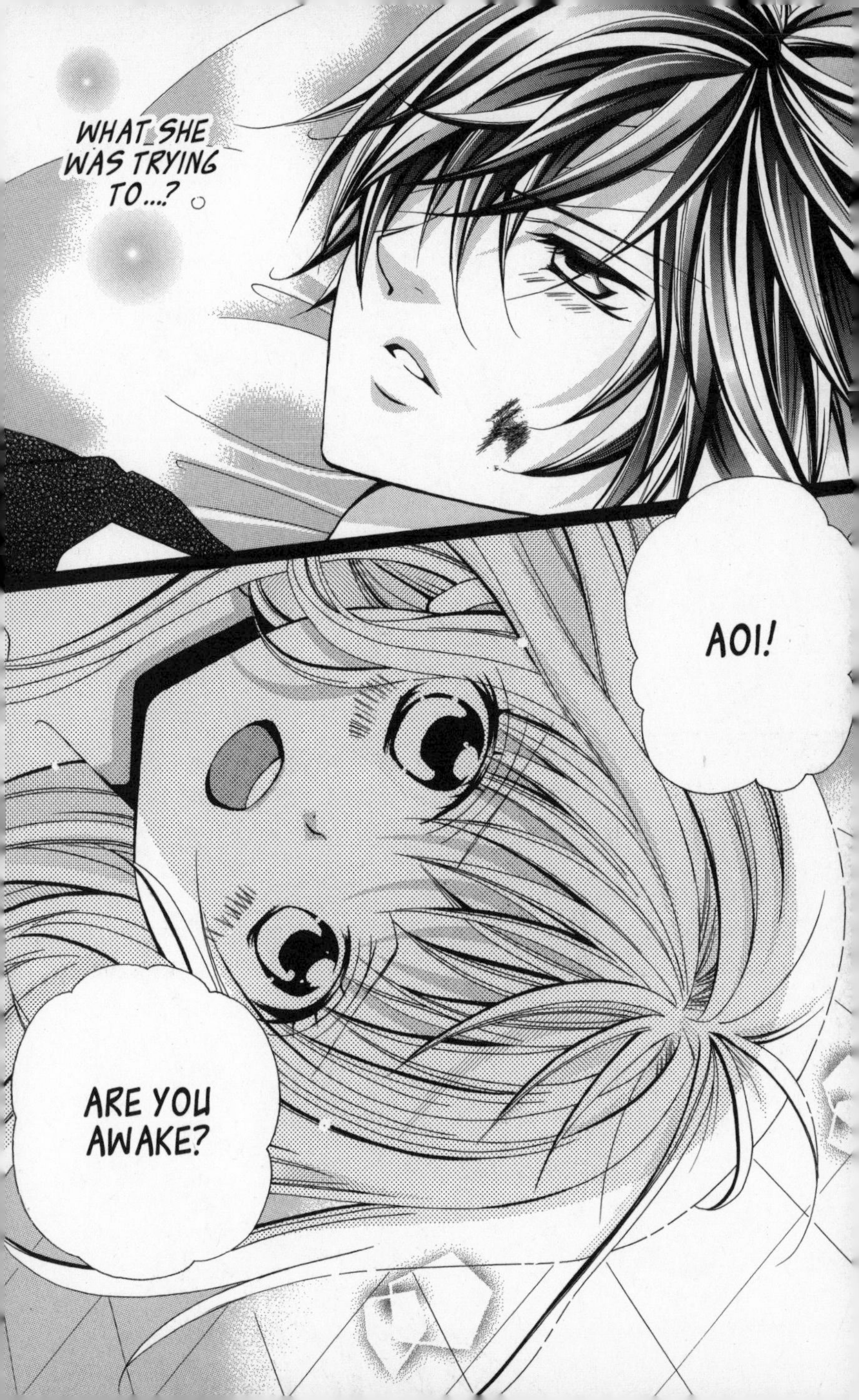
WHAT SHE WAS TRYING TO...?
AOI!
ARE YOU AWAKE?

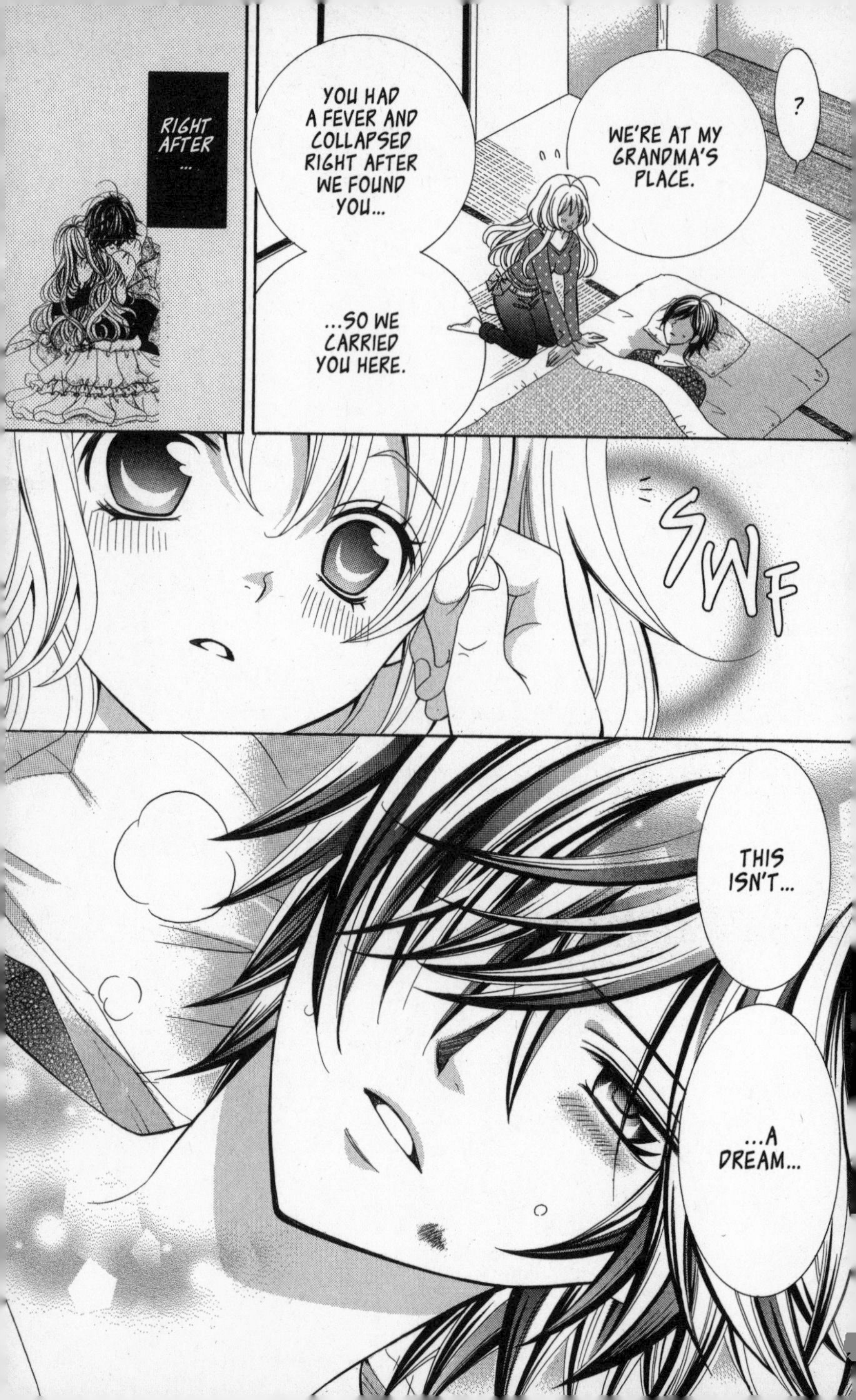
?
WE'RE AT MY GRANDMA'S PLACE.
YOU HAD A FEVER AND COLLAPSED RIGHT AFTER WE FOUND YOU...
...SO WE CARRIED YOU HERE.
RIGHT AFTER...
SWF
THIS ISN'T...
...A DREAM...

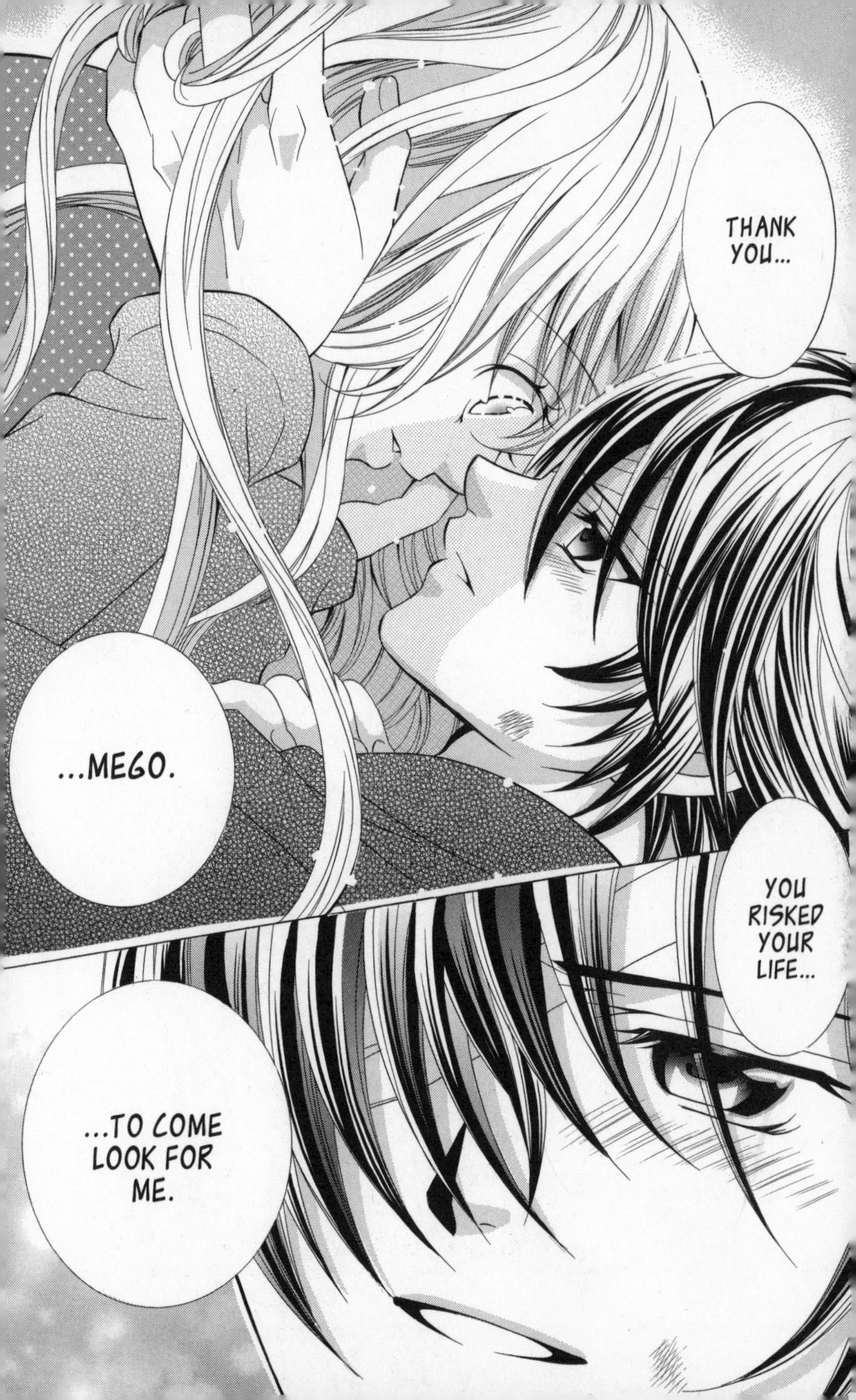
THANK YOU...
...MEGO.
YOU RISKED YOUR LIFE...
...TO COME LOOK FOR ME.

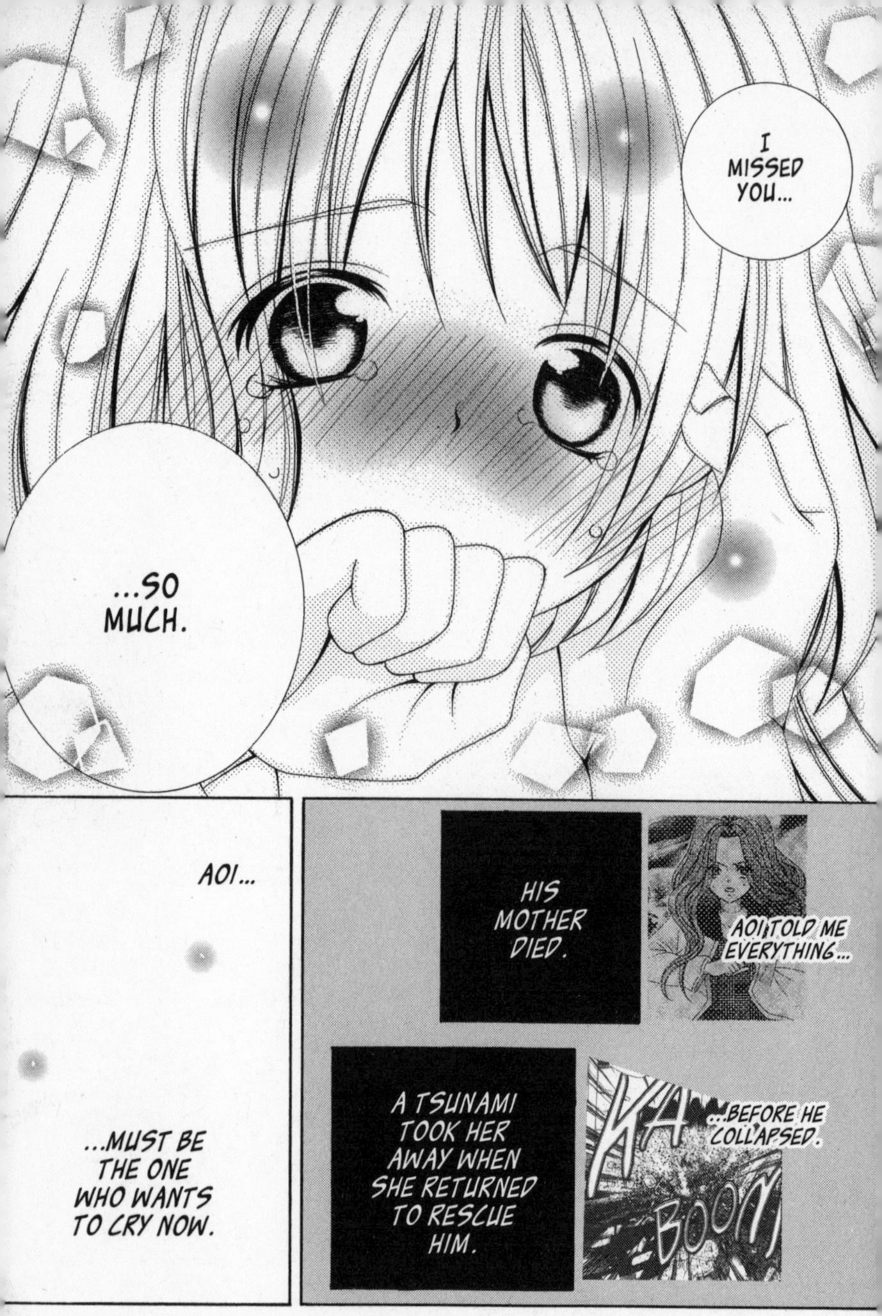
I MISSED YOU...
...SO MUCH.
AOI TOLD ME EVERYTHING...
HIS MOTHER DIED.
...BEFORE HE COLLAPSED.
KA
BOOM
A TSUNAMI TOOK HER AWAY WHEN SHE RETURNED TO RESCUE HIM.
AOI...
...MUST BE THE ONE WHO WANTS TO CRY NOW.

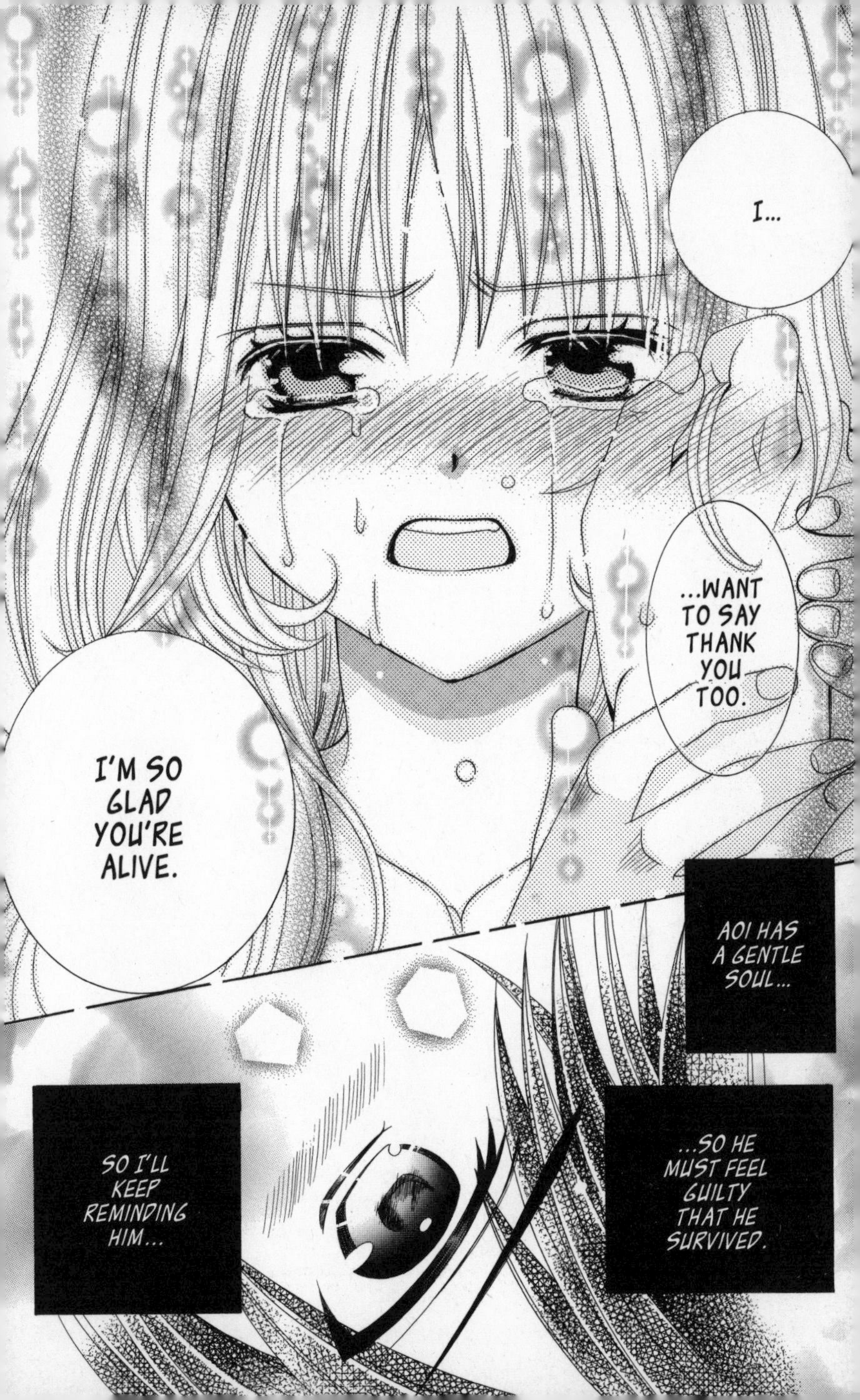
I...
...WANT TO SAY THANK YOU TOO.
I'M SO GLAD YOU'RE ALIVE.
AOI HAS A GENTLE SOUL...
...SO HE MUST FEEL GUILTY THAT HE SURVIVED.
SO I'LL KEEP REMINDING HIM...

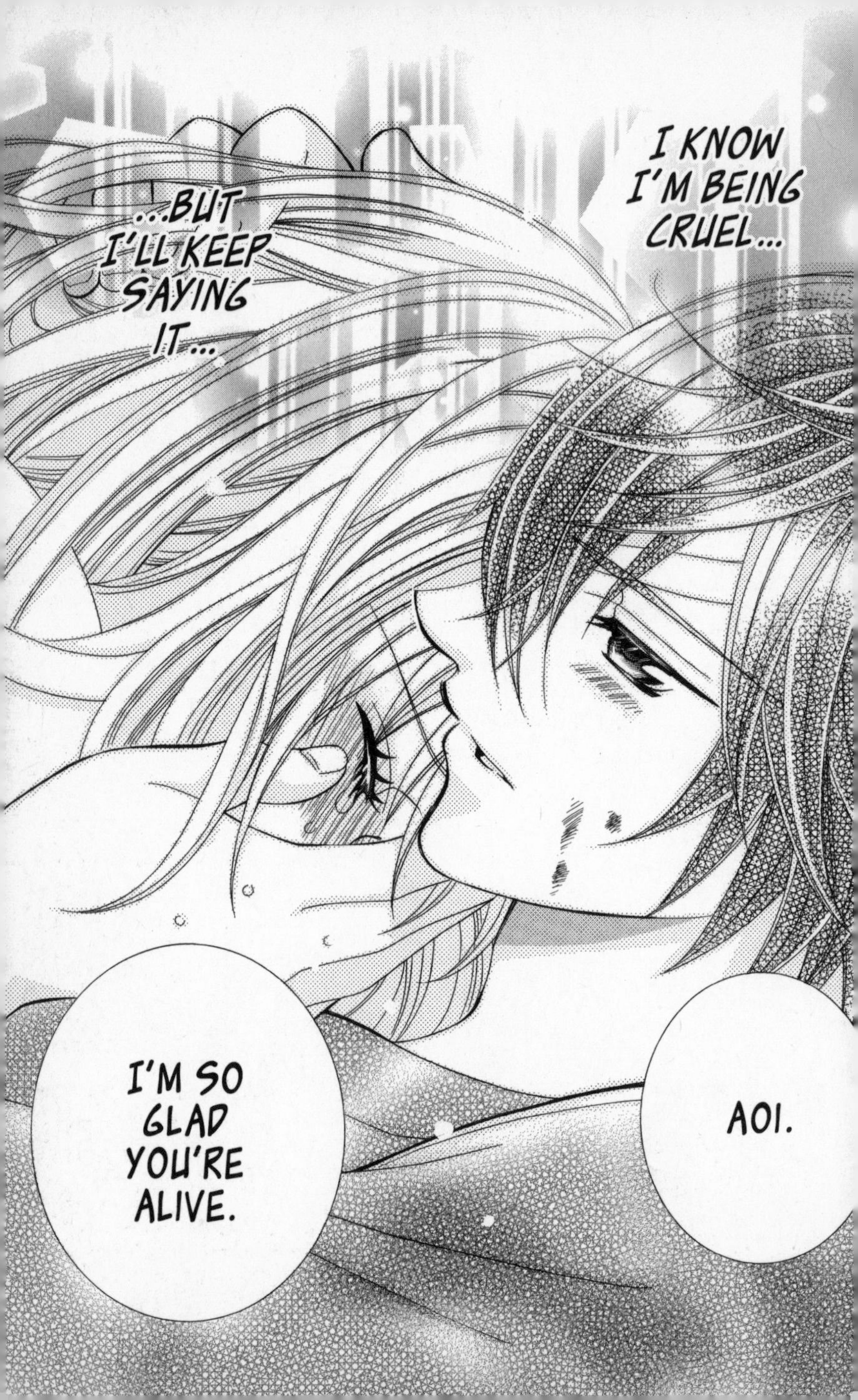
I KNOW I'M BEING CRUEL...
...BUT I'LL KEEP SAYING IT...
AOI.
I'M SO GLAD YOU'RE ALIVE.

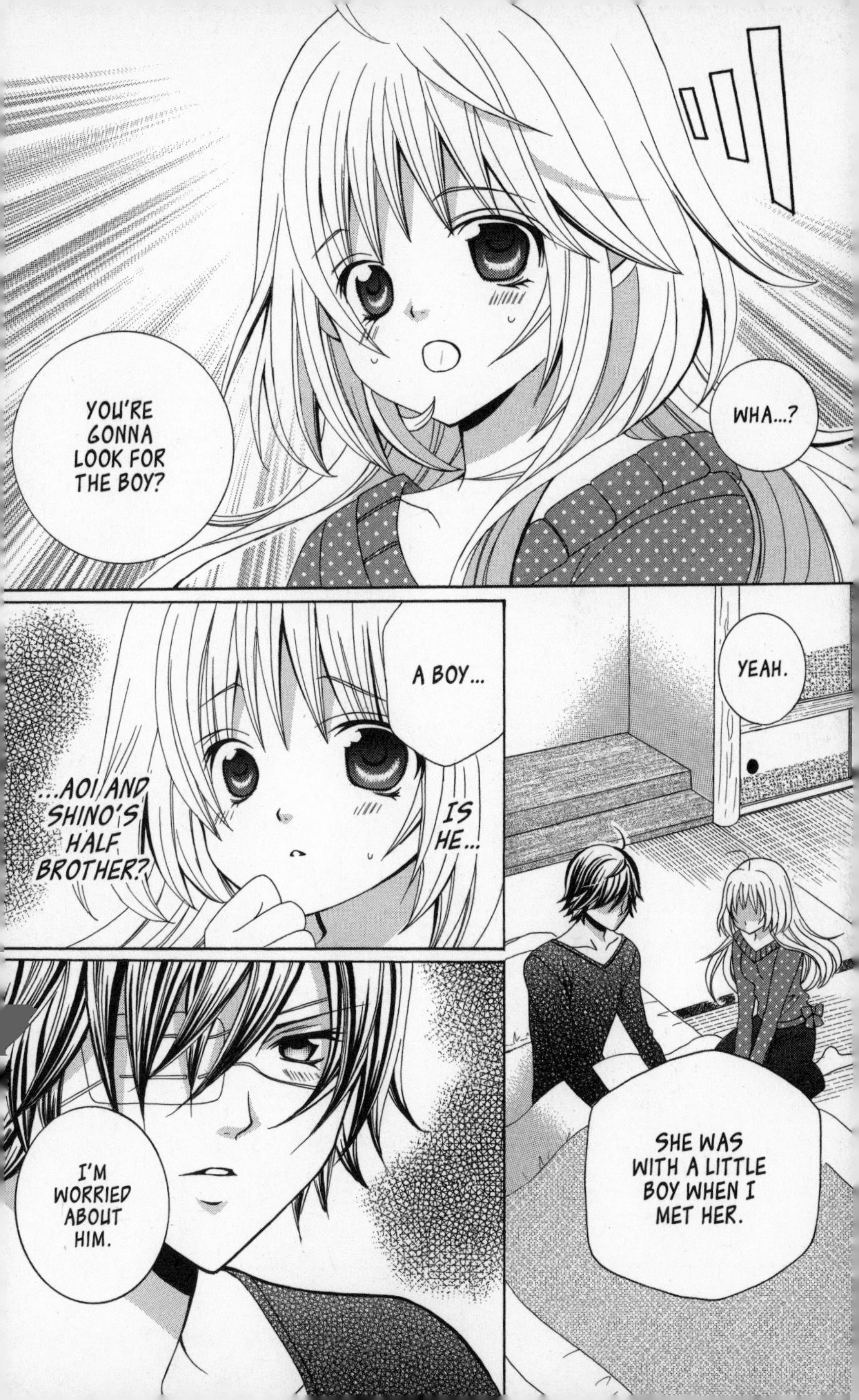
WHA...?
YOU'RE GONNA LOOK FOR THE BOY?
YEAH.
SHE WAS WITH A LITTLE BOY WHEN I MET HER.
A BOY...
IS HE...
...AOI AND SHINO'S HALF BROTHER?
I'M WORRIED ABOUT HIM.

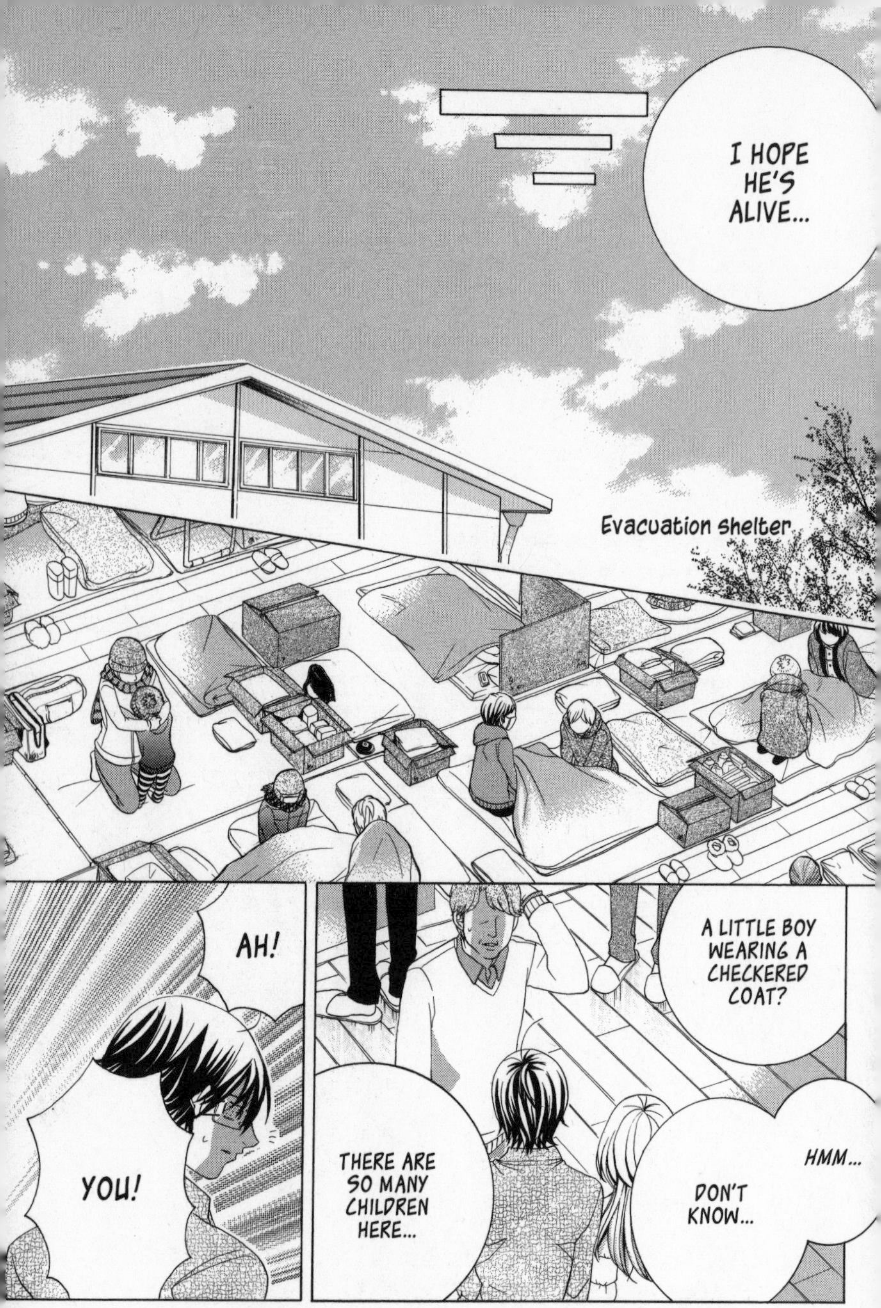
I HOPE HE'S ALIVE...
Evacuation shelter
A LITTLE BOY WEARING A CHECKERED COAT?
HMM... DON'T KNOW...
THERE ARE SO MANY CHILDREN HERE...
AH!
YOU!

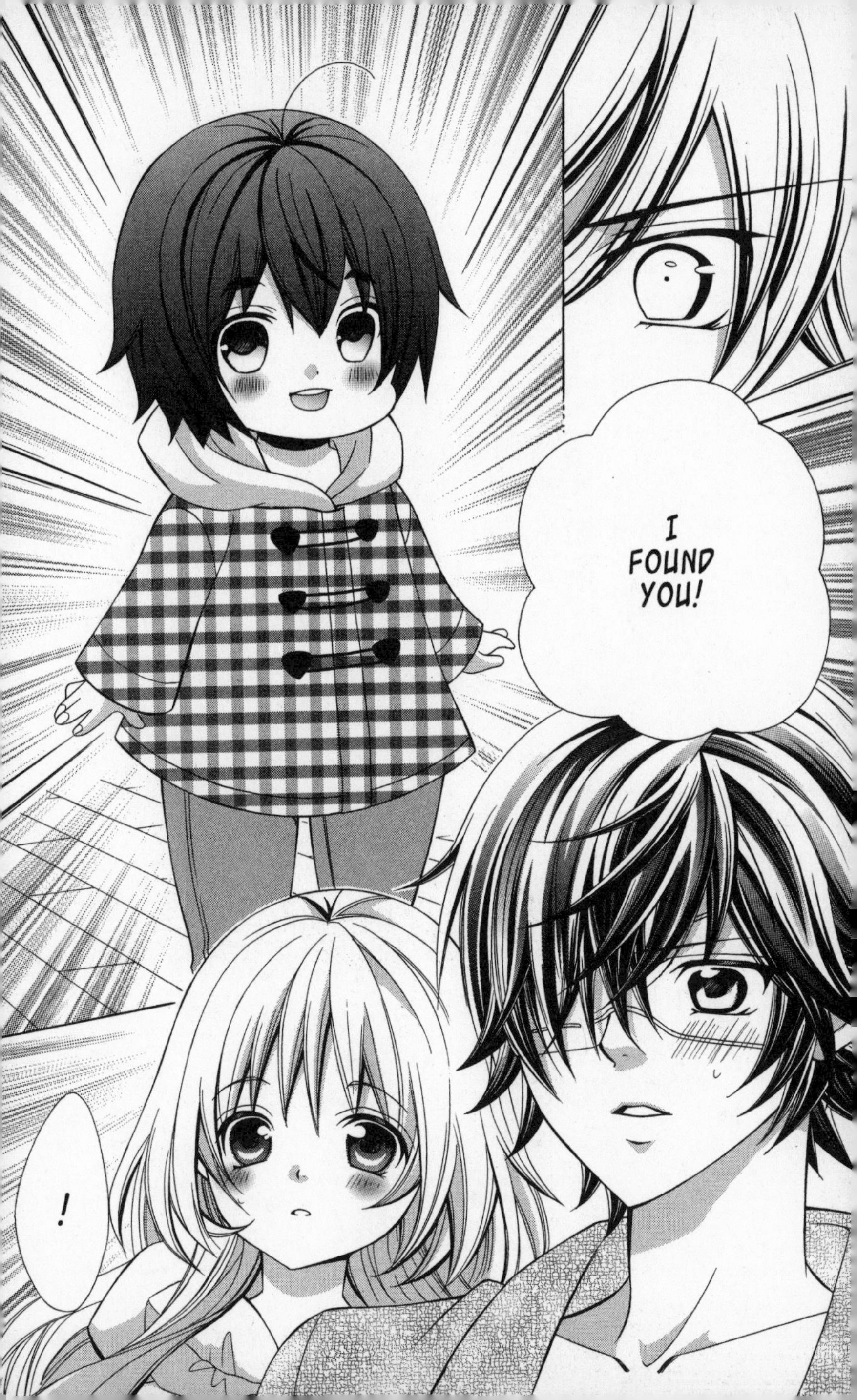
I FOUND YOU!
!

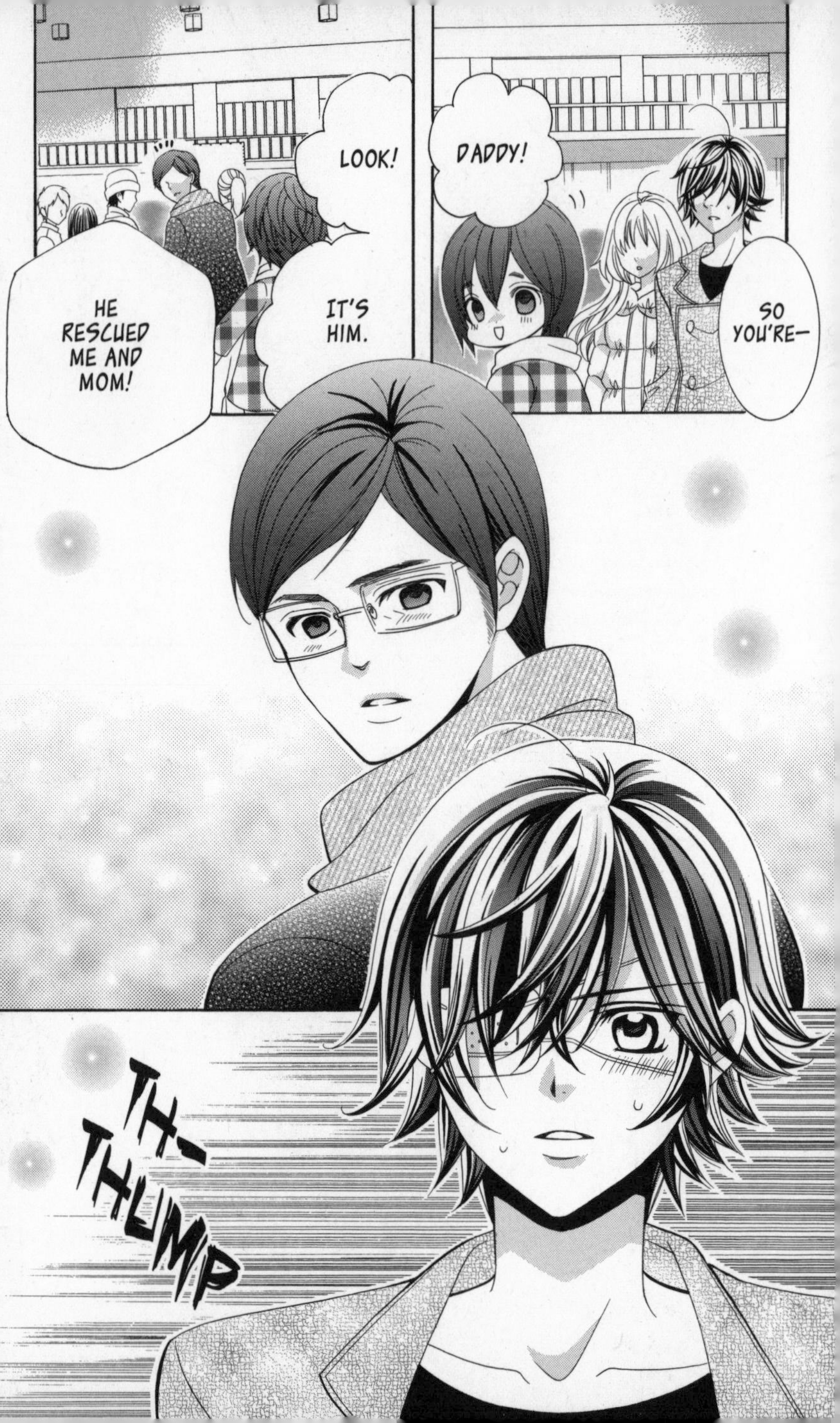
DADDY!
SO YOU'RE—
LOOK!
IT'S HIM.
HE RESCUED ME AND MOM!
TH-THUMP

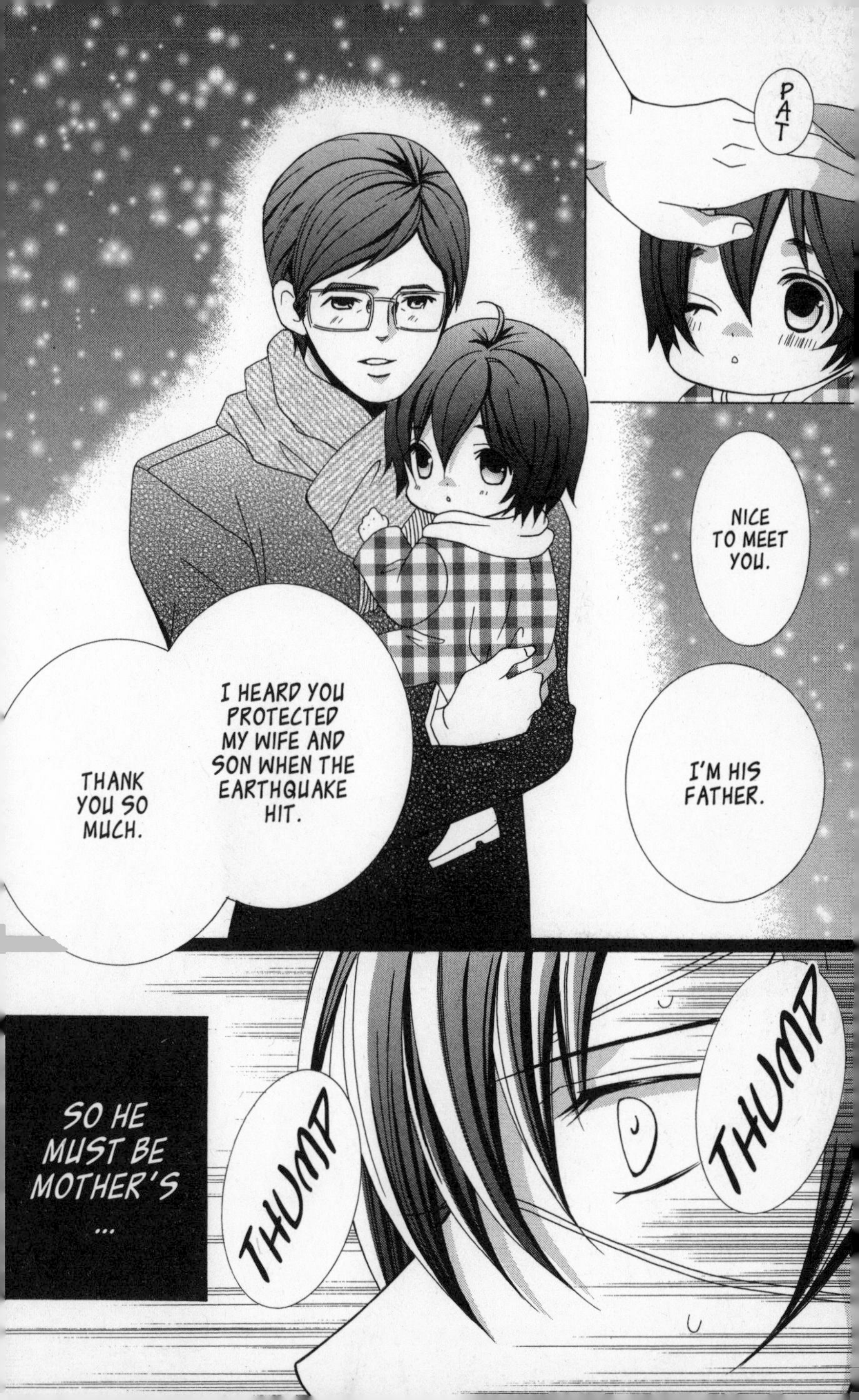
PAT
NICE TO MEET YOU.
I'M HIS FATHER.
I HEARD YOU PROTECTED MY WIFE AND SON WHEN THE EARTHQUAKE HIT.
THANK YOU SO MUCH.
THUMP
SO HE MUST BE MOTHER'S ...
THUMP

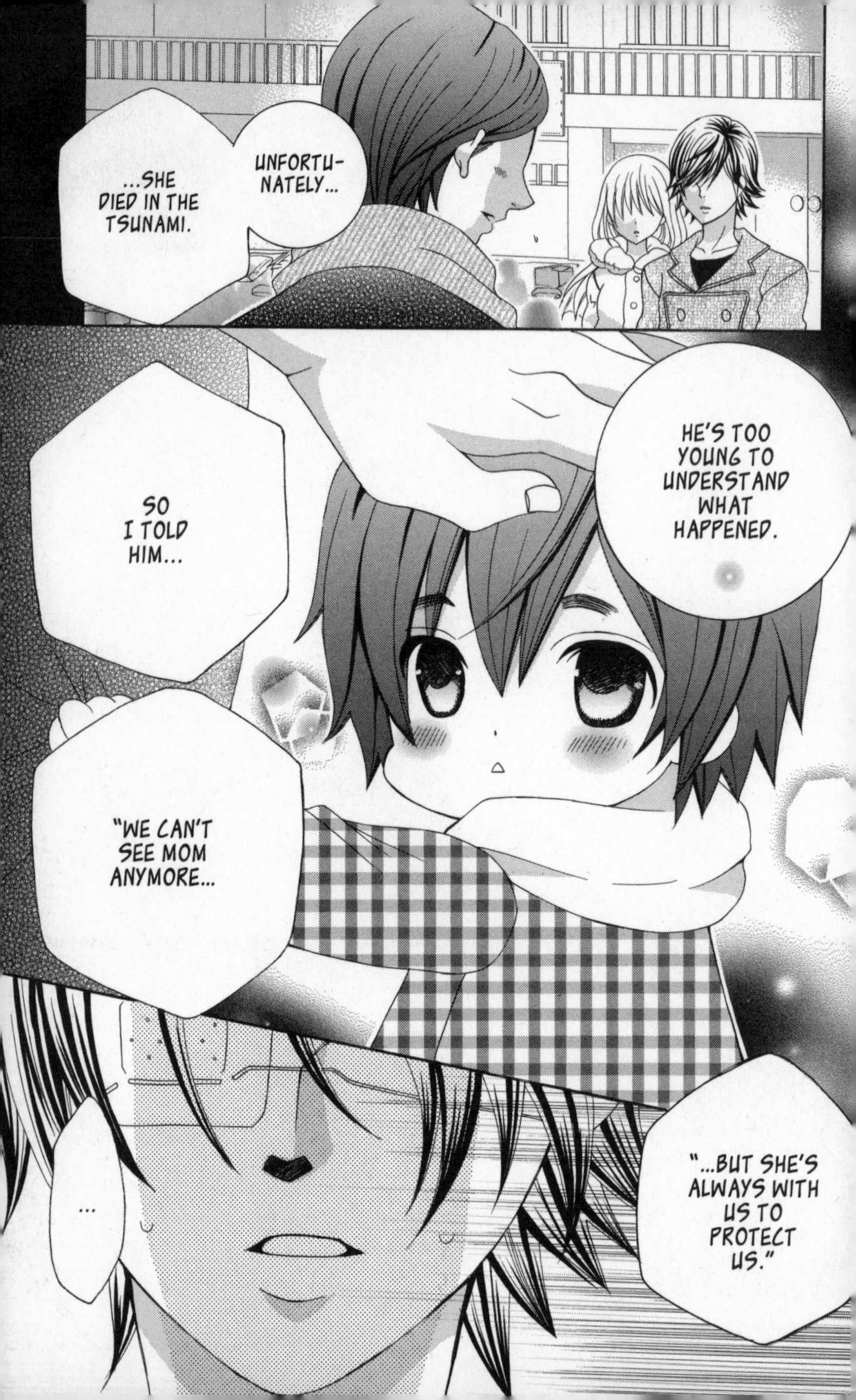
UNFORTU-NATELY...
...SHE DIED IN THE TSUNAMI.
HE'S TOO YOUNG TO UNDERSTAND WHAT HAPPENED.
SO I TOLD HIM...
"WE CAN'T SEE MOM ANYMORE...
"...BUT SHE'S ALWAYS WITH US TO PROTECT US."
...

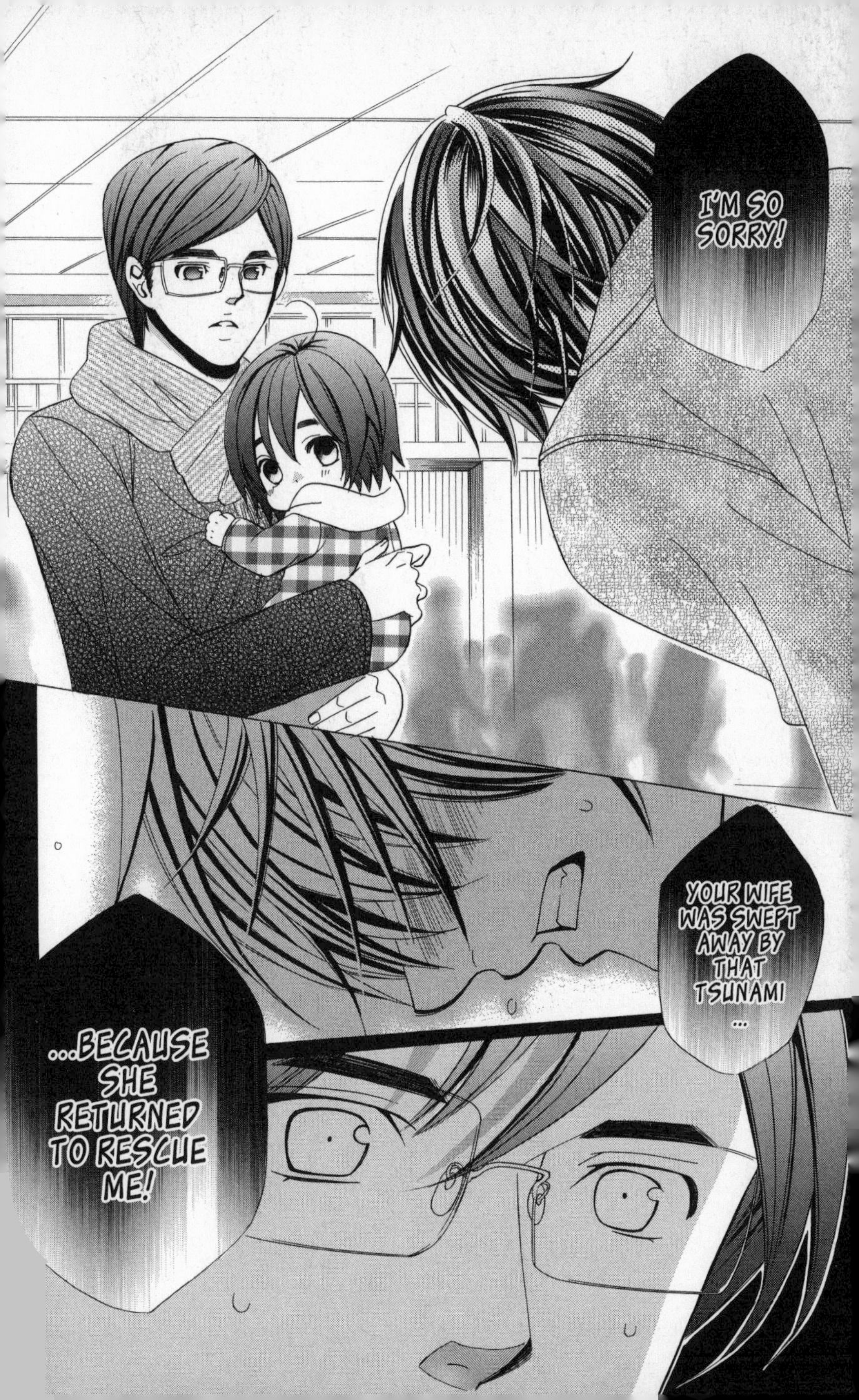
I'M SO SORRY!
YOUR WIFE WAS SWEPT AWAY BY THAT TSUNAMI ...
...BECAUSE SHE RETURNED TO RESCUE ME!

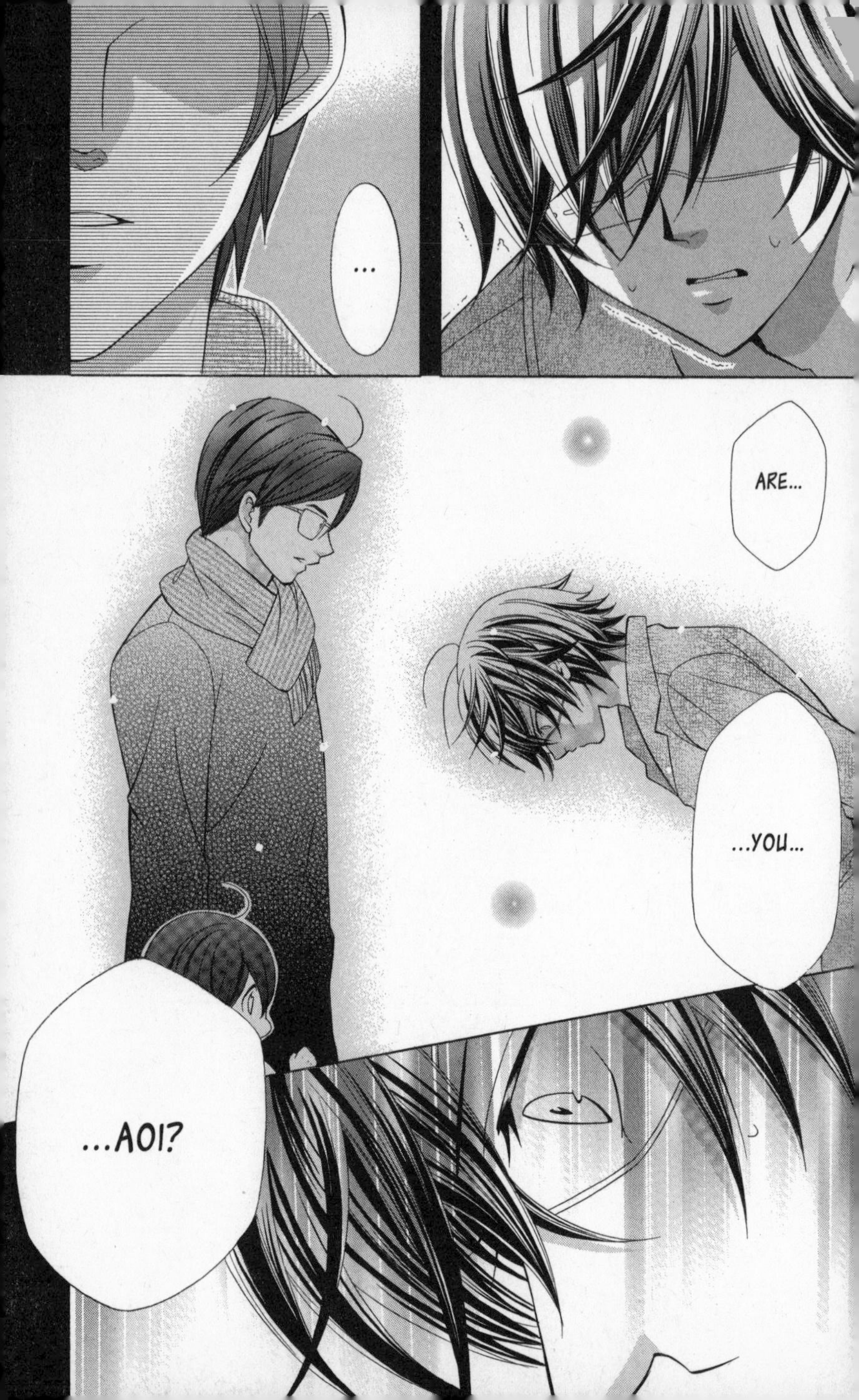
...
ARE...
...YOU...
...AOI?

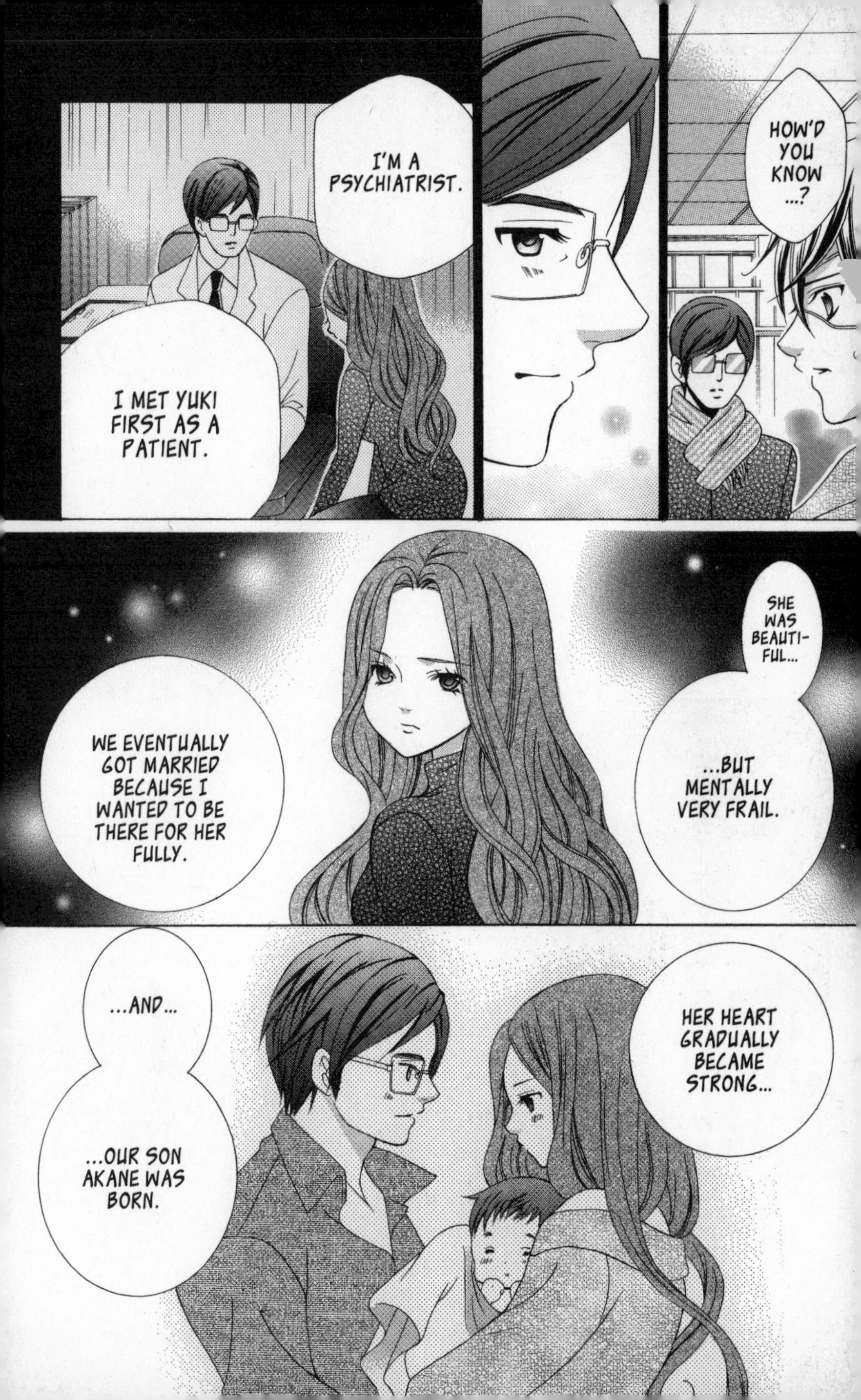
HOW'D YOU KNOW ...?
I'M A PSYCHIATRIST.
I MET YUKI FIRST AS A PATIENT.
SHE WAS BEAUTI-FUL...
...BUT MENTALLY VERY FRAIL.
WE EVENTUALLY GOT MARRIED BECAUSE I WANTED TO BE THERE FOR HER FULLY.
HER HEART GRADUALLY BECAME STRONG...
...AND...
...OUR SON AKANE WAS BORN.

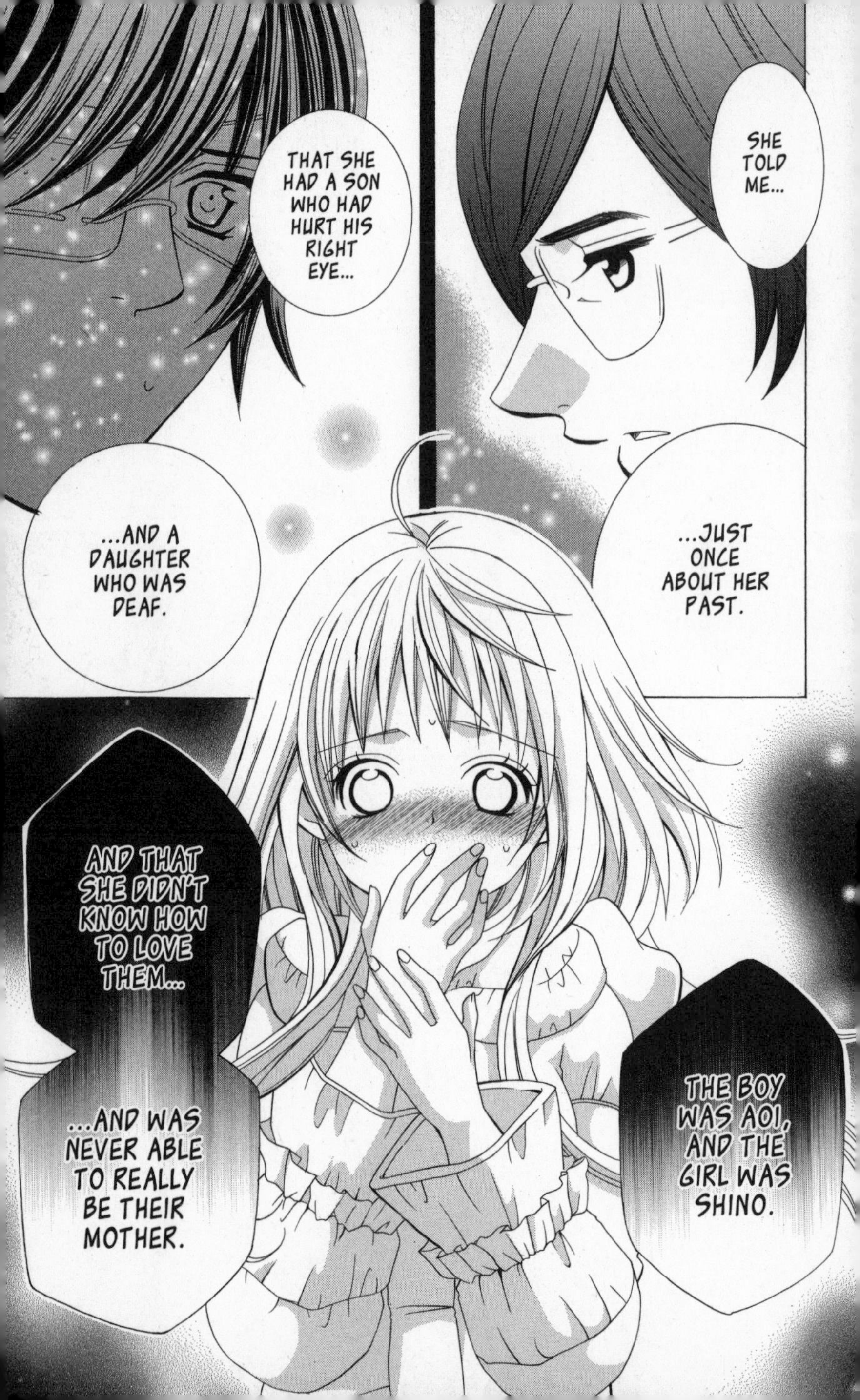
SHE TOLD ME...
...JUST ONCE ABOUT HER PAST.
THAT SHE HAD A SON WHO HAD HURT HIS RIGHT EYE...
...AND A DAUGHTER WHO WAS DEAF.
AND THAT SHE DIDN'T KNOW HOW TO LOVE THEM...
...AND WAS NEVER ABLE TO REALLY BE THEIR MOTHER.
THE BOY WAS AOI, AND THE GIRL WAS SHINO.

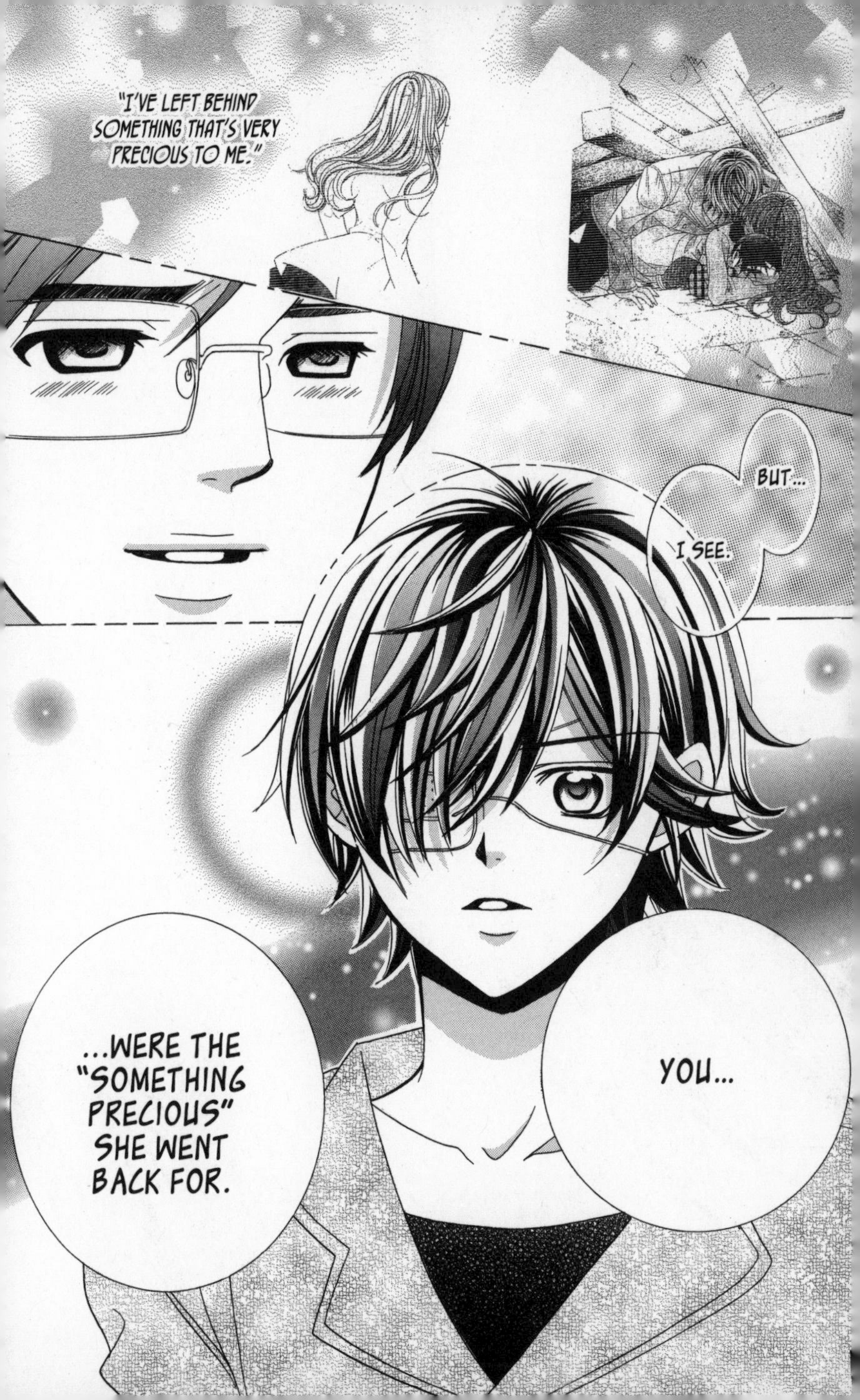
"I'VE LEFT BEHIND SOMETHING THAT'S VERY PRECIOUS TO ME."
I SEE.
BUT...
YOU...
...WERE THE "SOMETHING PRECIOUS" SHE WENT BACK FOR.

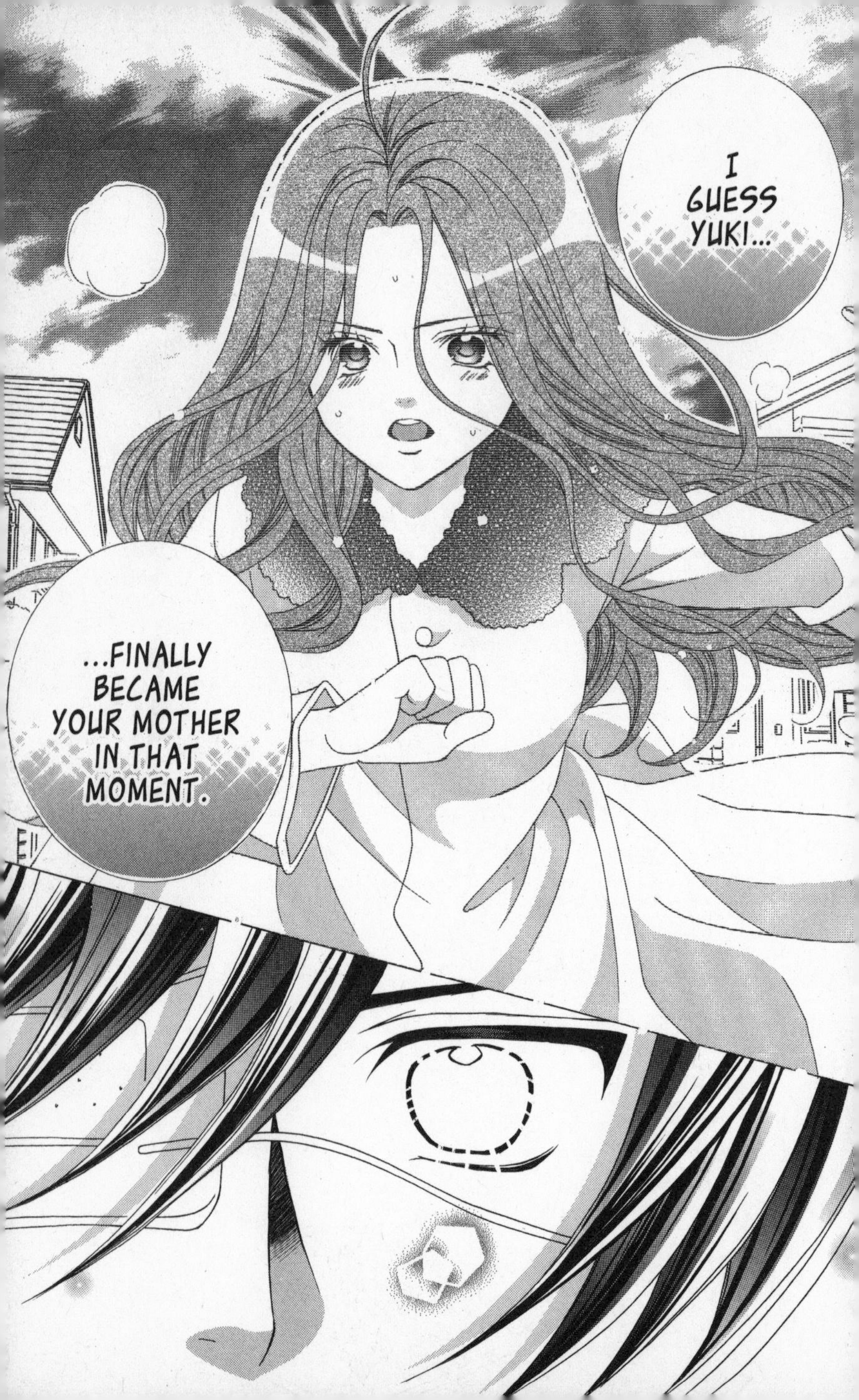
I GUESS YUKI...
...FINALLY BECAME YOUR MOTHER IN THAT MOMENT.

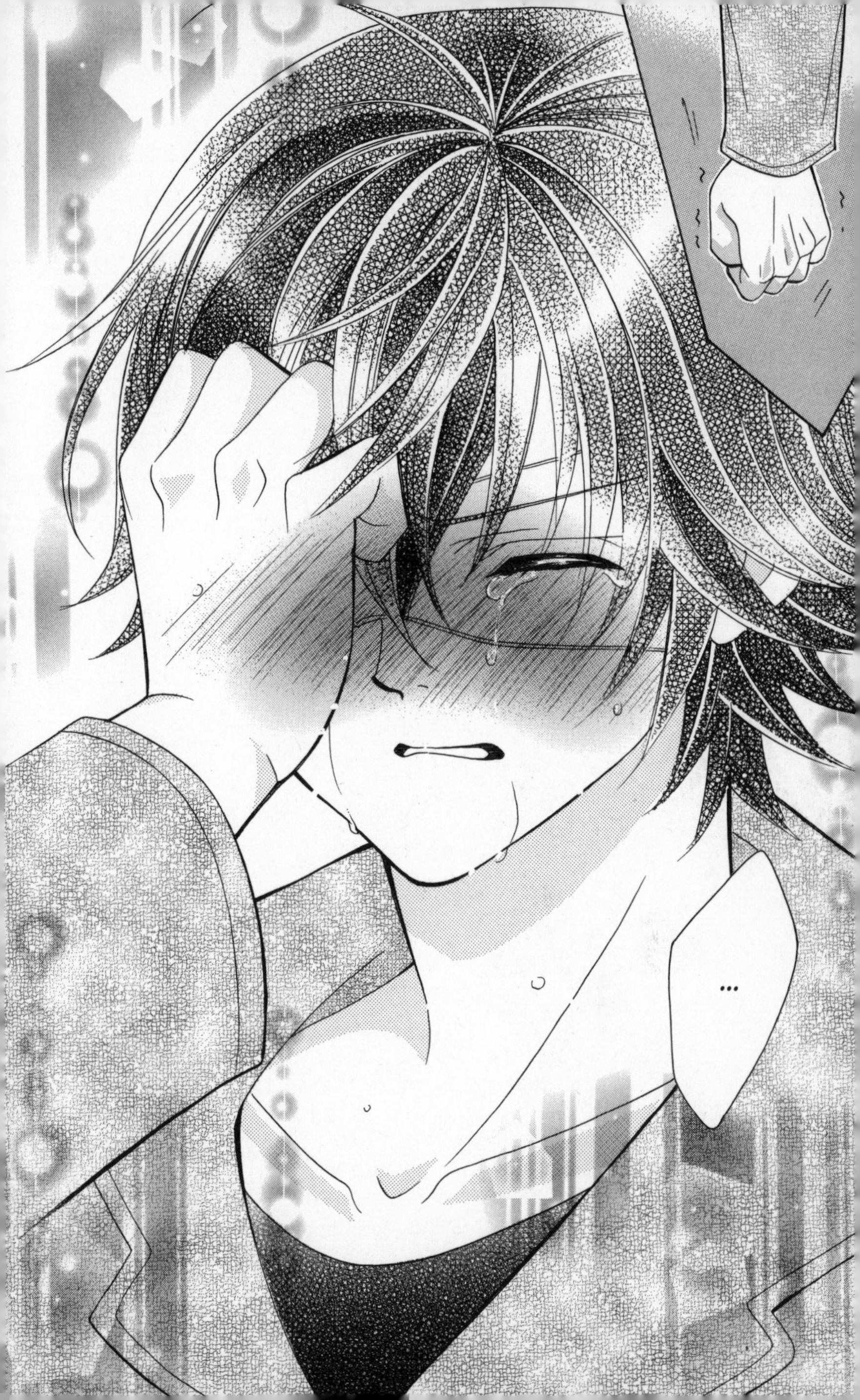
...

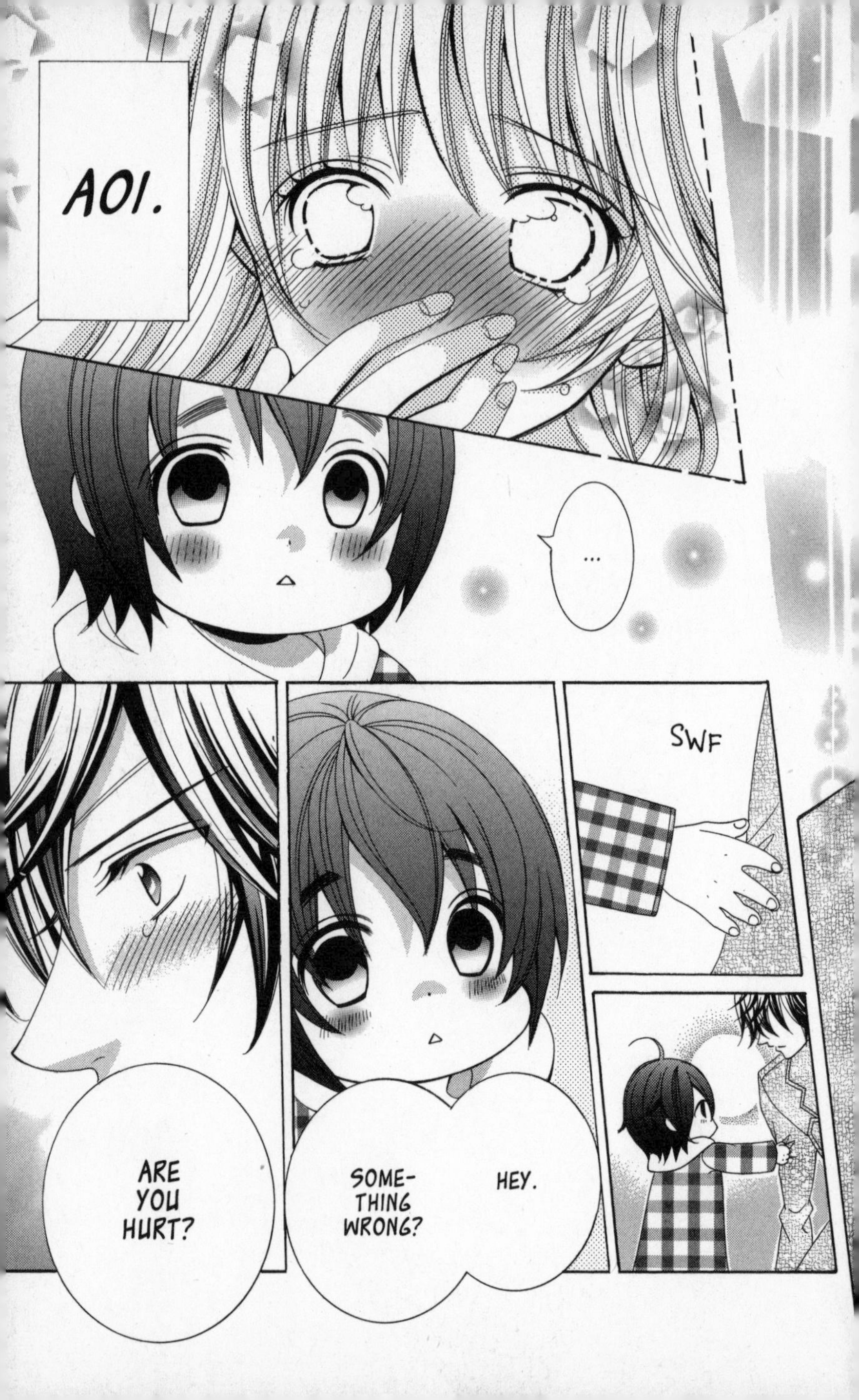
AOI.
...
SWF
HEY.
SOME-THING WRONG?
ARE YOU HURT?

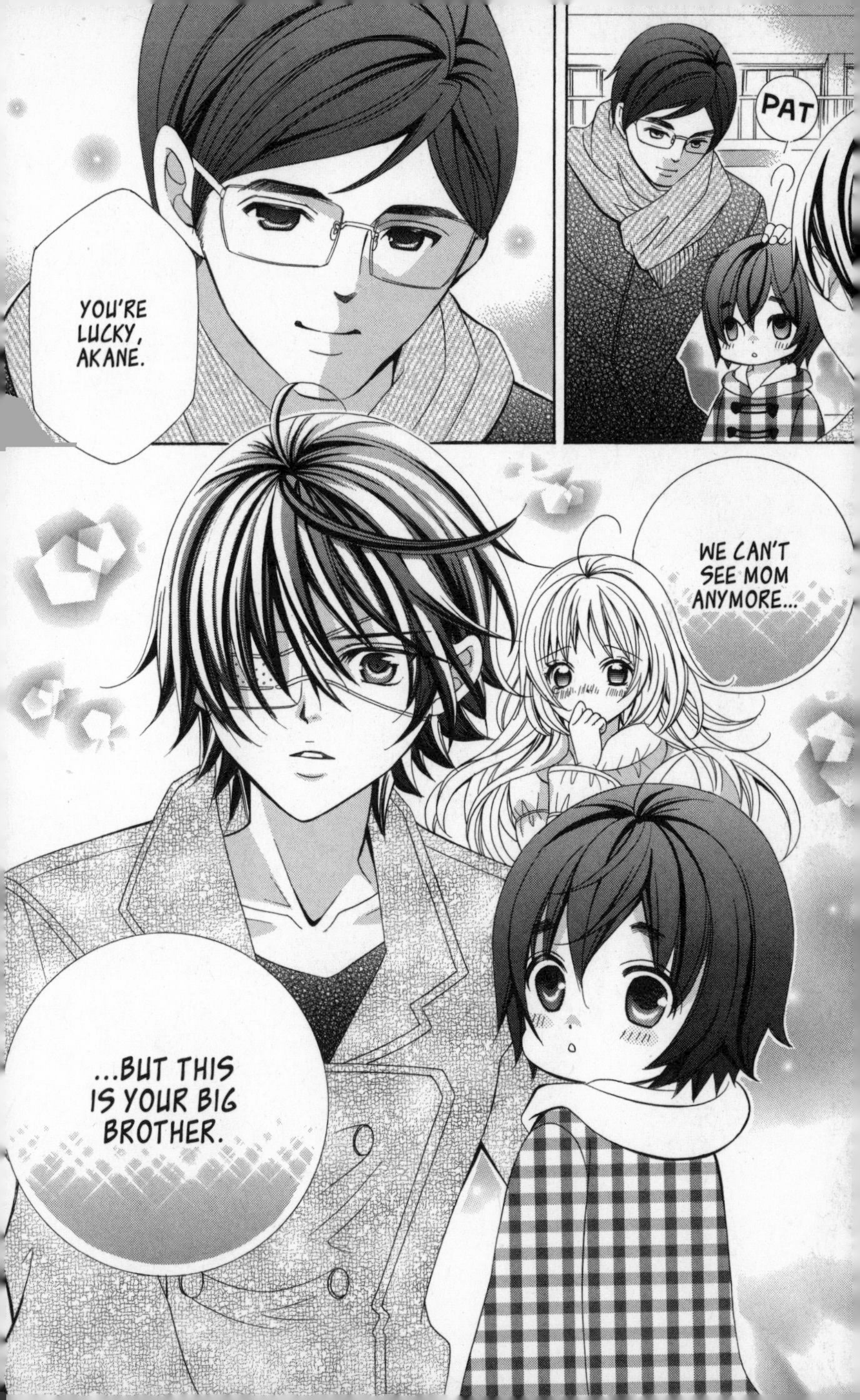
PAT
YOU'RE LUCKY, AKANE.
WE CAN'T SEE MOM ANYMORE...
...BUT THIS IS YOUR BIG BROTHER.

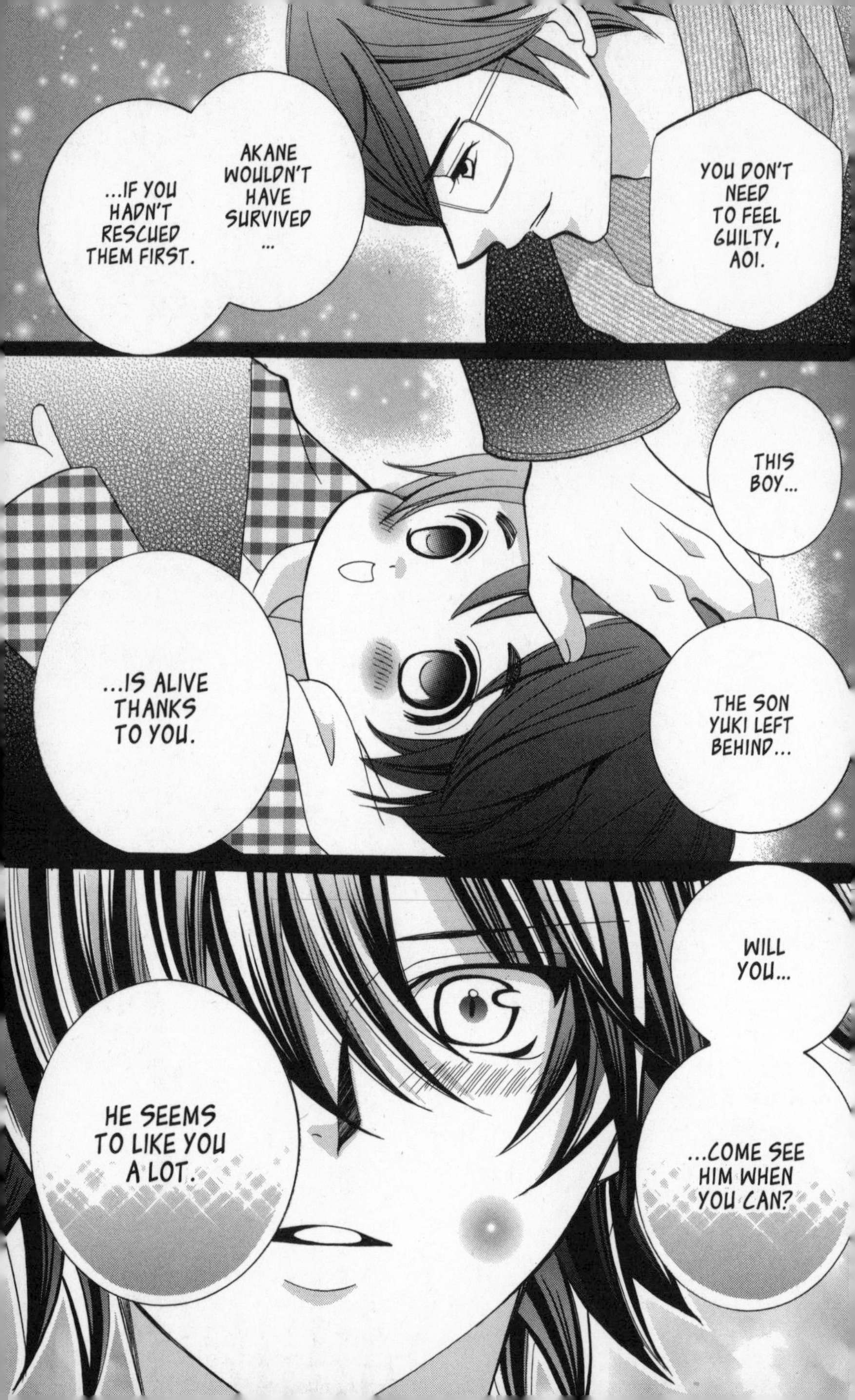
YOU DON'T NEED TO FEEL GUILTY, AOI.
AKANE WOULDN'T HAVE SURVIVED ...
...IF YOU HADN'T RESCUED THEM FIRST.
THIS BOY...
THE SON YUKI LEFT BEHIND...
...IS ALIVE THANKS TO YOU.
WILL YOU...
...COME SEE HIM WHEN YOU CAN?
HE SEEMS TO LIKE YOU A LOT.

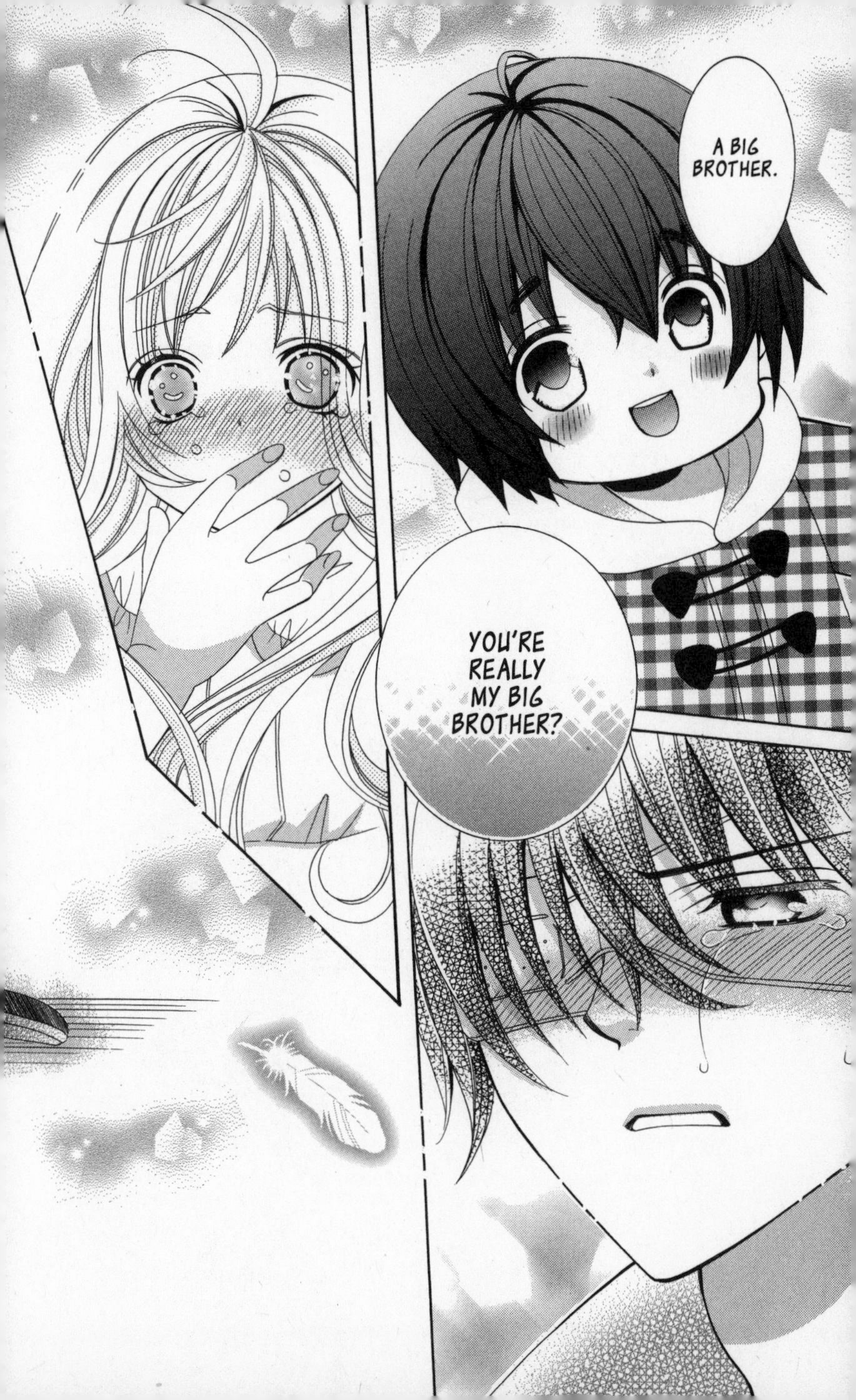
A BIG BROTHER.
YOU'RE REALLY MY BIG BROTHER?

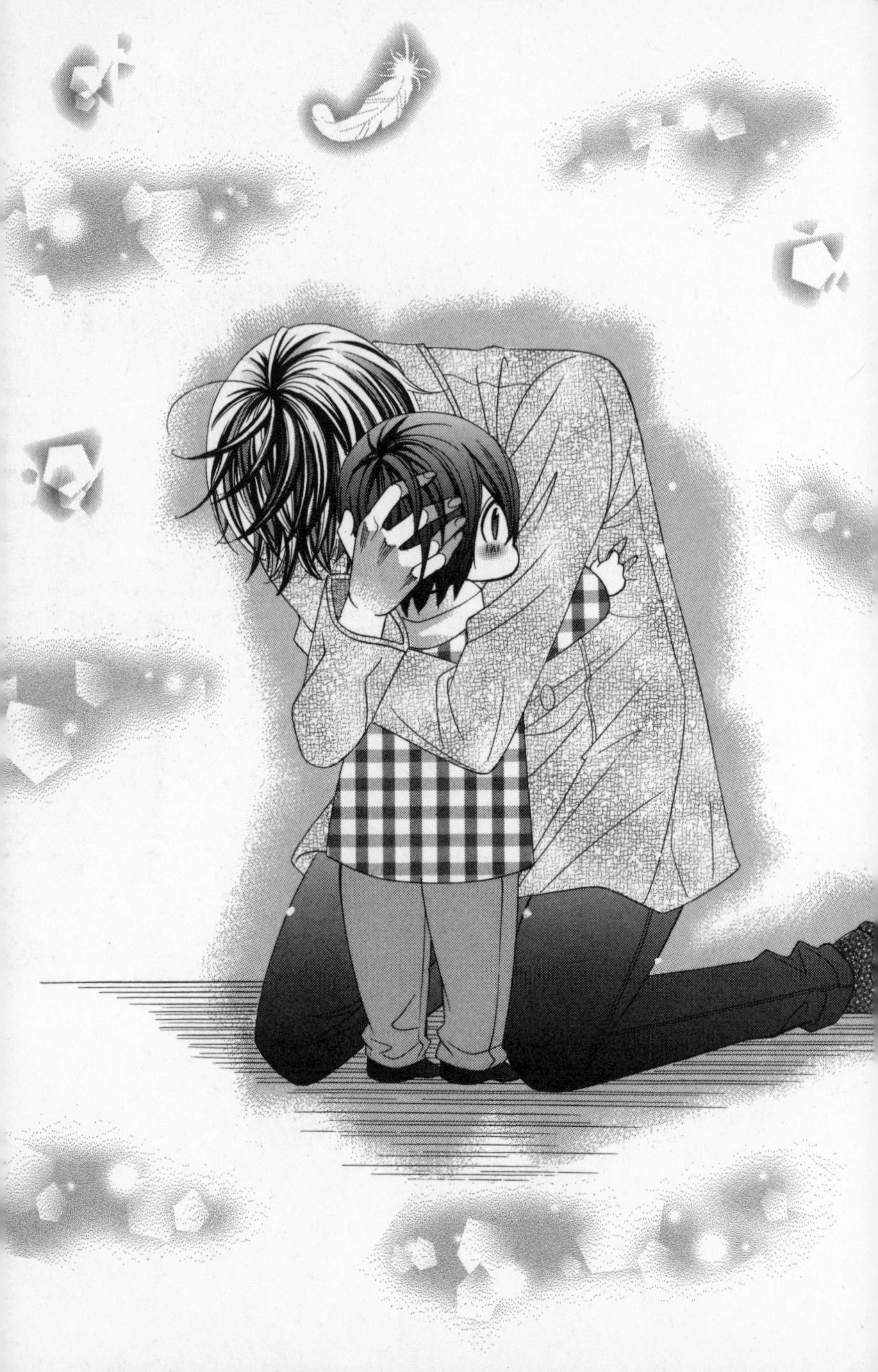

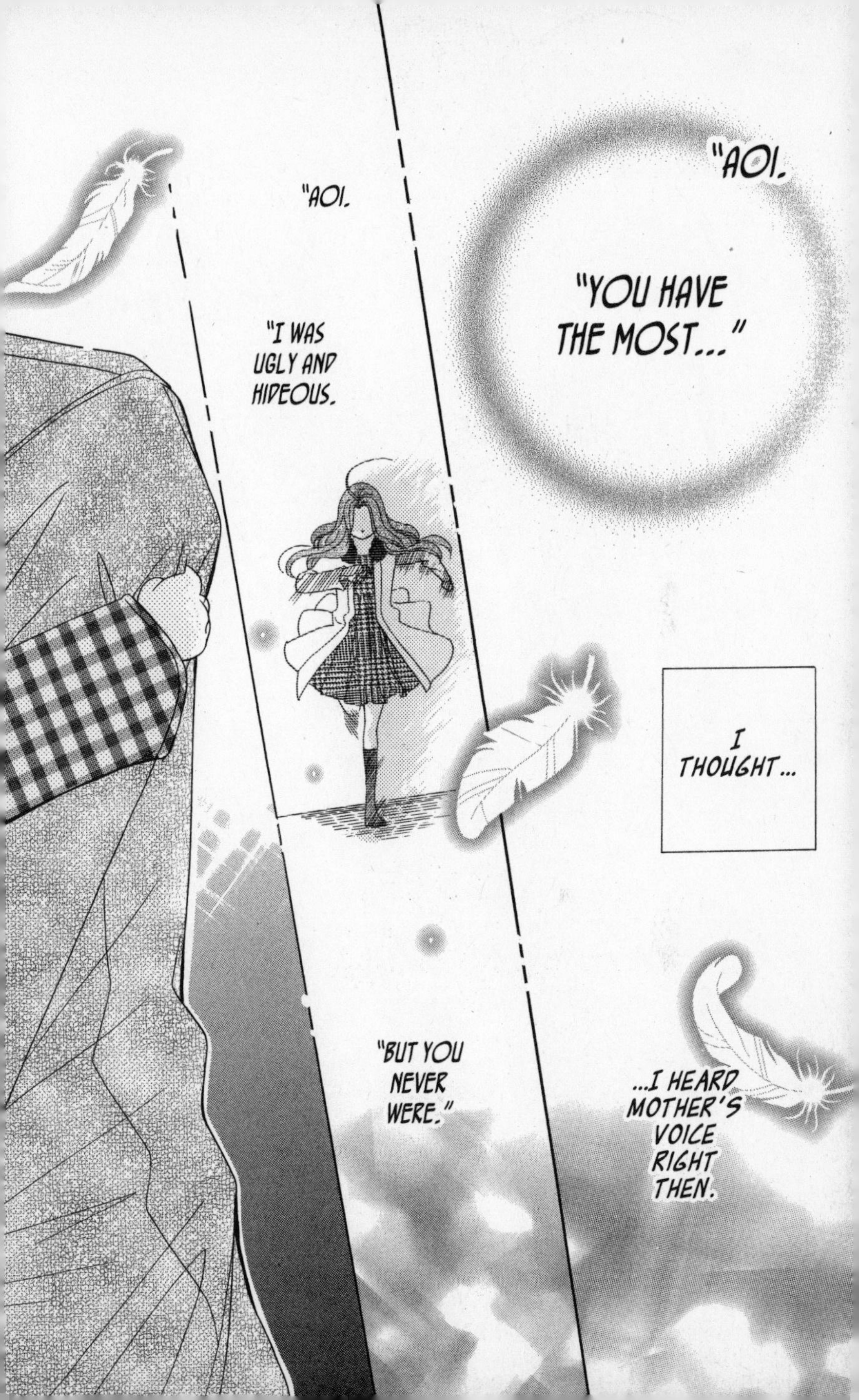
"AOI.
"YOU HAVE THE MOST..."
I THOUGHT...
...I HEARD MOTHER'S VOICE RIGHT THEN.
"AOI.
"I WAS UGLY AND HIDEOUS.
"BUT YOU NEVER WERE."

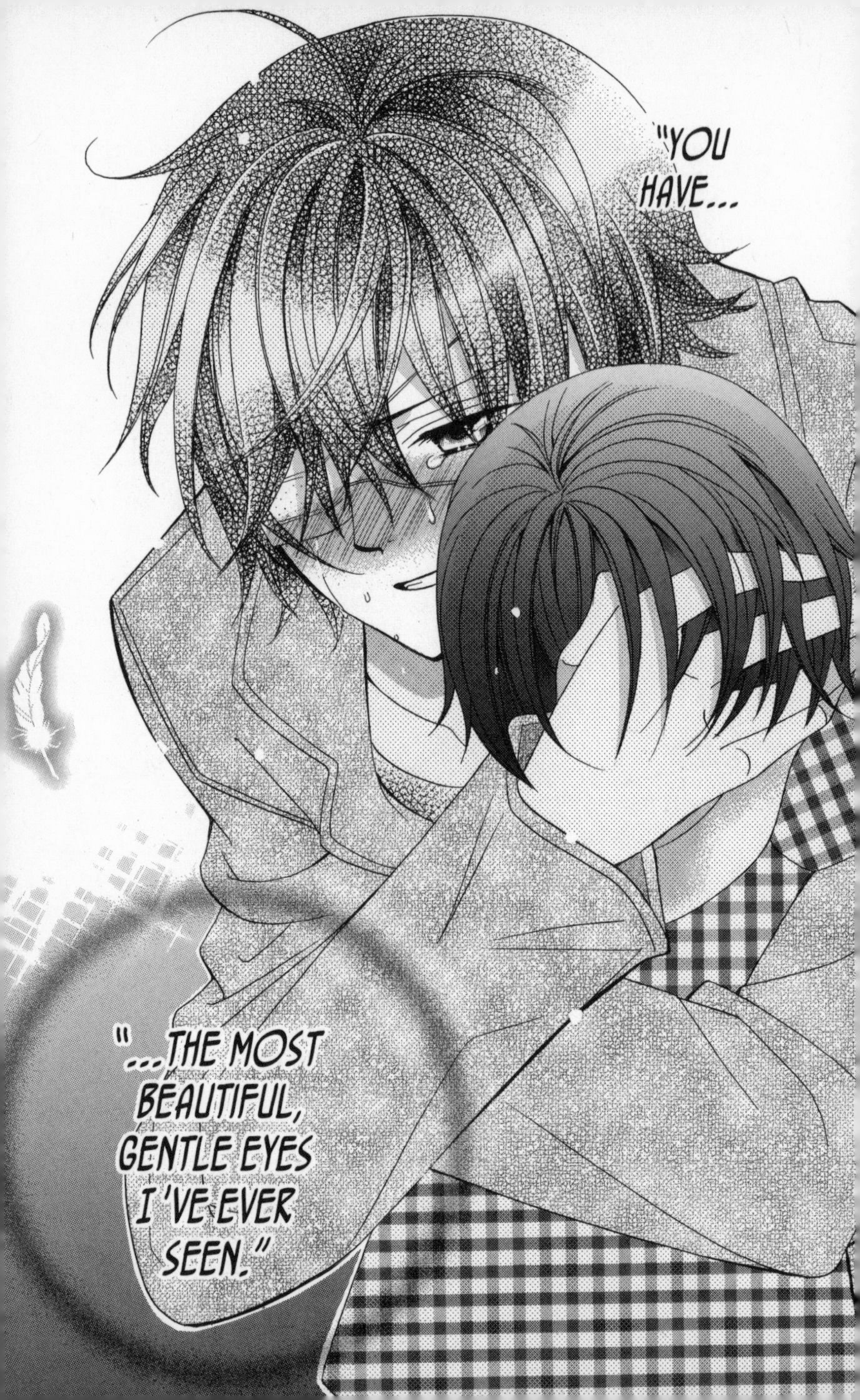
"YOU HAVE...
"...THE MOST BEAUTIFUL, GENTLE EYES I'VE EVER SEEN."

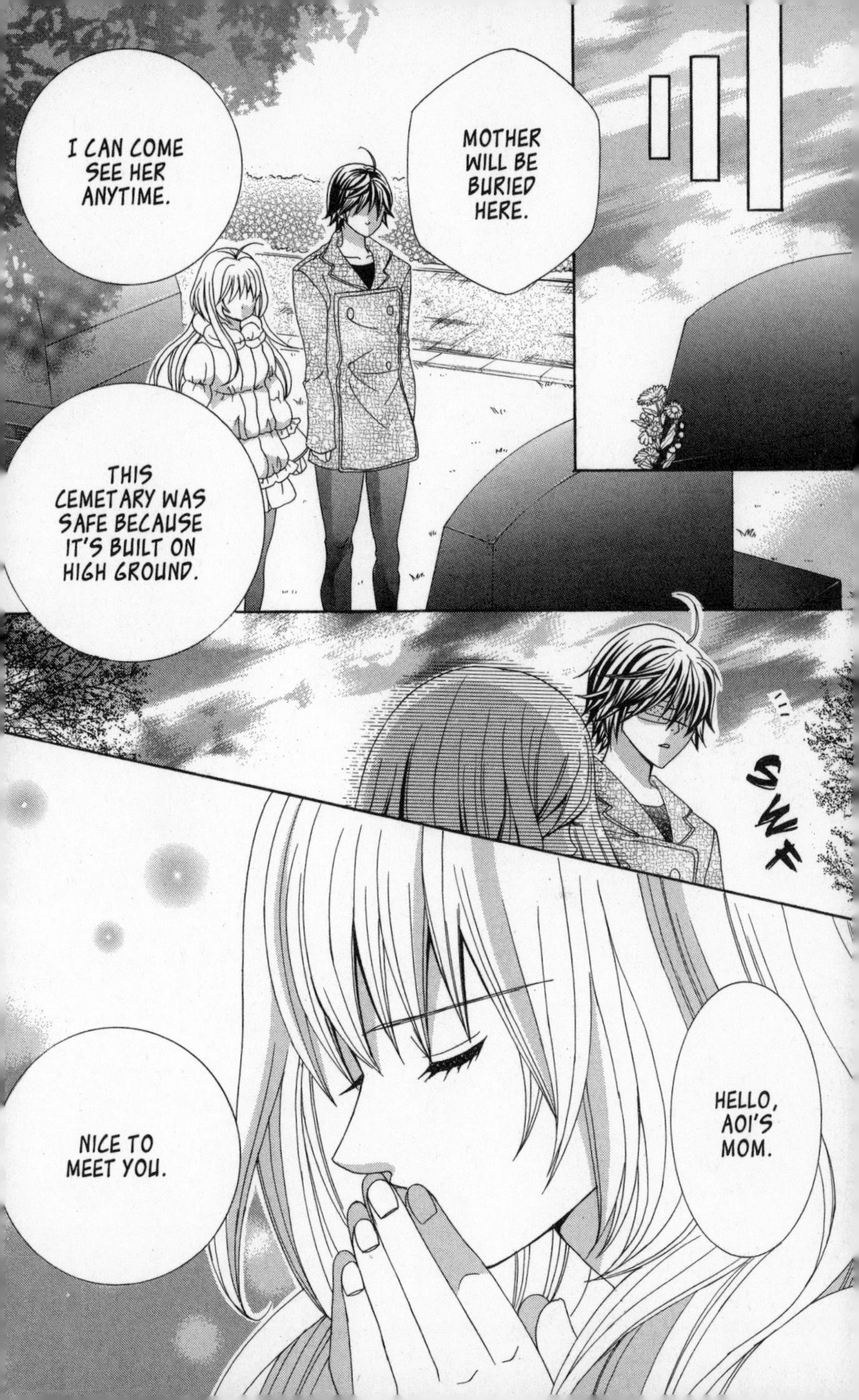
MOTHER WILL BE BURIED HERE.
I CAN COME SEE HER ANYTIME.
THIS CEMETARY WAS SAFE BECAUSE IT'S BUILT ON HIGH GROUND.
...
SWF
HELLO, AOI'S MOM.
NICE TO MEET YOU.

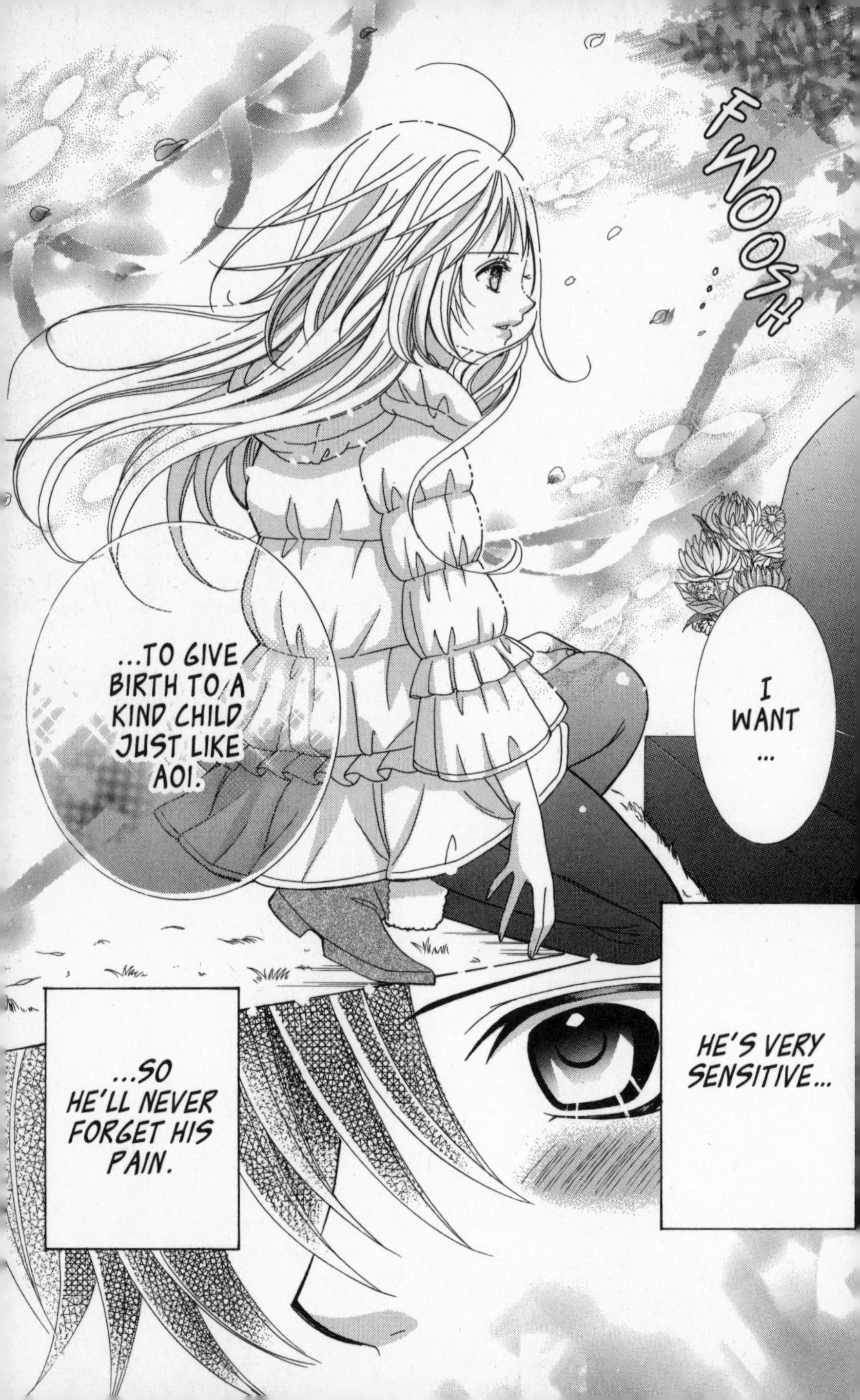
FWOOSH
I WANT ...
...TO GIVE BIRTH TO A KIND CHILD JUST LIKE AOI.
HE'S VERY SENSITIVE...
...SO HE'LL NEVER FORGET HIS PAIN.

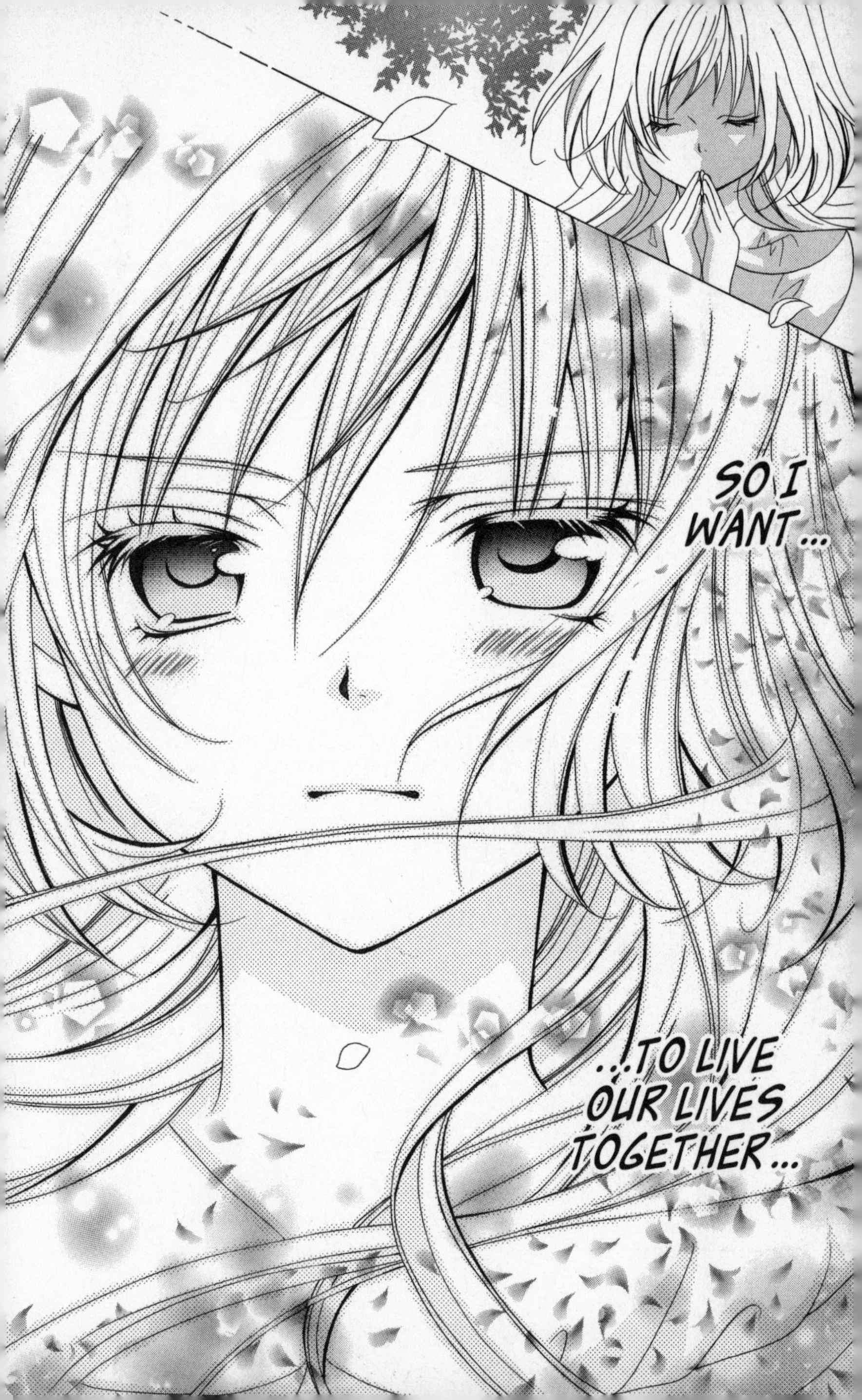
SO I WANT...
...TO LIVE OUR LIVES TOGETHER...

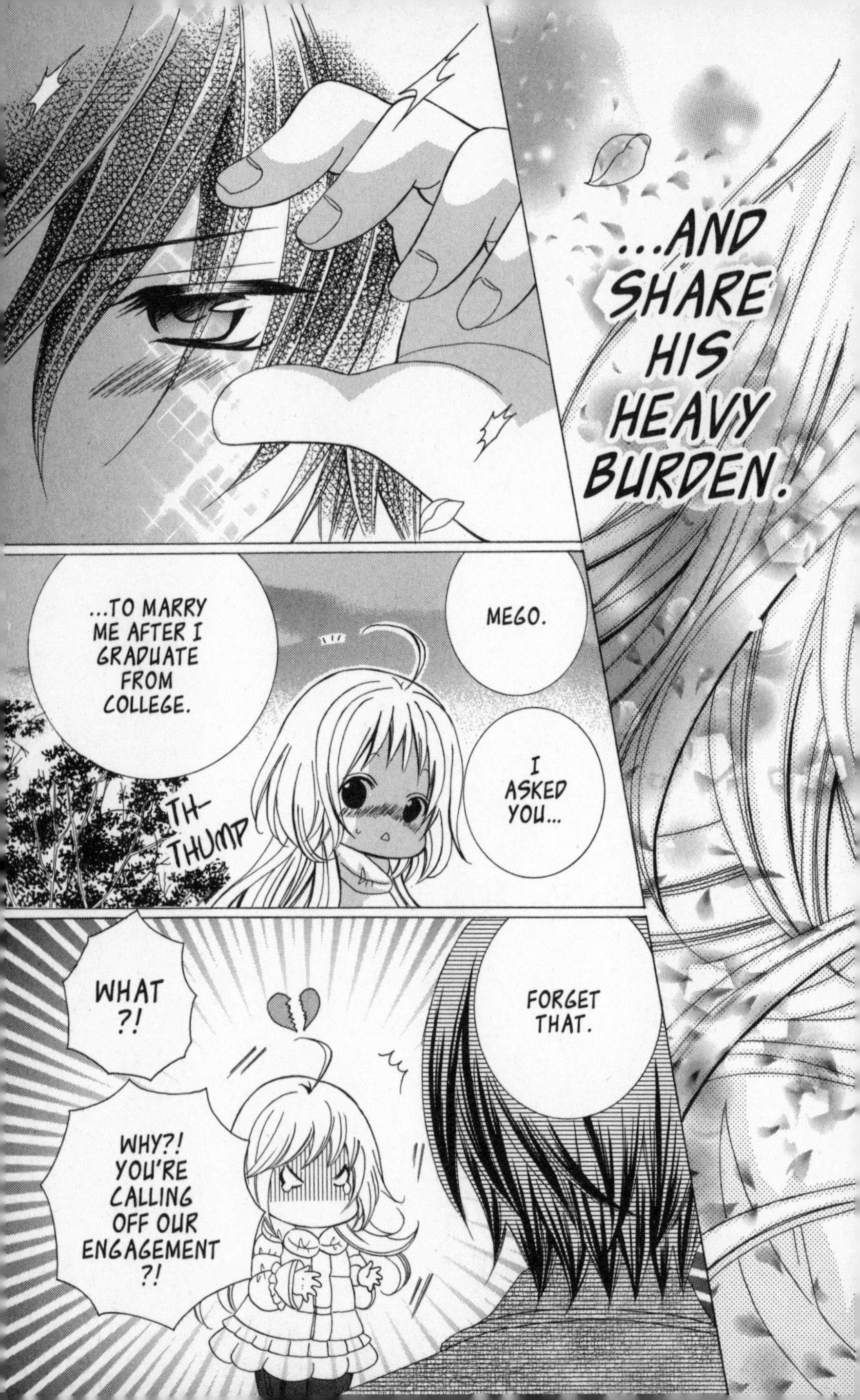
...AND SHARE HIS HEAVY BURDEN.
MEGO.
I ASKED YOU...
...TO MARRY ME AFTER I GRADUATE FROM COLLEGE.
TH-THUMP
FORGET THAT.
WHAT?!
WHY?! YOU'RE CALLING OFF OUR ENGAGEMENT?!

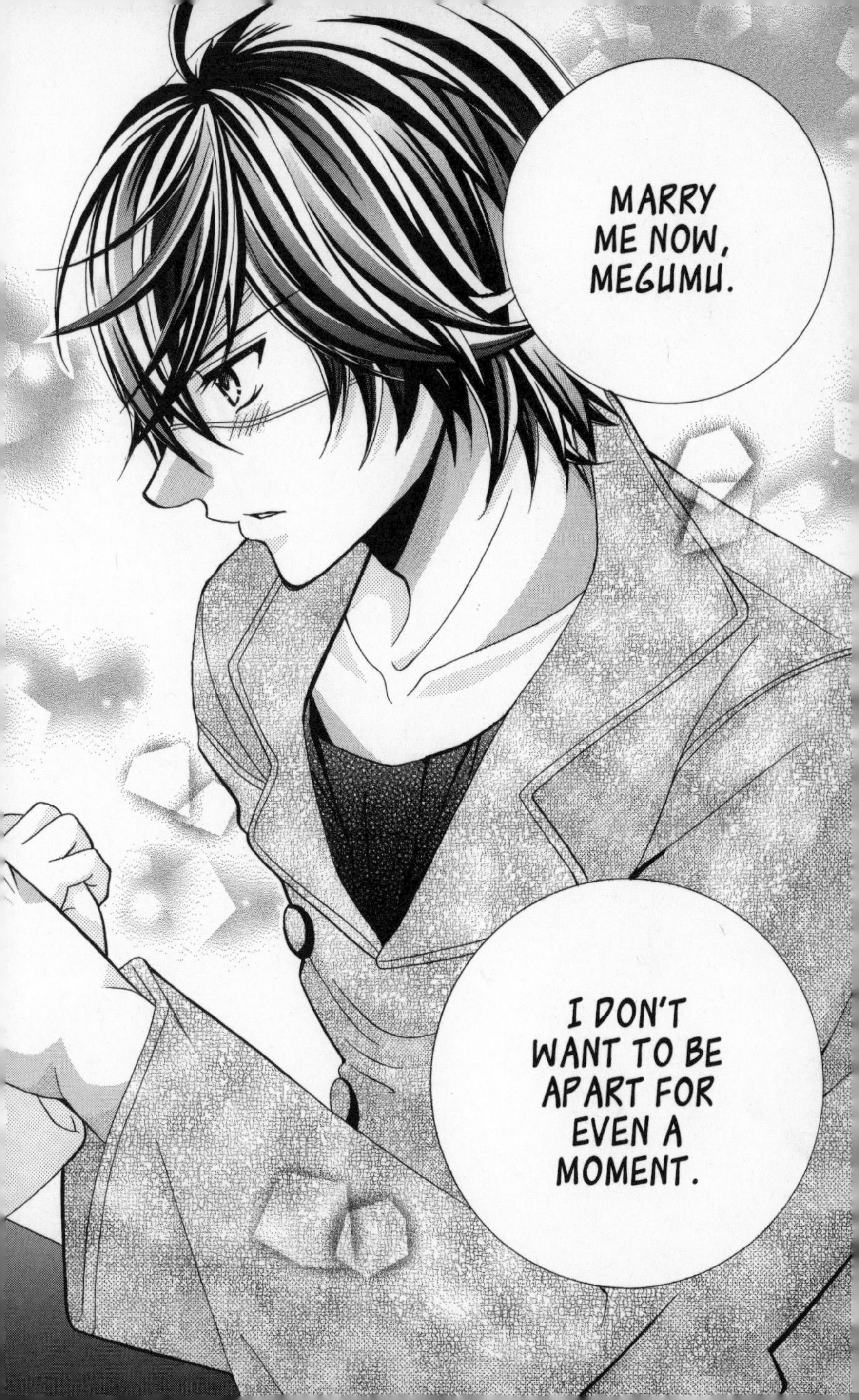
MARRY ME NOW, MEGUMU.
I DON'T WANT TO BE APART FOR EVEN A MOMENT.

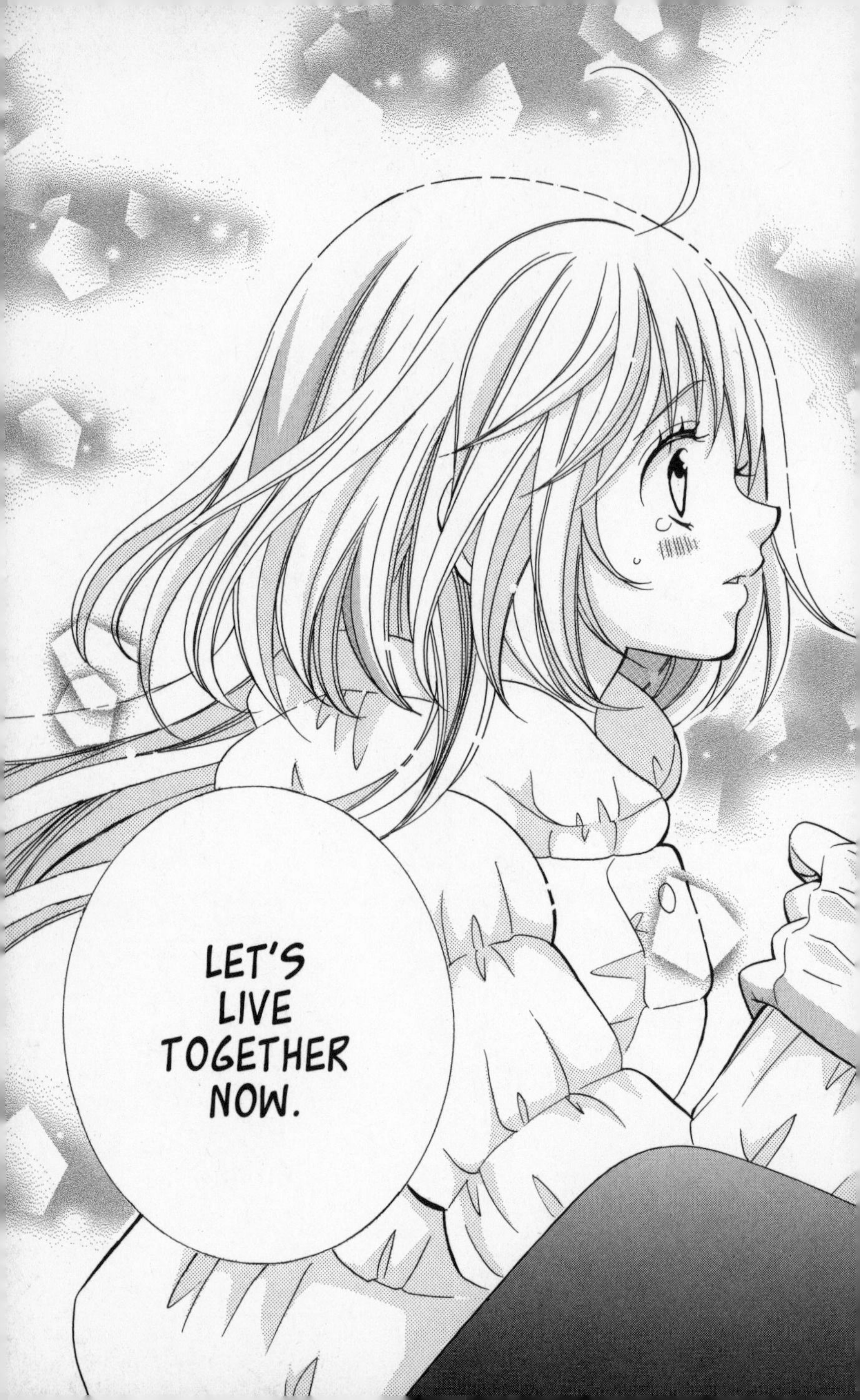
LET'S LIVE TOGETHER NOW.

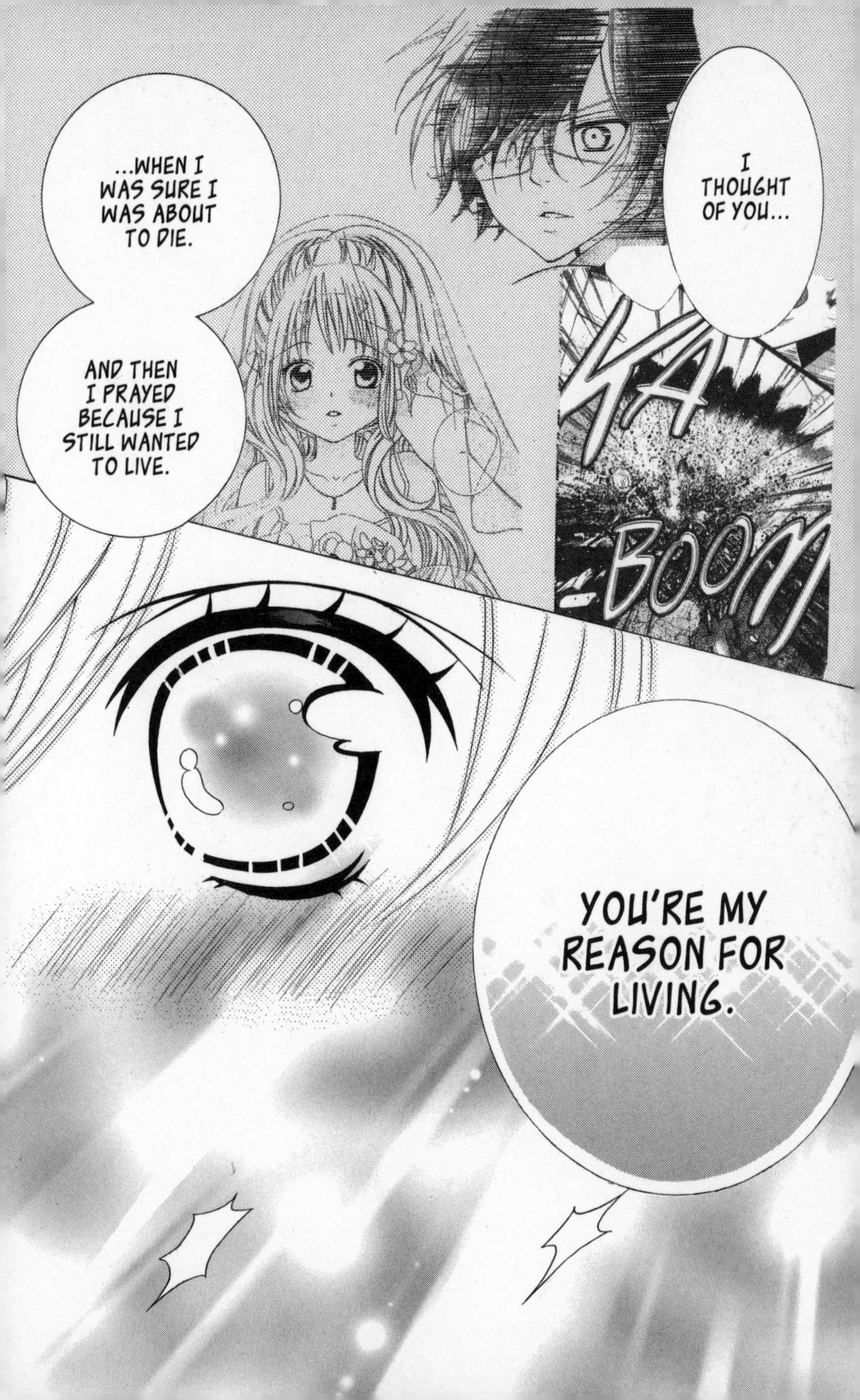
I THOUGHT OF YOU...
KA-BOOM
...WHEN I WAS SURE I WAS ABOUT TO DIE.
AND THEN I PRAYED BECAUSE I STILL WANTED TO LIVE.
YOU'RE MY REASON FOR LIVING.

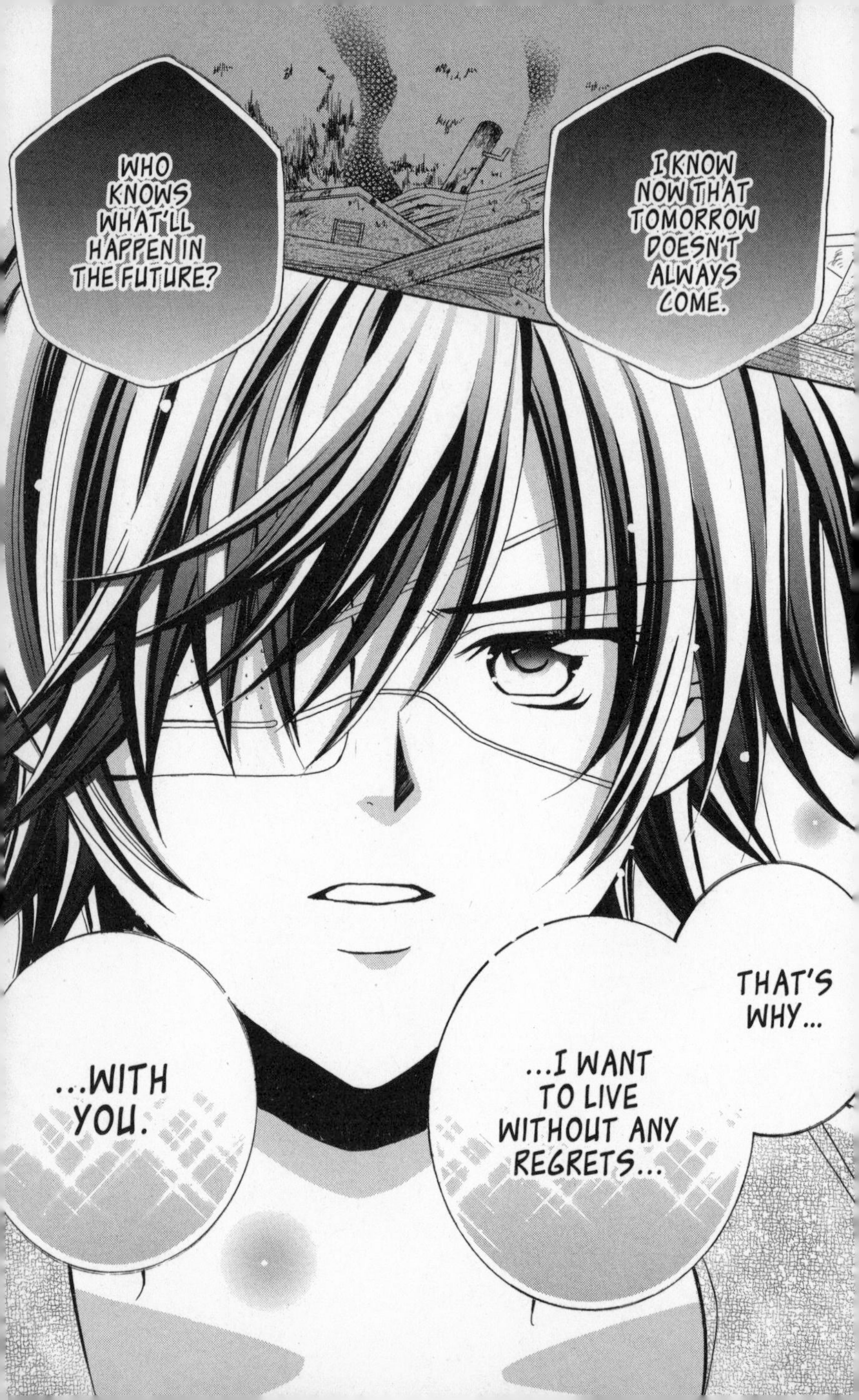
I KNOW NOW THAT TOMORROW DOESN'T ALWAYS COME.
WHO KNOWS WHAT'LL HAPPEN IN THE FUTURE?
THAT'S WHY...
...I WANT TO LIVE WITHOUT ANY REGRETS...
...WITH YOU.

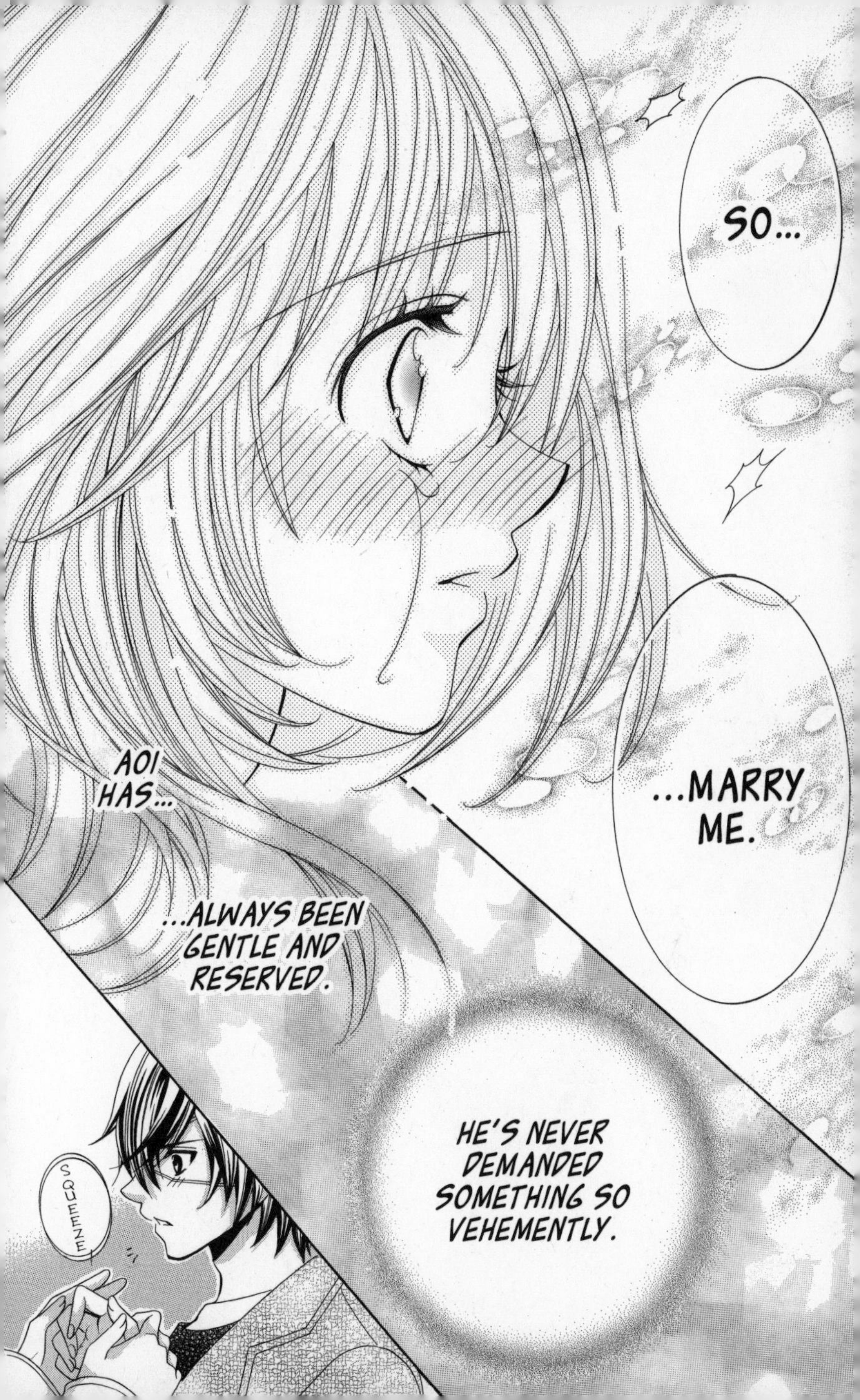
SO...
...MARRY ME.
AOI HAS...
...ALWAYS BEEN GENTLE AND RESERVED.
HE'S NEVER DEMANDED SOMETHING SO VEHEMENTLY.
SQUEEZE

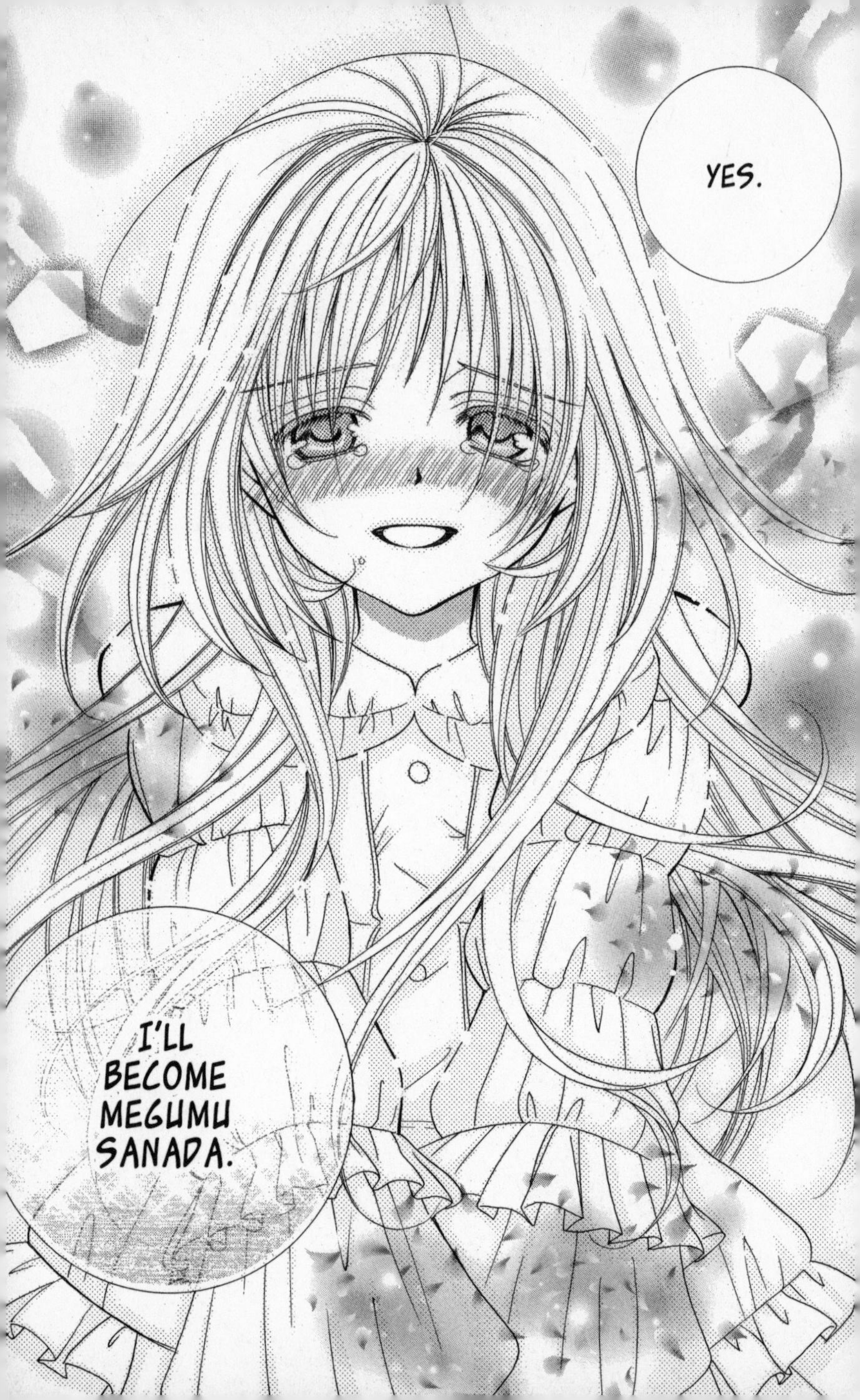
YES.
I'LL BECOME MEGUMU SANADA.

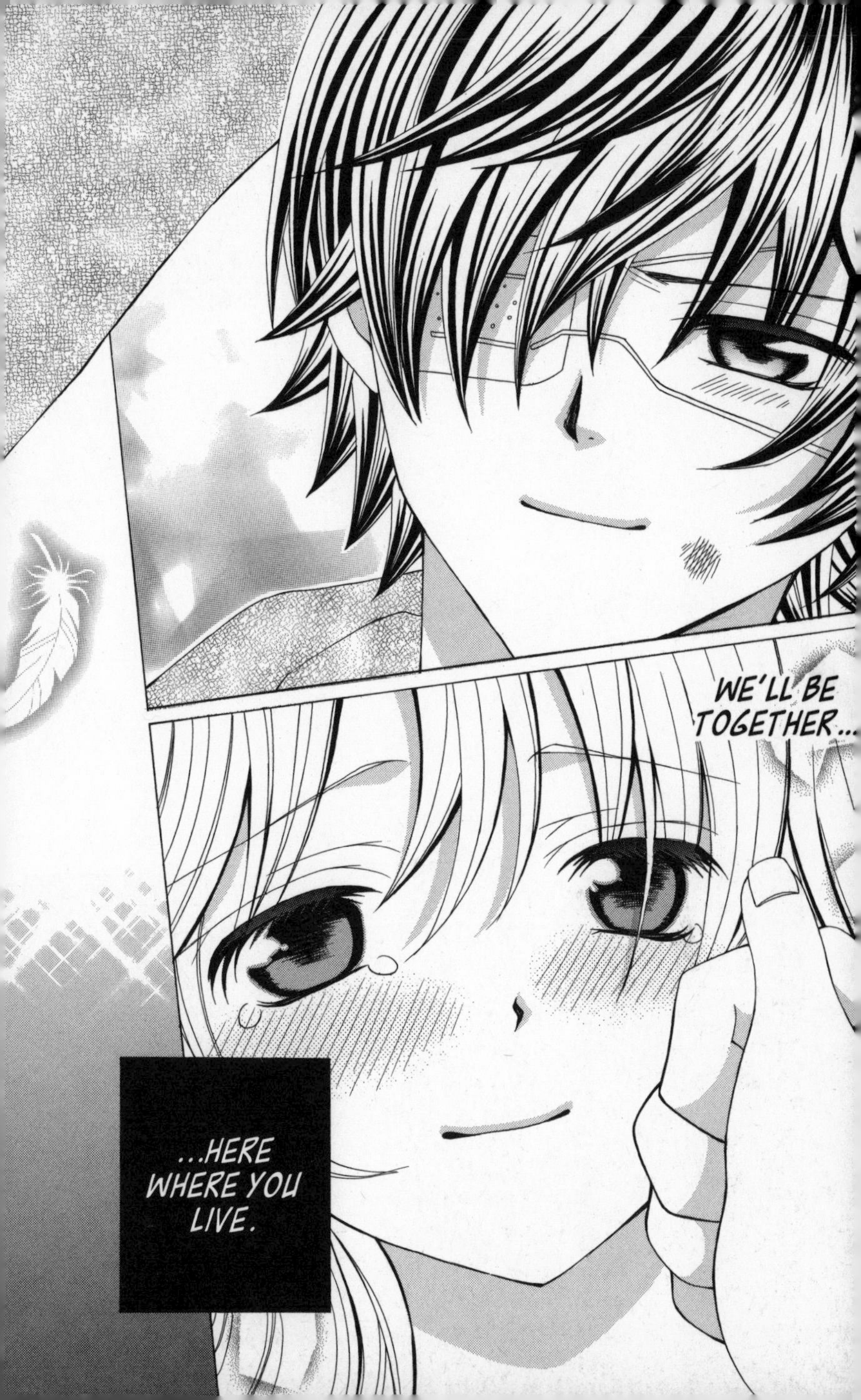
WE'LL BE TOGETHER...
...HERE WHERE YOU LIVE.

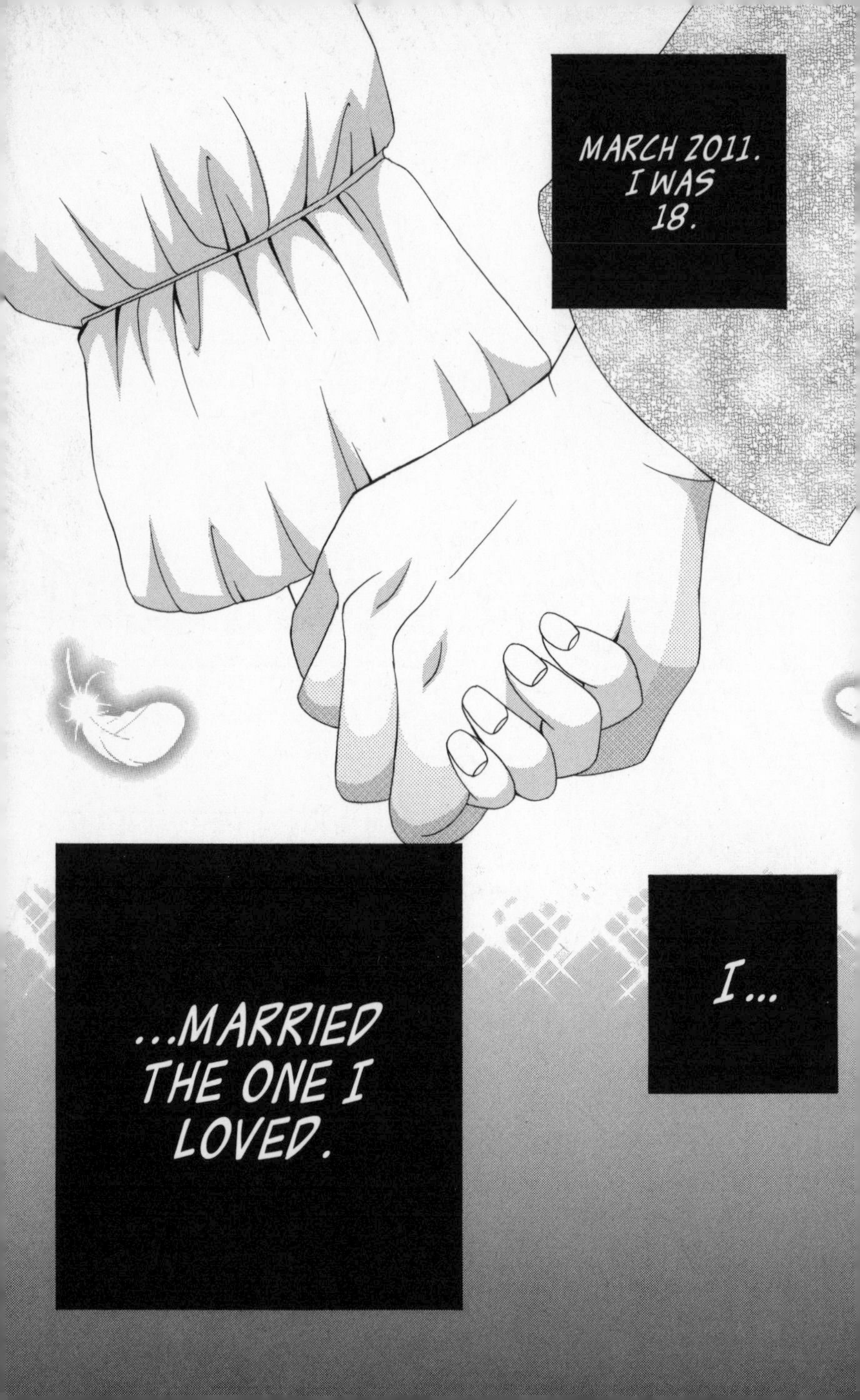
MARCH 2011. I WAS 18.
I...
...MARRIED THE ONE I LOVED.

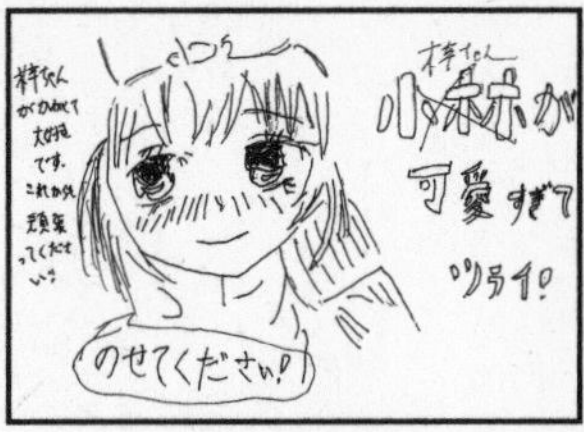
梓ちゃん
小林が
可愛すぎて
ツライ!
梓ちゃんがかわいくて大好きです。これからも頑張ってください。
のせてください!

Rai Yozakura (Chiba) ←
Ed.: People love Azusa. ♥ I wanna be popular too. (><)

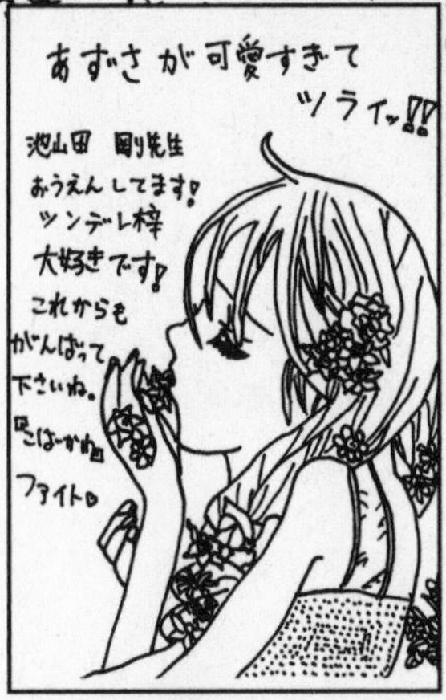
あずさが可愛すぎて
ツライッ!!
池山田 剛先生
おうえんしてます!
ツンデレ梓
大好きです!
これからも
がんばって
下さいね。
『こばかわ』
ファイト。

Yuma Washino (Ehime) ←
Ed.: Azusa in love... a memorable scene.

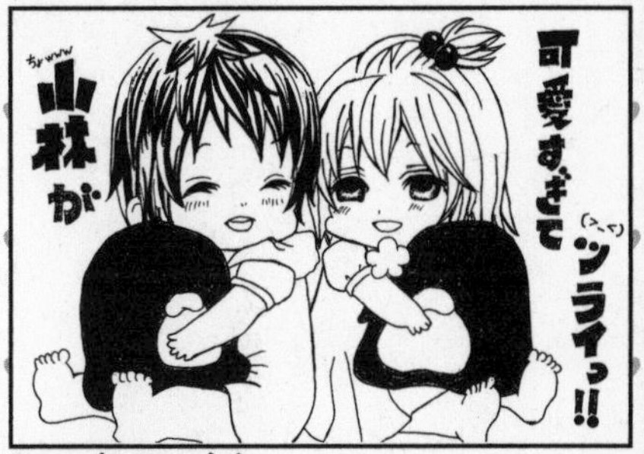
ちょwww
小林が
可愛すぎて
(>_<)
ツライっ!!

Ryoma (Saitama) ↑
Ed.: The little twins! So cute!!

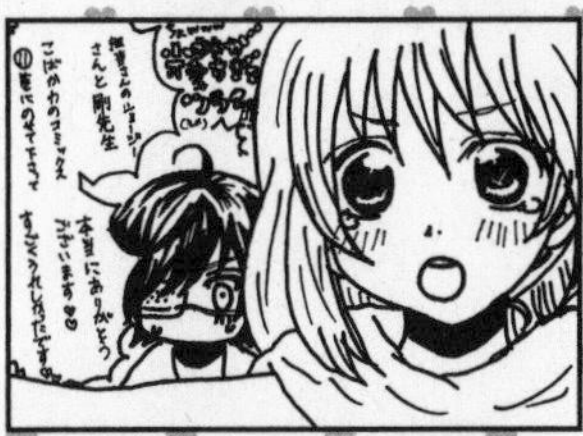

Wakana Matsumoto (Miyazaki) ←
Ed.: Aoi looks surprised!!

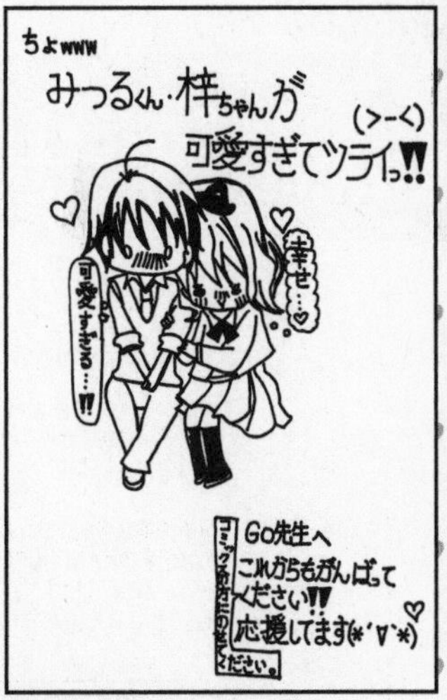
ちょwww
みつるくん・梓ちゃんが
(>-<)
可愛すぎてツライっ!!
幸せ…
可愛すぎる…!!
Go先生へ
これからもがんばってください!!
応援してます(*'▽'*)
コミックス表紙にのせてください。

Yui (Kanagawa) ↑
Ed:. I wanna watch over them forever. (><)

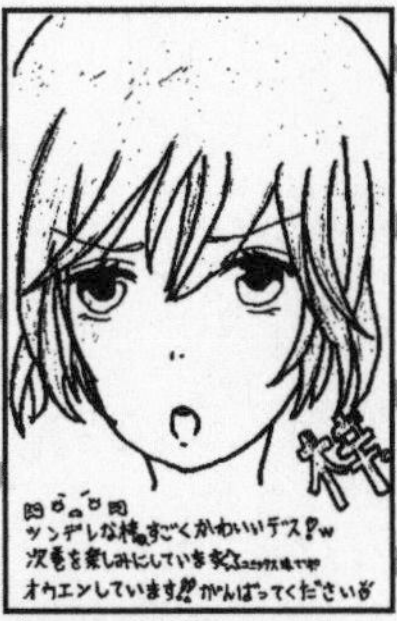
ツンデレな梓すごくかわいいデス!w
次巻を楽しみにしています☆
オウエンしています!! がんばってくださいね

Chikayasu Umeki (Osaka) ↑
Ed.: My heart flutters at the blushing Azusa. ♥

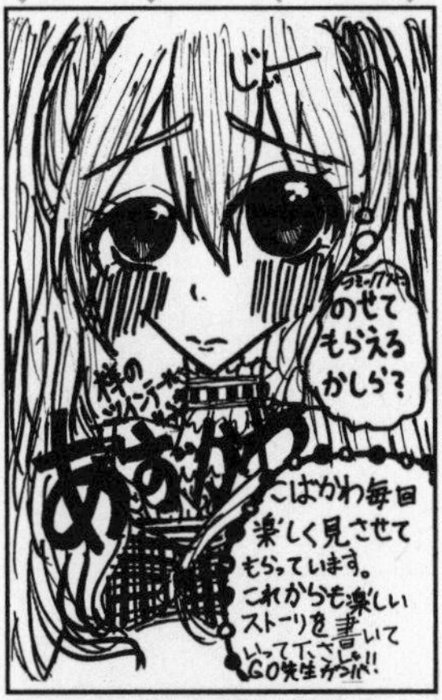
じー
のせてもらえるかしら?
あおか
こばかわ毎回
楽しく見させて
もらっています。
これからも楽しい
ストーリを書いて
いって下さいね!!
GO先生がんば!!

Honoka Sekiguchi (Niigata) ↑
Ed.: Her drooping eyebrows look super cute!!

Send your fan mail to:

Go Ikeyamada
c/o Shojo Beat
VIZ Media, LLC
P.O. Box 77010
San Francisco, CA 94107

Chapter 71

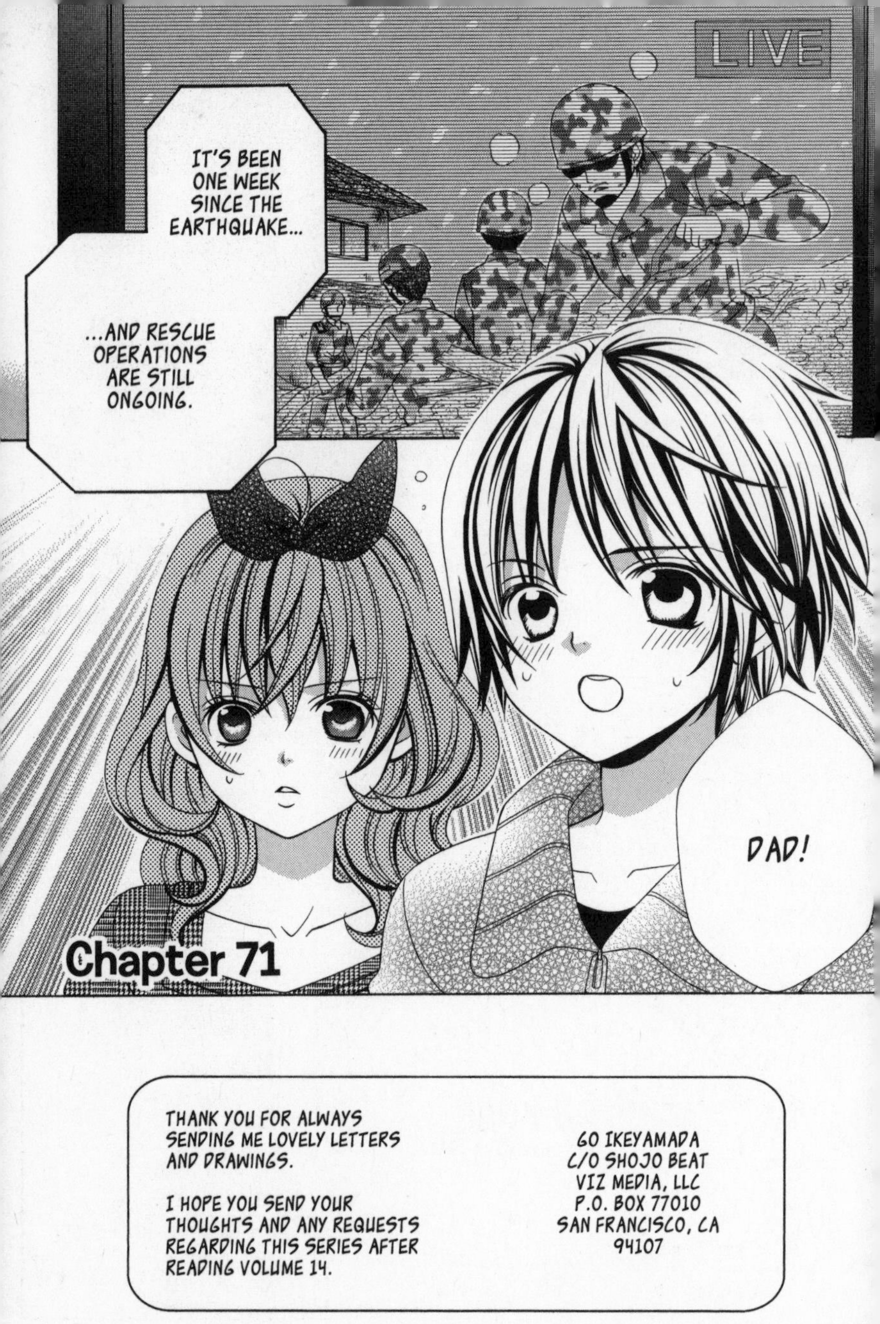
LIVE
IT'S BEEN ONE WEEK SINCE THE EARTHQUAKE...
...AND RESCUE OPERATIONS ARE STILL ONGOING.
DAD!

THANK YOU FOR ALWAYS SENDING ME LOVELY LETTERS AND DRAWINGS.

I HOPE YOU SEND YOUR THOUGHTS AND ANY REQUESTS REGARDING THIS SERIES AFTER READING VOLUME 14.

GO IKEYAMADA
C/O SHOJO BEAT
VIZ MEDIA, LLC
P.O. BOX 77010
SAN FRANCISCO, CA
94107

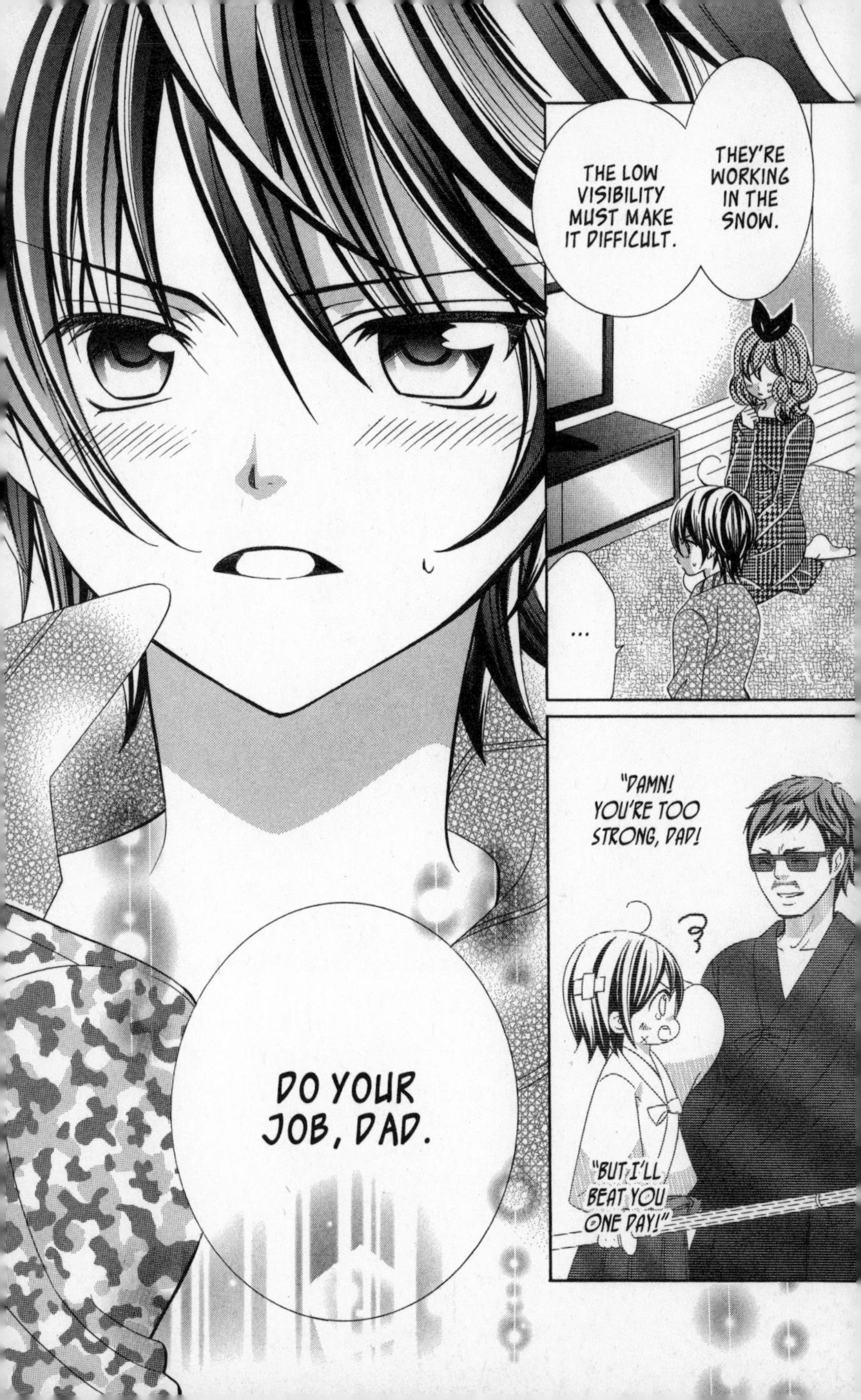
THEY'RE WORKING IN THE SNOW.
THE LOW VISIBILITY MUST MAKE IT DIFFICULT.
...
"DAMN! YOU'RE TOO STRONG, DAD!
"BUT I'LL BEAT YOU ONE DAY!"
DO YOUR JOB, DAD.

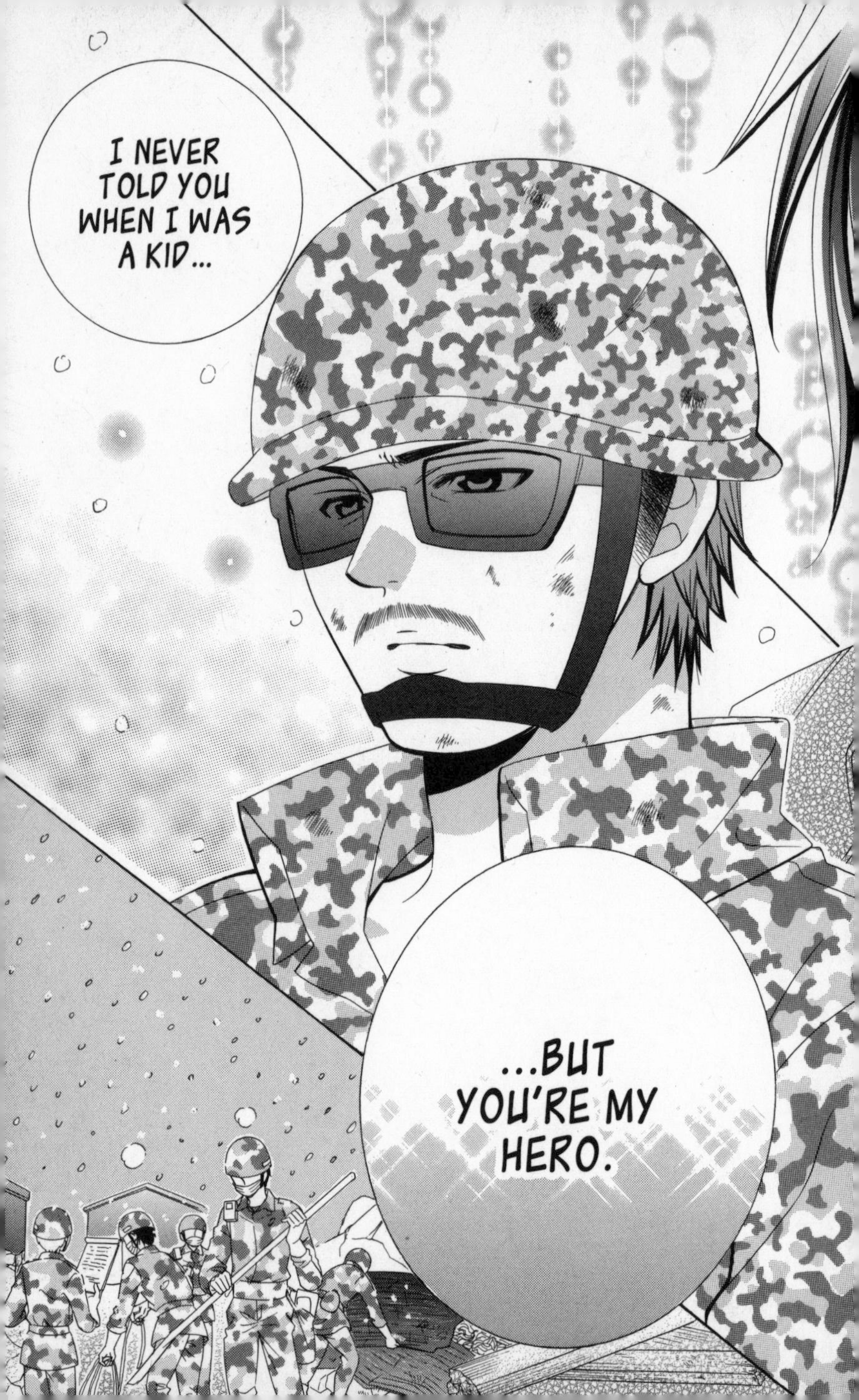
I NEVER TOLD YOU WHEN I WAS A KID...
...BUT YOU'RE MY HERO.

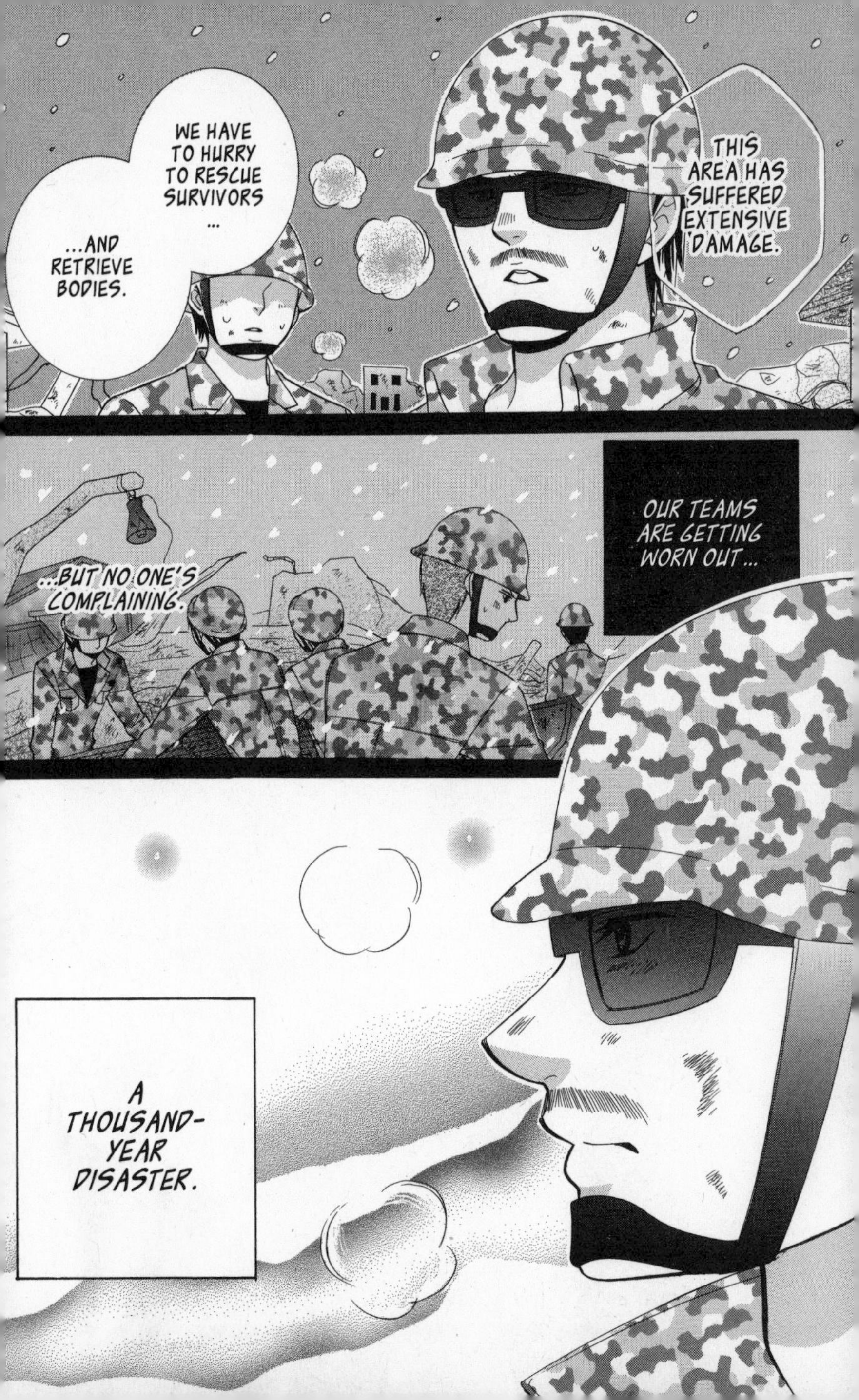
THIS AREA HAS SUFFERED EXTENSIVE DAMAGE.
WE HAVE TO HURRY TO RESCUE SURVIVORS ...
...AND RETRIEVE BODIES.
OUR TEAMS ARE GETTING WORN OUT...
...BUT NO ONE'S COMPLAINING.
A THOUSAND-YEAR DISASTER.

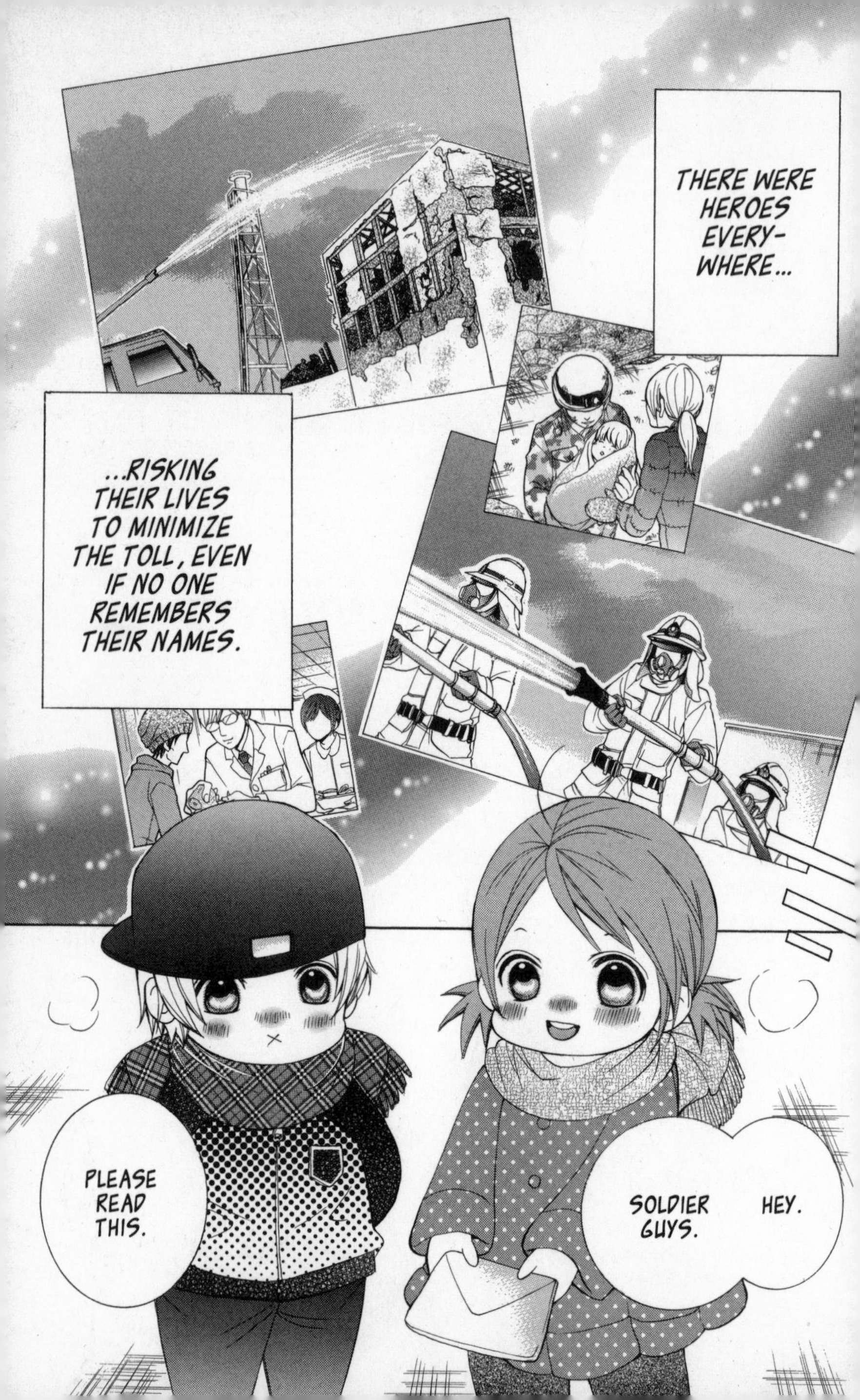
THERE WERE HEROES EVERY-WHERE...
...RISKING THEIR LIVES TO MINIMIZE THE TOLL, EVEN IF NO ONE REMEMBERS THEIR NAMES.
HEY. SOLDIER GUYS.
PLEASE READ THIS.

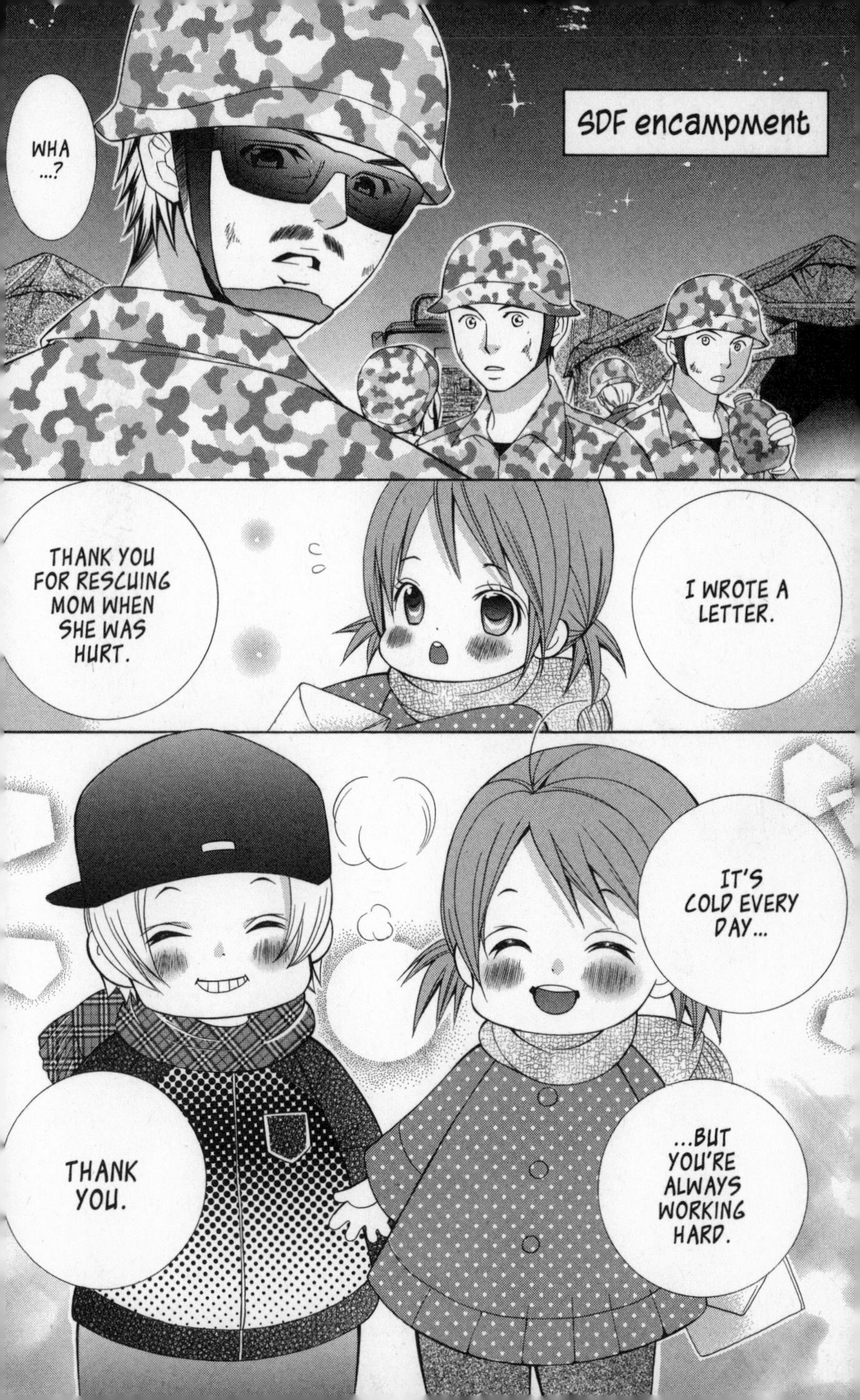
SDF encampment
WHA ...?
I WROTE A LETTER.
THANK YOU FOR RESCUING MOM WHEN SHE WAS HURT.
IT'S COLD EVERY DAY...
...BUT YOU'RE ALWAYS WORKING HARD.
THANK YOU.

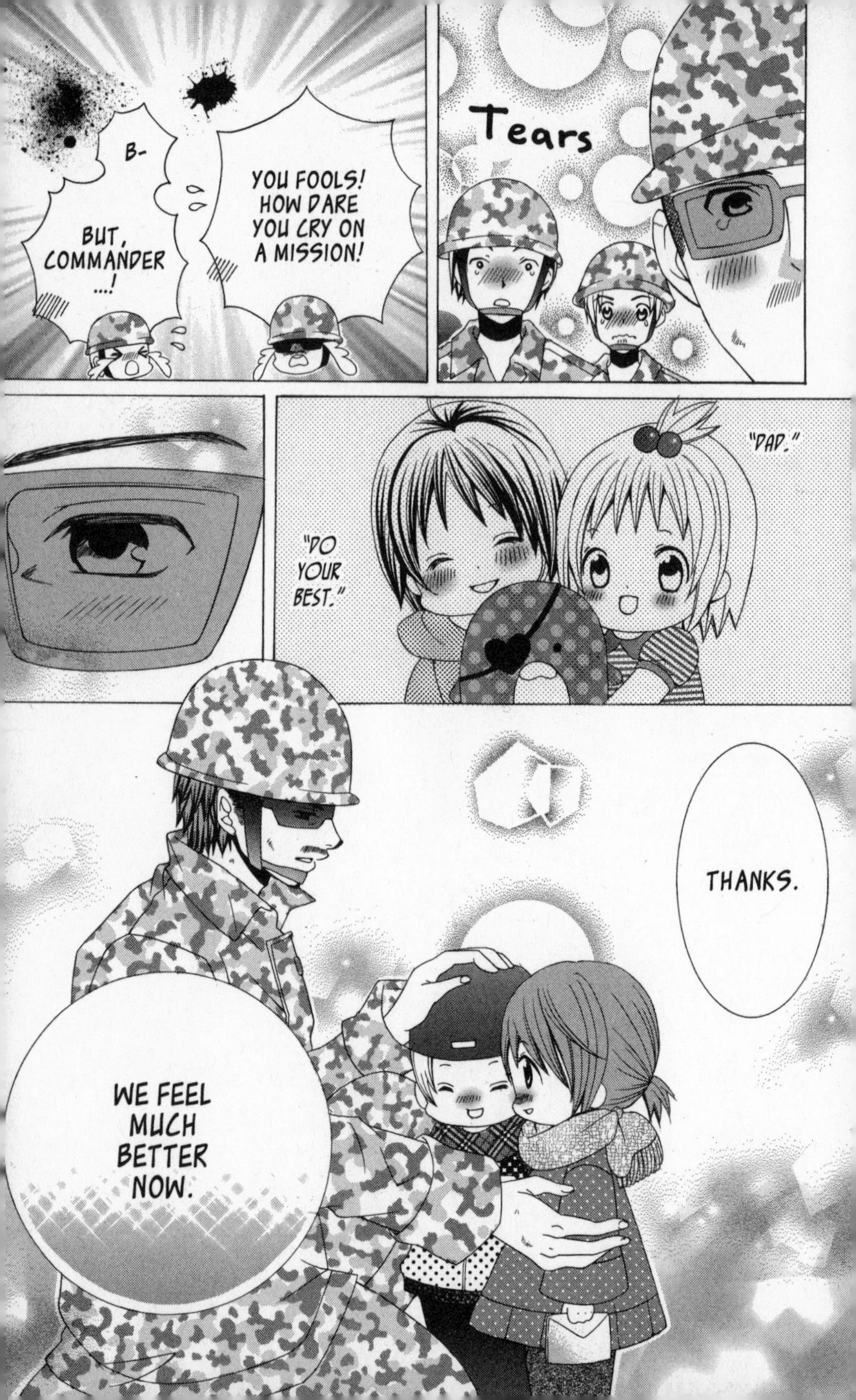
Tears
YOU FOOLS! HOW DARE YOU CRY ON A MISSION!
B-
BUT, COMMANDER ...!
"DAD."
"DO YOUR BEST."
THANKS.
WE FEEL MUCH BETTER NOW.

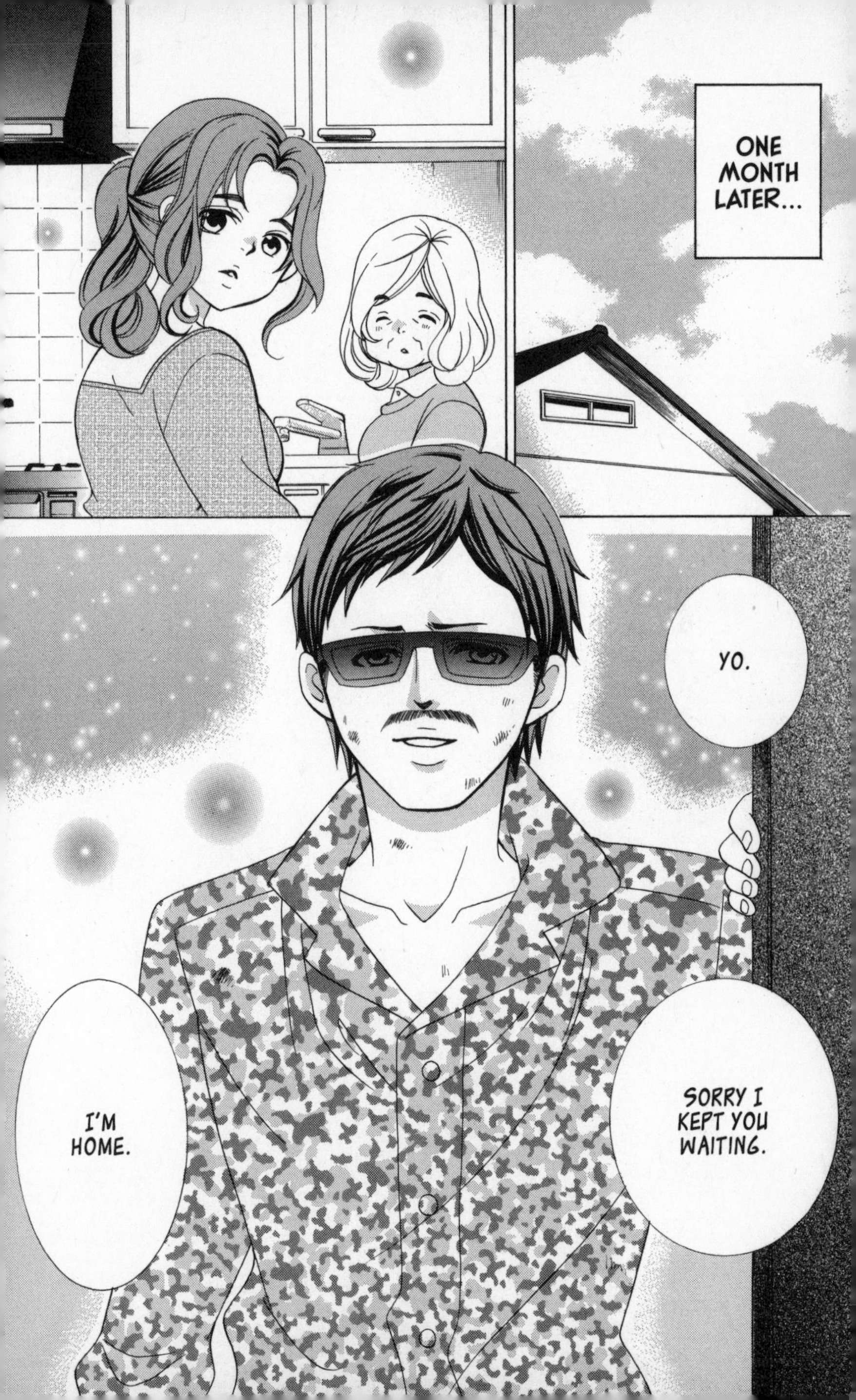
ONE MONTH LATER...
YO.
SORRY I KEPT YOU WAITING.
I'M HOME.

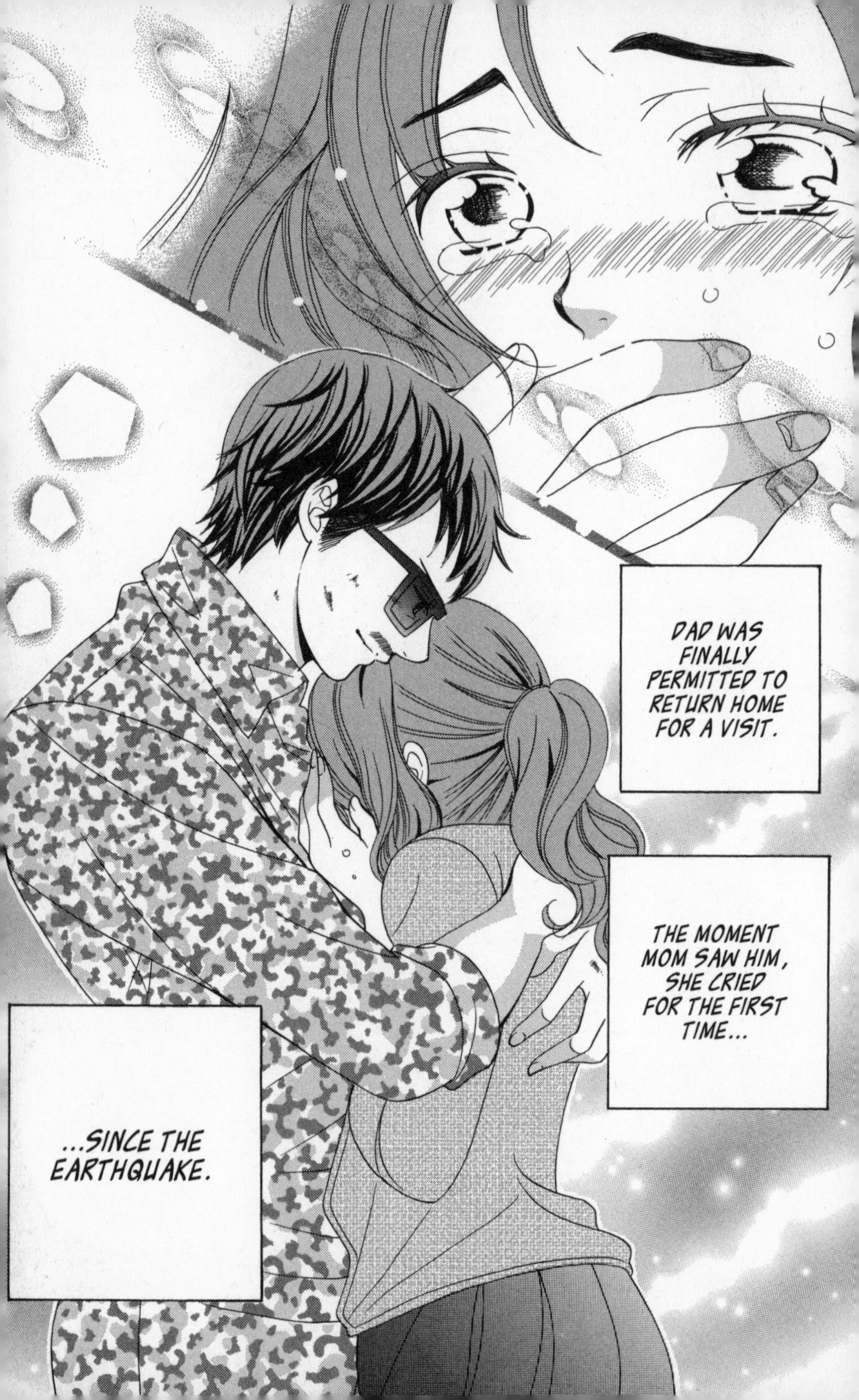
DAD WAS FINALLY PERMITTED TO RETURN HOME FOR A VISIT.
THE MOMENT MOM SAW HIM, SHE CRIED FOR THE FIRST TIME...
...SINCE THE EARTHQUAKE.

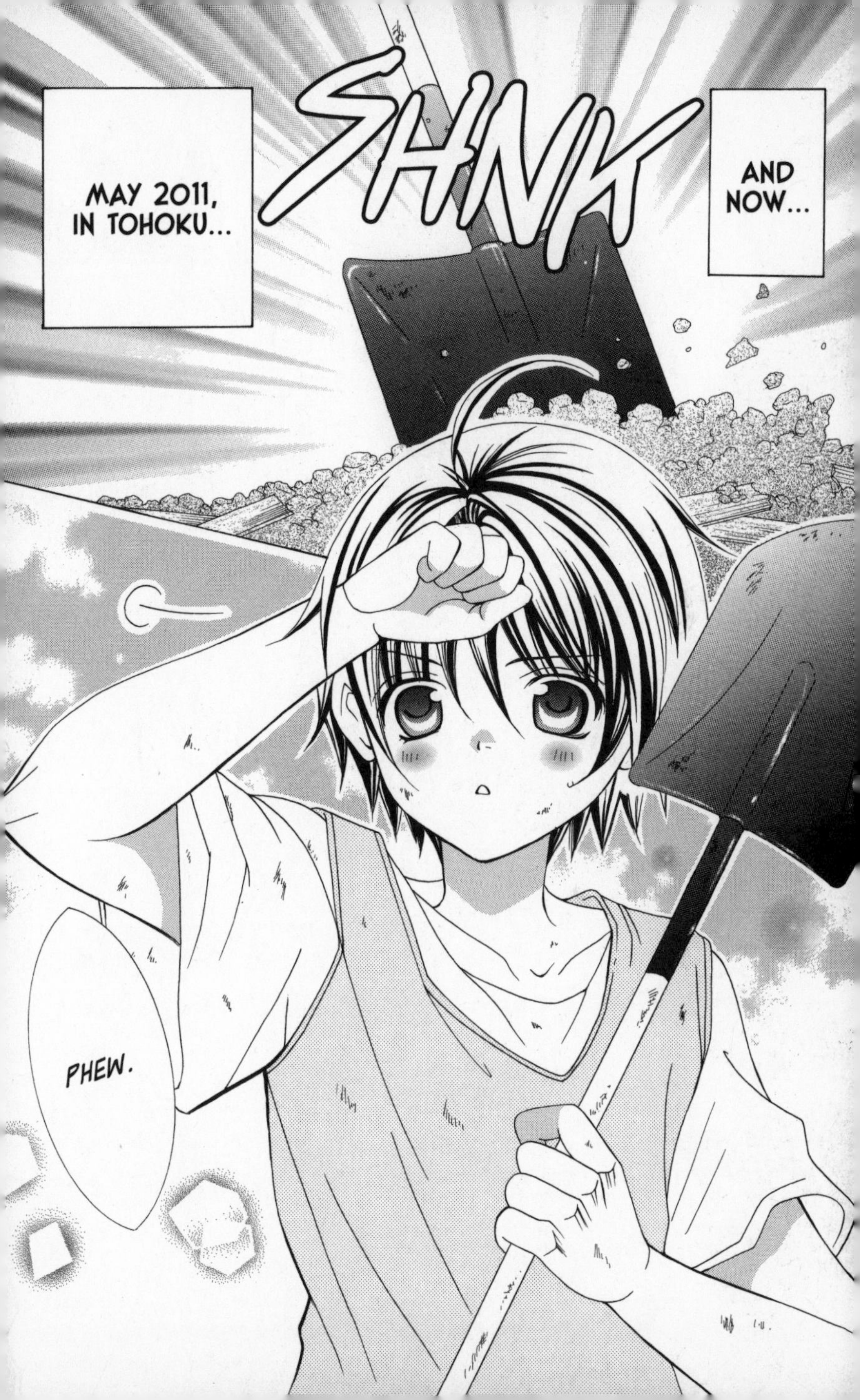
AND NOW...
SHINK
MAY 2011, IN TOHOKU...
PHEW.

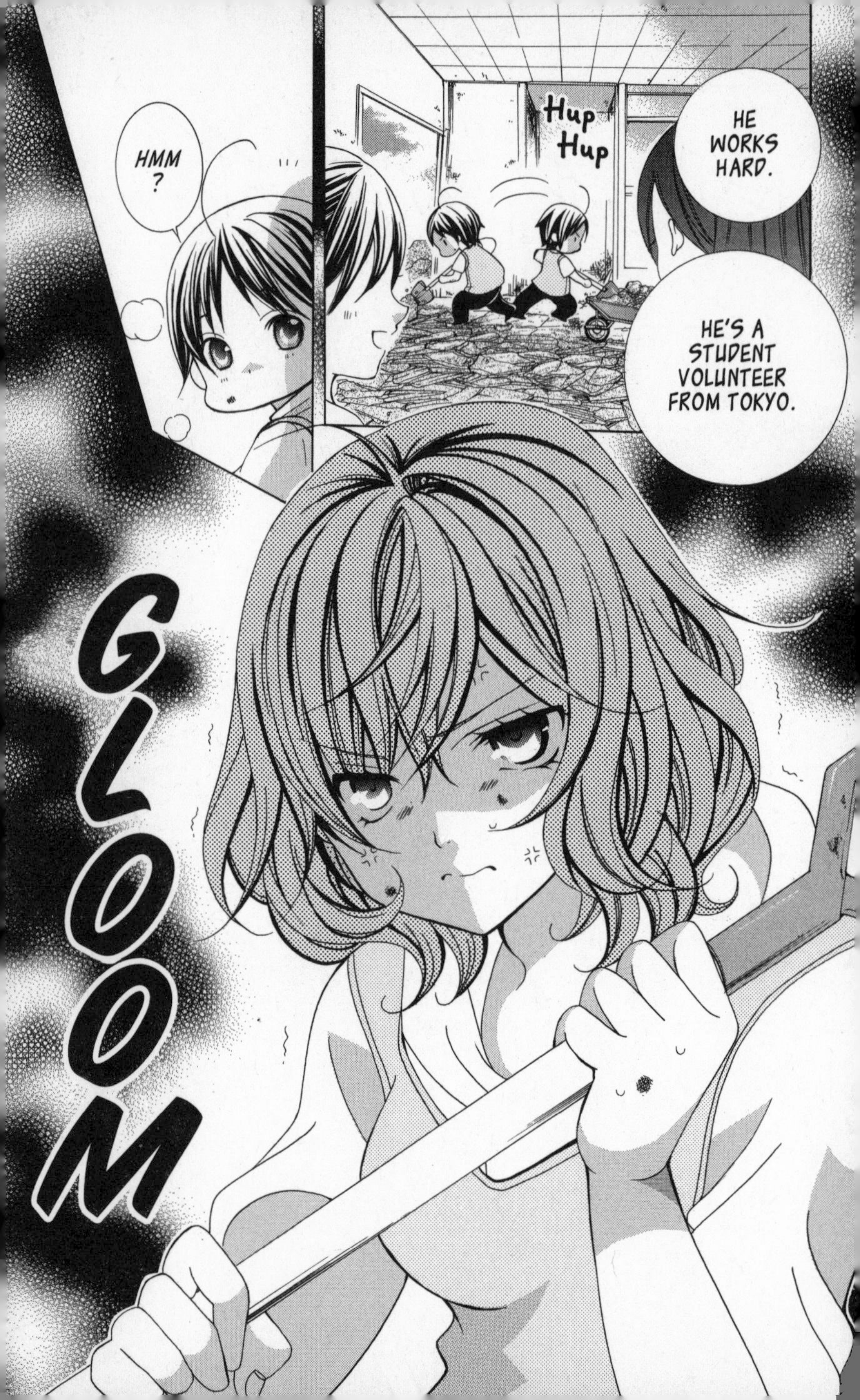
HE WORKS HARD.
Hup Hup
HE'S A STUDENT VOLUNTEER FROM TOKYO.
HMM ?
GLOOM

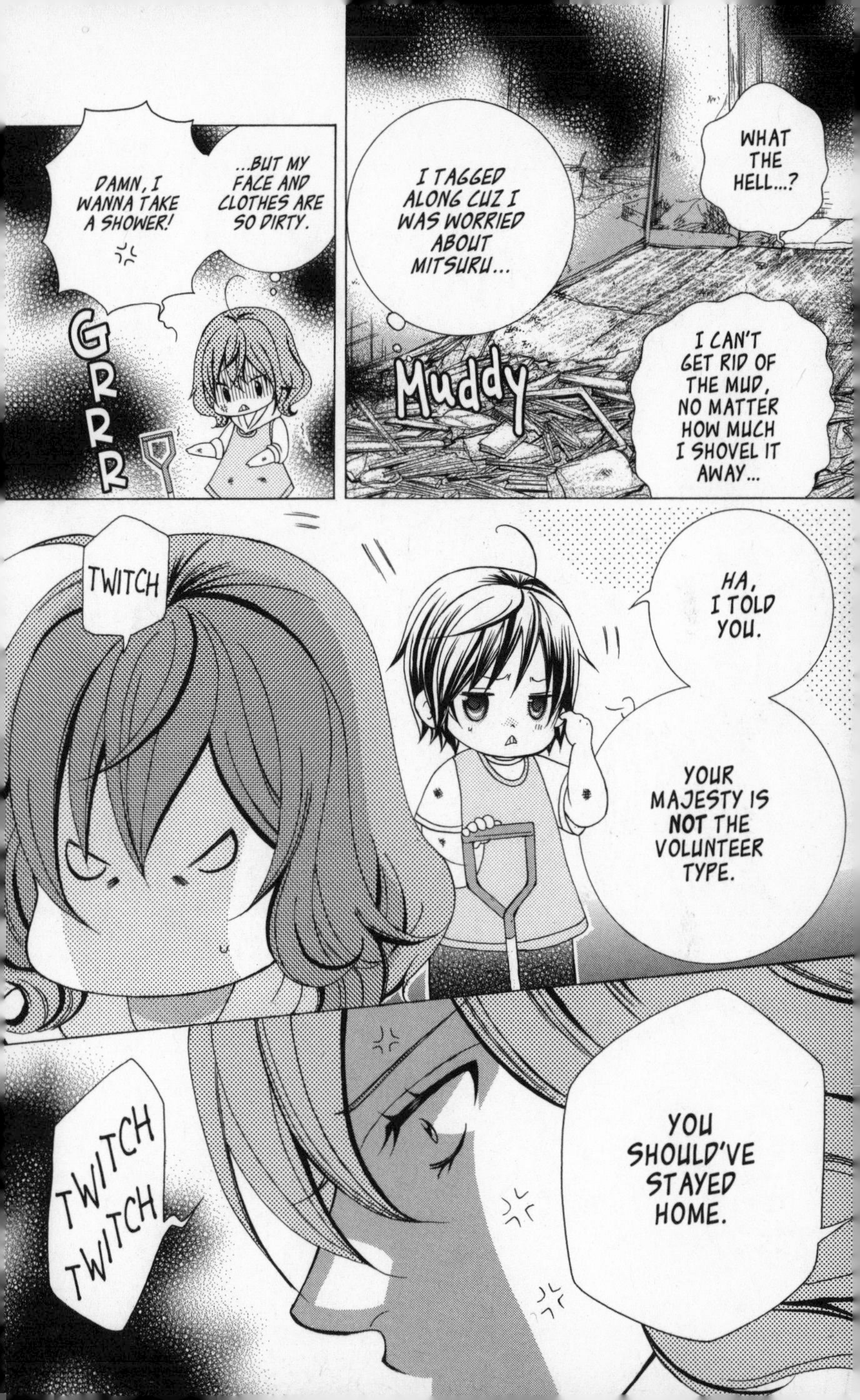
WHAT THE HELL...?
I CAN'T GET RID OF THE MUD, NO MATTER HOW MUCH I SHOVEL IT AWAY...
I TAGGED ALONG CUZ I WAS WORRIED ABOUT MITSURU...
Muddy
...BUT MY FACE AND CLOTHES ARE SO DIRTY.
DAMN, I WANNA TAKE A SHOWER!
GRRR
HA, I TOLD YOU.
YOUR MAJESTY IS NOT THE VOLUNTEER TYPE.
TWITCH
YOU SHOULD'VE STAYED HOME.
TWITCH TWITCH

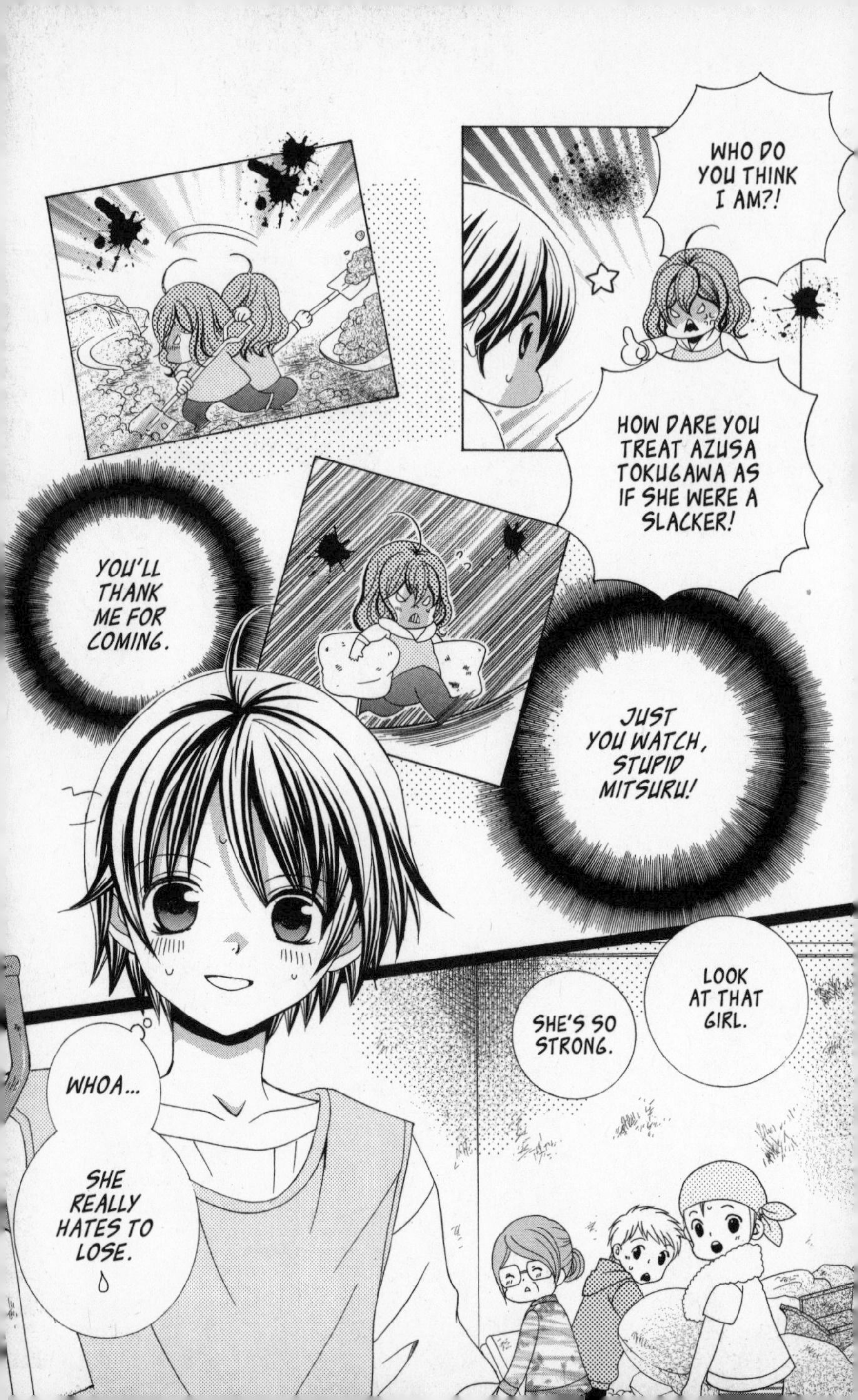
WHO DO YOU THINK I AM?!
HOW DARE YOU TREAT AZUSA TOKUGAWA AS IF SHE WERE A SLACKER!
JUST YOU WATCH, STUPID MITSURU!
YOU'LL THANK ME FOR COMING.
LOOK AT THAT GIRL.
SHE'S SO STRONG.
WHOA...
SHE REALLY HATES TO LOSE.

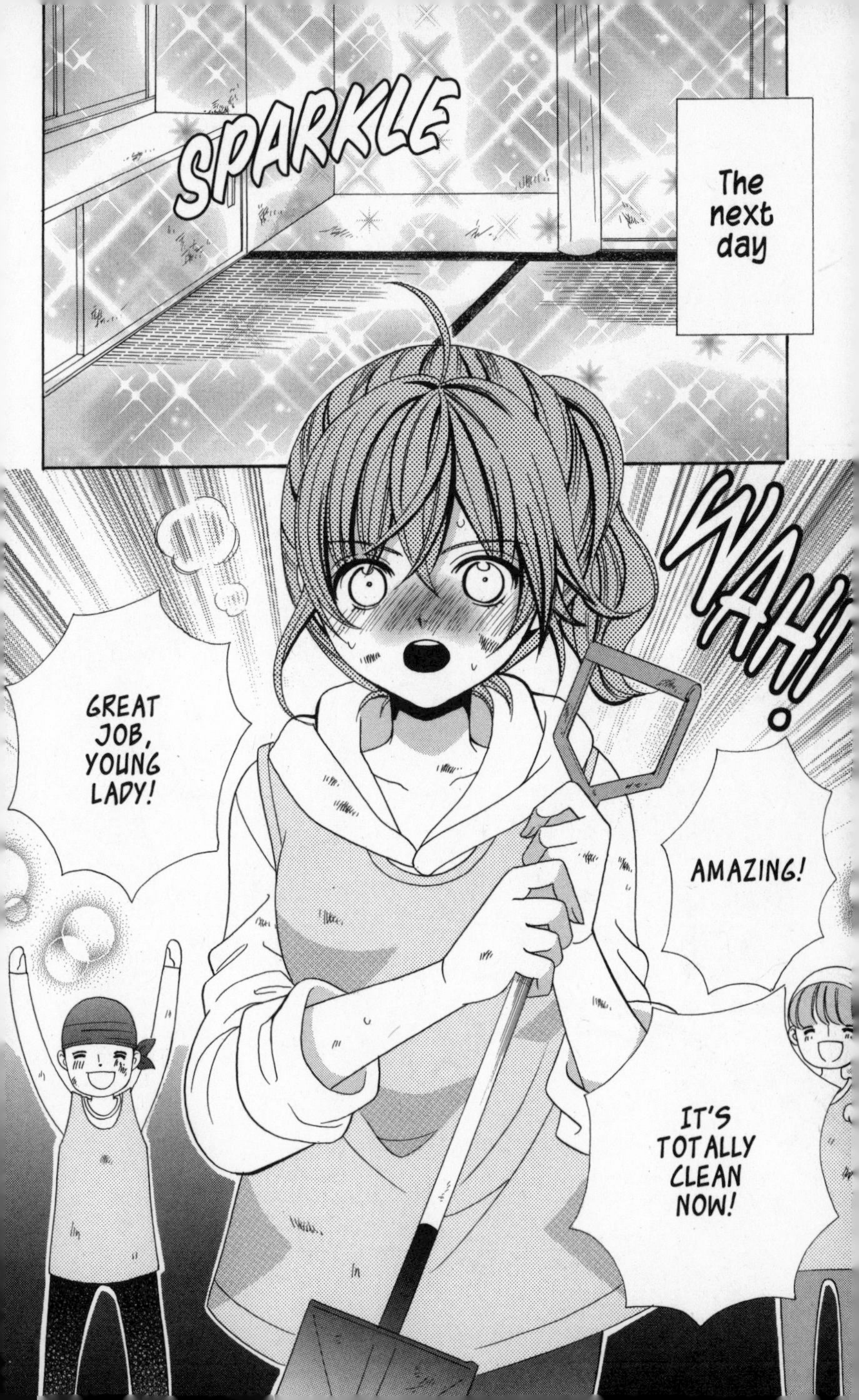
The next day
SPARKLE
WAH!
AMAZING!
GREAT JOB, YOUNG LADY!
IT'S TOTALLY CLEAN NOW!

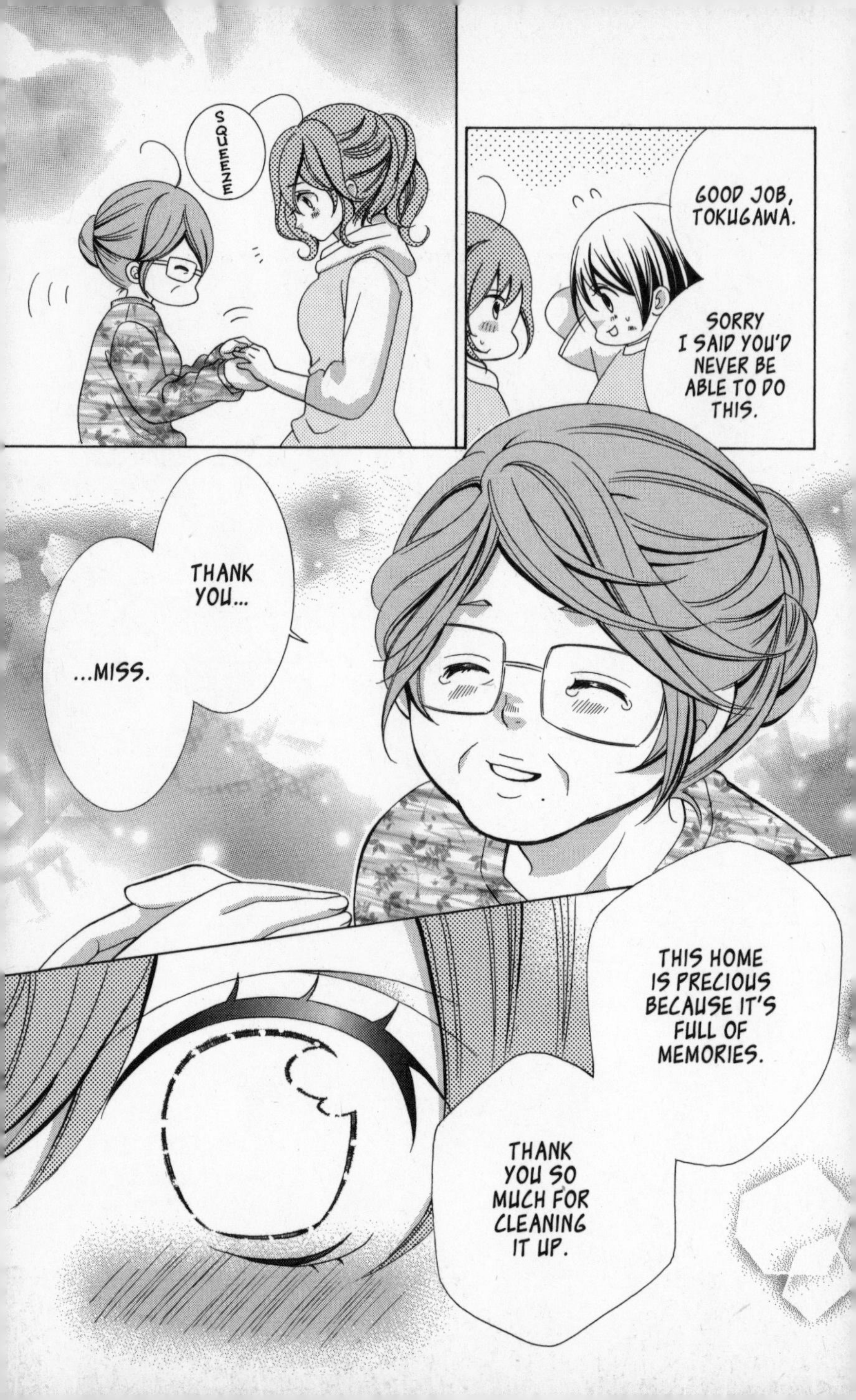
GOOD JOB, TOKUGAWA.
SORRY I SAID YOU'D NEVER BE ABLE TO DO THIS.
SQUEEZE
THANK YOU...
...MISS.
THIS HOME IS PRECIOUS BECAUSE IT'S FULL OF MEMORIES.
THANK YOU SO MUCH FOR CLEANING IT UP.

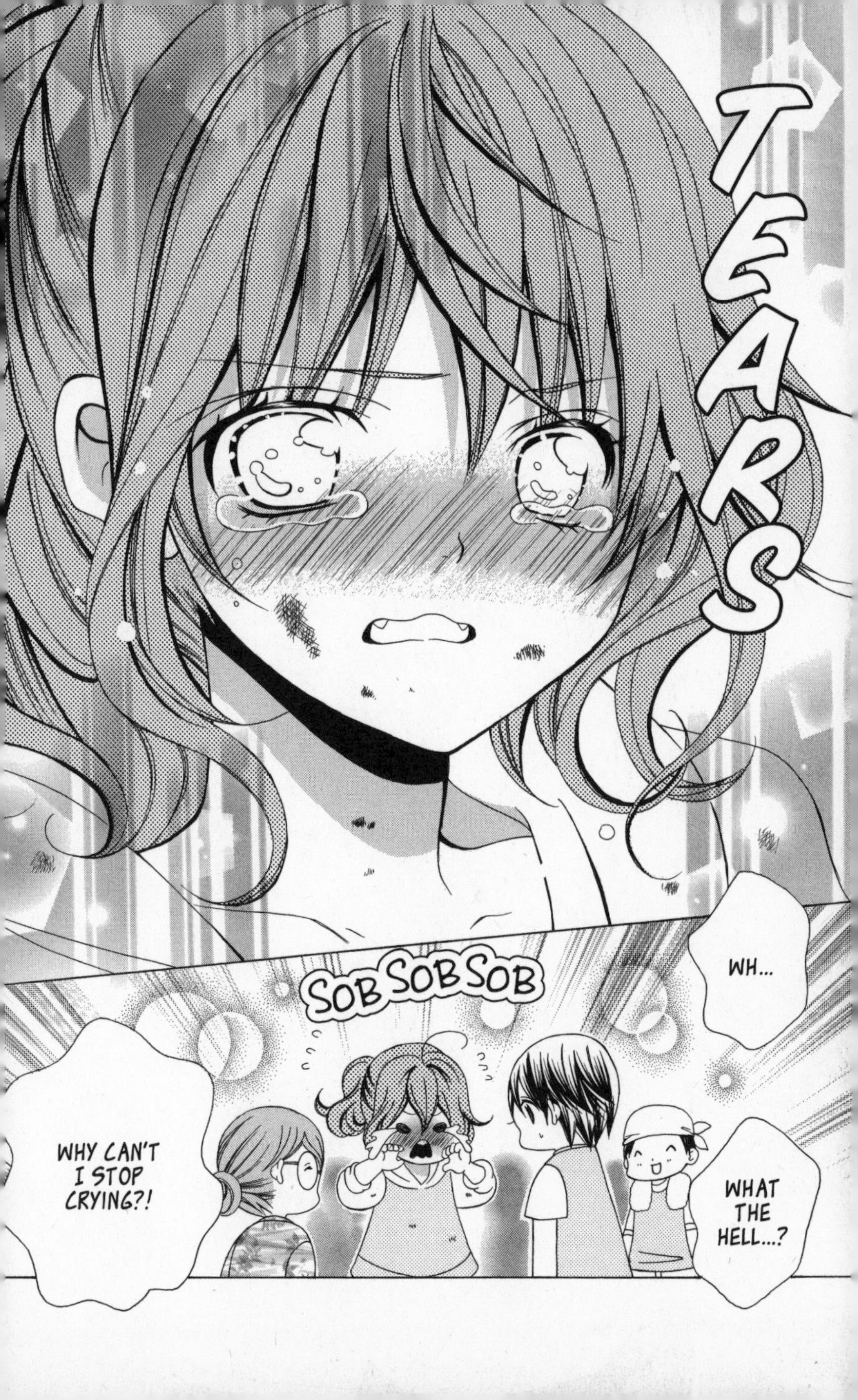
TEARS
WH...
SOB SOB SOB
WHAT THE HELL...?
WHY CAN'T I STOP CRYING?!

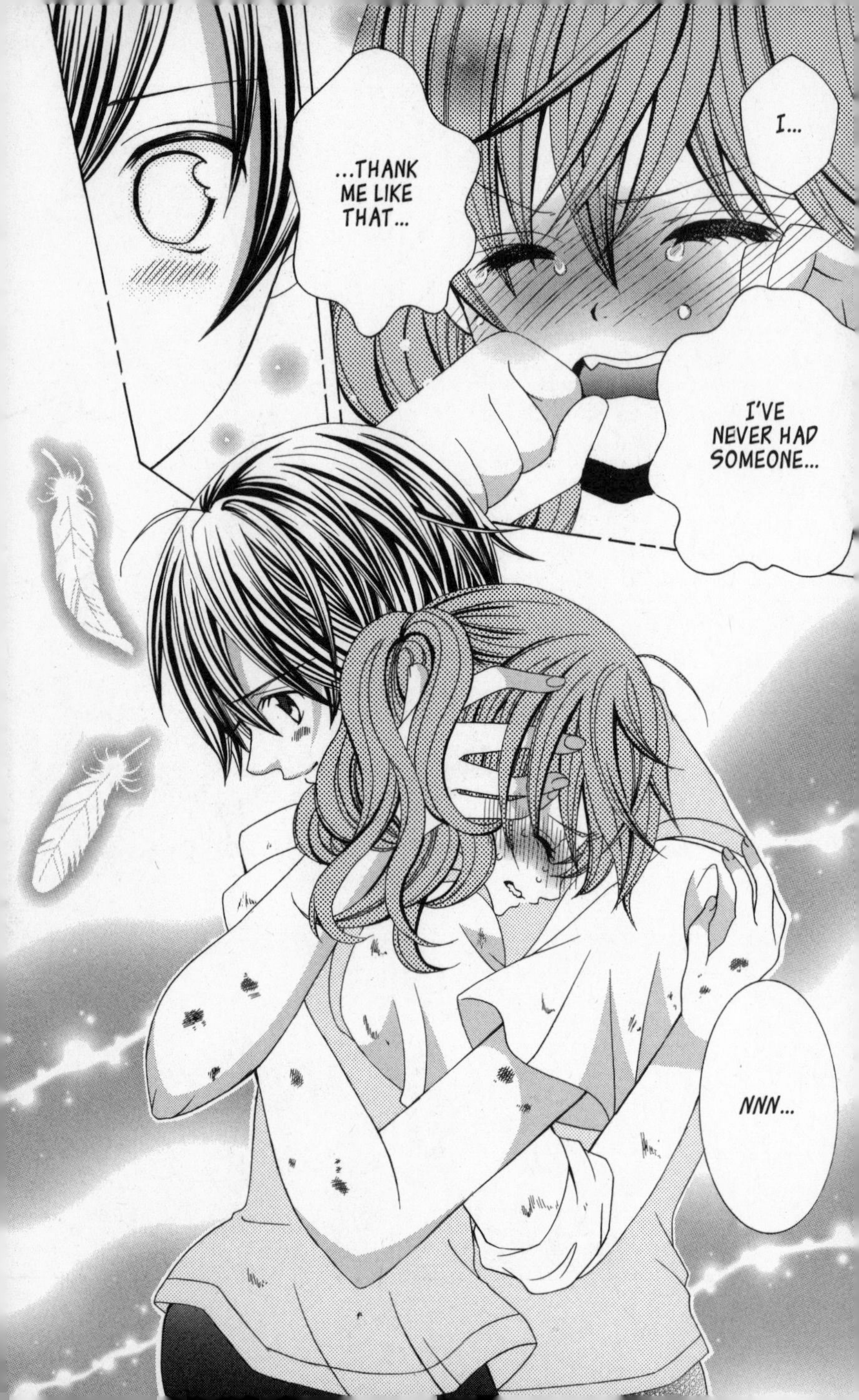
I...
I'VE NEVER HAD SOMEONE...
...THANK ME LIKE THAT...
NNN...

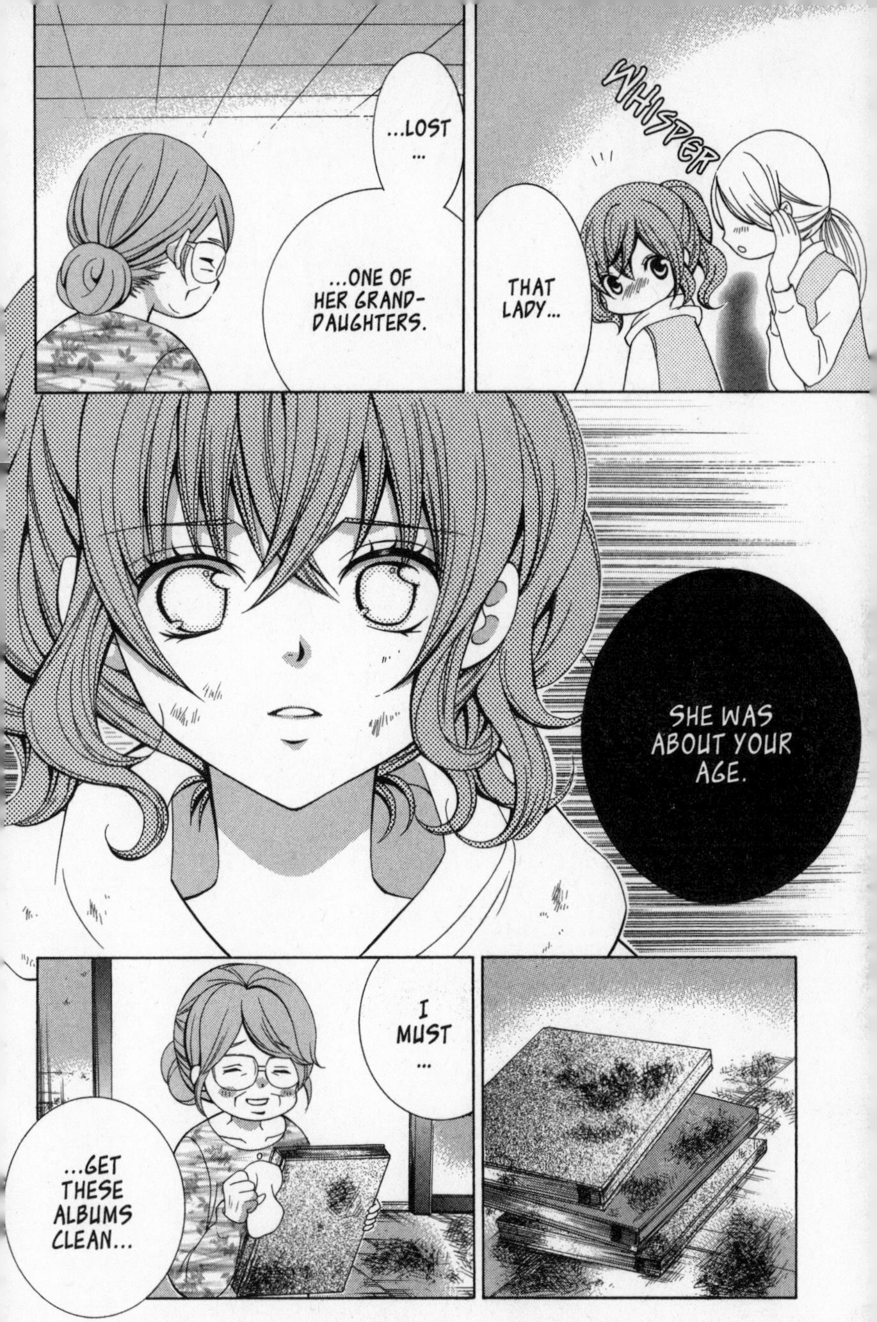
WHISPER
THAT LADY...
...LOST ...
...ONE OF HER GRAND-DAUGHTERS.
SHE WAS ABOUT YOUR AGE.
I MUST ...
...GET THESE ALBUMS CLEAN...

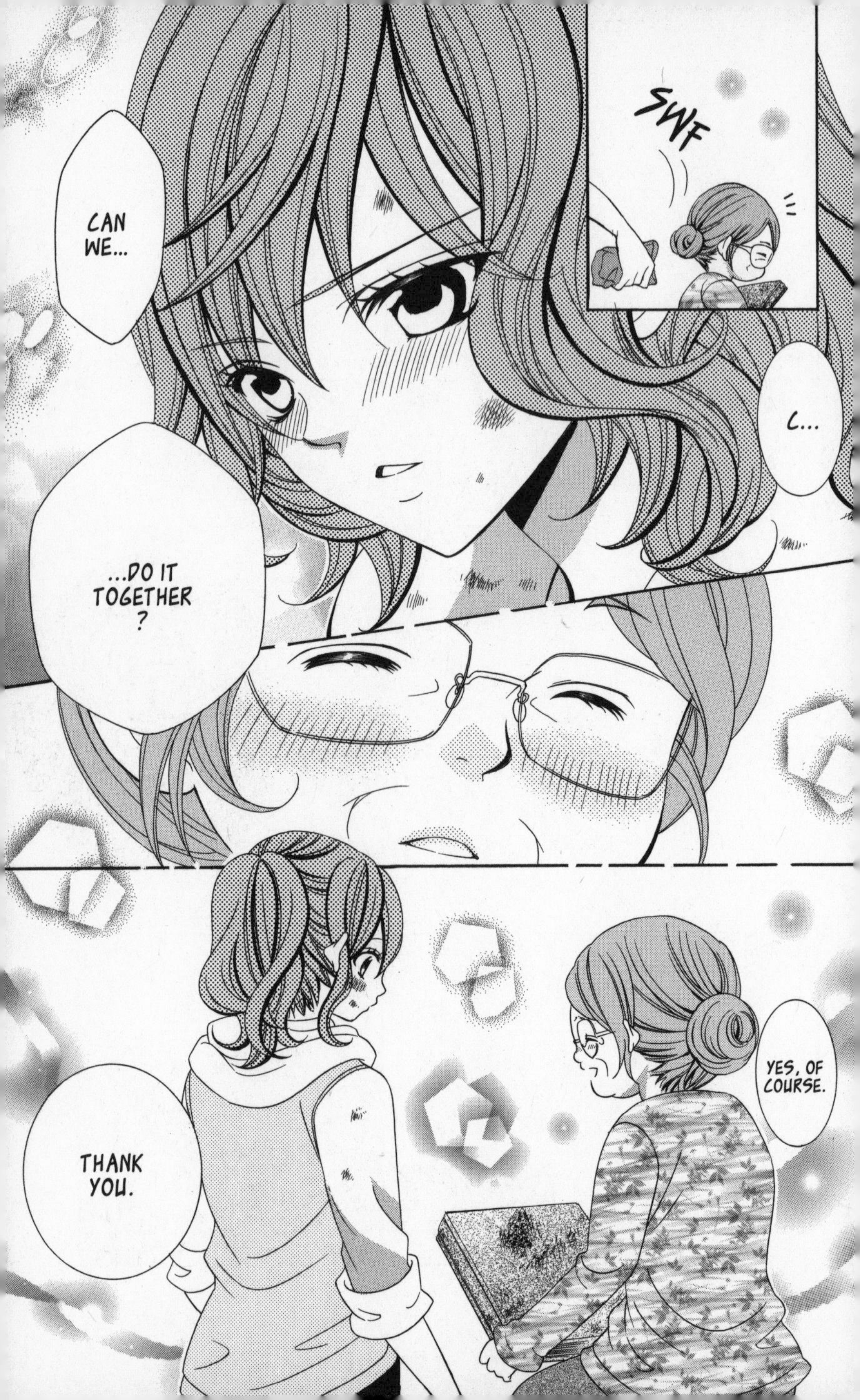

SWF
C...
CAN WE...
...DO IT TOGETHER?
YES, OF COURSE.
THANK YOU.

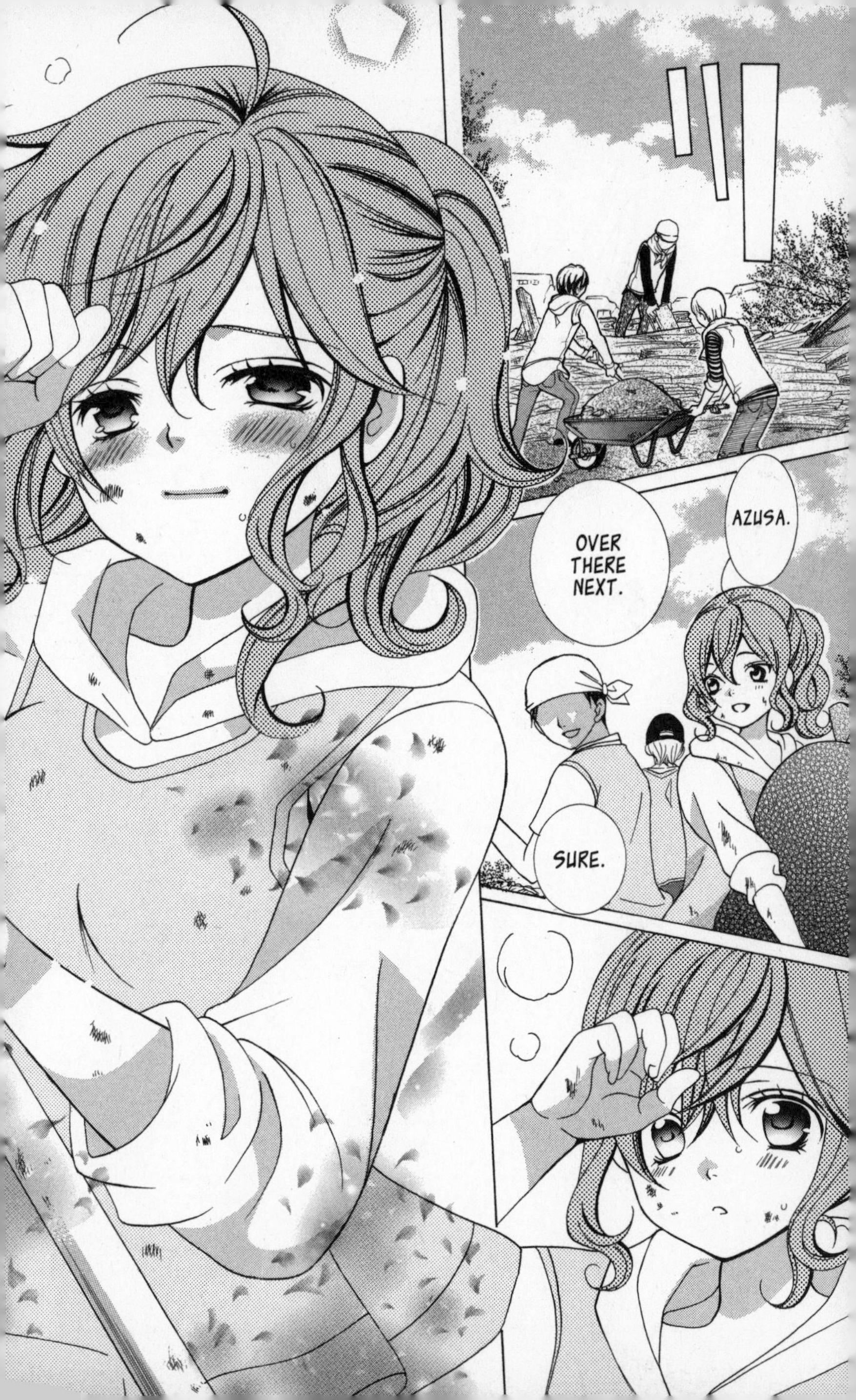
AZUSA.
OVER THERE NEXT.
SURE.

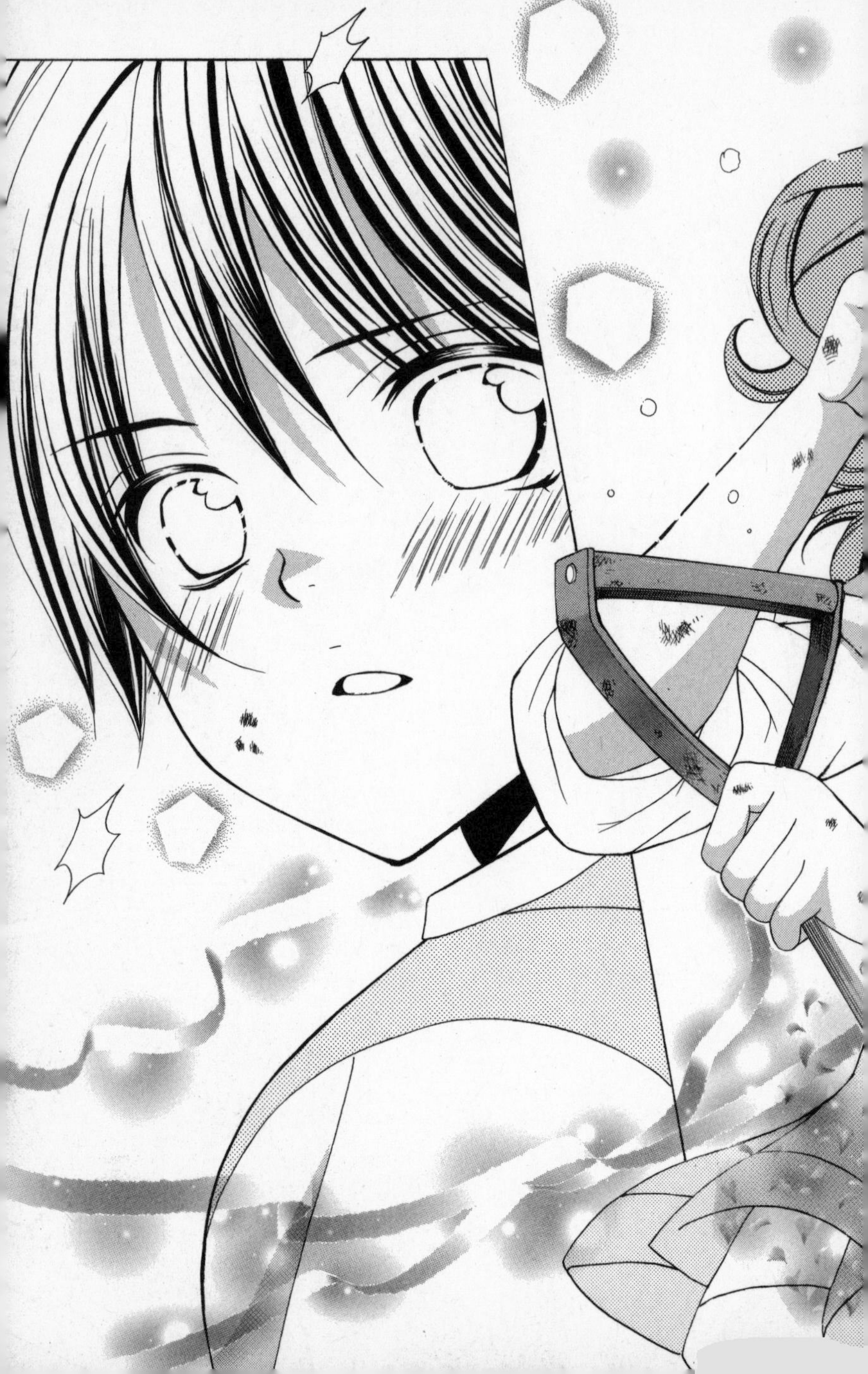

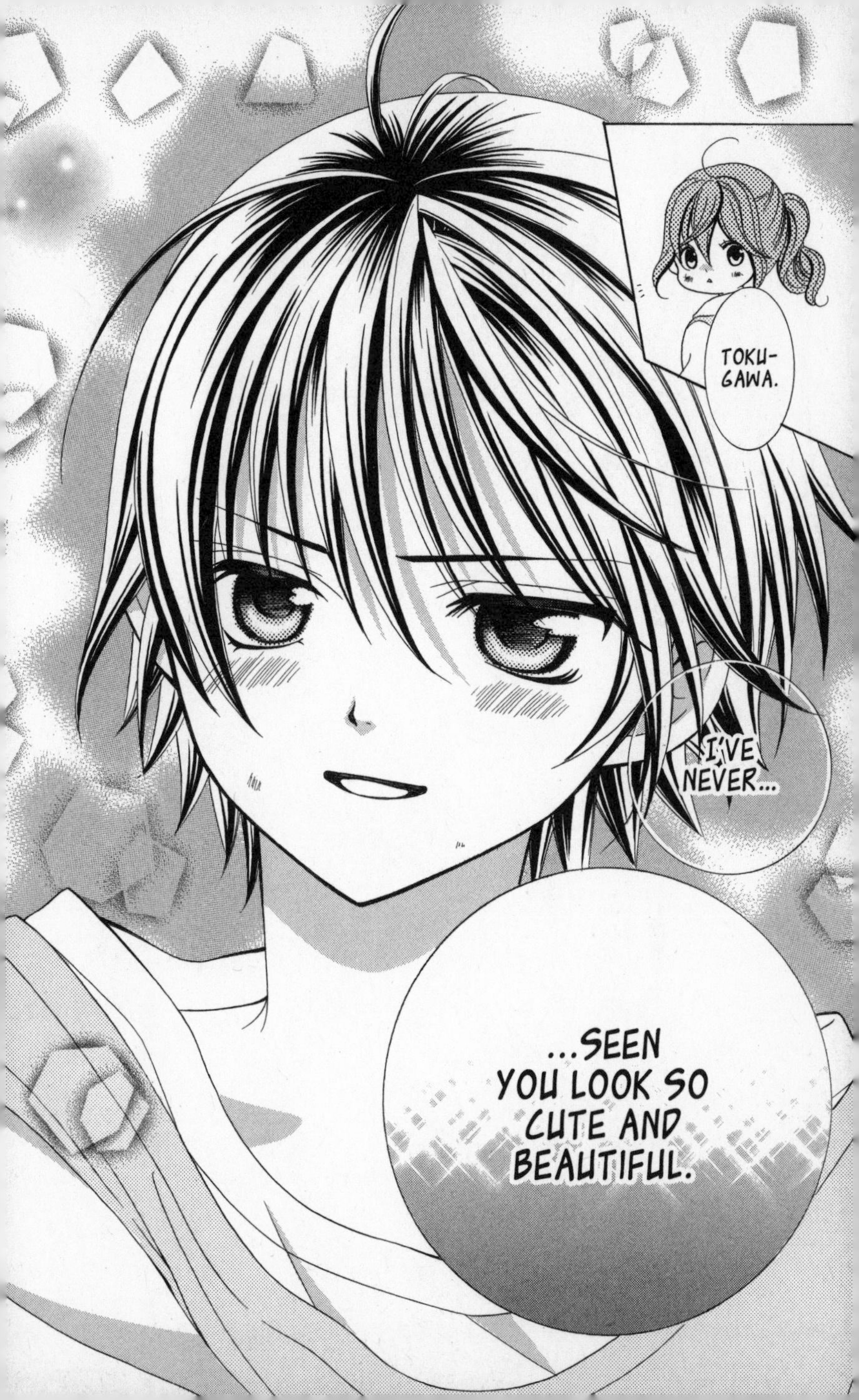
TOKU-GAWA.
I'VE NEVER...
...SEEN YOU LOOK SO CUTE AND BEAUTIFUL.

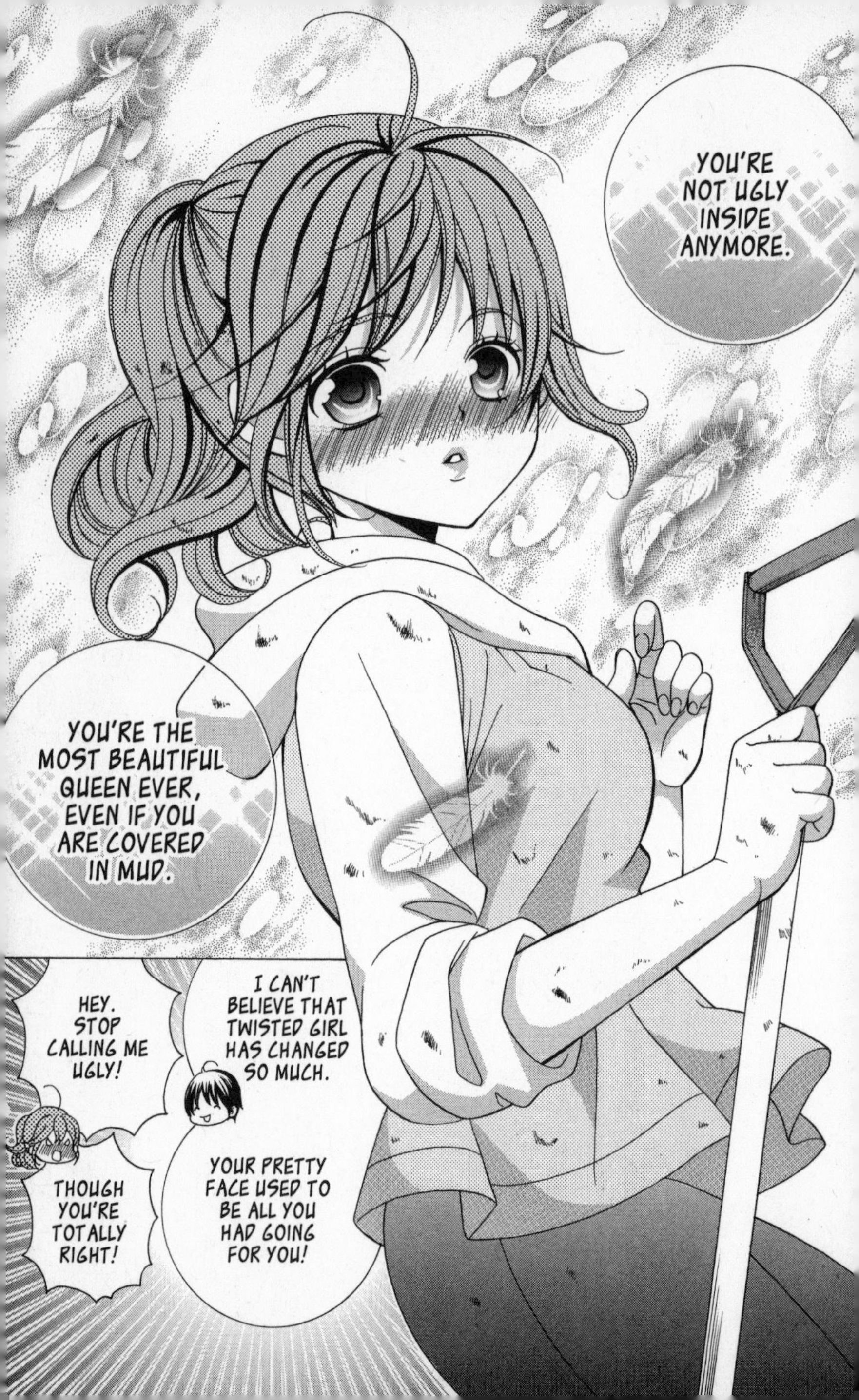
YOU'RE NOT UGLY INSIDE ANYMORE.
YOU'RE THE MOST BEAUTIFUL QUEEN EVER, EVEN IF YOU ARE COVERED IN MUD.
I CAN'T BELIEVE THAT TWISTED GIRL HAS CHANGED SO MUCH.
YOUR PRETTY FACE USED TO BE ALL YOU HAD GOING FOR YOU!
HEY. STOP CALLING ME UGLY!
THOUGH YOU'RE TOTALLY RIGHT!

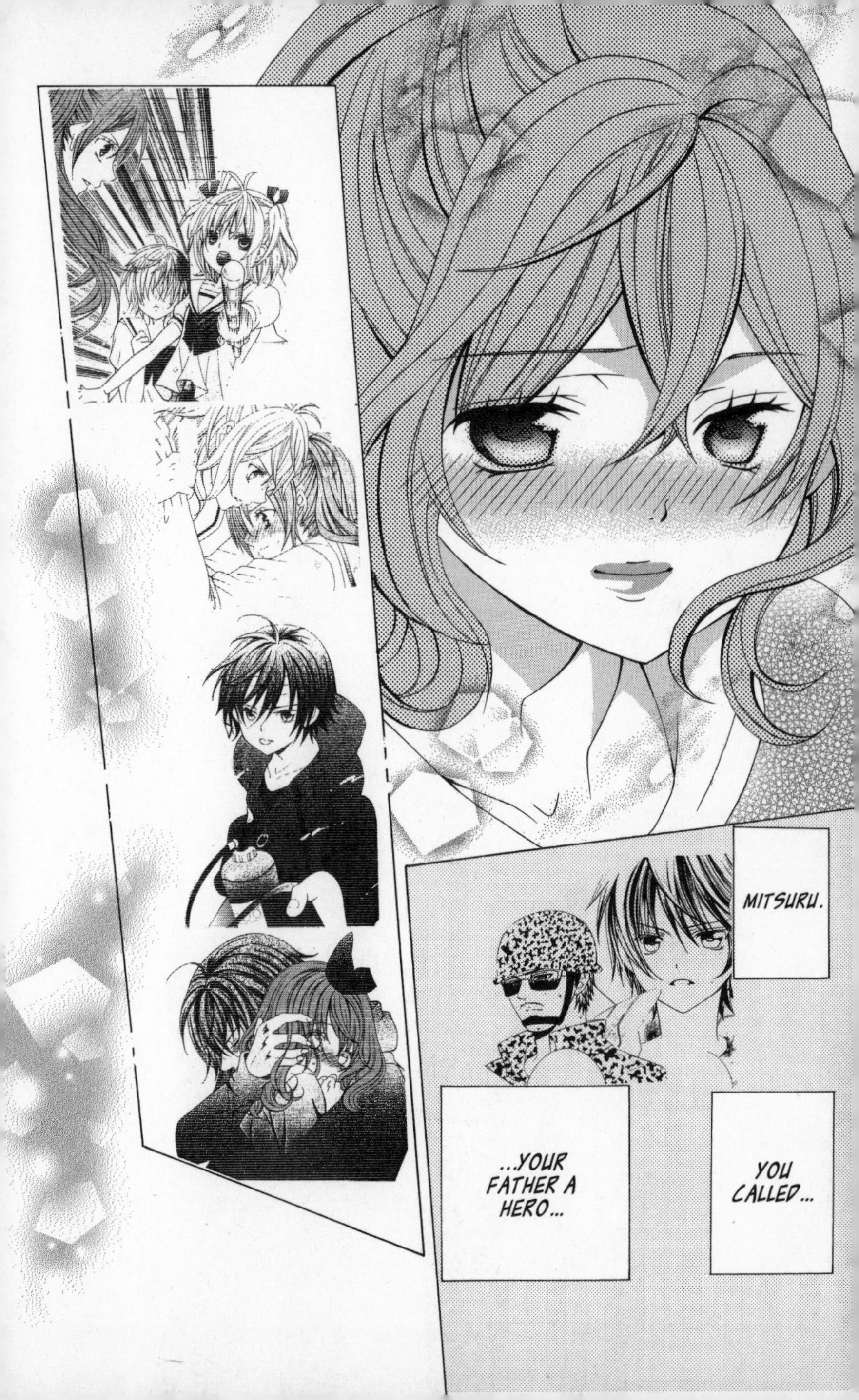
MITSURU.
YOU CALLED...
...YOUR FATHER A HERO...

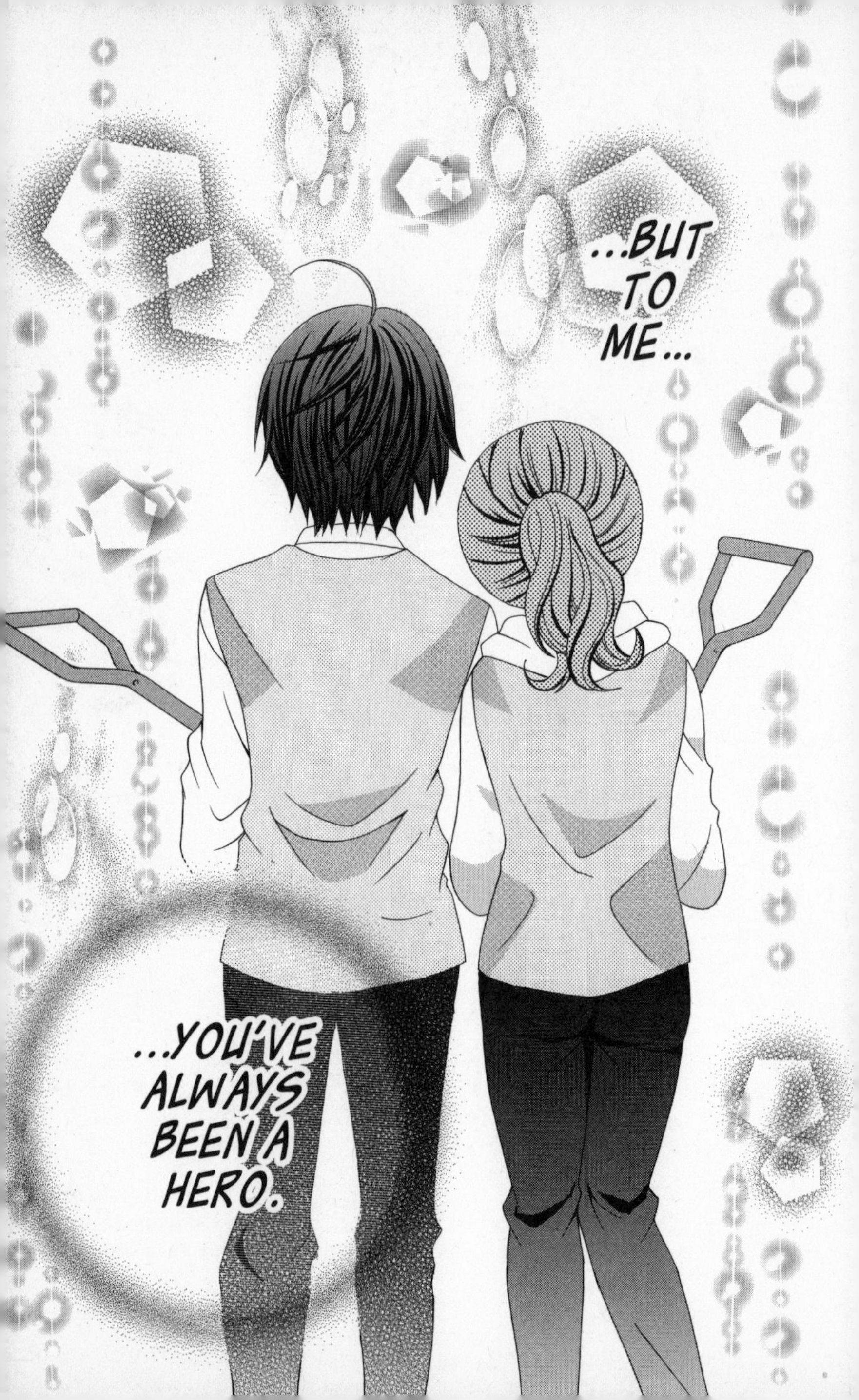
...BUT TO ME...
...YOU'VE ALWAYS BEEN A HERO.

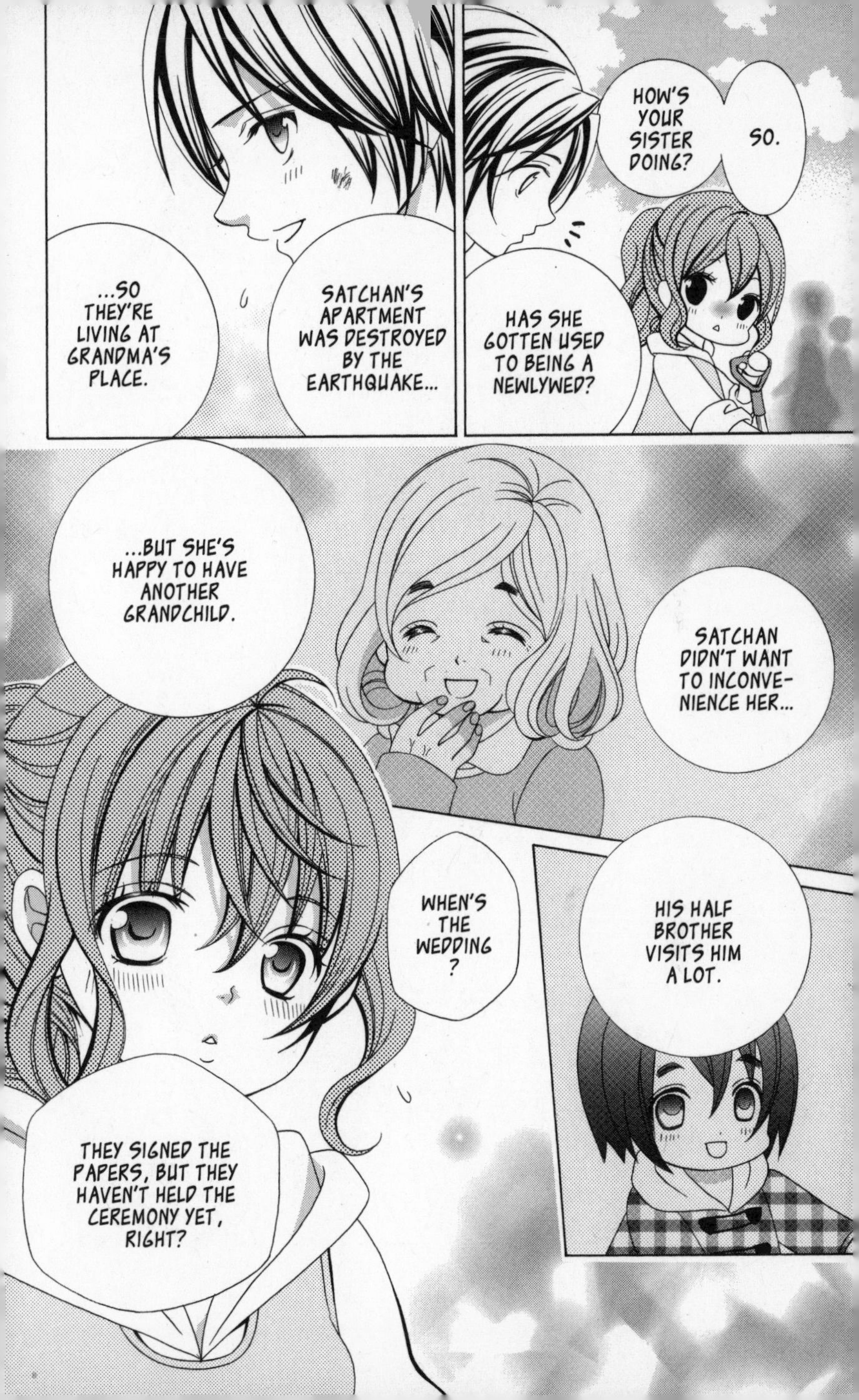
SO.
HOW'S YOUR SISTER DOING?
HAS SHE GOTTEN USED TO BEING A NEWLYWED?
SATCHAN'S APARTMENT WAS DESTROYED BY THE EARTHQUAKE...
...SO THEY'RE LIVING AT GRANDMA'S PLACE.
SATCHAN DIDN'T WANT TO INCONVENIENCE HER...
...BUT SHE'S HAPPY TO HAVE ANOTHER GRANDCHILD.
HIS HALF BROTHER VISITS HIM A LOT.
WHEN'S THE WEDDING?
THEY SIGNED THE PAPERS, BUT THEY HAVEN'T HELD THE CEREMONY YET, RIGHT?

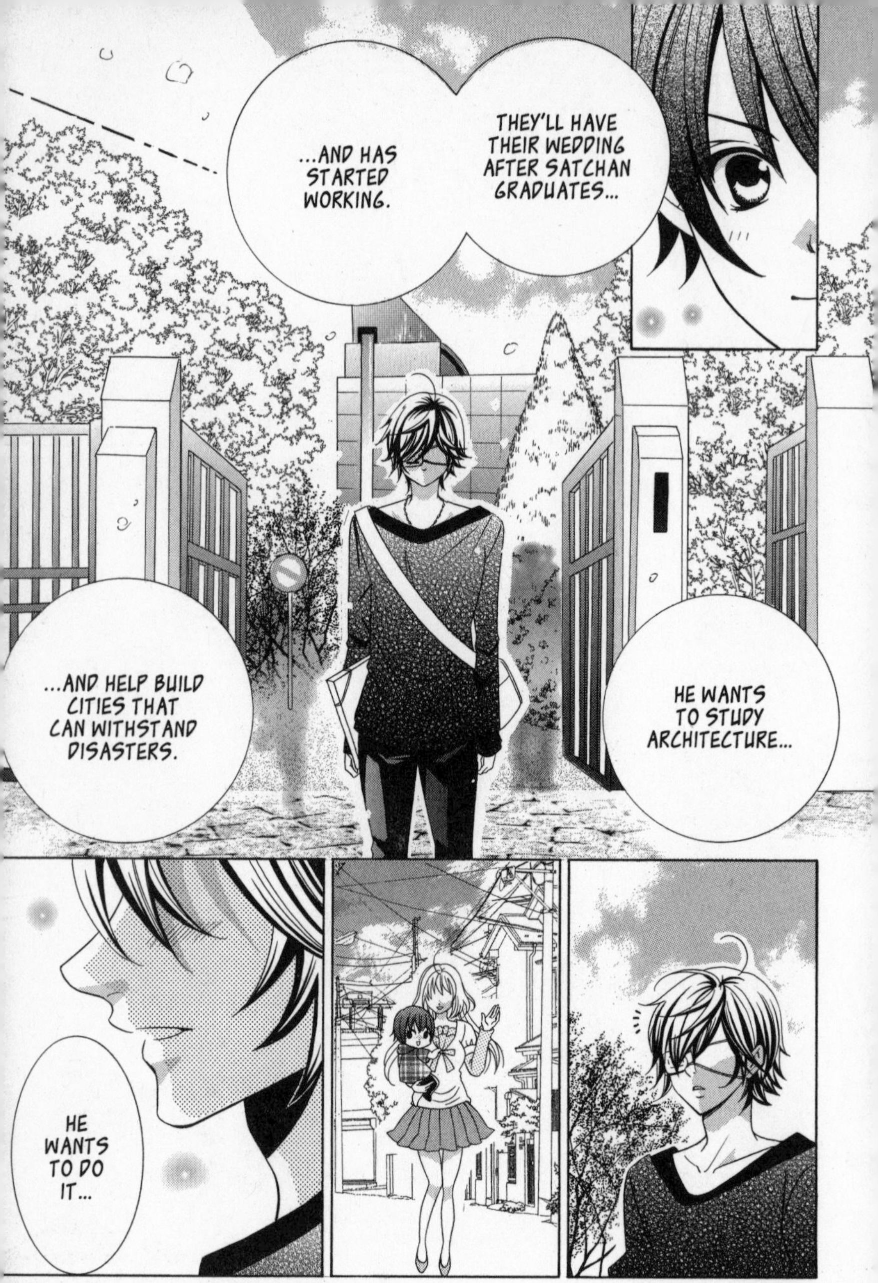
THEY'LL HAVE THEIR WEDDING AFTER SATCHAN GRADUATES...
...AND HAS STARTED WORKING.
HE WANTS TO STUDY ARCHITECTURE...
...AND HELP BUILD CITIES THAT CAN WITHSTAND DISASTERS.
HE WANTS TO DO IT...

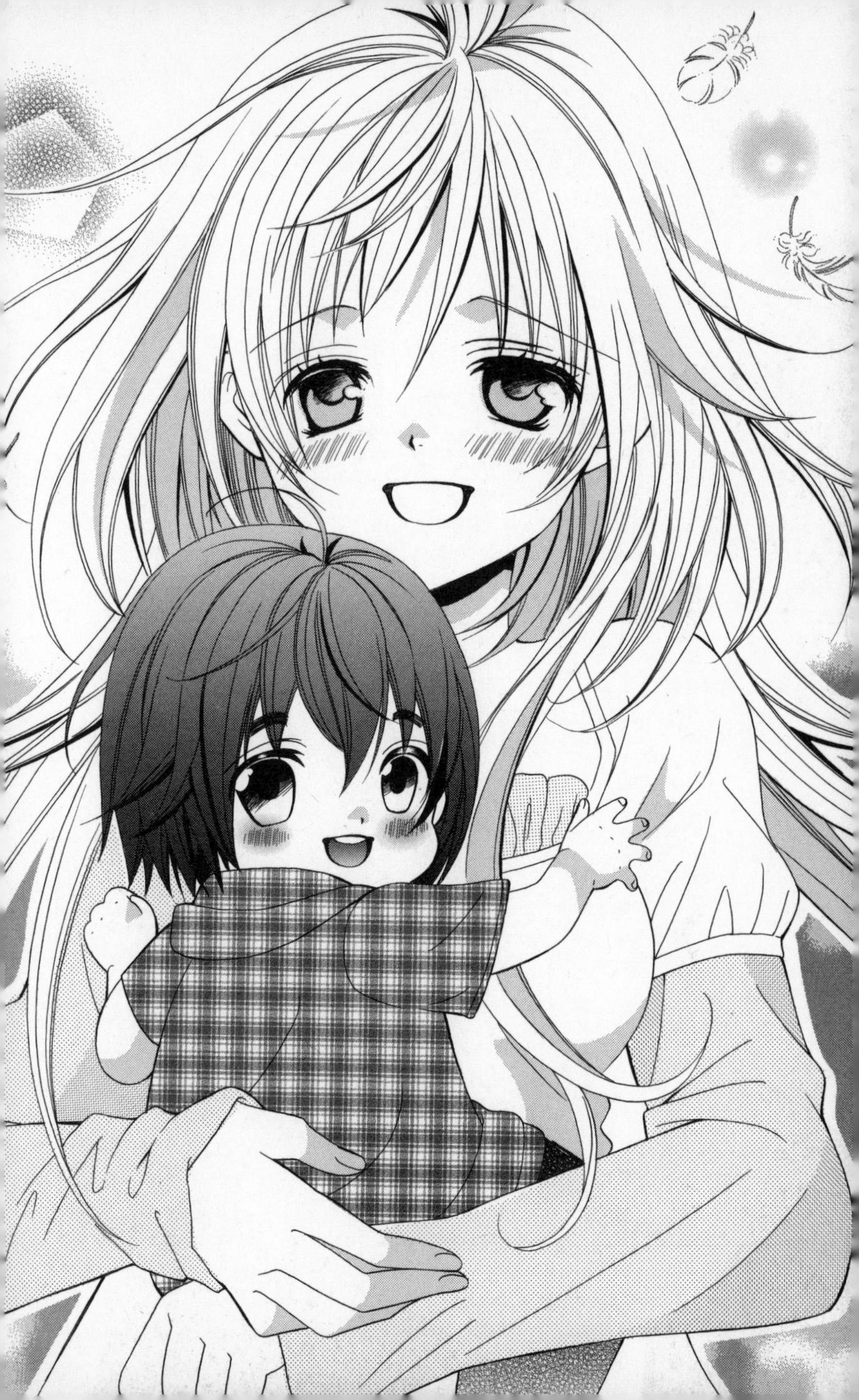

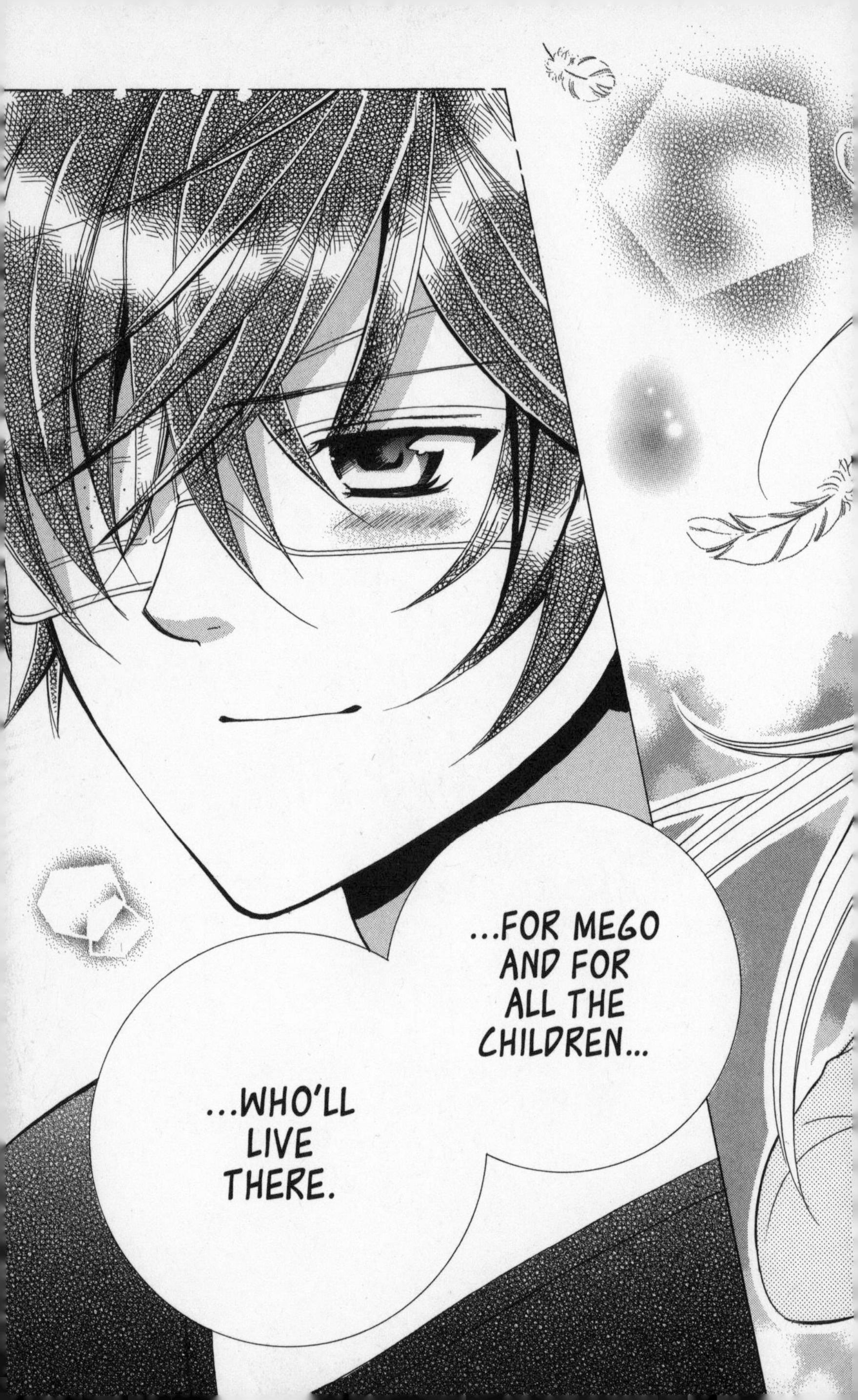
...FOR MEGO AND FOR ALL THE CHILDREN...
...WHO'LL LIVE THERE.

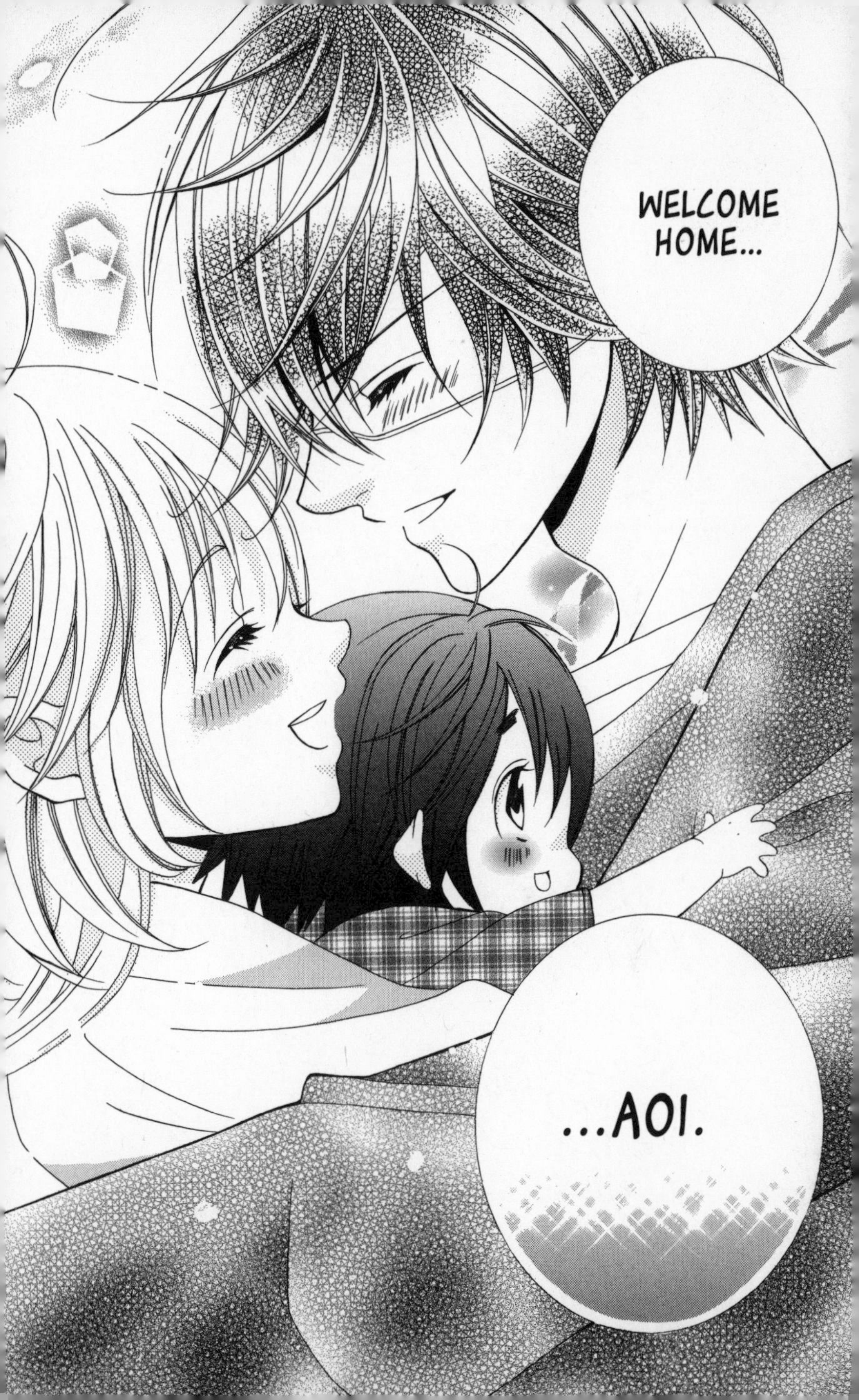
WELCOME HOME...
...AOI.

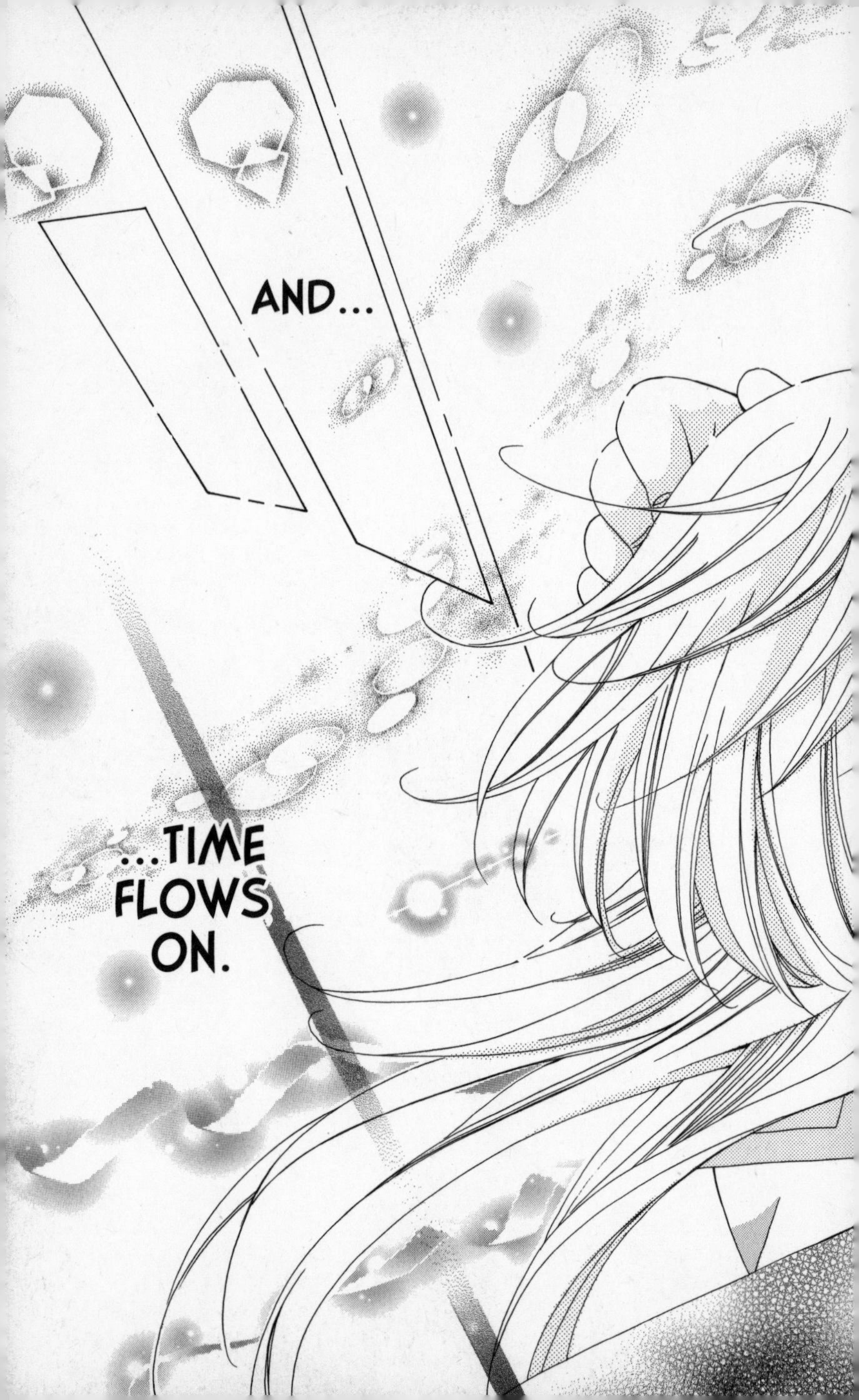
AND...
...TIME FLOWS ON.

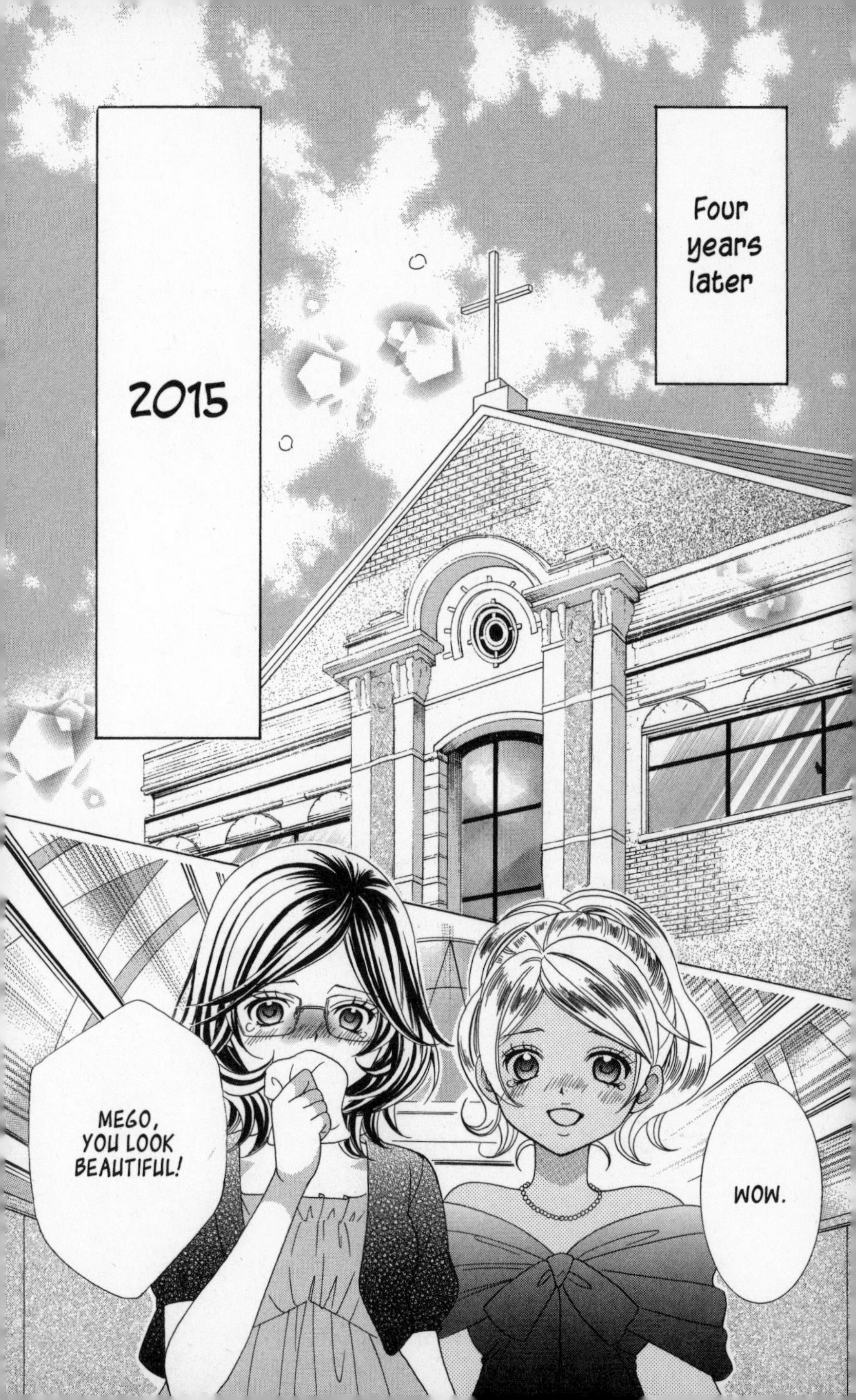
Four years later
2015
WOW.
MEGO, YOU LOOK BEAUTIFUL!

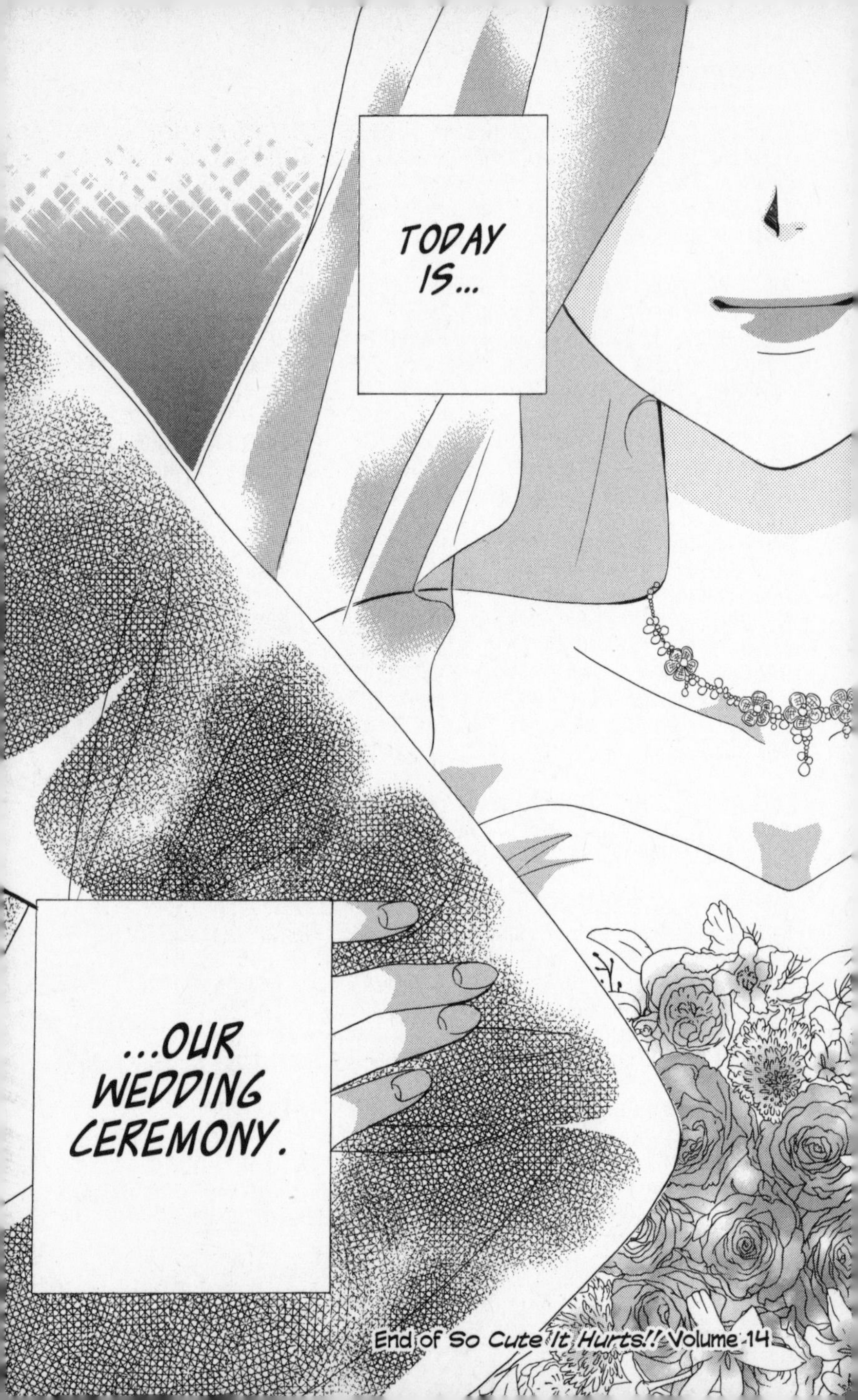
TODAY IS...
...OUR WEDDING CEREMONY.

End of So Cute It Hurts!! Volume 14

AFTERWORD

THIS IS MY 14TH YEAR WORKING AS A MANGAKA. I'VE ALWAYS WANTED TO DRAW A CHEERFUL MANGA THAT MAKES READERS FORGET THE PAINS OF REALITY. I MYSELF WAS SAVED BY THE JOY OF READING MANGA WHEN I WAS A STUDENT, EVERY TIME I WAS WORRIED ABOUT SOMETHING OR JUST WHEN I WAS TIRED.

AS I MENTIONED IN THE AFTERWORD OF VOLUME 13, I HESITATED AND AGONIZED A LOT WHILE WORKING ON SO CUTE! EVEN AFTER I'D STARTED THE SENDAI ARC. THIS NEVER HAPPENED WITH MY OTHER MANGA. I KEPT ASKING MYSELF IF I SHOULD REALLY BE DEPICTING SOMETHING SO TER-RIFYING, OR IF I SHOULD TURN A BLIND EYE AND NOT INCLUDE IT.

I HAD MANY UNFORGETTABLE ENCOUNTERS AND EXPERIENCES IN THE MEANTIME. ONE THING THAT GAVE ME COURAGE TO KEEP DRAWING WAS A TV DOCUMENTARY I SAW IN MARCH.

THIS MARCH MARKED THE FOURTH ANNIVERSARY OF THE EARTHQUAKE AND THE 70TH ANNIVERSARY OF THE TOKYO AIR RAID, SO THERE WERE MANY SPECIAL PROGRAMS DEDICATED TO THE TWO EVENTS. I WAS ESPECIALLY MOVED BY A WAR DOCUMENTARY I HAPPENED TO SEE WHEN WORKING LATE ONE NIGHT. THE DOCUMENTARY FEATURED PEOPLE WHO'D BECOME WAR ORPHANS AFTER THEY'D LOST THEIR FAMILIES IN THE AIR RAID. THEIR EXPERIENCES FELT RECENT, SINCE WHAT THEY HAD ENDURED WAS VERY MUCH LIKE WHAT THE EARTHQUAKE SURVIVORS WERE GOING THROUGH.

ONE OF THE WAR ORPHANS WAS A BOY WHO SURVIVED THE AIR RAID AND ALSO MANAGED TO SURVIVE WWII. HE MADE PAINTINGS OF THE AIR RAID AFTER HE BECAME AN ARTIST.

THE AIR RAID OCCURRED 70 YEARS AGO, SO ONLY BLACK-AND-WHITE PHOTOS REMAIN. HE'S BEEN DRAWING HIS TERRIFYING MEMORIES IN VIVID COLOR, AND I WAS AS OVERWHELMED BY HIS TERROR, ANGER AND SORROW AS IF I HAD BEEN WATCHING COLOR FOOTAGE. THE PAINT-INGS WERE TERRIFYING, BUT THEY MOVED ME BECAUSE THEY WERE SO TERRIFYING. I FELT HIS FIERCE DETERMINATION TO CREATE HIS PAINT-INGS IN ORDER TO PASS DOWN HIS MEMORIES TO FUTURE GENERATIONS.

"TO KEEP DRAWING ABOUT SOMETHING SO PEOPLE WON'T FORGET." IT MAY BE TOO EARLY TO DO THIS, BUT SEVERAL YEARS DOWN THE ROAD, PEOPLE WHO DON'T KNOW ANYTHING ABOUT THAT EARTHQUAKE WILL BE ABLE TO KNOW WHAT IT WAS LIKE. PEOPLE LIVING OUTSIDE JAPAN MAY WANT TO KNOW WHAT IT WAS LIKE. I FELT LIKE HE'D GIVEN ME THE COURAGE TO CONTINUE DRAWING.

I AGONIZED OVER HOW TO PORTRAY THE EARTHQUAKE AND ITS AFTERMATH IN THE MANGA. I COULDN'T FORGET *SO CUTE!* IS A SHOJO MANGA, BECAUSE READERS WOULDN'T WANT TO READ IT IF THE STORY GOT TOO GRIM. BUT IF I GLOSSED OVER REALITY, THE MANGA WOULDN'T BE WORTH DRAWING. I FUMBLED AROUND, FIGURING OUT WHAT I COULD PORTRAY WITHIN THE CONSTRAINTS OF SHOJO MANGA.

THE TERRIFYING "BLACK HANDS" NEWS VIDEOS PUSHED ME TO DRAW IT NO MATTER WHAT. THE STRUGGLES EVERYONE WENT THROUGH. PEOPLE WHO PUT OUT THE FIRES AT THE NUCLEAR POWER PLANT. ALL THE WORKING PEOPLE, FIREFIGHTERS, THE SELF-DEFENSE FORCES AND MEDICAL PERSONNEL WHO RISKED THEIR LIVES IN RESCUE OPERATIONS.

I WANTED TO TOUCH ON THE STORIES OF PEOPLE WHO SAVED LIVES BEHIND THE SCENES, EVEN IF THEY WON'T BE REMEMBERED AS HEROES. THE SDF MEMBERS WHO RISKED THEIR LIVES IN RESCUE OPERATIONS AND THEIR FAMILIES WHO HAD TO SEE THEM OFF—THAT WAS THE STORY I WANTED MEGO, MITSURU AND THEIR PARENTS TO PORTRAY. (I WISH I HAD BEEN ABLE TO DRAW MOREABOUT MEGO'S FATHER.)

AND THE PAIN OF LIVING AFTER YOU'VE LOST YOUR LOVED ONES. IT MIGHT BE EVEN MORE PAINFUL THAN LOSING YOUR OWN LIFE. BUT IF SOMEONE HAD TO DIE AND LEAVE THEIR LOVED ONES BEHIND, THEY'D PRAY FOR THE HAPPINESS OF THOSE WHO STAYED ALIVE... *I WANT YOU TO REMEMBER ME. I DON'T WANT YOU TO FORGET ME, BUT I ALSO WANT YOU TO LIVE AND BE HAPPY.* I BELIEVE THAT'S HOW PEOPLE WOULD FEEL...

THE STORY INVOLVING AOI, YUKI, AKANE AND HIS FATHER WAS VERY GRAVE, AND I STRUGGLED TO DECIDE HOW TO END IT, SINCE THERE'RE NO ANSWERS. I FEEL LIKE AKANE BECAME A SYMBOL OF HOPE IN THE STORY.

WHEN AOI PROPOSES TO MEGO, HE SAYS, "I KNOW NOW THAT TOMORROW DOESN'T ALWAYS COME. WHO KNOWS WHAT'LL HAPPEN IN THE FUTURE?" HIS WORDS ARE EXACTLY HOW I FELT MYSELF AFTER THE EARTHQUAKE. NATURAL DISASTERS HAVE CONTINUED TO OCCUR IN JAPAN EVERY YEAR, AND I SEE NEWS ABOUT CONFLICTS ALL OVER THE WORLD. I CAN'T STOP THINKING ABOUT WHAT IT MEANS TO LIVE.

VOLUME 14 TURNED OUT TO BE VERY SERIOUS, BUT THE STORY HAS ONE MORE VOLUME TO GO. I HOPE YOU'LL KEEP READING THROUGH VOLUME 15!

GO IKEYAMADA
DECEMBER 2015

lolololol

So Cute It Hurts!! (>_<)

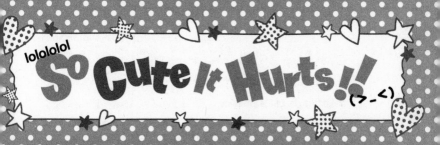